D1592646

WHICH BUSINESS?

Help in Selecting Your New Venture

BY **NANCY DRESCHER**

Published by The Oasis Press®/PSI Research
© 1997 by Nancy Drescher

This publication is designed to provide accurate and authoritative information in regard to the subject matter covered. It is sold with the understanding that the author and publisher are not engaged in rendering legal, accounting, or other professional service. If legal advice or other expert assistance is required, the services of a competent professional person should be sought.

– from a declaration of principles jointly adopted by a committee of the American Bar Association and a committee of publishers.

Editor and interior design by Karen K. Billipp, Eliot House Productions
Cover illustration and design by Steven Burns

Please direct any comments, questions, or suggestions regarding this book to The Oasis Press®/PSI Research:

Editorial Department
300 North Valley Drive
Grants Pass, OR 97526

(541) 479-9464
(541) 476-1479 *fax*
psi2@magick.net *e-mail*

The Oasis Press® is a Registered Trademark of Publishing Services, Inc. an Oregon corporation doing business as PSI Research.

Library of Congress Cataloging-in-Publication Data
Which Business? : help in selecting your new venture /
    by Nancy Drescher. -- 1st ed.
        p. cm. -- (PSI successful business library)
    Includes bibliographical references and index.
    ISBN 1-55571-390-4 (pbk.)
    1. New business enterprises. 2. Small business. I. Title. II. Series
HD62.5.D74   1996   96-47509
658.1'141--dc21   CIP

Printed in the United States of America
First Edition 10 9 8 7 6 5 4 3 2 1 0

 Printed on recycled paper when available.

Contents

Acknowledgments

Considerable credit goes to all those people mentioned throughout the book. Jon Drescher, Superintendent, Water Pollution Control Division, Bowling Green, Ohio and a leader in environmental issues, recommended exceptional environmental companies and gave input on the agricultural, engineering, and environmental chapters. Thanks to those who referred excellent companies, many which are mentioned throughout the book. Also, thanks to all those who read and gave input on the book including David Wing, business consultant, and others. Thanks to David Kaczorowski for originally suggesting the inclusion of pictures and for answering technical engineering questions.

Special thanks to the featured companies for spending substantial amounts of time plus many follow-up phone conversations with me. These companies are all experts in their fields. Without their input, this book would not have been possible.

Thanks to Karen Billipp for her editing suggestions and book design. The book is more effective through her editing and design expertise. Special thanks also to Steven Burns for his cover design and willingness to assist in the inclusion of company photos.

Introduction

S mall businesses are the future of our economy. More new jobs and innovations are occurring within the small business community than from larger companies. As larger companies cut their staffs, they limit their futures, shrinking their supply of original ideas and new product research. Many talented people, disillusioned with the profit-first attitude of companies, are taking their valuable ideas and starting their own ventures.

Owning your own business allows you to use your work experience plus other skills and talents. Many people have highly developed skills honed through hobbies and other non-job experience.

The difficult question is: Which business to start? This can be a frustrating and paralyzing experience. *Which Business?* will show you how to get past this indecision and on to starting your new venture. Once you have decided on your business, you will find plenty of start up help.

The purpose of this book is to give you ideas for your own business. The book begins with suggestions on where to find business ideas and how to research those ideas to see if they will sustain a business.

The next step is to focus on your areas of interest by exploring the different business sectors in Chapters 4 through 27. Read the sections that appeal to you. In each business section, trends are identified, opportunities are presented, and frauds or pitfalls exposed. Through the stories of over 50 small companies, you will learn how and where others got their business ideas. Once your curiosity about these companies is ignited, *Which Business?* will follow through and tell you how these businesses have grown.

Once you have an idea of the direction you'd like to explore, be sure to use the extensive resources in the back of the book. Each chapter has its own list of companies, organizations, and publications relating to that particular field. These will be invaluable in your search for your own venture. You will find contact information for the businesses discussed.

From the ideas presented and stories of existing successful businesses, you will be able to develop your own business opportunity. Give yourself plenty of time to identify and investigate your business. Good luck and enjoy your journey!

CHAPTER 1

How to Choose
Your New Venture

*T*his chapter will guide you through where and how to get ideas for your new business venture. Choosing a business that incorporates your interests, values, and enthusiasm will impel the growth of your business. Your commitment will give you the strength to deal with challenges that arise.

Beginning Your Search for Your New Venture

Identify Your Interests

You have activities that you do just because you enjoy doing them. These are your interests. Even if you were not paid or rewarded for doing these things, you would still do them.

One of your interests may be working with people. You readily accept opportunities to help, teach, or lead others. George Sieg, a NOVUS franchisee owner, likes to work with people. Although his core business is windshield repair, he comes into contact with a variety of people through the business.

Most talents are not inherited. Some physical characteristics may make an activity easier, such as height as an advantage in the sport of basketball. Still, someone is not a good basketball player just because of their height. They need to practice to gain the necessary skills. Motivation to practice is the result of enjoying the sport.

Your living environment may have had a strong influence on your interests. If people around you delight in certain pastimes, you may also find these activities enjoyable, focusing your attention on these interests. Throughout life, you encounter new experiences and find new interests. If you want to broaden your interests, continually try new activities, make an effort to meet new people, and travel to new places.

One of your interests may be music. You pay close attention whenever you hear music, listening for the elements you enjoy, humming the melody, harmonizing, or contemplating changes you might make in the music. You may expand your collection of compact discs and consistently listen to music in your car, at work, and at home. When you hear references to music, you pay attention. You may not even realize how much time you spend enjoying music. Inevitably, with all your time invested, you will know more about music than someone with little interest. In your search for a business venture, you may want to consider an idea that incorporates music.

Take time to write down your interests and the activities that you enjoy doing. As you go through your daily routine, make note of the activities that you choose to do first. Watch for those that are pleasant and include these on your list. Try to keep track of these activities for a week or more, realizing this list is not complete. You may also find new activities you have never tried that are enjoyable. Trying new things is a good way to expand your interests. Reading about the businesses in this book may help you discover new interests.

Know Your Values

Your values are your beliefs. Some common values are: honesty, generosity, quality, industriousness, and justice. These values determine how you react to the many situations you encounter daily. A business venture that reflects your values will allow you to pursue that venture enthusiastically, feeling good about what you do.

Incorporate Your Interests and Values into Your New Business

Now that you are aware of your values and some of your interests, you can try to incorporate them into a business.

The Body Shop, founded by Anita Roddick, is a cosmetic and skin care business. Roddick uses her business to support her interests and values: providing a marketplace for products from developing countries, serving the world community, and highlighting environmental issues. Natural Cotton Colours, which breeds different varieties of naturally colored cotton, is the result of Sally Fox's hobby of weaving. She discovered that Native Americans had grown naturally colored cotton and used it in their weaving. Passionate about her hobby and preserving the environment, she decided to develop her own varieties of cotton. Because her cotton is naturally colored, less chemicals are used in processing, reinforcing Fox's desire to preserve the environment.

Some of you may feel that you cannot do what you enjoy and still make a living. Your thinking may be too limited. Following your interests when choosing a business does not mean that the business needs to be exclusively focused around those interests. If you enjoy basketball, you can pursue basketball in many ways without actually being a professional basketball player. You could be a high school basketball coach, manage a sports arena, be a sports writer, or open a sports bar. You may decide that you want basketball to be a leisure activity, not your work.

Think of the possibilities writing has to offer. Besides the obvious ambition of writing novels, there are other ways to incorporate writing into your new venture. Perhaps you could start a small specialty publishing company. Do you like to write to persuade? Ad copy, speechwriting, magazine writing, writing your company brochures, and grant writing are just a few types of persuasive writing. Are you a researcher, too? Consider a business as an information specialist, independent specialty or law librarian, nonfiction writer, providing competitor intelligence for businesses, editor, fact checker for publishers, or publishing consultant. You may decide that you want to incorporate writing into your business without it being the main focus of your venture. Just because you love doing something does not mean that you want to do it most of the time. Fran Novak, co-founder of Training á la Carte, a computer software training business, enjoys writing the company training manuals and plans to write a book related to her business someday. But as co-owner of the business, she spends most of her time performing other tasks. Writing is just a small part of her business.

Many real business ideas are presented in this book. Read through the chapters and see what interests you. Later, in the chapter on market research, we will discuss how to further investigate if your idea could be a successful business for you.

Finding Business Ideas

Where can you find business ideas? The sources of ideas are all around you: your profession, your current job, your daily activities, existing businesses, your hobbies, talking with others, trends, and events. We will examine each of these sources.

Questions to Ask

Before looking for where to find ideas, let's discuss how to find them. Although the source of ideas is your everyday life, you may not be attentive to the opportunities. By asking yourself certain questions, you can focus your thinking and use the sources in your life to find opportunities.

When you examine the subsequent sources, ask yourself:

> ❖ *Do you have a unique idea?*
>
> ❖ *What are the problems?*
>
> ❖ *Is this an area of strong demand?*
>
> ❖ *Are there unmet needs?*
>
> ❖ *Are there wants that can be satisfied?*
>
> ❖ *Is there an unfilled niche?*
>
> ❖ *Can service be improved?*
>
> ❖ *Could the cost of this service or product be cut while still keeping the quality?*
>
> ❖ *Are there alternatives?*
>
> ❖ *Could this be more fun?*
>
> ❖ *Are there other applications for this product/service?*
>
> ❖ *Could this business be approached differently?*
>
> ❖ *Future scenarios?*

Do You Have a Unique Idea?

Do you have an idea for a new product that you want to develop into a business? Individuals that develop or distribute unique products benefit from a lack of competition and greater flexibility in pricing their products. Pachinko Paradise sells refurbished Japanese pachinko (pinball) and slot machines. Everything Earthly retails clothing and products made from environmentally friendly or "green" materials. Western Design Center designs and licenses custom microprocessor chips for special applications. As an alternative to a gun, Air Taser developed a product allowing individuals to incapacitate an assailant. Building their product line, they are developing a series of personal protection products.

Before basing your company on a single product, consider the potential for additional products, like Air Taser. Building a business on a single product is risky.

With a product line, you will have variety of products in the same market sector. You can use the same marketing channels for similar products, decreasing costs.

Baby Think It Over has one basic product, an infant simulator. Different editions of the dolls resemble varying nationalities. One of their dolls has a cry similar to that of a baby born to mother taking addictive drugs. Although they have one product, the variations open additional markets.

Providing a new service can also be a business opportunity. Be aware, though, that if you are successful, you will be copied. Services cannot be patented, but some products are patentable (although patents may be challenged in court). Plan in advance for competitors. Being first, you may design ways to dominate the market. If the number of competitors exceeds demand, everyone's profits may drop and competition may be predominantly on the basis of price.

Being first with an new idea has risks as well. You may spend an enormous amount of time and money developing your new product or service. Then others may later copy that idea, building on your efforts and incorporating changes that skirt any patents. This happened to a few companies mentioned in this book. To avoid this challenge, you must be prepared to grow quickly and obtain the additional capital to firmly establish your market. You also will need to continually improve your product or service to stay ahead of the competition.

What Are the Problems?

Most of us avoid problems. But many businesses were created to solve problems. Problems create opportunities. Many of us have such a negative attitude concerning problems that we miss looking at these problems for hidden possibilities. Changing your attitude about problems, viewing them as opportunities and learning situations, can make the situation less stressful and help you to discover possible business ventures. Problems demand solutions. Complete resolution may not be necessary.

For example, a few years back the medical profession was appalled by the Occupational Safety and Health Administration's (OSHA) extensive new safety regulations. All employees now need to have training about risks and marking of hazardous materials, wear additional protective clothing, and follow guidelines in the disposal of hazardous materials. But many new companies and jobs were created by these regulations. Employees need to have yearly training. Manuals were written, videotapes made, and companies who specialized in training were created. Supply companies profit by increased sales of protective clothing and devices. Laundries offer cleaning of uniforms that could no longer be taken home and washed. Medical facilities had to respond to OSHA's demands or face steep fines. Responding was cheaper.

Every business has problems. People have problems. Some dilemmas are long-standing; others caused by recent changes. Recent problems are usually easier to resolve, or at least partially solve. Long-term problems have resisted prior attempts for resolution, but that does not mean they are impossible. New technology may make these issues easier to resolve. If you can solve a problem that will increase profitability and decrease stress, you have the beginnings of a successful business.

BEST Institute is a company that was created to provide improved industrial safety and OSHA compliance for small- to mid-size companies. The company provides safety assessments and training. Often Workmen's Compensation rates can be reduced by using the services of BEST's consultants. The client company obtains the services of a specialist without having to hire a full-time employee. Jerry Beougher founded the business as a companion venture to a spin-off, a safety products distributorship, he purchased from his former employer. While still employed, he saw the need for safety consulting and was able to thoroughly investigate the companion venture.

Some needs are left unfilled because no one has yet found a way to make a profit on satisfying the need. Resourceful individuals find ways to build a business that helps solve a problem or meet a need. An example, American Traffic Systems has designed a business around drivers who speed or run red lights. Photo radar, an entirely new business in the United States, is the result. Resourcefulness in providing part of a solution to rising accident rates created a new business opportunity. American Traffic Systems has been copied and the competition to win city contracts is intense among photo radar companies.

The rising teenage pregnancy rate is a complicated and difficult problem. There is much agreement that something needs to be done, but changing behavior based on deep-rooted problems is difficult. The Jurmains had heard about attempts at educating teenagers about the demands of a baby by having them carry around sacks of flour. Certainly a flour sack is much less demanding than a real child! Mary Jurmain challenged her husband, Rick, to find a better solution. He did! Baby Think It Over, a doll designed as an infant simulator, helps young people form more realistic expectations. It does not solve the pregnancy problem and time will tell how effective the doll is, but it is a step toward working out a solution.

Increasing crime is a problem that demands multiple solutions. Air Taser modified the detonator for a protective device used by police departments. Their product provides an alternative for individuals who want protection from assailants, but do not want to use a gun. This device, the Air Taser®, allows individuals to incapacitate their assailant long enough for them to escape, without permanent harm to the aggressor.

Peter Hill's company, Traco International, wants to show individuals, especially women, that they can defend themselves. He developed a self-defense and self-esteem program called G.E.T. I.T. that teaches women how to cope with difficult situations.

Consider a non-profit organization. Certain businesses are eligible for non-profit tax status. Usually these are businesses that provide a socially beneficial service. Below is a partial list of organizations that may qualify:

✤ Private schools

✤ Charitable organizations

✤ Homes for aged

✤ Religious organizations

✤ Scientific research (unless for commercial operations)

✤ Amateur athletic organizations

✤ Child-care centers

✤ Community development organizations

✤ Animal shelters

✤ Business leagues

If you are interested and committed to one of the above causes, you can obtain more control and may increase your earnings by establishing your own non-profit business organization. Mary Sue Watson uses non-profit status for one of her child-care centers, which allows the center to receive more benefits. This can turn an unsuccessful business into a sustainable organization. The downfalls are increased paperwork and regulations.

Are There Unmet Needs?

Most of us have occasionally noticed a need for a product or service, commented on the void, but not acted to fill the need. Granted, you may not have had an interest in this type of business, but if that need was investigated, you may have found a viable business. Identifying unserved needs is an excellent way to focus your business. Many of the business owners that are profiled in this book based their business on filling a need.

Small businesses have historically had difficulty getting approval to accept credit cards. Banks want to work with established businesses. Home- and Internet-based businesses have found it nearly impossible to get set up for credit cards. The use of credit cards has become so prevalent that a company that does not accept these cards loses business. Enter the Access Group to meet this need. The Access Group not only works with start-up companies, but specializes in these businesses.

Dick Husta, Husco Engineering, designed his automobile armrest to make long drives more comfortable in his new car. Mike Byrnes and Devorah Fox of Mike Byrnes and Associates wrote training manuals for truck drivers so they could pass driving tests and to improve driver safety. LemonBusters inspects used vehicles prior to sale to help buyers assess the true condition of a car. SmartPractice produces patient incentives and practice management materials to help dentists, doctors, and other health professionals promote their practices in a very competitive environment.

Park Your Pool is the result of an unused pool in Lloyd Brunn's backyard. His inground pool required year-round maintenance and expense. He also realized that the pool added value to his home so he didn't want to in-fill it. Instead, he found a way to keep the pool without the maintenance while founding a new business.

Many companies are founded in response to meeting a need. Kelly Patterson, a registered nurse (RN) in a busy hospital intensive care unit, realized that constantly searching for frequently used items wasted time. He designed an apron, Nurse Pro Pack, to carry this equipment. Tired of wearing the same boring scrubs, Sue Callaway, another RN, made her own. Other nurses asked her to make scrubs for them, which gradually grew into a business, S.C.R.U.B.S. Most women have an assortment of clothes that they no longer want nor can wear, but are too good to throw out. Ann Siner opened an attractive resale shop, My Sister's Closet, to sell these clothes and enable women to buy quality clothes for less than the retail price. John Reinhardt was astonished to find that Arizona has many excellent lakes for fishing, his passion. Now his company, Sunflower Sales, publishes regional maps and books showing the locations of these lakes plus other recreational guides.

Fran Novak and Janet Corbisiero were computer trainers with a large computer retailer. At the time, training was included in the purchase price of a computer system. Both thought that people would pay extra for computer training. Their idea was to make training a separate profit center, but management laughed them off. So they set up their own training business and were profitable almost immediately.

Frequently a new business is founded by being alert to unmet needs. When you find a need, start researching ways to fill the void.

Is This an Area of Strong Demand?

In business sectors that are experiencing rapid growth, there may be pent-up demand for a product or service. Often this occurs with services that involve specialized knowledge, requiring time to become proficient. Eventually the need and demand will balance out as more qualified companies gear up to enter the market. But, for a time, the field may be very lucrative. Should you enter a field of strong demand? Sure, if you enjoy the work and have the skills. If you need to retrain, realize the demand will have eased by the time you are prepared. Still, if this is an area of interest, give it consideration.

In the mid-90s, businesses of all sizes are placing their computers on a network for immediate sharing of information and equipment. Chris Piraino of Granite Computer Solutions finds this a profitable area because of the huge demand for setting up and maintaining computer networks in small businesses. Once the network is set up, when additional equipment is added, Piraino's services will be required again. Eventually the demand may shift to new areas in computer technology, but Piraino, as a small business owner, will be able to adapt more quickly than a larger business.

Businesses are setting up shop on the Internet. They need experienced, knowledgeable individuals to design a web site, get them online, and then maintain that site. Since the World Wide Web is brand new, few people have more than two years experience in site design and management. The demand is great now, but it will ease as more companies enter the business. Currently, there are many inexperienced people trying to do this work, making clients cautious. Prepare a portfolio of your work and a reference list to substantiate your ability.

Are There Wants That Can Be Satisfied?

People prefer to buy what they want rather than what they need. Products or services that are unique and that appeal to our sense of individualism are in demand. Margie Frierson of Wacky Wires & Wonders finds that her customers want event decor and flower arrangements they can't find in stores. She is successful because she dares to experiment with new materials, giving her customers the unusual. Constantly thinking up new designs is challenging, but Frierson says that she finds ideas everywhere.

Arizona Bread Company also understands that people are looking for the distinctive and the unusual. Ordinary bread is boring and tasteless. Arizona Bread Company strives for memorable bread to keep customers coming back. They are opening their third store with only two years in business, proving that people will seek out the unique.

In everyday life, we encounter the ordinary. What would you splurge for? What would you go out of your way to buy, paying a premium? Keep these thoughts in mind in the search for your new venture.

Is There an Unfilled Niche?

Is there a niche within your field or interests that you could fill? A large business may overlook or dismiss small markets because they don't foresee enough profit potential. For you, as a small business, there may be plenty of business. And, as has happened before, the large company may have miscalculated. There may be more demand than they suspect.

Bill Mensch found his niche. His company, Western Design Center, designs custom chips derived from the 6502 CPU (Central Processing Unit), which he co-developed while working for a larger company. His own company now licenses these custom chips to other companies for special applications. He charges a small per chip charge for use of the design, which enables small companies and even individuals to take advantage of these custom chips.

Richard Scott of Everything Earthly defines his retail niche as environmentally-friendly. Market research prior to opening indicated that the demand for these products was not sufficient to support a retail store. Undaunted because of his commitment to his values of preserving the environment and community action, he opened the store anyway and works to build demand for these products. Finding a shortage of suitable products, he has formed a Western Hemisphere group, Green Retailers' Association, to develop and distribute environmentally-friendly products.

Sunflower Sales found a publishing niche. John Reinhardt publishes regional guides. Because the demand is primarily local, larger companies are not a threat; but there is plenty of business to support his company.

Can Service Be Improved?

Although providing excellent customer service receives lots of lip service, you probably have often found service lacking. Several small companies told me that they find it easy to surpass existing service of their competitors because they just don't deliver what they promise.

Ronni Anderson worked with an employment placement firm. Since her ideas for improving service differed from her boss, she embarked on her own, founding

Staff One Search. She finds that, although many businesses claim to place their client needs first, few consistently adhere to this policy. Staff One Search strives to always place client needs first. This policy has contributed to the firm's growth.

Realty Executives' mission is to improve service to real estate agents. By enabling agents to be more successful, they keep quality salespeople in the real estate business, resulting in better service to home buyers and sellers. John Foltz, Vice President, tells agents he is there to serve them. He asks them what they need to be more successful then finds ways to deliver.

Could the Cost of This Service or Product be Cut While Still Keeping the Quality?

Can you make the same product or provide the same service at the existing (or better) level of quality for less money? Cost cutting is a common basis for a new business in any field. Sauder Manufacturing in Wauseon, a small community in Ohio, has achieved astounding success in the furniture business by producing low cost, assemble-it-yourself furniture. Although lower cost is a primary success factor, the company is innovative in its training, respect, and trust in its employees.

By avoiding a retail storefront, a small business can cut costs and provide superior service while charging customers less. Wacky Wires & Wonders is located on the owner's homesite. Exceptional floral displays and gift baskets can be sold at a lower price because overhead costs are less. The company purchases products at wholesale, which allows it to organize a party or other event for nearly the same cost as if the customer did all the event work.

Providing Alternatives

Flies buzzing around animals and people are not only annoying, but they spread disease. Rick Frey of Arizona Biological Controls (ARBICO) realized that people would buy a product that would reduce the fly population. Pesticides and traps are not very effective against flies and toxicity is a problem. The company produces a harmless wasp which destroys fly larvae. ARBICO is the world's largest source of non-pesticide controls of insect pests. What alternatives could your company supply? What alternatives are available, yet not well-known? Like Frey, could you expand the use of these alternatives by finding ways to inform people of their availability?

Trojan Technologies produces alternatives to chlorine, which is coming under increased scrutiny for possible adverse health effects, for water and waste water treatment. Substitutes for toxic or less effective products presents opportunities.

Trojan Technologies and ARBICO understand that even though their products may be environmentally superior, cost effectiveness is also necessary.

The legal system in the U.S. is rooted in ability to pay. If people have enough money, it seems that they can buy themselves out of any crime. Ralph Wagner, a lawyer, founded Nolo Press to give people an alternative to legal counsel. If you can't afford or don't want a lawyer, Nolo Press provides information to help you take care of your own legal matters or at least be a better informed consumer.

Can This be More Fun?

We can all use a little more fun. Businesses that can incorporate fun have a distinct advantage. HEADSHOTS™ a fashion photography company, mission is to make having your picture taken be fun. How many of you really enjoy being photographed? But there are times when you need a flattering photo. Their photographic session uses a variety of wardrobe changes, poses, and flattering lighting in an enjoyable atmosphere to produce results that are complimentary.

Pachinko Paradise is in the fun business. The company imports Japanese pachinko machines, an electronic vertical pinball machine using dozens of small metal balls, and Japanese slot machines, a variant of American slots. Many are sold to game parlors, bowling alleys, and other businesses. Others are sold through catalogs to people everywhere. Doesn't that sound like fun?

Are There Other Applications for This Product/Service?

Home inspections are considered essential prior to the sale of a house. Buyers feel more comfortable with their purchase when they know the true condition of a house before buying. LemonBusters has applied the same concept to used car sales by conducting presale inspections assessing the true condition of a car. Buyers can then make a fair offer and sellers receive what the car is actually worth. Although this service may seem to favor buyers, sellers have the advantage of a confident buyer.

Look for other ways to apply a proven business concept in a new area to create your venture.

Could This Business Be Approached Differently?

You have spent many years in public (or private) school education. Each year, you found yourself with a new teacher, a new classroom or, in high school, multiples of each. And for that year, your exposure to learning was limited by the expertise of those individuals. Is there a better way? Gail Richardson, a former public school educator, wants every child to have access to the best teachers. He envisions bringing experiences to all classrooms that would otherwise be inaccessible. While technology has evolved, most schools have yet to take advantage of these advances. His company, Educational Management Group, provides programming to schools through satellite transmission. Children in locations throughout the U.S. can direct their questions to experts via phone. This is just the beginning of his vision for education.

Dale Rector envisioned a way to create a real estate agency that would attract the most productive agents. He decided to pay them 100 percent of the commissions they earned on sales. The agency, Realty Executives, provides and gets paid only for the services that the agents need. The agents are in control of their careers and earnings. Initially agents were hesitant to try this new approach, but his strategy, which has now been copied, works.

Changing the traditional approach to a business requires tremendous courage and commitment, making this strategy the most difficult to implement. But big changes often bring accordingly large rewards.

Future Scenarios?

Looking at different possibilities for the future and then charting your course based on one or more of these predictions is called scenario planning. Use scenario planning to predict the future direction of your specialty, then develop a business to meet future needs. Write down future scenarios that might affect your business. Which scenario do you think is most likely? Produce a plan that will help your company be successful given that scenario.

China Mist Tea Company used this strategy to found its business. Noting the decline in acceptability of alcoholic drinks for business meals, the founders, Dan Schweiker and John Martinson, bet that iced tea would take its place. They bet right!

Hank Vander Laan, founder of the Canadian company, Trojan Technologies, noticed that chlorine was increasingly coming under scrutiny for water treatment. He did his homework by talking with environmental experts. His company, which gained patent rights on UV disinfection by buying a metal fabrication plant owning these patents, is a leader in UV disinfection of water and wastewater worldwide.

Jerry Hansen of Ala Carte Productions helps other companies do scenario planning. The planning scenarios are often humorous and incorporate lots of audience participation while helping companies decide how they will deal with a challenging future.

Scenario planning may not only provide the idea for your new company, it can also be incorporated into the business to help chart future direction and unearth potential new opportunities.

Getting Started: Where to Find Ideas

Now that you know which questions to ask, you can go looking for business ideas. Where should you look? All around you. Your ideas will come from your everyday life. The opportunities are out there, you just need to be attentive and have an optimistic attitude. Try looking at these sources for business ideas:

❖ *People*

❖ *Your profession or current job*

❖ *Your hobbies and interests*

❖ *Your daily activities*

❖ *Other existing businesses*

❖ *Trends*

❖ *Travel and vacations*

❖ *Events*

People Are Your Best Resource

Have you made inside contacts in your field? People are your most valuable asset. A business can be successful if you have better contacts than your competitor. If you don't have contacts, start developing a people network. All businesses will benefit from a strong network.

How do you get these contacts? Be friendly, help when asked. Talk to people. Ed Karian at Laser Re-Nu received a big break when he cold-called a company, Ecotech, whose name he had seen in the news. Since Laser Re-Nu is a laser cartridge recycler, and Ecotech sounded like an environmental company, he thought they might be able to work together in some manner. Ecotech specializes in countertrade. When an exporter makes a large sale that will take financial resources from that country, the country's government will often ask for business in return, a countertrade. All due to this one cold call, Laser Re-Nu began working with Ecotech, providing countertrade by supervising building of laser cartridge recycling facilities abroad. This is now a large part of its business.

Hank Vander Laan of Trojan Technologies heard about the availability of a local business that held valuable environmental patents by talking with a fellow committee member at his neighborhood school. Conversations break you out of your set thought process. Another person's comments may change your viewpoint. Never underestimate the power of people. Rick Frey of ARBICO, obtained his business idea from his wife's ex-boyfriend. The friend had the product—beneficial bugs—but Frey was able to convert the product into a vision and a business.

Once you have selected your business, consider forming an advisory board for your new company. Companies that have tried this approach say that the effect on their business is very beneficial. Select advisory board members from different business sectors to get varied viewpoints. Try meeting at different intervals (quarterly may be the best compromise) over a paid lunch. At meetings, discuss your plans and any obstacles that you might be facing, then wait for your advisors' input.

Your Current Job and Profession

Working in your current job, you have an inside view of your company's operation. Around you are people who have expertise in varying capacities pertaining to this business. Keep alert for opportunities in your daily routine. Use your fellow employees for feedback to your ideas, though be cautious about mentioning your search for self-employment. You may find problems for which you can develop solutions, new markets, new services or products, and niche markets. Are there divisions that could be spun off as independent businesses? Can you find a growing area to specialize in? Your job is a gold mine of potential ideas.

If you are not currently employed, consider temping in businesses of interest. Being able to work in a business for a limited time is a great opportunity to find more out about a particular business. Many people are impatient about starting their own companies, losing out on opportunities to learn more about a business while on salary. Often a company will train you at its expense. Instead of rushing into a business where you have no experience, strongly consider working in another company first. While employed, you will have opportunities to make valuable contacts with other people. You will learn of the challenges as well as the opportunities in this business. Once you have your own company, you will probably be competing with other experienced, established businesses.

Broaden your perspective to include your whole profession. Each profession has opportunities to expand your skills and meet other professionals. Seek out these opportunities. You may be able to find growing areas or special interest areas that you can focus on, becoming a specialist. Your profession most likely has conferences at least yearly where you can see new products, take seminars from experts, and meet many interesting people. Conferences can break you out of your daily routine. Try to socialize with new acquaintances rather then staying with your company colleagues.

Position yourself as a specialist within your profession by giving presentations at meetings and seminars, writing for journals, and mentoring others. When helping others, you may find that you are the real recipient of benefits.

Pursue Your Interests

Just spending time pursuing your interests may bring business opportunities to you. Subscribe to periodicals and trade journals related to your interests and pay close attention to the advertisers. Advertisers already are in business in this interest area. Are there new ideas that could be the basis of your business? Can you modify existing ideas to create a new business?

Take seminars in areas of special interest. Talk with both the presenters and attendees. Join groups and organizations that bring you together with people who have similar interests. Talking with them and helping others may lead to the discovery of ideas or bring you together with a business partner, mentor, or future client.

When basing your business on your interests, try to be resourceful in identifying ways to turn these interests into a business. Jerry Hansen of Ala Carte Productions and Margie Frierson of Wacky Wires & Wonders found very unique ways to combine performing arts with business needs.

By specializing, you can create your own niche. Bill Mensch calls himself "the long, tall man," implying his in-depth knowledge of a narrow area. He understands the design and fabrication of computer chips in intricate detail from the physics through the conception and layout of a new chip. Building on his knowledge, he created his business, Western Design Center, which designs and licenses custom computer chips.

By choosing a business that relates to skills you already possess, you have a distinct advantage over new competitors. If you have interest, but not the skills, you can still consider the business. Just make sure that you gain the skills and as much experience as possible first.

Your Daily Activities

As you pursue activities in your personal life, keep your mind alert for potential opportunities. When running errands, meeting others, watching television, reading, and pursuing leisure activities, you will come across possible business ideas.

Other Businesses

Be especially alert to other businesses. When patronizing a business, think: What would I do differently if this were my business? What stands out about this business? What would improve the business? Could this business do better in a different location? What ideas could be borrowed from this company and applied to a completely different business?

Even if this is not a business of interest, you can learn much that could be applicable to your business. You may think of services or products which that company could use, finding a possible client for your new business. Talk to business owners; most love to talk about their endeavors. Compliment the owner concerning the aspects of the company that you like. Find out how they selected their businesses.

Events

When listening to news, reading the paper, listening to local business channels, and observing advertising, you may discover unfilled needs your new business could fill. Ed Karian of Laser Re–Nu learned about Ecotech through a local business newspaper. Watch for new legislation and regulations that might provide new business opportunities, as did Jerry Beougher of BEST Institute.

Travel and Vacations

Neglecting to take a vacation or travel to other locales, results in lost opportunities. It is important to occasionally break out of your routine to enable yourself to see beyond your small world. Some people and businesses get so wrapped up in themselves that they miss big chances. Also, many people come back from a vacation with renewed enthusiasm and a new perspective. To get these benefits from time away, look for opportunities to try new activities, eat in different types of restaurants, meet new people, change your schedule, and pursue those activities that catch your interest. The more change you encounter during your vacation, the greater the benefits.

Identifying and Timing Trends

Getting in quickly with new trends can give a business a fast start or bring new business to an existing company. Many trends have wide reaching implications, affecting many businesses. Look for trends within your interests. Margie Frierson founded her business, Wacky Wires & Wonders, by getting into the singing telegram business early. With only one competitor, business was plentiful for both companies. She has continued to thrive by being an astute observer of upcoming trends so she can provide these services early before she has an abundance of competition.

The founders of China Mist Tea Company found how critical timing can be for your business. Both partners were in the gourmet coffee business before the trend took off and both lost their businesses. With incredible courage, they jumped right back in, anticipating a trend for gourmet iced tea. Their China Mist Tea Company filled the void with a delicious, non-caloric beverage.

Trends, both good and bad, can lead to the development of a successful business. Rising crime led to the Air Taser® and the refocusing of Traco International, a martial arts company.

Align your business to take advantage of trends. Below are trends that may relate to your business idea. Use these trends to create new services or products for your clients:

- ❖ More women are working to provide income and increased financial security in an era of downsizing. Women's influence will bring about changes in the way business is transacted.

- ❖ With both spouses working, time is precious. Convenience in buying and services is important.

- ❖ Customers are increasingly demanding value in exchange for decreasing discretionary dollars.

- ❖ Individuals are having multiple, longer careers. Companies will find mature employees that possess valuable combinations of skills.

- ❖ Technology is changing at an increasing pace. This creates a need for continual re-education.

- ❖ Downsizing is forcing more individuals into self-employment. This is especially significant for older, experienced professionals who have more skills.

- ❖ Telecommunication and computers is permitting more people to work away from the office and congested cities.

- ❖ More businesses are pursuing a global marketing strategy to increase their markets. Some operations that are cheaper to run abroad are exported.

- ❖ Companies are outsourcing more work to avoid hiring additional employees, creating a demand for freelance professionals to fill specific demands.

- ❖ Increasing numbers of graduating lawyers continue to add to complexity of laws and increases litigation, thereby inflating costs of products and services while stifling some smaller businesses.

❖ The do-it-yourself movement is alive and well. As real wages decline, more people are doing work themselves for which they formerly hired contractors.

❖ A maturing population is seeking out youth-restoring products.

❖ Clothing designers who design fashions that are flattering for mature figures will thrive.

❖ People are living longer due to better healthcare and improved health habits. As people age, they tend to become more health conscious and more willing to invest in products and services to improve their health.

❖ As the world becomes more complex and personal challenges are encountered, people increasingly look for meaning in their lives.

❖ Crime is on the increase, the result of a variety of societal factors: breakdown of core family, lack of good paying jobs, and drugs.

❖ Our environment is a priority to most Americans, who have seen the aesthetic, health, and economic effects of lack of environmental controls in other countries.

❖ Entertainment is sought after in all economic climates. Comedy is king in tough times. Who needs more depression?

❖ Ethnic foods are becoming more popular with an increasingly diverse population. Predictions are that by year 2000, the population of Texas will be over 50 percent non-Caucasian. Ethnic food stores and restaurants will do better than non-specialty stores.

The Key to Finding Your New Business is to Match Your Passions and Skills With Other People's Needs and Wants

Your business needs to provide a service or product for which others are willing to pay the price. If your business incorporates one or more of these trends, your chances for success increase. Plan your business strategy to align yourself with these future changes.

Metamorphosis: Trial and Error as an Idea Incubator

Often the process of discovering business ideas is the result of trial and error. Jerry Hansen, Ala Carte Productions, found his niche in custom business conference productions through his dinner theater business. He noticed that although dinner theaters were profitable on weekend nights, conferences provided a seven day a week business. Although Hansen's career includes multiple sidetracks, the combination of occupations came full circle for him in his present business. If he had not had his abundant business experience, he probably would be much less effective writing his custom productions.

Bill Mensch, Western Design Center, has "closets full" of unsuccessful product prototypes. He tried many approaches before hitting upon the idea of licensing custom computer CPU (central processing unit) chips.

Trial and error is an effective means of market research. Many of the small businesses in this book mentioned that they constantly use trial and error as inexpensive market research. They add new ingredients to their business and observe the results. If it works, they keep it. If not, the idea is discarded or reworked.

ARBICO's Rick Frey calls his company a "plan, do, and review" business because they are constantly trying new things. Initially, ARBICO focused on fly control. Frey's wife, Sheri Herrera de Frey, came up with the idea of starting a catalog featuring not only their products, but those of other producers. Now they are the world's largest distributor of beneficial insects.

Why didn't an idea work? Failures have often led to success. Management consultants will tell you that if a person fails in his or her first business, the second business will often be successful. John Martinson and Dan Schweiker will vouch for this. Both went bust with their coffee companies, but loved the business. With alcohol losing acceptance for business lunches, they knew another beverage would take its place. They bet that beverage would be iced tea. So they started China Mist Tea Company, specializing in quality iced tea. Don't let go of your failures too quickly. Examine what you can take and transform into a new venture.

Possible Pitfalls in Your Search

Let's look at some potential pitfalls that can lead you down the wrong path. Searching for a good business venture takes time and patience. Many get discouraged and, when some of these pitfalls appear, give up their focused search and take the quickest or easiest path. These paths often lead to failure because they are not in sync with what you really want to do. If you are not immediately successful, you will likely give up. If, by chance you are financially successful, you may be unhappy, unsatisfied, and bored. Being less than committed, these feelings may result in only short-term success. Watch for these pitfalls:

❖ Prepackaged business opportunities

- Get rich quick schemes

- Considering only your skills and experiences, disregarding your interests

- Financially lucrative businesses that violate your values

- Following someone else's advice

- Going for the currently hot business

- Choosing your business from a list

- Seeking security

- Thinking that your new venture must be unique

- Doing something you don't want to do until you can afford to do what you want to do

Prepackaged Business Opportunities

If you are interested in starting a business, you have probably looked through the ads in the back of a business opportunity magazine or in the classified ad section of your local newspaper. Some of these ads are companies that are in the business of selling business opportunities. If the opportunity is so lucrative, why aren't they in that business rather than selling it? The answer is that selling the opportunity is more lucrative (and easier) than running the business.

Although you may already realize this, chances are you have considered responding to one of these ads. You would like these ads to be true, although intuitively you know this is not a good opportunity. Trust your intuition.

Ads for prepackaged opportunities for medical billing services are currently common in business opportunity magazines. However, large billing companies are past their growth years, with many downsizing or selling out. Medical billing, despite the no experience needed ads, requires knowledge of medical procedures and insurance experience.

Commit yourself to finding a business that fits you: your interests, your skills, your values, and your lifestyle. A prepackaged business, even if it were viable, is unlikely to produce a business that will be uniquely yours.

Get Rich Quick Schemes

You've seen the ads or heard the hype, "Easy money, no experience needed, no work. Products sell themselves. $100 thousand a year, the first year." Okay, so if there is no work and the products sell themselves, why do they need you? If you've had any work experience, you know there are not any easy jobs that pay $100 thousand a year to start with no experience. So why do people fall for these ridiculous ads that are all hype?

Everyone's dream is to win the lottery. Many play although they know the odds are overwhelmingly against them. The lower your income, the more likely you will take the chance. Well, the more lost or desperate you are, the more likely you are to respond to such an ad. Keep focused on finding a business that includes your interests. Spend the time and money researching your own business. You won't have time to be tempted into trying one of these ventures.

Considering Only Your Skills and Experiences, Disregarding Your Interests

A common route to seeking a business is to look at your skills, those abilities you have gained through life and employment, and trying to put them together into a business. Other people advise that since you are such and such you should use those skills in your business. The word "should" is dangerous. It may make you feel guilty. After all, you did graduate from college with a degree in this field and spend fifteen years working in that particular field. Maybe you should use this experience.

Well, maybe you should, but maybe you shouldn't. You may have hated every moment of those fifteen years. And because you hated it, you may have not developed your skills or kept up with current changes. The world is changing rapidly. The field you loved may be vastly different than fifteen years ago. New skills, skills that you dislike, may be needed. You may just want to try a dream you ignored previously because of finances, location, or family responsibilities. Now you may have the time, financial resources, or confidence to pursue this dream.

Having a computer or other equipment is not the basis for a business. Equipment is a tool that you can use once you have selected which business you want to start. If you don't have the equipment you need, you can buy, lease, or borrow it. But using your existing equipment to pick your business is even more foolhardy than looking only at your skills to choose your venture.

If you love your career, but just want to have more control or to pursue another direction, don't give it up. Make the adjustments needed. Refocus your goals. If your skills and interests are in sync, this field is a good match for you. Having skills and experience will help you be successful and your business grow more quickly.

Financially Lucrative Businesses That Violate Your Values

You have your own unique values that guide how you live your life: how you respond to daily challenges and what decisions you make. These values are not easily changed. They are what you believe in, what you hold sacred. If you believe honesty is always important, even a small lie will make you uncomfortable. If you believe in preserving the environment, you won't be a person who throws trash out your car window.

Some businesses may not be in harmony with your values. Some people have left a job because they didn't believe in what their company did or made. While at that company, they probably performed at less than their abilities because of this disharmony.

When you select a business, ask yourself if it will be in harmony with your values. If it is not, you will probably be less successful. You will feel uncomfortable, dissatisfied, and guilty. These feelings do not allow you to give a 100 percent effort. You may avoid those activities that violate your values and spend less time building the business. Choose a business that allows you to give your best efforts.

Following Someone Else's Advice

When you tell others you want to start your own business, be prepared to receive advice as to which business. Friends and family may have a personal interest in your decision. Although your advisers may mean well, they cannot make this decision for you. You know best what you enjoy doing.

Discussing your interests with friends and family may be helpful if you just consider their ideas as part of your input. Often more casual acquaintances can provide new insight without bringing in their personal interests. A brainstorming session may bring out ideas that you haven't considered. Meeting someone with similar interests may lead to a mentor or a partnership. Discussion helps relieve some of the tension and pressure. Consider others' ideas, but when a decision is made, make sure it is yours.

Going for the Currently Hot Business

Starting a business because it is currently in vogue will probably result in a short-lived venture. If you don't enjoy the business, you won't give your best efforts or be very successful. If the business is very popular, you will find yourself in cut-throat competition with many other competitors. You may become involved in intense price wars. You will need to find ways to distinguish your business from these competing businesses.

The business may be trendy, with a short lifespan. Will you be willing to start anew when the demand is dwindling or gone? Will you stay with the business long enough to be successful? Most businesses require time to grow. Some people jump from business to business, but they never stay with a business long enough to make it successful. When they do not experience immediate success, they jump to another hot business, losing the time and money invested in the previous business. Is this something you want to stay with? Is the business worth the start-up cost and effort if it has a limited potential? Will large companies jump into the market, making competition tough for a small business?

Ignore predictions concerning future demand businesses. If you are unconvinced, look back at a business opportunity list from a publication several years old and check the predictions against the present. Use your own observations. Talk to those already in the field.

Is this late in the business cycle, with the market already saturated? If prepackaged business opportunities are available, you are probably late in the market cycle. If the business appears on lists of best small or home businesses, you have missed the growth phase. Jumping in at this point, you will be participating in the decline, not the rise, of the business. If you are going to start a trendy business, get in early so you can take advantage of the increasing market. Before you start, stop and ask yourself if you are really going to enjoy this business.

Choosing Your Business from a List

Starting your search for your new venture from a list found in a magazine or book may lead you to a business that does not match your interests. Many lists are compilations of "hot" businesses. Others are not viable businesses. Businesses listed tend to be those that have reached their peak growth. Niche markets are usually ignored. When you choose your business from real needs and wants, matching these with your interests, you will have the start of a viable business. Starting from the list is going in reverse and you may not end up where you want, with a viable business.

Seeking Security

Starting a business to gain more control of your career and financial future makes sense. Be sure that you are not selecting a business just because it seems like a secure business. Starting a business involves substantial risk. No business is secure. By choosing a business that incorporates your interests, values, and passions, you'll have more resilience to get through the challenges that all businesses eventually encounter. If times get tough, you will at least be doing something you enjoy, which will help sustain the business. You will be more likely to find new markets and directions for your company rather than abandoning it and jumping to a new business. Security is best gained by utilizing your interests and skills to become an expert in your field. You will find ways to adapt to the inevitable changes in your market.

Thinking That Your New Venture Must Be Unique

Your business doesn't need to be unique or new. Look around your town for successful businesses. How many of them are based on a totally new product or service? You can build a company by improving existing service or products.

In fact, by building on what is already out there, you get a head start. Marketing has already been done. You benefit from this marketing because customers now know the service or product exists and someone else paid to get that message out there.

This doesn't mean that your company should be a "me too" business. If your company is indistinguishable from others, you may be forced into intense price competition. Make your venture your own by improving the service, specializing, or finding a niche, adding fun, or using any other ways to make the business unique. Metamorphose your company by using trial and error to constantly experiment with ways to make the business unique. Many of your changes will not produce results and can be abandoned. But a few of these experiments may be successes. The world is constantly changing and a successful business must change with this evolution. In the process of your experimentation, you may hit on a wildly successful idea, but first, get into a business you enjoy. Then experiment your way to success.

Doing Something You Don't Want to Do Until You Can Afford to Do What You Want To Do

Urgency is one of the key success factors for businesses. Urgency is a call to action. If your business idea is sitting on the back burner, chances are that is where it will stay. The world is changing and ideas need to be acted upon.

This doesn't mean quit your job and start your business right now. Instead develop a plan of action that will work within your life and meet your needs. Then start working on that plan. Read the next chapter to research your idea. Develop a step-by-step plan to get it going. Keep your plan flexible, because once you get started you will need to make adjustments and may find unexpected opportunities. Commit to getting started now.

You have a start on your list of ideas for your business. As you read through the book, you will expand on this list. How can you determine if your ideas will develop into a successful business? To find the answer, read on to the next chapter, Market Research.

CHAPTER 2

Market Research: Increase Your Chances of Success

*R*ead an entrepreneurial magazine, attend a franchise show, or browse a "how to start your own business" book and you will find a lot of business ideas. Separating real business ideas from unprofitable ones can be a challenge! Many ideas would incorporate well into an existing business as an added service, but on their own, just don't have market potential. Confirm all information, advice, and numbers given to you by another party. It is your time and money that will be invested, so check out the facts. How do you determine which ideas can provide a profitable business?

Once you have defined your business idea, market research will give you a reality check, indicating your initial chances of success. By spending a little time and effort, you can often save much time, effort, and money. Not only will a little research indicate possible success, these efforts will also help you better position your business in its market.

Before You Start Your Venture

Define Your Business

Write down exactly what service or products your business will produce and describe your potential customers. This sounds simple, but is probably the most difficult step. Having a very clear vision about the nature of your business is a key to your success. This vision will evolve as your business grows, but you need to define where you will start.

Be Flexible

Old style businesses always had a separate location, traditional, inflexible hours, and a conventional mode of operation. In today's competitive world, flexibility is important. Many service-type businesses can operate most profitably from a home. An office may be your car, equipped with phone and computer. Think of how you can best provide value for your clients. Use technology to take the place of unneeded overhead.

Allow for flexibility in your planning. An advantage of being small is quick decision making, which allows you to respond more quickly to opportunities that arise. When you spot an opportunity, jump on it before the larger companies can respond.

Make Sure That the Profit Potential Is Worth the Risk

The more time and money that will be invested in your business, the more market research you need to do. Make sure the risks you are taking are in line with the potential for profit. Many service businesses can be started with a small amount of money. You can try different markets and develop your business where you find the most opportunity.

Identify and Survey Your Customers

Before you invest in a business, it is wise to research the market. Who are your customers? How will you reach them? Talk to people who you identify as potential customers. Do they need and want your product or service? Are they willing to pay a fair amount for what you offer?

There are many needs that remain unfilled because potential customers are not willing to pay a fair price or cannot afford the services. For instance, you may have the noble goal of providing software training for people who are unemployed. If they cannot pay you, how will you stay in business? A business such as this needs grant money for support. To obtain grants, you will need to set up a non-profit corporation or subcontract with an existing agency. If you have enough paying clients to make a reasonable profit, you may want to donate time to working with those who cannot afford your fees. From the start, your goal is to become profitable so that your business will be successful.

For what services are your potential clients willing to pay? What are their unfilled needs and wants? How do you find the answers to these questions? Identify, then survey your customers. Do your surveying by phone, with a written survey, or even online. The questions will vary depending on your business. For example, let's use a personal computer trainer. These are some questions you might ask:

✦ Have you ever attended a seminar or training session for a computer software program?

✦ Do you feel computer expertise will make you more successful?

✦ Under what circumstances might you seek software training?

✦ Which is more important to you: cost or class size?

✦ Would you prefer a one-day training session or multiple, shorter sessions?

✦ Is follow-up from the trainer important to you?

✦ Would you prefer a one-on-one session?

✦ How much would you be willing to pay per hour for a personalized session?

✦ Would you prefer someone come to your home or you go to his or her location?

✦ How would you find a computer trainer?

✦ What do you feel is most important in selecting a trainer?

✦ What problems have you encountered in previous training?

✦ What do you feel could be done better?

✦ For which software might you benefit from training?

Keep your survey short and you will get a better response. This list of questions is too long for most surveys, especially written surveys. You might divide the questions. Ask questions that determine if there is a demand for your service to one survey group. Then ask more specific questions to a second group. From the survey results, you will find if there are enough people who will pay for your service. The survey results do not guarantee your success, but may save you from investing time and money in an unprofitable business.

Asking the right questions is part of the secret to a valuable survey. How you interpret the results is the other significant part. Really listen to what people are saying without trying to make a quick judgment. Try not to influence their comments. They may not say what you want to hear. Accept their observations. Delay interpretation until you have spoken to all the people you are surveying.

For a new product, use a similar survey. Surveying is most effective if you have a prototype so potential buyers can see the actual product. Producing the product in a limited quantity and test marketing is a great way to gauge your demand. If you want to assess an existing market, go to companies already selling the product to estimate potential sales. From this investigating, you can get ideas for product improvements and marketing ideas.

Surveying your clients can be an ongoing process that helps you identify and meet their changing needs. You might offer your clients a small reward for returning your surveys, but often this is not necessary. The easier you make completion of the survey, the better your response rate. A short multiple choice questionnaire is easy. Make sure you leave room for an alternate choice as it is frustrating when none of the choices is appropriate.

Check out your competition. Most businesses are not unique. Find businesses similar to yours through the yellow pages (your local and others), advertising in trade publications, trade shows, and associations. Ask your potential customers who they presently use for your proposed service.

Survey Similar Businesses

Can't find a similar business? Unless you have a very unique enterprise, there are similar existing businesses. Talk to suppliers, your local and national organizations, and look through local business directories. Most states have directories of small businesses. A directory of local businesses may be available for your own community. The new CD-ROM phone directories are excellent for tracking down similar businesses. You can search for a particular business type. Your library may have this service.

If you can't find a similar existing business, it will be difficult to gauge your chance at success. You may need to spend a great amount of time and money educating clients. Make sure that you have the funding to do this. If your business is original, you'll need to be very thorough with your customer survey. This may be your sole predictor of success.

If your business will be strictly local, you can call and visit similar businesses in other locations. Since you will not be a competitor, most will be happy to talk with you. Even locally, you will find people who enjoy sharing their experience. Ask questions. Using our computer software personal trainer as an example, the questions might be:

❖ Has software training been a fulfilling business?

❖ What do you like best about training others in software?

❖ What organizations have been helpful to you?

- ✦ Where can I get more information about software training?

- ✦ What experiences have been most valuable in preparing you to train others?

- ✦ For which software is there the most demand for training?

- ✦ Who are your customers?

- ✦ Where do you get your customers?

- ✦ Tell me about your competition.

- ✦ How long did it take for you to become profitable?

- ✦ What advertising has been most profitable?

- ✦ What have your customers asked for that you do not want or have not been able to supply?

- ✦ What is most challenging about the business?

- ✦ What are some of problems?

- ✦ How do you view the future of software training?

- ✦ Would you start this type of business again?

- ✦ If you were to start again, what would you do differently?

- ✦ Do you have any advice for me?

- ✦ Can you recommend anyone else with whom I might speak?

It is best to start with easy, positive questions, queries likely to get a "yes" answer. Let the owner become comfortable speaking with you. When you have gained rapport, ask more personal and complex questions.

Pose as a Customer

Another way to survey similar businesses is to call posing as a customer. Ask the type of questions that a client would ask. You will discover their availability and customer responsiveness. Inquiring may provide clues regarding how to position your business more competitively.

Will People Buy Your Product or Service?

Probably the biggest mistake made in start-up is to choose something you like to do regardless of whether others will pay you for the service. Keep an open mind and listen carefully to what others say. Play the devil's advocate and try to think of all the reasons your business might not be profitable. What can you do that might change these factors? Even after you do this market research, you still cannot be ensured that people will buy until they actually do.

Work in a Similar Business

Try working in a similar business either as an employee or volunteer. If you are considering a temporary help business, for example, try to find a position in a similar company and learn as much as possible. Make contacts within the business. Watch for problems that your new company can solve. Look for areas that are underserved or unrecognized.

Time Spent Investigating Is a Good Investment

This may seem like a lot of work, but it is worth the effort. The information gained is extremely important to the success of your business. You will avoid spending time and money in unprofitable ventures. Finding a niche is important in this competitive world. Information obtained should provide clues regarding where efforts would be best concentrated.

Being self-employed gives you more control over your future. Employees at all salary levels lack power over their position and the company's future viability. You control the future of your business. You can adjust to changing trends. Putting more time and effort into your work increases your satisfaction and financial rewards. This is why people choose to own their own companies.

After speaking with many business owners, the one factor that all successful businesses seem to share is persistence. All businesses will have crisis and difficult times. Expect this from the start. You will have competition and possibly bad publicity and criticism. Decide from the beginning how you will deal with these challenges. Watch cash flow so you can survive through tight times. Most of all, you must be totally committed to making your business work. When you are committed, you will continually seek out ways to help your company thrive. Bill Mensch, Western Design Center, experienced a tremendous challenge very early in his business. His only customer stopped doing business with him. He tried many things to make his business successful before he found success in licensing his custom chip design. If he had given up and become an employee again, he never would have experienced his current success. Persistence and commitment seem to be essential to success in small business. Hang in there.

Position Yourself for Success

Find a Mentor

Align yourself with a successful business owner. When you establish rapport with an owner, ask if you may call later with other questions. There are many advantages to having someone you can call. They might have more work than they can handle and refer some to you. You might have different strengths and be able to work together. Start building alliances with other businesses immediately.

Suppliers come into contact with many businesses and are often happy to provide information if they think they will be gaining a customer. Ask them which businesses do well and what makes them successful. Get the names of these business owners and call them.

Be a Salesperson

Why are people so hesitant to sell? If you see a movie you enjoy, don't you tell others? You are essentially selling that movie. When you eat at a restaurant with great food, you naturally tell others. Tell others about your business. If you are not enthusiastic about your business, how can you expect your customer to be interested in doing business with you?

If you are in a one-person business, you will have to be a salesperson. If you have a good product or service, then why hesitate to tell others about it? If you don't think you have a good product, make it better prior to starting. Whether you have a retail business or seek clients for your service, you must sell yourself and your product.

Be Positive

People are attracted to positive people. Positive individuals make us feel good while negative people do not. Be the type of person that attracts others. You want to attract people to your business to become your customers.

This does not mean that you should not be realistic. All businesses have their own problems. Instead of complaining, look for ways to meet these challenges.

A note on problems: Most people go out of their way to avoid problems, but fewer people would have businesses and jobs today if there were no problems. Problems create work. People who avoid problems do not make good entrepreneurs.

Instead of avoiding problems, look for better ways to handle them. Think of what your business can do with these problems. Is there an opportunity for you to help find solutions? Baby Think It Over founders, the Jurmains, could have avoided working with one of our most overwhelming social problems, teenage pregnancy. Instead, they faced the dilemma head-on, realizing that their infant simulator may not be a total solution, but a partial solution gets us headed in the right direction.

Learning to work with problems makes much more sense than avoiding them. It is difficult to make a living without problem-solving skills and these skills are best developed through solving real dilemmas.

Trust Your Instincts

If information you hear or a situation doesn't feel right, check it out yourself. Every day we are bombarded with information and much of the information is skewed to the advantage of the perpetrator or just plain inaccurate. Sometimes important information is missing, changing the overall view.

Be Charismatic

Some people just attract others. These people are positive, enthusiastic, and exude energy. Energy, at times, seems like magnetism, drawing others. They are flexible, adapting rather than insisting on their own way. They have a "Let's work together" approach. Being charismatic has made individuals without experience or even special knowledge successful. Of course, to stay successful, you'll need to get that knowledge.

Rick Frey of ARBICO, is a charismatic individual. With a background in biology, he just loves being able to run a business he believes in. Whether you are interested in the environment or not, he'll get your attention. Because of his personality, he continues to grow a successful business that started with only two cups of bugs.

Create a Win–Win Situation Between Your Clients and Yourself

Most businesses depend on repeat customers. Having to continually bring new customers into your business is expensive. Keeping existing customers is more cost-effective. By rewarding current customers and making them happy with your products and services, they will not only continue to come back, but will send new customers to you. Make sure that your customers get a good deal so they continue to come back. Electronic Materials and Computers uses the goal of win-win deals as its business mission.

Help Others

When you help others, you often gain as much or more as the person you are help-ing. Your knowledge and skills increase as you explain concepts to them and they may be able to return the favor.

Ways to Get Into Business

Be flexible when determining how to start your business. You have multiple choices:

❖ Find a partner(s).

❖ Be an independent contractor or distributor.

❖ Buy an existing business.

❖ Buy into an existing business as a partner.

❖ Buy a franchise.

❖ Buy a business package, a nonfranchise business opportunity like Snap-On Tools™

❖ Be a consultant.

❖ Start part-time or moonlight.

❖ Incorporate.

❖ Work as an associate for a business owner with a buy-out agreement.

❖ Buy a portion of the business where you work.

❖ Form alliances.

In Japan, business alliances are common. An alliance combines the strengths of multiple companies for a more effective and powerful organization. In the U.S., a weakness of our intense competitiveness is that companies are often too suspi-cious to trust others. By combining strengths, small, synergistic companies can create more value for their customers.

Trojan Technologies convinced the maker of its power supplies for its wastewater UV disinfection system to align with a European company, encouraging idea exchange. Both companies gain knowledge and skill. Trojan gets a superior prod-uct by creating a win-win situation. Alliances promote idea-sharing and can cre-ate new markets for the involved companies.

Small companies have limited resources. By pairing with another company to handle part of the business, costs can be kept down and each company can concentrate on what it does best. Air Taser uses another company to assemble its protection devices; then a second company, Insight Distribution Network, to ship its products. This company concentrates on making the critical component, the probe cartridges, to ensure high-quality control.

Remember that Microsoft started out as a tiny, two-person company. Their alliance with IBM enabled them to find their pathway to success.

Keep Your Priorities

Many new business owners get so wrapped up in the day-to-day operation of their business that they lose sight of the big picture. Don't forget to keep priorities that will enable your new business to succeed.

You Must Make a Profit

At first you might not be profitable, but over the long-term you must make a profit if this business is going to support you, your family, and your employees. Make decisions that keep your company in business.

You Must Provide Services and Products That People Want, Need, and Are Willing to Pay For

If you want to make things for yourself, that is a hobby, not a business. Use your passions to provide those products and services that people will want to purchase.

You Must Commit to the Business

When you decide what your business will be and have done your market research, commit to the venture. Decide that you will do whatever it takes to make this business successful. To keep the business profitable, you will need to make it a very high priority in your life.

Keep the Broad Picture In View

Sometimes you become so focused on your small business sector, that you miss the broader issues that impact the business. Occasionally zoom out with your focus to note what is happening in related fields and larger trends.

Maintain People Contact

People will give you feedback, tell you their needs and wants, shift your viewpoint, and help you maintain balance. Keep some contact with people even if you work from home as a sole proprietor.

Get On With Your Business

Anyone can have a great idea. Each person has unique experiences. Other people's ideas are not better than yours, just different. Instead of envying the ideas of another, use your own ideas. In the next chapters, you'll read the stories of the businesses already mentioned. Reading these stories, you will see these are people like yourself. If they started successful businesses, so can you.

I wish you great success in your new business. Once you have established your new venture, please write and describe your business. Perhaps your company will be included in a future edition of this book.

CHAPTER 3

Real Business Ideas

*I*n the subsequent chapters, you will discover individuals, some similar to yourself, who created successful businesses using their ideas and interests. Reading about how they chose their business ventures will give you business ideas. If they were able to select and build a thriving business, you, too, can choose and grow your own business.

Read through those chapters that interest you. After the real life business stories, you will learn about related business opportunities. When you find a business that sounds interesting, combine this opportunity with your own unique ideas and experiences. Talk with other individuals and businesses. Use the information in the previous chapter on market research to evaluate market potential where you live.

Some of these businesses are still very small; all started with only a few people. Many prospective business owners find the concept of a large business overwhelming or unattractive. A few of the businesses discussed prefer not to have employees. In busy times, they bring in freelancers or temporaries.

Some of the businesses are home-based. ARBICO, the world's largest distributor of beneficial insects, could be classified as home-based. Although their business is not in their home (with bugs, thank goodness), it is on the grounds of their 10-acre homesite. Business is just a few steps from home.

While some are happy with the current size of their businesses, others have big plans to grow. Some have already experienced this growth. A few want to take their companies public or franchise. One has been bought out by a much larger business, giving an infusion of capital and propelling rapid growth of the company.

A few of the stories are about new businesses, less than three years old. Others have 20 years of experience. By reading about a variety of companies at different stages in their growth, you can discover the challenges that they have faced and see the opportunities.

All the businesses discussed in this book are successful, although the level of success varies. Some people measure success by financial returns. No matter how great a business is, to continue to provide its service or product, it must make a profit. When you work hard and provide a service or product of value, you deserve to be compensated. All the companies I spoke with mentioned that they paid close attention to costs and earnings. Though profit may not be primary for these businesses, they are successful in part because they realize that they need to be profitable.

All of these business owners, though, have goals beyond financial return. Think about your own goals. One great part of having your own business is that you can build the business in harmony with your own goals and values.

From these businesses, you will see that there are many paths to becoming a business owner:

❖ Some made a product for their own use, then others requested that product: Husco Engineering, S.C.R.U.B.S., and Nurse Pro Pack.

❖ One decided to meet the needs of an abandoned market sector: Access Group.

❖ Two bought part of the company for which they worked: BEST Institute and Arizona School of Real Estate and Business.

❖ Others actively sought to start their own businesses to get out of the corporate world: HEADSHOTS, My Sister's Closet, Sunflower Sales, Granite Computer Solutions, and Laser Re-Nu.

❖ Some had a great idea: Husco Engineering, Air Taser, Baby Think It Over, HEADSHOTS, and Styles On Video.

❖ Several business owners decided to take control of their own futures when their companies wanted them to relocate: Electronic Materials and Computers, Husco Engineering, HEADSHOTS, and others.

❖ Businesses that found a better solution to help solve a problem: Air Taser, Baby Think It Over, LemonBusters, Traco International, ARBICO, Trojan Technologies, N-Viro, and Park Your Pool.

❖ Filling a need would include many of these businesses, but especially: Access Group, Children's Campus, Educational Management Group, BEST Institute, Mike Byrnes and Associates, My Sister's Closet, On Assignment, Precision Home Inspection and others.

❖ Finding a better way to do something is a great route to your own business: Realty Executives, Trojan Technologies, Educational Management Group, Arizona School of Real Estate and Business, Training á la Carte, China Mist, and Ala Carte Productions.

❖ Several used their community activism to promote a better environment: Everything Earthy, ARBICO, Natural Cotton Colours, and Nolo Press.

❖ Seeing an opportunity: Sunflower Sales, Pachinko Paradise, and Mina International.

❖ Following a hobby or talent: Ala Carte Productions, Wacky Wires & Wonders, Roy's Train World, Nancy's Notions, Mesa Aquatics, Western Design Center, S.C.R.U.B.S., and Natural Cotton Colours.

❖ Do you think that you can run the business where you work better than your boss? Some have put this to test by actually starting a similar business: Ky-ko Roofing, Wacky Wires & Wonders, Staff One Search, and Training á la Carte.

❖ For some, the dream of having their own business is the reason for the business: Arizona Bread Company, Fidelity Monitor, and My Sister's Closet.

❖ A few entrepreneurs found themselves out of a job and decided to get more control of their futures: Corporate Arts, Access Group, Mike Byrnes and Associates, and Baby Think It Over.

Why were these businesses selected? Each business has an unique story that can help other start-ups. Many of the businesses described in this book are located in the Southwest because of their proximity for discovery and personal visitation, yet they could just as easily be located elsewhere. People have similar needs and wants in communities worldwide. Technology enables very small companies to do business from locations that are sometimes remote. Some of these businesses, even a few home- and single-person businesses, are global enterprises. Indeed, technology—computers, networks, and e-mail, advanced phone systems and fax, and efficient shipping—has enabled small businesses to be competitive.

Most businesses were very receptive to sharing their stories. They immediately recognized that telling their company stories is an unique opportunity. Successful business owners are pros at seeking out opportunities, especially those that provide free marketing. However, this was not the only reason they agreed to be included. Most genuinely wanted to share their experiences to help others.

Some businesses are easier to start. They require less start-up money and fewer special skills. Some can be started in your home although many will grow beyond this space. Network marketing and some service businesses are examples of easy entry opportunities. Be cautious of businesses that promise little effort and huge profits. These businesses, because of ease of entrance, may have many companies that come and go quickly. When the new owner realizes the amount of work necessary to sustain the business, he or she may give up. Transient businesses tend to tarnish the image of those that remain. Ease of entrance may not be the best criteria for choosing your business. Businesses that require more effort may pay higher rewards, both financially and in self-satisfaction. Rather than choosing the easiest path, choose a business that has good long-term prospects and which is a good fit with your interests.

Non-profit corporations are an often overlooked opportunity. If you have a passion for an area that qualifies, a non-profit corporation may allow you to do the work you love, while making a living and having more control over your work.

Many of the business owners related that they never would have started their business if they had known the difficulties ahead. But they all were happy that they had stuck with the business. None would go back to being an employee. Yes, they have strenuous days and face challenging problems, but the business is still satisfying. Expect difficulties as you get started. Use these challenges as opportunities to forge the best path for your new enterprise. Be flexible to shifts in direction to adapt to a changing market.

A resource list is included at the back of this book for each chapter. Much information may already be available from the professional association representing your business field. These associations can provide a wealth of people contacts as well as providing you with current information through their periodicals. Subscribe to a few in your business sector to keep current.

The business ideas presented are meant as examples of how others founded successful companies. The pace of change in business has accelerated. The route these companies followed may not be the best path now, but note their passion and commitment, essentials for success. Formulate your own business venture. Since you want to avoid being a "me, too" company, use your own unique ideas, abilities, and talents to customize your venture. Taking a business idea from a list, as mentioned under Pitfalls in Chapter 1, will likely lead you astray. Your ideas are valuable, but you need to act upon them to be successful.

The biggest factor for success in business is action. After reading this book, set up a plan to select your business, then take steps to get started. You may at times feel uncomfortable while searching, researching, and starting your business. Expect this. To be successful, you need to reach beyond your comfort zone. Although you are reaching out, you don't need to risk everything. Taking a loan against your home is probably unwise. Find ways to leverage your risks. If necessary, start part-time. Go ahead and get started on your search for your future business!

CHAPTER 4

Agricultural Businesses

*F*armers have had an increasingly tough time maintaining profitability. Approximately one-third of U.S. farms are not profitable. Most of these are small farms, which makes profitability more difficult. Some of these are "lifestyle farms," farms that are not the primary family income source, but are farmed part-time for a rural lifestyle. Farming is a business demanding the same management, cash flow, and marketing skills as any other business.

Consider an agriculturally-related business if:

❖ You have a farming background and are aware of the challenges.

❖ You have a biological science, environmental, farm management, or agricultural degree in addition to farming experience.

❖ You have management skills: knowledge of cash flow, marketing, and negotiating.

❖ You have strong contacts in the agricultural business.

❖ You are interested in an environmental business.

Despite the challenges that face agricultural businesses, the following two businesses are successful because the founders are passionately committed to their endeavors. They feel they are really making a difference by improving the environment and producing exceptional products. Both effectively use the media to inform others about their unique, environmentally-friendly products.

Arizona Biological Controls (ARBICO)

The inspiration for Rick and Sheri Frey's company, ARBICO, came one day when an ex–boyfriend of Sheri's stopped by the Frey home with two bags of bugs. The visitor was raising beneficial insects for fly control. "Lights flashed before my eyes," described Frey. "I knew this was what I wanted to do."

A biology instructor and graduate of University of Arizona, Frey approached the head of the livestock program in the cooperative extension program, offering to draw up a biological fly control research program. He received the nod for the contract and went to work with the University of Arizona as his first customer.

March 4, 1978 is a day Rick Frey remembers vividly. That day, he released his first beneficial insects with coverage by local television in Tucson, which was subsequently syndicated across the U.S. This promotion sparked the growth of the company and illustrated vividly to the Freys the power of publicity. Since then, publicity through television features and articles has provided millions of dollars in free advertising for ARBICO, effectively using the media to promote Frey's vision.

On a part-time basis, and while maintaining his teaching position, Frey started selling his fly control program to local livestock raisers. The first nine people he talked to bought the program. Now Frey's program is used worldwide for fly-infested areas. ARBICO's customer base has doubled in the past two years and the company is now the world's largest distributor of beneficial insects.

Frey initially funded his business by refinancing his Dodge Ramcharger. Combined with some money from Rick and Sheri's parents, ARBICO was founded, headquartered in an Airstream. As the business grew, an inflatable building was added. Relying on its own profits, ARBICO has pursued a slow growth path. In 1980, the Frey's moved to their permanent location on 10 acres in the foothills of the Catalina Mountains just north of Tucson, Arizona.

Since 1980, both Frey and his wife, Sheri, a business graduate of the University of Arizona, and co-visionary, devote all their time to the business. Prior to this, they had just one employee, an entomologist. In 1980, they added two of Rick's brothers, one for sales and the other for maintenance and production. Throughout the 1980s, fly control was the company focus.

Often when clients ordered fly control products, they would ask if ARBICO had any products for other pests such as aphids. Frey knew that other companies were producing biological control alternatives and decided to investigate other pest problems. Sheri came up with the idea of a catalog featuring not only their own products, but those of other companies. ARBICO has expanded to a broad line of biological alternatives. Their product line also includes soil enrichment, habitat refuge plants for beneficial insects, and pest monitoring.

ARBICO's catalog has evolved to its present full color, thirty-plus pages, and a circulation of hundreds of thousands. To increase delivery speed, products are drop shipped from individual suppliers. Starting locally, they now ship throughout the U.S., plus 15 countries and are growing worldwide. Exporting insects internationally has opened new opportunities plus subsequent challenges.

The company employs 15 employees year-round, expanding to 30 during the spring and summer growing period. Their own fly control products are about 60 percent of their business, the remainder, from other suppliers whose products are featured in the catalog. ARBICO is unique among the environmental alternative companies because it buys products from other producers. The company brings together a worldwide web of bug suppliers, a one-stop source of environmental alternatives. "ARBICO does not have solutions for all pest control, but engages itself in the areas where the solutions lie," explains Frey. "What we're doing is educating and re-educating people that insects are a good part of life. We were raised to believe that the only good insect is a dead insect."

Frey is passionate about providing options in pest control. His goal is to win the Nobel Peace Prize for giving people worldwide choices in pest control. In 1994, the Environmental Protection Agency awarded the company the Apple Award for its educational efforts. The Freys travel extensively, giving speeches and providing exhibits for conventions and organizations. Helping customers formulate a complete pest control program is ARBICO's mission. This involves discovering the customer's goals, pest monitoring, soil analysis, and formulating a continuing program for biological pest control. Biological pest control is frequently more cost effective than chemicals, but timing for release of products is critical to success.

In 1980, ARBICO introduced Ruidosa Downs Racing and Hialeah Racetracks to its fly control program. The University of Arizona offers a degree program in Racetrack Management, and a yearly conference brings worldwide racetrack owners to Tucson. Frey spoke at the 1981 conference. His presentation was followed with a talk endorsing ARBICO's products by the director of the Santa Anita Racetrack. With this recommendation, ARBICO began selling products to racetracks worldwide.

"ARBICO is a plan, do, and review company," explains Frey. Products and programs are tried and they keep the most effective. On their acreage, the Freys farm an organic garden and raise two horses. That way they can experiment with new product innovations on-site. He developed a pod which attaches to a remote controlled aircraft for faster and easier insect dispersal. This automatic dispersal of insects takes minutes to do a job that previously took hours. Another invention is a solar flytrap which cleverly entices flies into the trap using a bait and when the flies are unable to find their way out, they dehydrate. Their "Delectables" line of dead insects from the solar flytraps are attractively packaged and marketed to pet stores and zoos.

Located near Biosphere II, ARBICO helps with the project's biological control needs. When a large retirement community was built nearby, Frey introduced the management to ARBICO's products to help maintain the golf course. ARBICO is also assisting a nearby world-class resort with compost management, organic crops, and beneficial insect controls. Other clients include dairies, cattleyards, horse tracks, commercial growers and landscapers, researchers, pest control companies, retailers, and backyard gardeners worldwide.

ARBICO has entomologists and consultants on staff to answer questions relating to sustainable growing practices. Whether you are a homeowner, apartment dweller, greenhouse or animal owner, or farmer, and use traditional or organic growing methods, ARBICO can answer questions relating to soil, fertilizer, lawn care, cover crops, disease, and pest control.

Natural Cotton Colours

Sally Fox also has been able to develop her passion into a successful business. Fox is the patent holder and original developer of FoxFibre®, the first machine spinnable naturally colored cotton. Historically, the naturally colored cotton strains used by Native Americans had a shorter fiber length and poorer strength when used in automated spinning. Two centuries ago, the switch was made to white cotton because it lent itself, due to longer and stronger fibers, to modern textile processing. Better, though less healthy for the environment, dyes became available to provide the color artificially.

With her background in entomology and as a hobbyist weaver, Fox became interested in the naturally colored cotton and has painstakingly developed strains that have superior strength and longer, machine spinnable fibers. This cotton requires a longer growing season, which limits growing locations to Arizona and Southern

California in the U.S. Originally some of her colored cotton was grown in Texas, but the narrower growing season resulted in shorter fibers.

Fox has bred chocolate brown, reddish brown, and sage green colored cottons, all trademarked as FoxFibre® Other colors are in development. As the cotton matures, and with repeated exposure to washings, the colors deepen rather than fade like dyed cottons. Colors can be interwoven to add depth to the fabric, a result that dying can't duplicate. This interwoven cotton can mimic the appearance of silk or wool.

Fox first began developing the patented cotton in 1982 and continues to work on refining the cotton's qualities and adding colors. The process of developing new colors is slow. Fox must find a plant with the desired color then interbreed it to develop the preferred characteristics. This requires generations of crops, taking the seeds of one generation and selectively breeding them with seeds from another plant until the result is satisfying. Fox has bred her cotton organically so that it is selected to thrive with organic farming methods, decreasing use of chemicals and conserving water. Some varieties are naturally fire retardant.

Sales of naturally colored cotton apparel, which commands higher prices, have been profitable. Companies such as Levi Strauss and L.L. Bean received tremendous response to products made from these fibers. Despite this excellent response, the challenges in getting this cotton to retailers have been extraordinary.

Some farmers worry that colored cotton fields planted near white cotton could result in cross pollination, contaminating white cotton fields and vice versa. If a mill processes both cottons, there can be some intermixing during processing. These are challenges that can be dealt with, but financial constraints have limited ways of working through the process.

The traditional white cotton industry depends heavily on fertilizers and pesticides. Based on total land use, the cotton industry is one of the largest users of chemicals and water. After harvesting the cotton, further chemical treatment is used to bleach, then dye the cotton. Dyeing is an expensive process and, in the U.S. and other regulated countries, toxic effluent from dyeing must be purified prior to discharge.

Originally Fox developed and grew her colored cotton on her farm in Southern California. A ban from the cotton growers association in California forced a move to Arizona where the government has been more supportive. Since relocating to Arizona, Fox says that growers have been more businesslike and less provincial.

Getting the colored cotton to market has been slow. FoxFibre® commands high prices from retailers so has greater profit potential for farmers. Resistance from spinners is the primary obstacle in getting more naturally colored cotton to market. Fox feels that patience is needed in the introduction of these new varieties of cotton and that, with time, her cotton will be more accepted.

Although Fox understands the concerns of traditional cotton farmers, she believes that naturally colored cotton is better for the environment. She is committed to the breeding of this cotton despite the challenges. Fox believes that "we do not need to wear out the Earth to have something to wear." FoxFibre® demonstrates that having a superior product, even a product in demand, is not enough in itself. Resistance by the traditional cotton industry has hindered growth.

Although marketing of colored cotton in the U.S. has been difficult, the Israeli government, copying Fox's ideas and breeding, has strongly supported growing of naturally colored cotton in its region. There seems to be greater appreciation of the market potential for these cottons in Israel. They are Fox's main competitors.

Fox would like to be a seed supplier for the naturally colored cotton industry. Being a small and private company, she can afford to think long-term, with less concern for immediate return of investment. She enjoys this business because it incorporates her values with her work and allows her to make her own decisions.

Getting FoxFibre® in more apparel will require a larger commitment from spinners to process the cotton. With more financial backing, Fox could lobby on behalf of this cotton and work with more farmers. Since the market response has already been tested with very positive results, less risk is involved.

"Stay out of areas of which you are unfamiliar," Fox advises new businesses. "Concentrate on what you know; find your niche and do it to the best of your ability. Commit to the long haul." Even a great product may be difficult to get to market, but commitment will increase your chances.

❖　　❖　　❖

Both ARBICO and Natural Cotton Colours do business internationally. U.S. farmers compete with farmers worldwide, price being the overriding factor. Companies that assist farmers in increasing their competitiveness globally will find market demand.

Agricultural Opportunities to Explore

NAFTA eliminates most tariffs between the U.S. and Mexico, increasing agricultural trade. Mexico exports coffee, live cattle, fruits, and vegetables. With direct investment by U.S. firms, more processed foods are produced in Mexico. The U.S.

exports grains, meat, and dairy products. These product differences help balance trade. The Farm Bill, passed in March 1996, allows more versatility for farmers to select their crops. With this increased flexibility, farmers can choose crops that demand higher prices in the international market and avoid those that place them in competition with products that can be produced at lower cost elsewhere.

Increasing Competitiveness Through Larger Farms or Cooperatives

The trend in the U.S. has been toward larger, more professionally managed farms. An alternative for smaller farms is forming a cooperative: sharing equipment, resources, and skills. Farmers can buy in bulk plus share marketing expenses, and in turn, decrease costs. When farmers work together as professionals managing a business, they increase their ability to compete domestically and internationally.

New Farming Methods

New farming methods will become more mainstream as techniques improve, lowering costs. Consider a business that provides products and services related to these new methods.

ORGANIC FARMING: Demand for organically grown produce continues to grow as the population becomes more health conscious. Younger people are growing up with a greater awareness of the influence of diet on their health. As fertilizers and pesticides continue to deplete the soil, the need to replenish the soil will shift the focus more to organic techniques, supplemented with selective use of chemicals.

Companies that are producing seeds bred for organic farming, beneficial insect and other biological control companies, composting, and soil moisture retention products will continue to benefit. Both ARBICO and Natural Cotton Colours are examples of this trend.

PRECISION FARMING: Using global positioning systems (GPS), satellite imaging, and a technique called remote sensing, hypothetically, crop yields can be improved and costs decreased. These techniques are part of a new approach called precision farming. GPS systems are coupled with on-the-go rate controls for seed, fertilizer, water, and pesticides. Software is already available to integrate the data. Early results indicate that chemical costs decrease. Whether yields and profits subsequently increase is still being evaluated. For committed individuals, this market is creating business opportunities.

SELECTIVE BREEDING OF LIVESTOCK: With artificial insemination, farmers can select the qualities that they want to breed. Livestock farmers will need companies to assist them with these techniques.

AQUACULTURE (FISH FARMING): Fish is gaining in popularity because of its nutritional value, resulting in shortages of some varieties. Shrimp is one of the most lucrative and largest markets. Retail fish prices have been rising faster than meat and poultry.

To increase production and decrease costs, fish will be increasingly raised on fish farms rather than through offshore fishing. Ornamental fish will also be farmed rather than brought in from other countries where harvesting may be restricted.

Distance Learning

Many farmers live some distance from towns with educational resources. Farming demands continual learning, demonstrated by the trend toward precision farming. Agricultural companies might consider courses for farmers via satellite television, bringing information to the farmers.

The Internet and online services are also great sources of information. The Internet provider market is crowded in cities, but resourceful companies can still build businesses in more rural or small town areas.

New Crops

New crops will be developed that are beneficial to the environment. An example of a promising new crop is salicornia, a hardy succulent that was found growing in salt water marshes. Ninety-eight percent of the world's water is salty. Salicornia thrives on saline water and poor, sandy soil. Salicornia is prized as a gourmet vegetable, but the primary planned use is to extract the oil from the seeds. After the oil is removed, the crushed meal makes a high protein livestock food or flour. Besides all these benefits, the plant is effective in removing carbon dioxide from the air. Ideal climates for growing salicornia are: Australia, Mexico, Pakistan, Saudi Arabia and the southern U.S. states, especially Florida and Texas. This crop has attracted investment dollars worldwide.

Genetically engineered seed that is resistant to pests is already available. Further development of new plant strains will decrease pesticide use while increasing yields. Sally Fox of Natural Cotton Colours breeds her naturally colored cotton to grow best organically. The cotton is naturally more resistant to insects. Plants develop a more intricate root system. This results in a healthier plant that can more effectively use moisture and nutrients in the soil.

New Uses for Existing Crops

Some businesses produce ethanol from corn. Other sources such as yard wastes, city wastes, agricultural byproducts, and crops like switchgrass may also be used by companies to produce ethanol. Companies are developing new uses for other plants, such as paper made from kanaf.

Use of New Energy Sources

Farms and rural areas are logical sites for alternative energy due to their abundance of land, increased need for energy, distance from utility companies, and sensitivity toward environmental issues. Solar power technology is becoming safer and more cost effective. Once the cost-effectiveness issue is lessened, alternative energy companies catering to farmers could provide opportunity for new businesses.

Increase in Home and Business Landscaping/Computer Imaging

Demand is growing for specialty landscaping plants and trees as homeowners and businesses become more aware of how landscaping increases the value, beauty, and energy efficiency of their property. Using computer imaging helps clients visualize the completed appearance of a landscape design. Coupling this service with a landscaping business will increase sales.

Produce Trucks

Instead of selling to distributors, why not have your own produce truck and go directly to consumers? Trucks provide access to a larger market, making more sense than farmers' markets where customers must come to you. Include fresh milk, bread, and baked goods for increased sales. This idea worked in the past and is worth trying again. You may find that a route including businesses, plus evenings and weekends for residential areas, is most productive.

Conservation and Purification of Water

Farming run-off has been one source of water contamination. Farmers understand the importance of good quality water to their survival. Efforts to optimize water use and decrease run-off will increase. Irrigation systems with soil sensors automatically provide water as needed. Some are solar powered. Electrostatic sprayers charge the water mist so that plants attract the water. Further development of water optimization techniques and products by businesses will continue.

Raising Specialty Livestock

Some farms are raising ostriches and buffalo for their meat, which appeals to customers seeking the unusual. The Mad Cow disease in England has increased the popularity of other types of meat. These are risky and trendy endeavors, so proceed carefully.

Ostriches can yield up to one hundred pounds of boneless meat and produce as many as one hundred eggs a year. One trendy use of ostriches is for racing. Several communities have yearly Ostrich Festivals, featuring the odd bird. Buffalo, which require an abundance of grazing land, are raised for their meat and hide.

Llamas are being used in place of horses to carry equipment for long, multi-day hikes. They can't carry as much as horses, but will eat the vegetation along the trail, are sure-footed, and have nice dispositions.

Partnership Between Agriculture and Entertainment

Farming can also provide leisure activities for its patrons. Many farms use entertainment seasonally, such as Halloween or fall harvest, when people come to their farm stores. Hayrides, tours, contests, and demonstrations not only educate the public but increase sales.

An interesting example of this combination is a Rainbow Trout farm located in wooded Oak Creek Canyon alongside a rocky mountain stream near Sedona, Arizona. Nestled between high, beautiful red cliffs, you can fish in the ponds at the hatchery for a fee, but without a license. "Hook'em and cook'em" is offered on site with drinks and snacks available for a complete meal.

Surplus and Parts for Farm Equipment

Farmers are innate recyclers. Opening a business that provides surplus equipment close to farming communities can fill the need to lower costs. Being resourceful, farmers will find uses for recycled equipment.

Farm equipment often needs repair. Businesses that can supply parts, such as a tractor parts business, for older equipment are providing a needed service.

Less Aid to Farmers

Most of the recent farm programs established by legislation expired at the end of September 1995. New farm legislation was included in the budget bill, which came to an impasse. Farmers were left in limbo for the 1996 season.

The Agricultural Market Transition Act (Farm Bill) was passed by Congress in late March 1996. This legislation encompasses dramatic reforms in agriculture by replacing current subsidy programs with declining market transition payments over the next seven years. These payments will not be linked to market conditions as they were in the past. Other provisions include granting increased flexibility in selection of crops in exchange for complying with other programs such as conservation and establishment of a committee to study what farm programs, if any, the government should provide.

For a future scenario in farming, expect farm subsidies to decline. Farmers need to concentrate on making a profit without dependence on the government. Products and services that help farmers increase profits, compete globally, and decrease costs will be in great demand.

CHAPTER 5

Business Equipment, Supplies, and Transportation

*B*usinesses need a variety of equipment and supplies, but many of the manufacturers and suppliers are highly capitalized companies. In this chapter, we will examine ways smaller companies can participate in this huge market. Businesses everywhere are greatly dependent on transportation to get their products distributed throughout the U.S. and worldwide. As the trend accelerates to a global economy, transportation needs are growing. You'll want to avoid direct competition with large companies who have name recognition, quantity advantage, and high capitalization.

Business equipment and supplies may be a good area for your business if:

❖ You are a successful salesperson who enjoys selling to businesses and professionals.

❖ You have identified an underserved market or unserved needs.

❖ You have experience in a specific industry and feel that you can better meet the industry's equipment needs.

❖ You can repair and service business equipment.

Transportation may be a good field for you if:

❖ You enjoy travel and flexible hours.

❖ You have an excellent driving record and find driving nonstressful.

❖ You are familiar with the business and can provide superior service.

The following two companies found opportunities in this sector. Both faced significant challenges and changing markets. Possibilities for businesses are abundant, often combined with substantial competition.

Electronic Materials and Computers

Bud Levey, a chemical engineer, started Electronic Materials and Computers, to avoid company relocation. His employer, Georgia Pacific Chemical Manufacturing, wanted him to move elsewhere, but he did not want to relocate. EMC started as a sole proprietorship in 1986, building on a network of acquaintances in the electronics field. The original focus of the company was precious metal recovery, primarily gold and silver from manufacturers' scrap. Founded as Electronic Materials and Recovery, Levey has since shifted the focus.

The reprocessing equipment cost $15 thousand, which was funded by a family loan. Levey felt confident he could survive for a while without a salary because his expenses were low. His car was paid off and he had a small monthly mortgage payment. Company equipment was purchased used through auctions and other resale sources.

At first it was difficult to gain the confidence of large manufacturers so he began working with smaller companies. He explained the company's positive capabilities and used his credentials as a chemical engineer. Sometimes, he would get a client by offering to do a split shipment. Part of their scrap would go to the present recycler, part to him. This gave him the opportunity to demonstrate his company's service. Perseverance in repeatedly going back to manufacturers would sometimes get their business. There was no place to advertise so he had to rely on the telephone and his own presentations.

About six months after going into business, he was approached by a former employee of a recycler in Northern California that had gone out of business. The man had good contacts, but no place to process his metals. For a while they did deals together and finally became partners.

While looking at materials for reprocessing, Levey saw other scrapped equipment. He inquired where that equipment was going. When he found that this surplus equipment was for sale by bid, he called contacts in other businesses. Levey found that a demand existed for this equipment and located publications where he could advertise. He would go to his buyers and find out how much they would pay for items. Then he went back to the company to make a lower bid.

The Environmental Protection Agency (EPA) started regulating metals recycling more closely, decreasing profits. Metal recovery is now a minor part of the business with the focus on the sale of surplus equipment. Levey buys equipment in large lots, then tests and cleans it. They refurbish equipment, not remanufacture it, and usually give a warranty. This equipment is primarily computer and test equipment.

During the first few years, it was easy to grow rapidly. People would stop by the store and ask if equipment was for sale. Using only word-of-mouth, customers came back repeatedly and referred others. Soon they outgrew their portion of the building so they expanded to their current storefront. A second, then third location were opened, but both have since been closed. Levey explained that it was difficult to get enough good quality PCs to adequately stock each store. The additional locations took customers away from the original store. Time was spent running from store to store. Another problem was finding dependable employees. When the three stores were opened, they often had to pull an employee from one store to cover an absence in another.

Used equipment has become more acceptable. Levey feels that it is easier to make money on wholesale than retail. Profit is made on the buy so it is important to buy low. Their business is currently 20 percent wholesale and 80 percent retail. Some companies need parts from older equipment for their service contracts. Even larger companies are more open to buying used equipment.

Levey has started paying employees a nominal wage then adding commissions and profit-sharing. He feels this brings a higher quality employee and makes employees feel more responsible to the business.

"Success in business" explains Levey, "is through creating win-win situations both for clients and employees. If the deal will not be good for both parties, it should not be done." He doesn't expect vendors to sell at or below cost. They also need to make a profit. Customers must get a good value. If not, they won't return. He builds the company on repeat business, not one-time deals.

Employees are told to always be fair and honest. If they know a computer system won't be ready tomorrow, they don't promise it tomorrow. If they tell someone they will do something, they must follow through and do it. His mission is to treat customers fairly.

When visiting in California, he saw businesses holding periodic swap meets at their stores, but no one was doing this in Phoenix. Bimonthly, Electronics

Materials now holds a computer swap on Sundays in its parking lot. Levey rents out spaces to other people for sales. Often people come to him, wanting to sell equipment. Sometimes this is not a win-win situation. In the swap market, they can sell their own equipment and get the best price. At first, this made the store more well-known, but now he feels that it may actually take some business away from him. However, he feels that it is a way to help out those with part-time, new, or home-based businesses, and it builds goodwill within the community. Swaps draw about 100 vendors and bring in about 3,000 to 5,000 people.

As the business has grown, the focus has been changing. Levey allows new ideas to be tried, sometimes growing a business within the business. He didn't plan to get into the PC business, but customers dictated the shift. "Listen to your customers," he advises.

Cell Phone Extensions

Maybe the worst misfortune for a small business is to get drawn into litigation, especially with a much larger entity. Cell Phone Extensions, a franchise of protected territories across the U.S., was on this path from the very beginning. These individually-owned companies clone cellular phone IDs that permit cellular phone users to have more than one phone on a single cellular number. This allows a cell phone user with a fixed car phone and portable phone to take a portable phone on out-of-town travel while leaving the car phone for the family. Good idea? Yes, for users. But the cellular phone companies feared loss of profits and threatened to sue.

A small company cannot compete with a highly capitalized phone company. Litigation can be extraordinarily expensive, wiping out a small company overnight. This appears to be the fate of the local Cell Phone Extensions. Their phone has been disconnected. A month prior, the local newspaper had run an article about the company. The owner, believing he was operating legally, promised to fight for his business. Some of these franchises may still be in existence in other areas. But in legal battles, the odds are overwhelming against the small guy.

Be sure your new business is not in a head-on battle with a larger entity that you cannot afford to fight. Starting a new company is challenging enough without complicating matters.

Business Equipment and Supplies: Opportunities to Explore

Independent Sales Representative

Independent sales representatives sell equipment and supplies for manufacturers who either do not have their own sales forces or wish to supplement their sales people, perhaps in geographical areas that cannot support an exclusive rep. Small companies may sell through independent reps. Many companies begin their international sales efforts using independent reps, specializing in their field. Some companies continue to market internationally using reps for cost-effectiveness. If you enjoy sales and have sales experience, becoming an independent sales representative is a way to have your own business and more control over which products you sell.

Niche Markets

If you have developed a product for a small market or a unique product, you may be able to build a business in this niche. Cost control and cash flow will be challenging. Start with a prototype and thorough market research.

Used Industrial and Computer Equipment

Used equipment markets have been good opportunities for small businesses. Larger companies have generally avoided this equipment because of the hassles involved. Dealing with used equipment can be labor intensive. Equipment may need testing and refurbishing. Larger companies prefer remanufacturing, replacing defective components with new parts, because it is quicker and they already have the components.

Recently, the used industrial and computer equipment markets have become more competitive. Industrial equipment often holds its value for a longer time. Computer equipment has a very short life, but some surplus computers and computer peripherals may be quite current. There are still some cities that are not saturated, but locations with many manufacturers of this type of equipment are highly competitive. Equipment is generally acquired by bidding. The more bidders, the higher the prices. Opportunity now may be best found by trucking surplus equipment to less competitive areas. Electronic Materials and Computers is an example of how a company enters the used equipment market.

Used Office Equipment and Furniture

There has always been a market for used business furniture since many businesses can't afford or don't need new equipment. This demand will increase as more individuals start businesses. The supply of used equipment and furniture varies somewhat depending on the economy. Equipment is obtained through auctions, bankruptcy sales, moving and storage (including mini-storage) companies, and bidding from larger companies who are refurbishing. Maintain contacts with large companies in your area so that you will be notified when equipment becomes available.

Swap Meet Organizer

Swap meets are immensely popular. Racetracks, drive-ins, parking lots plus indoor sites are good locations. The larger swaps provide food, beverages, restrooms, bank teller machines, and entertainment. Many individuals operate businesses that are based almost entirely on swap-meet sales. Organizers, who charge for spaces and sometimes admission, make money while giving others the opportunity for a start-up or part-time business. Patience is needed in building a successful swap market. Consistency in advertising, services, and providing a win-win environment for client-businesses and customers will increase your chances of success. In most areas of the country, indoor booth space is important due to frequent cold and wet weather. Successful swaps can be located outside urban areas in cheaper, yet convenient locations. These more rural locations attract serious shoppers. Make your swap-meet unique and fun to visit.

If you have swap-meet organizing experience, consider consulting and writing manuals on starting a swap market. Good information is scarce. Start an organization for swap market organizers.

Equipment Leasing

By investing in equipment, you can than lease this inventory to others. To avoid competition with larger companies, find a specialized area. Use your knowledge of your own field to look for opportunities. Examine your special interests. An example is setting up a two-way radio communications repeater, which picks up and rebroadcasts radio signals. You can then lease two-way radios to local businesses. For radio communications, many frequencies require licensure which, after study, can be obtained at low or no cost.

Qualifying your clients by thorough financial checks is important. Leased equipment often involves a large financial investment so make sure you have experience in the business before starting out on your own.

Short-Term Equipment Rental

Equipment takes up valuable storage space, requires maintenance, and eventually becomes obsolete. If the equipment is used only infrequently, businesses may find renting cost-effective. Equipment requiring special expertise to operate may demand contracting for both the equipment and operator. Look at your industry to determine equipment needs.

Equipment Repair

Although much business equipment is under service contract, older equipment is less likely to be under contract. Smaller businesses may not purchase service contracts. Quality, fast, repair work will always be in demand. The greatest challenge may be in marketing, getting word out you are in business. By targeting specific businesses and equipment, you can network through organizations and word-of-mouth. Direct mail advertising may also beneficial.

Supplies

Paper Direct, a specialty paper company catering to the needs of small businesses, was started when one of the founders looked for bright paper to print a flyer. He couldn't find anything, but knew that he had found an unmet need. Paper Direct was founded to fill that need. In your work, think about supplies that would expand the use of your equipment or facilitate your work. You may be able to specialize in providing better or customized supplies. Consider making better service the focus of your business.

Transportation Opportunities to Explore

Because of the cost of vehicles, transportation businesses usually involve high start-up costs. These are also highly competitive markets. However, transportation is more important today with markets located at greater distances.

Limousine and Courier Service

In some areas, a limousine service is profitable, but you'll need to have a stable customer base to even out the one-time wedding and special event customers. Courier services deliver for hospitals, laboratories, and businesses. Check your local area for competitiveness and demand. Look for niche areas such as catering to specific businesses if you live in a very large metropolitan area.

Fleet Maintenance

While start-up costs are greater, maintenance of trucking fleets provides a steady flow of business once contracts are negotiated.

Trucking Broker

When businesses have products that need to be shipped, often time is of essence. A trucker is needed to transport their goods to market. Trucking brokers match businesses with truckers, serving the needs of both. By knowing your market, making contacts on both sides, and being committed to providing round-the-clock service, you can build a business that will serve the needs of both truckers and businesses.

Independent Trucker

Independent truckers require enough capital to purchase their vehicles. Although there is a need for competent truckers, the costs are high, especially for long distance routes and profit margins are often low.

Local Moving Company

Starting a moving company demands a large truck. Even then, you will probably be limited to local moves and will need to compete with national companies even for short moves. Catering to businesses for local moves may be more lucrative.

Baggage Delivery and Airport Shuttle

Baggage delivery services may be contracted out by airlines. All you need is a van or truck to get in this business. Check with local airlines for availability. If you are in an area without an airport shuttle service and airport parking is limited, check out the feasibility of starting a shuttle. High vehicle and insurance costs require substantial capital and finding quality employees to work around the clock can be difficult. Combining these two businesses may increase profitability.

Aviation Service and Parts

If you have experience in aviation, you may be able to find a niche market in servicing airplanes and helicopters. Some businesses specialize in parts for older aircraft, which are used in foreign countries.

Future Opportunities in Equipment, Supplies, and Transportation

Business equipment and supplies are a strong market. Small businesses are a growing sector of this market. Some businesses focusing on the small and home-based market have been very successful. Because profit margins have been historically higher with business compared to many personal products, companies find this market attractive. With the trend to smaller companies, margins have decreased, but new opportunities are available.

Transportation is essential to get products to market. Finding innovative and more efficient ways to get products to market has led to the success of a number of companies. One new automobile transportation business uses closed rather than the traditional open trucks to transport vehicles. Dealers, transferring their transport needs to this new company, are impressed with this more secure transportation. Business equipment and transportation tend to be capital-intensive businesses, but, with a solid business plan, funding is more readily available than in the past.

CHAPTER 6

Business Services

The trend toward outsourcing work continues to open new possibilities. The first area to look for opportunity is your current job. Can you perform your same responsibilities more efficiently as a separate company or as a consultant? Your present employer could be your first customer. The most important factor in the early success of a business is cash flow. To have a positive cash flow, you obviously need clients. If you can start your business with a major client, you can jump start your business.

The business service market is so broad that some services have their own chapter in this book. These are: Accounting/Financial, Business Equipment and Transportation, Computer Services and Products, Import/Export, Legal Services and Products, and Marketing and Event Planning. In this chapter, you'll learn about services not covered in those individual chapters.

Business services may provide opportunities for you if:

❖ You have work experience and have developed specialized skills.

❖ You enjoy working with other business professionals and have a network of business contacts.

❖ You have specialized, in-demand computer skills.

❖ You have extensive business contacts in a specific market or market segment.

❖ You have international business experience or have worked abroad.

❖ You work in professional services and provide a service businesses need.

❖ You have manufacturing, construction, or trade skills and present yourself as a professional.

❖ You have superb people skills and enjoy working with difficult people, negotiating, or sales.

❖ You have creative ability and business experience.

Two of the following businesses were started by breaking off with a former employer. One, BEST Institute, bought a portion of his former company. Ronni Anderson of Staff One Search had ideas, which differed from her employer, for providing better customer service. Each of these owners knew their businesses thoroughly, facilitating start-up. On Assignment is a specialty temporary services firm. The company struggled at first, not staying within its niche. Once a new CEO took over, the company refocused on its core services and found ways to constantly improve its own service. When you find a niche, stay with your focus and, like On Assignment, strive to constantly improve your services through continual experimentation.

BEST Institute

BEST is an acronym for Business Education Safety Institute. BEST assists companies in assessing their safety training and product needs. Most smaller companies cannot afford and do not need a full-time safety director. However, they do need a safety program, training, and products. BESTs target market is small- to mid-size industrial companies with less than 100 employees and no in-house safety director.

Jerry Beougher, owner, spent most of his career in the corporate world, rising to vice president of Zee/McKesson, a large company in the drug and consumer products business. In a downsizing move, Zee/McKesson sold off many of its company-owned safety products distributorships to independent distributors. This division, called Zee Service, Inc., distributes first-aid and safety products such as stocked first-aid cabinets, first-aid products, hearing and eye protection, and eye wash stations. Beougher, familiar with the division, bought a distributorship with the intention of adding educational safety programs. While working for McKesson, he came up with the idea of incorporating education and safety and saw Zee Service as providing an instant client base. Because of his position at McKesson, he was able to investigate the potential of the Zee

Service distributorship. There are 85 Zee Service distributorships, all protected territories.

BEST is separate from Zee Service. Clients are given a variety of sources to purchase needed products; Zee Service is just one on the list. His company has two Occupational Safety and Health Administration (OSHA) certified instructors and one certified safety professional. His consultants do work site evaluations utilizing a 300-point check list. Recommendations for safety products and training are given. The company will set up OSHA compliant training programs and bring in outside consultants if hazardous materials are involved. CPR classes are also offered.

Hiring qualified employees is sometimes challenging. When BEST was started, government safety regulations were on the increase. Now the government has started backing away from the trend of increasing regulations. OSHA, with its poor funding for enforcement, provides little motivation to increase safety. OSHA is changing its focus towards functioning as a consultant rather than stressing compliance. The agency's previous emphasis was investigating injuries and employee complaints. State OSHA requirements overrule federal if they surpass federal standards. Litigation related to safety issues is much more of a threat. Beougher works with local insurance companies for risk management. The ability to lower Worker's Compensation costs is another benefit from BEST's services. BEST promotes increased worker productivity as a direct benefit from increased safety.

Initially Beougher thought he would nationally franchise the business, but has realized that his success is directly tied to his client base from Zee Service, so has presently abandoned the idea of franchising.

Beougher advises potential new business owners to realize that the emotional ties you have to your own business are like an extended family. When employed, you do not often have this much emotional commitment.

❖   ❖   ❖

Starting a business related to your employment uses your experience and knowledge of the field. This is a lower risk route to owning your own business. Knowing the problems and trends in an industry is valuable and minimizes unexpected surprises. Companies are increasingly spinning off divisions to be run as independent businesses, often by former employees. These divisions may be less profitable for the company, but, with inside knowledge, you may find ways to increase profitability.

Staff One Search

Starting a business similar to one you have worked in is a natural transition. Ronni Anderson, owner of Staff One Search, worked for almost two years for an employment placement firm prior to founding her own firm in 1983. Differing with the management style of the owner, she thought she could provide better service on her own. Client service is the focus of Anderson's business. She strives to provide consistent, quality service to every client, whether business or individual.

Like many business owners, Anderson says, in retrospect, that if she had known what she was getting into, she probably would have never started. She was unable to get a loan, so she financed start-up with her own money. Her vision was to have a small business with only a receptionist. However, people she knew in her previous position kept coming and asking if they could work for her. This was not what she had in mind! Finally, she agreed to let some of these people work with her as independent contractors. But, because these contractors did not want to worry about the rent and other business responsibilities, they soon switched their work status to being employees, working on salary.

Staff One Search grew quickly. In retrospect, Anderson feels she should have adhered more strictly to a budget, spent less, and hired fewer employees. In 1986, the company relocated from very small quarters to a large, spacious office in a more centrally located office building.

The original focus of her business was permanent placement and recruiting for administrative, support, sales, and accounting positions. Often, a client would request temporary personnel until a permanent hire could be found. She initially referred these requests to another company, but soon realized she was losing business. Since she was unfamiliar with temporary placement, Anderson hired a woman who had managed a recently-closed temporary placement company. The temporary placement end of the business balances the permanent staffing division, creating less fluctuations in the overall business.

Anderson had a large percentage of clients in the real estate and development business. When these industries took a downturn locally in 1986, she saw profits drop. Learning from this lesson, she worked to diversify her clientele.

Computerizing her business, starting with the temporary side, has increased efficiency and exchange of information in the office. This expenditure, which eventually resulted in a computer on every desk, was well worth the cost, she explained.

Anderson has recently added employee leasing to the business. Because of litigation, government regulations, and access to better benefit plans, employee leasing is becoming more prevalent. For small businesses up to 100 employees, leasing can save money and enable a company to offer competitive employee benefits. Leasing can take compliance and liability responsibilities off the employer. Most leasing companies are co-employers, which leaves liability with the original employer. However, a few leasing companies, under a program called sole employer, take on the liability. To do this, they must provide a representative on-site who is an employee of the leasing company.

Anderson offers employee training, sometimes paid by the candidate and other times by the employer, for her clients. In late 1996, her business bought a computer training company to provide this service. She has found that often an employee will have most of the qualifications requested by the employer, but not all. Gaining the lacking skill would make that person a successful candidate.

A client-first policy has made Anderson successful. If she has a candidate that has most of the qualifications, but not all, she tells the employer. If she can't find a suitable candidate, she is honest with the employer and discusses why the candidate they desire is difficult to find. Although this at first seems obvious and simple, Anderson relates that surprising few businesses are this honest with their clients.

Anderson understands the importance of good internal communication and strives to have Staff One Search employees define their personal wants and needs. "Have things right on the inside of your company so things will be right on the outside," Anderson reiterated.

On Assignment

In 1985, two chemists working in a lab in Los Angeles discovered a need for scientific lab workers to work on short projects. With an infusion of $1 million dollars of venture capital money, they founded a business placing lab workers on a temporary basis, mainly in Southern California. Their idea was sound, but they made a common error, not focusing on their  initial niche. The two tried to do a little of everything, from consulting to headhunting, instead of concentrating on the company's initial temporary placement focus.

In three years, they lost $1.5 million and the venture capital firm decided to step in and find a professional manager to run the company. Tom Buelter was brought in to turn around the company. Buelter immediately focused on the temporary lab personnel aspect of the business, abandoning the others. Account managers, all of whom had actual lab experience, began to assist clients throughout the recruitment, placement, and follow-up to increase client service. Instead of concentrating on bringing in new business, account managers work closely with company clients and temporary staff, ensuring well-placed workers.

After a few months with Buelter's management, the company became profitable. In 1992 when the company went public, the venture capital company made $11.7 million on its $1 million investment. The two original co-founders did fine; one sold out, the other has a share worth over $5 million. In 1995, revenues increased 28 percent and income per share was up 29 percent.

The company's local offices, called Lab Support, are located across the U.S. The offices focus on placing temporary professionals in labs in the biotechnology, chemical, environmental, food and beverage, petrochemical, and pharmaceutical industries. Because of the increased difficulty in finding quality, highly skilled lab workers, On Assignment receives a higher percentage of salaries paid than the temporary placement industry standard. Many of the personnel placed are later offered full-time positions.

Now that On Assignment is on track, Buelter is creating a broad vision, a temporary placement delivery system applicable to other specialized, professional markets, for his company. His next application is the collection business. He thinks there is a need for experienced temporary employees in that field, targeting the special needs of different types of businesses. Recently, he bought two small businesses to use as a base for this endeavor. In 1996, in addition to expanding Lab Support, the company will develop Finance Support, offering personnel for banking and credit-related companies, and Advanced Science Professionals, providing professionals with specialized science-related experience. Buelter sees additional opportunities in the legal and health care markets.

With the company thriving, Buelter intends to stay within his niche, applying this delivery systems where he discovers a need. On Assignment has a proven system and now is concentrating on applying this system to appropriate markets.

❖   ❖   ❖

Business services is one of fastest growing business sectors. In addition to outsourcing by large companies, the thousands of small businesses springing up need the assistance of experts to supplement their core talents. Small companies cannot usually afford, nor do they need, these experts full-time. This opens opportunities for other new small businesses. An opportunity is right for your new venture if it fills a need while allowing you to work within your interests.

Business Service Opportunities

Niche Markets

Niche businesses are the experts of their market. By focusing on a small segment of a broader market, you can provide superior service by zooming in on this segment's unique needs. Once you define your niche market, stay with it unless you have saturated the niche. Instead of broadening your market, look for ways to exceed your own service. Being a specialist in your market segment makes your business exceptional.

Unique Services

Being first to provide a service is more risky, but if the need is present and other businesses will pay for it, being first may make it easier to find clients. Do your market research and, if there appears to be demand, go for it.

Superior Service

Can you find ways to improve a business service? After speaking with other businesses, will they pay for this improved service? Superior service will distinguish your business. Many companies told me that they found it easy to provide a better service. So many companies promise service, but they simply don't deliver. Superior service must be delivered consistently. If your service varies, you will lose clients. Put a system in place to ensure that service is consistently excellent.

Ronni Anderson, Staff One Services, stresses she always tries to focus on the needs of her clients. Clients are encouraged to call her when they are dissatisfied. She will then find ways to resolve the situation. When you are receptive to hearing about problems, clients will be open with you. This gives you the chance to regain that client's trust.

Win-Win Situation

Creating win-win situations is one of the great secrets for success in life, both business and personal. Make sure that your clients get as much benefit from your business relationship as you do. Make sure they get their money's worth or, better, more value.

Small Business Needs

Besides larger companies outsourcing work, the growth in small businesses has created needs that can be served by other small businesses. While large

companies may have specialists on staff, smaller companies often need specialists infrequently.

Smaller companies are usually run by individuals with special expertise. They need
the assistance of other specialists for the mechanics of running the business. They
may need assistance in retirement planning, accounting, marketing, public relations, management, insurance, staffing, environment concerns, and other areas.
Since small business needs are sometimes quite different from a large corporation,
specializing in the small business market may be the niche for your new business.

Human Resource Services

Human Resource Specialist

Smaller companies can't afford a human resource specialist full-time, but are in
need of many of their services. If you have a background in human resources,
offer your services on a consulting basis, as needed. Some of the services a small
business may need are temporary staffing, employee leasing, an employee benefits program, employee testing, drug testing, employee credentials checking, credit checking, and OSHA compliance and safety programs. Consultants provide
training for employees in leadership, teamwork, diversity (people with varied
backgrounds working effectively together), and job skills.

Temporary Employment Services

Many companies, small and large, are using temporary employees to adjust to
varying workloads. Temporary employment services provide screened employees
to meet these needs. Some companies are hiring full-time employees through a
temporary agency in order to have a trial period to see if the individual is a good
fit with the company. Although many large companies have entered this market,
in some locales there is still a need.

The best opportunities for temporary services may be in specialty areas. Tom
Buelter of On Assignment, cut services that were deviations from On Assignment's
niche and made the company profitable. "Employers today hire for valleys, or slow
periods," explains Buelter. Companies have a core work force. When demand
increases, they bring in temporary personnel to supplement their full-time workers.

Employee Leasing

Employee leasing has advantages for both employers and employees. In small
companies, management often lacks the time and negotiating power to set up an

employee benefit plan. By offering benefits, a company is more likely to keep its employees. By leasing employees, a company can take advantage of the larger pool of workers represented by the leasing company and procure better benefits for less cost. The employer, in addition to a more stable workforce, is spared of the task of researching and setting up a benefits program and keeping track of governmental regulations. Employee lease firms should relieve the employer of liability for noncompliance. Not all employee lease firms provide this protection.

Employee Benefits Consultant

If a company does not want to lease employees, an employee benefits consultant can help put together the best and most cost-effective benefits package. If the company is very small, the consultant may be able to pool the company's employees with other businesses to have more negotiating power.

Healthcare insurance is especially complex. A specialist should be aware of which insurance companies plans have the best records and most satisfied policyholders. A consultant can help you avoid selecting a company with a poor record, plus advise you of differences and voids in coverage.

As this area gets more complex, employee benefits consultants will be in greater demand. To specialize in this area, you will need work experience in employee benefits. You may want to specialize in just one type of benefit, such as healthcare insurance. Or you may specialize in one industry segment and its unique needs.

Employee Testing and Training

Some businesses set specific minimum standards for employees. Training firms can test prospective employees to ensure that they meet these standards. If an individual is lacking a certain skill, but is otherwise a good candidate, a training firm may be able to provide the necessary training.

Employee training is becoming increasingly necessary. Employees are receiving more training, more often. A small business will need to focus its training services to one type of training or one market. Because the quality of the instructor is so critical, training companies need a stable group of competent instructors. Training á la Carte, a computer training company, started with the two co-owners as the sole trainers. As the company grew, they hired other instructors. They have concentrated on identifying and implementing ways to keep a core group of excellent trainers.

Large companies with many instructors and instructional courses are already in this field. Your best bet is to be first to offer a training for a new technology.

However, when the next new technology comes along, you will need to be prepared to offer training for those skills. Another good strategy is to train employees in a small industry segment.

If you offer distance learning, you can train more people at a lower cost. Small companies often can't afford to close down for a day while employees are trained. Distance learning brings courses to the employees and can supplement on-site training. Of course, live instruction is more dynamic, but distance learning works well for motivated employees.

Hands-on instruction will usually give better results than a lecture type seminar. Remember that your training company will be judged by how well clients learn. By becoming more effective in conveying information and being able to observe the employees at task, your company will get better results and a superior reputation. This is an example of a win-win situation. Training á la Carte offers hands-on computer training. By being able to observe the students at work on their individual computers, instructors can see where additional instruction is needed. The company purposely adds stumbling blocks into training courses to see how students handle these situations. They want to ensure that, when students return to work, they will be able to work through new situations on their own.

Drug Testing

Many companies are doing pre-employment and random drug testing to discourage the use of drugs. This service is crowded in most cities, but perhaps you could pair testing with a prevention program. Make sure you are insured against possible litigation and maintain strict quality control.

Credit and Background Checking of Prospective Employees

By providing credit and background checks on prospective employees, hiring mistakes are minimized. Find a way to distinguish your business from the others in this segment. This is a potentially litigious area should you give false or inaccurate information.

Safety Compliance

BEST Institute specializes in safety programs for industrial companies that cannot afford a full-time safety specialist. BEST offers services such as safety training and assessments, CPR training, and noise level assessment. If you are considering a similar business, find ways of improving profit margins or a niche market that you can serve. Watch for new regulations because they create new opportunities for compliance training.

Employment Psychologist

This is an interesting and very challenging area for psychologists. Businesses are using psychologists who specialize in workplace conflict and interpersonal relationships to create a more productive and harmonious workplace. Success in this business will depend on how effective you are in conflict resolution.

Wellness Programs

The original creator of wellness programs found the concept a tough sell. Companies did not feel that spending money to change health habits would pay off. Changing habits is effective in reducing health costs, but it is difficult to get permanent lifestyle changes. Continued business for a wellness company requires results—a decrease in healthcare costs. Since better health habits may not be immediately reflected in reduced costs, employers often get impatient and drop the programs.

Insurance companies have noticed that by motivating individuals to improve their health habits, their pay-outs decrease. Instituting wellness education makes good business sense for them. Unless you can come up with highly-effective programs and show significant benefits, you should avoid this type of business.

Self-Insurance Benefit Programs

Self-insurance means that a company sets aside a pool of money to cover healthcare costs for its employees instead of using an independent insurance company. This type of insurance is appropriate only for larger companies with adequate resources. One liver transplant can cost a couple hundred thousand dollars and, if a company self-insures, the company must pay. This niche is for experienced insurance professionals only.

Telecommuting Specialist

As employees are more frequently working from locations other than the office, a person knowledgeable in telecommuting will be needed to select appropriate employees and set policies for companies employing telecommuters. You will need to devise ways to ensure that employees are maximizing their time out of the office.

Lie Detection and Fingerprinting

More companies are fingerprinting employees and using lie detectors in their business. While there is a need for these services, they would be best incorporated in an employee placement or screening business.

Diversity Training

Diversity training is hot right now. The work force is becoming a blend of more nationalities and age groups. As this trend continues to accelerate, so will the need for training on how to interact successfully with people who are different from yourself.

Outplacement

As companies downsize, outplacement firms get busier. These companies provide career counseling and job search advice for those employees who have been laid off. Many areas are saturated with outplacement firms and the market fluctuates. Combining outsourcing with training may increase market breadth and even out fluctuations in the economy.

Employment Ad Screening

With so many people seeking employment, job ads generate huge numbers of replies. This has created a business opportunity answering telephone inquiries and screening applicants. This business could easily be run from home. If applicants need to be screened in person, a business suite can be rented on a daily basis.

Creativity Consultant

There are so many creativity consultants it may be difficult to establish an identity. Companies will always seek out new ideas and if you can help them generate them, you have a business.

Marketing Opportunities

Since there is an entire chapter on marketing, only a few services are discussed here. If you have marketing experience and want to use this experience to build a business, fast forward to the chapter on Marketing.

Mystery Shopper Service

Although anonymous shoppers have been used for some time as a means for businesses such as restaurants to assess their quality of service, independent firms are cropping up that are applying the mystery shopper concept to new areas. One service specializes in sending anonymous individuals to dental offices to report to the dentist owner(s) the quality of service. Another way to use the service is to send shoppers to competitors to compare service level.

Marketing on the Internet

For those who have the skills to design, develop, and maintain World Wide Web pages, there is a tremendous need for your services. In the chapter on Computer Products and Services, this business is explored.

Fund Raising

Non-profit businesses employ approximately 10 percent of workers. Most non-profits need fund raising activities to raise money for continuing operations. Although a challenging field, individuals who are creative and enjoy sales can build a business around assisting these organizations.

Business Site Management Opportunities

Maintaining the premises of a business location requires a variety of services. Because many services are needed infrequently, outside firms are hired for those periodic tasks.

Prior to start-up, architects and designers may be contracted for the office layout. Then contractors are brought in to do the build-out. Specialists are hired for specific portions of the construction such as security systems, computer network design, landscaping, and heating and air-conditioning. Demand for these services varies by location. Don't dismiss slow growing areas as there can be a shortage of contractors once the economy picks up.

Property Inspection

There is an abundance of home inspectors of varying qualifications. If you have a commercial construction and engineering background, inspection of commercial properties may be more lucrative. A Phase 1 Environmental Assessment of property, which involves researching past use of the land, is a necessity when businesses are purchased with a bank loan. New owners assume liability for all past contamination unless an assessment is performed and banks require the assessment prior to a loan. In many locations, this market is already well-represented so check for demand. Needless to say, this is a highly litigious area demanding competent individuals and good insurance.

Indoor Air Specialists

As our knowledge of pollutants grows and pollution increases, demand for specialists in air, water, soil, and industrial pollutants rises. These specialties are covered in more detail in Chapter 13. Pollutants from carpeting, construction materials, industrial materials, air conditioning systems, and other sources are becoming a greater problem with increasing air tight, energy efficient buildings. Teaming up with a physician specializing in respiratory or environmental medicine would be a good match.

Indoor Environmental Design

Creating workplaces more conducive for working is a business opportunity. Pleasant environments make employees more efficient. By documenting your results, you can show businesses that by incorporating a variety of ambiance-enhancers such as pleasant, low volume music or sound, aroma dispersal, live plants, aquatic design, good quality air and temperature control, good interior design, and favorable lighting that they can achieve increased productivity. You'll need to create a team or an alliance of specialists to assess and implement these environmental changes.

Security Service and Systems

Increased crime provides a business opportunity for security companies. While litigation and regulations are a potential pitfall, security demands are escalating. With a background in law enforcement or government security, consider marketing yourself as a security consultant. You may find your best opportunities in businesses with high security needs. Recently, there has been a large increase in the theft of computer chips. Because of their small size, they are easy to steal. This is a difficult problem, but potentially lucrative for individuals who can help solve the problem.

The security guard business has high employee turnover due to low pay, poor hours, risk, and a negative stigma. Look for ways to overcome these difficulties. Equipping your guards with an Air Taser® (See Engineering: Air Taser, Inc.)

provides them with a means to secure threatening individuals without personal harm, decreasing risk. Increased use of technology instead of people in potentially dangerous situations will make the security business more attractive.

The security systems business is crowded, but there is still opportunity especially for systems that provide crime deterrents. There is an overabundance of alarm systems companies, but the true challenge in this market is to deter crime not to announce its occurrence. Check the legal implications of your systems carefully.

Self-protection seminars are good investments for businesses that have a high crime potential. Learning to recognize and deal with potentially dangerous people can improve outcomes, as law enforcement individuals already know. Although all situations cannot be avoided or successfully handled, outcomes can be improved. Individuals with martial arts or law enforcement backgrounds may have the experience to start a self-protection business. You will need to do extensive marketing and education since many companies may not immediately see the value of your services. OSHA is preparing guidelines for violence prevention for businesses with a high crime potential, such as convenience stores. Companies will need assistance to implement their guidelines, once finalized.

Traco, International is a martial arts company that has developed a personal defense program. Emphasis is on determining your own and others' motives, then developing methods to deal with potentially dangerous situations. Peter Hill, program developer, stresses the need to protect yourself rather than your property.

Maintenance Service

Companies that can offer cost-effective, quality repairs, and maintenance are always in demand. Communicating and demonstrating competent service are an initial challenge in gaining new clients. Find ways to get an opportunity to demonstrate your services then put a system in place to make sure the service is consistently excellent. Be more available than other similar businesses and work on obtaining business service contracts. Look for ways to distinguish your company from others: immaculate company trucks, competent, polite employees, quick response time, and similar attention to details will contribute to your success. Never underestimate the importance of the details.

Janitorial

Many businesses use independent cleaning or janitorial services. This is an easy business to get into, but, as with most easy entry business, is very competitive. Develop a company that has distinguishing service and look for specialized markets.

No one enjoys cleaning restrooms. Consider a restroom cleaning business. You might specialize in restaurants, gas stations, or another unserved niche.

Parking Lot Cleaning and Striping

The market for trash clean-up is huge. Small businesses with parking lots need regular cleaning with occasional recoating and restriping of the pavement. Cleaning and maintenance could be a separate business or paired together. In colder climates, snow removal can be added to provide work during the winter.

Metal Detectors

A recent trend is toward installation of metal detectors and signage prohibiting weapons in company buildings. Check your locale to see if there is opportunity here for a business.

Signage

The vinyl sign market is well saturated with franchises in most areas, but creative individuals can find opportunity painting seasonal and sale signage on store windows. The great part of this business is that there is so much repeat business. Windows will need to be repainted with each new sale or season.

Building Enhancements

Businesses seek ways to attract clients. Often fairly inexpensive design enhancements can make a big impact. In warm climates, awnings add a bright touch and can also be used as signage. Neon lights, inside and out, focus attention. Provide improvements that increase client business for a win-win relationship with your business customers.

Auctioneer

As the number of surplus businesses increases, the number of auctions seems to be somewhat decreasing, Why bother with the hassle of an auction when businesses will bid on entire lots? Auctions make sense when the items are of higher value, to maximize returns. Look for new markets that have not often used auctions to get rid of no longer needed equipment. Still, this business might be best tied in with a synergistic business such as surplus equipment.

Snack Truck

A company with a fleet of food trucks can establish regular routes to businesses, private schools, and other locations, selling snacks and lunch items.

Other Maintenance Businesses

Businesses such as leak detection, uniforms, landscaping, vending service, bottled water, phone service, and pest control are crowded. However, if you can find ways to distinguish yourself and are knowledgeable in these areas, give them consideration.

Secretarial and Miscellaneous Opportunities

The less specialized knowledge needed for a business, the greater potential for overcrowding. Businesses such as answering services and print shops are endangered by advances and availability of technology. Desktop publishing, with its wide appeal, is dependent on a unique application. Courier, shipping, and teleconferencing services abound.

Storage Centers

Although there is an abundance of mini-storage centers, many locations still have demand. Increases in home-based businesses, housing without basements, and population mobility fuel this demand. If you can get initial funding, the return on investment per square foot is high. Downsides to this business are the necessity to live on-site, with someone on premise 24 hours a day. This restriction can be handled by using retired individuals and rotating duty among multiple individuals.

Document Storage

Too much paper is a dilemma of many businesses. Storing documents on microfiche or, more recently, CD-ROM helps alleviate space and retrieval needs. To make this service cost-effective, scanning documents needs to be highly automated and fast. Special high speed scanners coupled with document organization and retrieval programs are available for this market.

Service Center for Home-Based Businesses

Professionals who work from their homes need to present a stable, professional appearance. They require a business address, answering service, package delivery address, and other amenities similar to office-based businesses. Responding to this need are service centers that are available for a monthly rent plus the additional cost of added services. These centers can give a home-based business an address, mail pick-up location, and conference rooms for meeting with clients. The cost of these services is often surprisingly low. If there is a need in your locale, consider starting your own center.

Future Opportunities

As businesses become more lean, they will look to outside companies to provide the services they do not need a full-time in-house person for. Look at your job and those of your colleagues. Could any of these jobs be outsourced? What other services would help the efficiency and profitability of the company? Small businesses will find more ways to serve other businesses in the future. Providing one of these services could be the start of your own company.

CHAPTER 7

Computer Services and Products

*T*he computer industry exemplifies change. The expansion of this market in the last 20 years is almost unprecedented. Computers have created many new business opportunities and substantially impacted the way we live and work.

Despite widespread computerization, the majority of people are still intimidated by computers. An individual may feel comfortable with word processing programs, but that same individual balks when it is time to install new memory or a CD-ROM drive. This fear creates work for those who are comfortable and competent with computer hardware. Many feel comfortable with prepackaged software, but customizing a system pushes them to seek help from a professional. Chris Piraino, Granite Computer Solutions, predicts more work for his business in this growing market.

Consider a computer-related business if:

❖ You have expertise in computer systems, computer or electrical engineering, and system troubleshooting.

❖ You have programming expertise.

❖ You are artistic and have combined your interest with computer expertise.

❖ You are at ease with using computers and enjoy teaching others.

❖ You have specialized experience in the design of electronic equipment.

In this swiftly changing market lies opportunities for both large and small companies. Small businesses look to other small companies for help in setting up office computer systems. Granite Computer Solutions is successful by focusing on this market. With the variety of software available, it is unreasonable to expect every individual to be familiar with every software package. Training is most effective on an individual, hands-on basis. Small companies such as Training á la Carte have thrived in this niche.

Granite Computer Solutions

For some people, the goal of being in your own business is making your own decisions and controlling your own future. Chris Piraino, owner of Granite Computer Solutions, had worked for large companies and decided this was not for him. Bootstrapping on this experience, he relocated then spent six months working for computer repair companies to learn the business. During this time, he legally set up his company and started building a client base on his own time. He decided that when his part-time work started impinging on his full-time job, he would quit his job. Six months later, he was on his own.

The first month on his own, Piraino made no money, but he has grown ever since. Granite Computer Solutions moved from Piraino's home to an office suite in 1995, the third year in business. The first two years in business his income was below his previous salary, but Piraino's motivation is not solely money. He enjoys making his own decisions and having control. Now past his third year, his business continues to grow as his library of prewritten code (specialized computer programming written by Piraino) increases in size. With this large repertoire of prewritten code, he is able to provide custom accounts receivable packages quickly and inexpensively yet with more powerful features. This creates a win-win situation with clients.

Piraino finds that small businesses often are happy with off-the-shelf accounting software except for the accounts receivable portion. Businesses often prefer to adapt a portion of the accounts receivables by customizing invoices, customer and product information databases, and sales trend tracking to meet their individual needs. Piraino's business specializes in helping meet these needs.

His interest in computers began as a hobby in high school. Starting with arcade games, he bought his first PC at age 13. Armed with a degree in mechanical engineering emphasizing data acquisition, Piraino can tackle either hardware or software. His software focus is database applications, currently using Microsoft™ products. He works on hardware projects from repairs to upgrades to networks.

Piraino's target market is primarily small businesses with under 50 users, but on occasion he has done work for companies such as Prudential Insurance and General Motors. He validated his credentials by becoming Microsoft certified. "Certification by the appropriate manufacturers is very important in establishing your competence," explains Piraino.

In exchange for office space, Piraino has a subcontractor who does some work for him, specializing in systems hardware. Having a separate person assisting in the hardware aspect of networking helps Piraino increase services and focus on software. He tried hiring an administrative person, but found his business losing its intended focus. He envisions his company with about a dozen employees in the future, but wants to stay small.

Since Piraino is comfortable with sales and feels technical expertise is necessary to sell his services, he has no plans for another marketing person. Business is by referral only. Piraino has done no advertising or telemarketing. He belongs to a leads (business referral organization) group, which has been very helpful, especially since his group is self-directed. He advises people to start their own groups. Joining chambers of commerce was costly and not effective for him.

Besides finding clients, understanding business taxes and accounting has been a big challenge. Hours are sometimes long, but he enjoys his work. Piraino is happy with his company's growth and has no desire to return to the corporate world. People find computers intimidating, which creates work for him. He views the computer market as continuing to grow, especially for client/server applications.

Training á la Carte

In 1985, Fran Novak and Janet Corbosiero were software trainers for a major computer retailer. Training was offered for free to buyers of computer systems. Novak and Corbosiero thought the training should be a separate profit center. They approached management with the idea of starting a separate training company within the reseller company. When management laughed them off, they decided to leave and start a training business of their own. At the time, everyone said that an independent software training company could not succeed. Their business, Training á la Carte, was profitable by the third week.

They started in a 500 square foot building with six computers. For the first two years, the two did all the marketing, administration, and training. Later they began hiring other instructors. At first instructors were independent contractors, but later all trainers became company employees.

In the past 10 years, Training á la Carte has expanded to multiple facilities and 31 instructors. The main office has 7,000 square feet of classroom and administrative space. Most satellite offices approximate 3,000 square feet. Top notch training with a personal touch is the company's focus. Originally, class size was six students per trainer. Subsequently, that number increased to eight and, more recently, to 10. This is still one of the lowest student/trainer ratios in the industry.

Classes focus on IBM and IBM compatible PC software. The top selling classes are word processing and spreadsheet, but the company also teaches e–mail, graphics, project and sales management, groupware, and database software.

Their 50/50 partnership has flourished because of the complementary strengths of the two women. Both partners agree neither could have built and managed the business without the other. Corbosiero breezes through technical problems and administrative challenges. Novak is a successful technical writer with a mania for quality and customer service. Mutual respect for their unique abilities has kept the partnership strong.

The partners admit much of what they know about business, they learned on the job. In growing the business, they made their share of mistakes. For example, on occasion they developed training materials for software products that didn't sell. Once they failed to read the fine print on a computer lease and wasted $2,500. They diversified into Macintosh training, but soon found that the market share was insufficient for profitability. When they made a mistake, they would lament it for two or three days and then just forget it and move on. They keep what works and cut their losses with what doesn't.

To start the company, each partner borrowed $5 thousand from family. After their initial investment, they grew the company from profits. Although they had excellent credit, they were reluctant to borrow. Each partner was the family breadwinner and neither had a second family income as a safety net.

Many of their original clients are still customers today. Their primary source of new business is competitive bidding and referrals from satisfied customers. About 98 percent of their clients are businesses who send their employees for company-paid training.

Novak and Corbosiero have developed computer training methods that work. Their training materials are tested on live audiences, and they welcome feedback from their customers about what works in the classroom. They intentionally introduce software problems into their training materials so that students can develop problem solving techniques. They don't want their students to flounder the first time they encounter a software challenge back at the job. Both partners encourage students to keep asking questions until they are certain they have mastered a concept.

Corbosiero has a background in special education. At 19, Novak started her training career as a teaching assistant at a state university. When PCs were introduced in the early 1980s, Novak was one of the first in her office to use personal computers. Later she taught fellow employees how to use them.

For a long time, Novak and Corbosiero did everything themselves. In retrospect, they wish they had taken more risks, expanded faster, and shared some of the management responsibilities sooner. "When you're a doer by nature, it's tough to manage rather than do it yourself," explains Novak. Eventually the company grew too large for the partners to do everything. "Each time we passed a function along to someone else," she reflected, "it invariably improved."

Keeping good instructors is a challenge. They tend to hire entrepreneurial individuals who may go on and start their own companies. To keep quality instructors, they maintain a flexible policy, hiring both part-time and full-time instructors. Both understand the need to accommodate home responsibilities and special interests.

In the last two years, Novak and Carbosiero have moved out of instructing, with management and developing new products taking more of their time. Novak occasionally teaches the introductory computer course. They network closely with their clients, strongly encouraging clients to offer suggestions or share criticisms. "We can fix what we know about," comments Novak.

Small companies are constantly changing. Recently, Corbosiero and Novak sold their company although they remain as trainers with the new organization. "We couldn't be happier with the new owners," explains Carbosiero. Their success demonstrates that ethical people who love what they do can be successful in their own small business.

Opportunities will continue to open up in the computer field. If computers are your passion, you will find work available. Keep changing and searching for better ways to serve your customers. Like Training á la Carte, try new things and see what works. Keep what does and just abandon the others. But keep looking for new and better methods and continue to refine your products.

Computer Business Opportunities

Computer Network Installation

With lower cost components and new operating systems, networking computers has become easier. Despite that, many businesses still need assistance in setting up their networks. Once you have installed a network, you have a client who will continue to need your services when new equipment or software is added.

Granite Computer Solutions provides network design, installation, and maintenance. Chris Piraino notes that many small business people are intimidated by putting together systems, creating a perfect environment for his expertise.

All these networks need components: networking cards, hubs, etc., but also simpler items such as cables. One local business seems to be doing quite well selling only custom cables.

Network security is another need. Companies want to ensure their databases are secure. In large companies, one or more individuals may have this responsibility, but smaller companies have similar concerns. Specialists can create a security hierarchy for companies to protect sensitive information and prevent fraud.

Automation in Industry

Industry is rapidly automating many routine processes. Computerization is the core of this automation. This is currently a very exciting and lucrative area for companies that combine teams of hardware, software, and other specialists. If you have one expertise, seek out individuals who can provide the other skills.

System Maintenance

Many small businesses do not need a full-time person on staff to handle computer upgrades, maintenance, and problems, but do need someone who can perform these services as needed. Often, a smaller company will forgo prepaid equipment maintenance contracts, preferring to pay for services if needed.

With technology changing so rapidly, companies need to upgrade so frequently that repairs are less often required. Their preference may be to spend dollars on new equipment rather than repairing. Still, outside help is often needed for selection, installation, and integration of new technology.

Computer Helpline

With the abundance of software and hardware available, users are experiencing problems with conflicts between the multitude of product combinations. An individual computer manufacturer cannot possibly test all combinations. Online services have forums which bring users together from widespread geographic locations. This is helpful yet only exposes the breadth of the problem. Solutions have been attempted, but the need continues to grow.

Data Recovery

Although more computer users have learned to routinely back-up their software (probably from past experience), there is still a need for data recovery. A couple of years ago, some individuals were doing recovery on nearly a full-time basis, but now this would be best considered as just one of your offered services.

Independent Programmer

If you are adept in one of the higher level languages such as a variant of C or Unix, you may want to consider working independently as a programmer. With the variety of computer programming languages, one individual cannot be adept in more than a few languages. You might want to form a consulting group, pooling individuals with different capabilities and referring work among members or working jointly on larger projects.

Software Seminars

With in-depth knowledge of a particular software program, giving seminars on the software is an option. For example, if you are a graphics arts company and have in-depth experience with a program such as Adobe PhotoShop™, you could extend your company's services by adding seminars. The seminar business requires a closely targeted market to cut advertising costs.

Specialty Software

Software is a tough market with much competition, but, if you find a niche that needs custom software, there is opportunity. Look for specific small business and automation markets.

CD-ROM

The CD-ROM market is growing rapidly as companies seek ways to train employees and store their records. Hardware and compression limitations had previously limited recording video on CD-ROM to motion jerkiness and small-sized windows. These limitations are improving. Recent products are evidence of the advances.

CD-ROMs have a large storage capacity. With the lowered prices on CD-ROM recorders, small businesses are appearing that do single CD recording. A company may want to put its employee manual, a software manual, or other materials on CD. Other companies have overflowing record files and are transferring these to CD-ROM to reduce needed storage space. Records will not get misfiled once they are recorded on CD.

Digital video discs (DVD) is the next technology. Although DVD will be available in late 1996, recorders are still a couple years off.

Computer Training

Computer training is a crowded market, but children's training seems a bit less competitive. Public schools are still lagging in computer availability and anxious parents want to be sure their children are computer literate. Although a children's only center is very limited, consider having concurrent classes for children and parents. Another possibility is a center that lets young adults work with programming and put together systems.

Mobile Computer Service

After watching numerous individuals hauling their systems into computer stores, there seems to be a need for computer repair person who makes house calls. Whether this is a workable full-time business in your area requires market research.

Computer Graphics, Animation, and Video Production

Computer graphics is one of those "hot" careers that has become very competitive. If you are truly passionate, plus talented in art and computers, you may be able to find a niche for your talents. Developing a distinctive style and specializing in several software programs will help you be successful. Develop a career plan, but be flexible, taking advantage of opportunities you encounter along the way.

Having a special interest coupled with acquired skills in video production is a strong combination. One self-educated freelancer began with a short animated video, sold to a local television station. The story told by the video was integrated with an explanation of how the animation was produced. Now that he has demonstrated his abilities, companies come to him for projects. At the same time, he is working on a long-term project researching a special interest that could eventually develop into a movie or television special.

In communities with movie studios, very talented and experienced independent animators can do well. Getting that experience requires real commitment. Rhonda Graphics, an animation studio, entered the animation market early when equipment and software costs were still high and captured a substantial portion of its local market. Being first in a market is risky, but the advantage is fewer competitors.

Video Law Services started in the wedding videography market, but discovered an unfilled niche in providing video and animation for law practices. Michaela Miller, Video Law founder, produced a documentary video on the use of video in the legal profession. She exhibited at legal meetings which generated new business.

With the advent of lower cost video editing systems, a number of video production studios are appearing. The key to being successful seems to be defining your market. Flexibility and resourcefulness will help you find niche markets. If you are not a salesperson, put together a demo tape and let someone else do your marketing.

Online Services

Everyone seems to be getting into the market of putting business home pages on the World Wide Web. The Web provides good exposure for companies and can provide customer service and product information. Tremendous demand exists for individuals who have the skills to design and maintain web sites. Since this is a completely new field, few individuals have formal training, so developing skills on your own is the norm. If you are interested in this market, you can develop your skills by designing and maintaining web pages for free or at low cost to get the necessary experience. Start with small jobs and build your skills.

Some companies have been burned by "webmasters" who took their money without delivering the services. Make sure you develop your skills before entering this market as a business. Disreputable individuals make business more difficult for reputable companies. The potential is good in this market, but only if you have credible references and have patiently developed your skills. If you do decide this business is right for you, keep your vision on future directions as changes will happen quickly in this market.

Computer Leasing

With rapidly changing technology, some companies find it more cost-effective to lease rather than purchase equipment. For a start-up company, leasing can lower upfront costs. Previously leased equipment can be sold after the lease expires for additional profit. Leasing requires substantial capital or can be started as a part-time business and built up slowly.

Future Opportunities

The computer market will continue to thrive. Many of us cannot envision working without computers. Because of the difficulty in keeping pace with the fast changes in this sector, the demand for skilled professionals will continue. For those with the interest and skills, this field will continue to provide an abundance of business opportunities.

Consulting

onsultants are paid for their specialized knowledge. Consulting lends itself to highly knowledge-intensive areas and experienced individuals who have in-depth knowledge, extensive credentials, and specialized skills.

Consider becoming a consultant if:

+ You have specialized knowledge and experience, especially if this knowledge is in an area that most companies do not need in-house.

+ You have established a network of contacts who are potential clients.

+ You have, in addition to experience, credentials to back up your qualifications.

+ You have some sales or marketing experience in addition to your specialized skills.

+ You are active in your professional organization, have written articles, or given seminars in your specialty to get your name known.

We generally call a person a consultant if he or she provides highly specialized services, especially if that person does much of the work at the client's location. Providing certain services, especially short-term technical or management advice, falls to the expertise of a consultant. A consulting business may be structured virtually identically to other small companies.

We'll examine three successful consulting practices then consider other opportunities in consulting.

Environmental Management Consultants

Sometimes the transition into consulting is a natural path from employment. Jack Akin started his career as a project engineer with a small industrial company. After a year and half, he moved to a larger company to fill a position as plant and environmental engineer. Since it was difficult to find an environmentally-trained engineer then, the company provided this training. They sent him to train with a group of attorneys specializing in environmental law. During this time he visited industrial plants to gain knowledge of the problems encountered in manufacturing. Because of this experience, he was often asked to speak at Society of Manufacturing meetings.

Following these meetings, he was frequently asked for advice and assistance, resulting in outside consulting jobs. With his company's knowledge, he found himself taking on more and more consulting. During this time, he also earned a Masters in Environmental Engineering, took post-graduate work in geology, public health, physical chemistry, and gained a number of certifications required by his state for removal, inspection, and installation of storage tanks, asbestos inspection, cathodic protection, soil matrix analysis, plus incident commander certification for environmental emergencies.

He took a half-time environmental engineering position with another company and devoted the remainder of his time to consulting. Finally, he formed his own full-time consulting company, Environmental Management Consultants, and has been very satisfied with this decision. In conjunction with his consulting, he also set up a testing laboratory for water—ground, surface, and drinking—and soil. He is less satisfied with the decision to set up his own laboratory, which has required large expenditures for equipment.

Akin says the environmental field has become very competitive, resulting in lower fees for consultants. Opportunities exist, but they vary between municipalities. Environmental issues are especially significant for the manufacturing industry. Companies, in part because of potentially huge liabilities for creating environmental contamination or buying environmentally-contaminated properties, need the assistance of experienced, certified individuals. Besides an environmental engineering background, Akin says that geologists, especially hydrogeologists, are in demand.

Human Resources Center

Prior to entering consulting, Dr. Jerry Eisen was senior vice president with a prominent hotel corporation. He had worked with many consultants during his career and noticed that most seemed to enjoy their businesses while earning a good income. About two years prior to leaving his job, he started to notice a change in the business climate within his organization, gearing more toward profits and less toward people. This shift, plus his work experiences with consultants, and the challenge of starting his own business, resulted in his decision to enter consulting. During his last two years of employment, he stepped up his already busy schedule of speaking commitments and article writing, focusing on making contacts which would prepare him for consulting. He used this time to research, through talking with small business owners and reading, the mechanics of starting a business.

During his investigation, Eisen discovered a niche in human resource consulting for small businesses. No one was assisting small business owners with their human resource needs. He attributes his immediate success to discovering and filling this need, plus his abundant network of contacts, his assertive personality, and a knack for marketing. "Small business owners are closely tied to their employees, usually having hired them," commented Eisen. This people-awareness attracted Eisen, noting the contrast from his previous position.

Eisen knew he did not want to be home-based, feeling this would be distracting and less professional. He rented a two-room office, one floor down from his attorneys. At start-up, he consulted with his attorney-advisors, and asked if they could provide any help in start-up. They volunteered use of their library and other aids. Since his work involves much correspondence, he immediately hired a typist and equipped her with a word processor. Five years later, he brought in a second consultant, expanding now to five others besides himself.

When Eisen left his employment, he already had his first client. Many people worry about other aspects of their business, but he astutely realized that having clients is most important. Through his work years, he had traveled extensively and knows many people, including attorneys and newspaper contact people.

At first, loneliness was the major challenge. Although there was an abundance of business due to his market niche, he had no place to go to get together with others. Consulting was not as prevalent; today it is the one of the top five fastest growing industries. Because of this growth, organizations, such as the Institute of Management Consultants, were founded to bring consultants together to share their experiences. Last year, Eisen was president of the local chapter and this year he serves as chairman.

Eisen feels that credentials are important, although your credentials may not win the job. Besides his Ph.D., Eisen has earned both Certified Management Consultant (C.M.C.) and Senior Professional in Human Resources (S.P.H.R.)

certifications. Another consultant in his company has credentials as a Certified Employee Benefit Specialist and is completing requirements for Certified Compensation Specialist. "Companies feel more comfortable working with a consultant that has a Ph.D.," he reflected.

Eisen attributes the growth in the number of consultants to bringing more people into the business. Experienced, professional people who are down-sized near the end of their careers find consulting a way to duplicate their prior earnings when they are unable to locate another position similar in pay and responsibilities.

In his small business management consulting, Eisen assists in labor relations, compensation and incentive programs, executive search, and prevention of employee litigation.

Peg Lovell Consulting

Peg Lovell, a dental practice consultant, has held many positions in dental offices. She started as a dental assistant, then was in charge of office finances, progressing to managing an entire office. From there, she held a position in marketing for another office. In that office, she encountered a dental practice consultant and immediately knew this was what she wanted to do.

She set forth to find out everything she could about dental consulting by talking to anyone remotely related to dentistry. She spoke with vendors, business supply companies, and dentists. Her goal was to find out how to get established in consulting.

A business supply company referred her to another company, Practice Consulting Group. She joined the group as a consultant, finding this an excellent way to learn the skills required. After this position, she became an independent consultant while working part-time for another dental consulting practice. Through her work with the consulting companies, Lovell made valuable contacts, learned how to establish herself as a consultant, and started to build her credentials. Now she has clients in Southern California and the entire state of Arizona.

Lovell has continued to expand her credentials. She finds that many dentists have had negative experiences with consultants, making it more difficult for those that are committed and qualified. She is the only female Certified Management Consultant in Arizona. Lovell is a member of the American Academy of Dental Management Consultants, National Institute of Management Consultants, National Speakers Association, and Vice President of the Arizona Chapter of Certified Management Consultants.

Dentists consult her primarily for help in overhead control and team management. With a small staff that has many roles to fill, dentists need assistance in developing teams that can step in and handle the variety of situations encountered daily. They also need support in finding, training, and keeping qualified personnel.

Her depth of experience in dental offices has proved valuable. When Lovell is advising the staff of an office, they know that she can empathize with their daily challenges since she worked as a dental assistant herself. She finds that the staff more readily accepts the advice of someone who has been in their position.

Lovell finds it important to discover upfront how receptive the dentist is to change because sometimes the doctor is part of the office problem. She discloses this possibility directly to the dentist before taking an assignment. Presenting possible challenges initially makes the situation easier to handle when these problems arise later.

Lovell gains new business through referrals from current and past clients. Much of her business, though, is repeat business. She is very satisfied with her decision to become a practice management consultant.

Consultants need to master many business skills in addition to their specialized knowledge. Many consultants, due to the technical nature of their work, do their own selling, fee setting, billing, and collections. A dilemma facing numerous individual consultants is falling into a roller coaster of work, sales, work, sales, with no steady stream of jobs. Jack Akin, Environmental Management Consultants, advises that one way to avoid this cycle is to take a large number of smaller jobs rather than concentrating on large jobs, with long periods of no work in between. Dr. Jerry Eisen advises that consultants always need to "keep one eye on the work and the other eye opened for future jobs." Some consultants work on multiple assignments at the same time, lasting for variable time lengths. Peg Lovell works with multiple clients during a typical week.

Communication is extremely important when the business is you. A consultant must not only assess a situation and make recommendations, but communicate these ideas effectively to the hiring company. Akin says that often communication is easier for a consultant, though, because people often hire you to support their ideas. Employees must work through office politics to get their ideas implemented.

Establishing relationships with your clients is important. You want to have repeat business. Client referrals may be your main source of new business. A consultant often works with companies during difficult periods. Listening carefully to what the client says will help uncover the true concerns. Your job is to help remedy those concerns. Clients often have difficulty clarifying their real problems and needs. Obtaining a clear objective will enable you to proceed towards a solution. Proceeding too quickly, before the situation is known, will probably result in an unhappy client and no future relationship. At best, time will be lost. Consultants benefit from being people persons, which helps in developing good client relationships.

Consultants may work alone or in groups. Peg Lovell indicates that "one of the most difficult parts of consulting is that you have no one to bounce ideas off." She began working in a group, but when she relocated, she went on her own. Lovell networks with other consultants to share ideas. In a small group, individual consultants could work out of their homes, conversing by phone or through periodic meetings. Larger groups can share support staff. An advantage of a group is that consultants with multiple specialties can share referrals and knowledge.

Consulting demand varies with trends so watch for changes in your field. By identifying a need early, you benefit from less competition, a larger demand for your services, and the ability to charge higher rates. Compensation for consulting services can be per project, per diem, per hour, or even a percentage of profits. For a well-defined project, the cost is often quoted on the whole job. The more unknowns that exist, the more likely a consultant will want an hourly rate.

In-Demand Consulting Opportunities

Current demands in consulting are especially strong for technical consultants, those with in-depth knowledge of the latest technology. The generalists think that a variety of skills are necessary to get enough work locally, so specialists may find themselves traveling. Since technology is changing so rapidly, a consultant will need to stay on the cutting edge to keep in demand.

Employee Compensation

Companies are moving toward paying employees based on productivity. Dr. Jerry Eisen of Human Resources Center identifies employee and CEO compensation as currently one of the hottest areas for human resource consultants. Compensation based on results and productivity attracts higher quality employees, according to business owners who have tried this method of compensation. Besides better employees, efficiency and results often improve.

Overhead Control and Employee Benefits

Cost cutting has caused companies to focus on ways to decrease expenses and employee benefits, especially healthcare insurance, are receiving scrutiny. A multitude of new options is available and someone with a background in setting up benefit plans should be able to find opportunities. The trend is toward a menu of benefits with the exact combination selected by the individual employee.

Short-sightedly, overhead control for many companies means cost-cutting. Employing this narrow definition often results in limiting the future competitiveness of companies. Alternately, a consultant may be able to re-focus on increasing profits by creation of exciting new products and services, changing management's viewpoint, and fashioning a more conducive work environment.

Work Teams

When people work well together, project results can be enhanced. Working in teams involves many issues such as defining team roles, communication, and working with a diverse group of people and skills. These issues can be challenging and an independent consultant can be valuable to facilitate group functioning.

Computer Network Design

Designing and installing computer networks in businesses to allow sharing peripheral equipment, databases, e-mail, and other information is currently a booming area. Once the network is established, when additional equipment is added or the software needs updating, your services will again be required. Repeat clients are great because they eliminate the need to constantly search for new business.

Chris Piraino has taken advantage of the computer networking trend in his business. He writes custom accounts receivable packages for use on client/server systems, often updating the network in the process.

Engineering

Engineers find consulting opportunities in designing, testing, safety, environmental, construction, infrastructure, telecommunications, and inspection. By watching for trends and niches while reading trade journals, attending trade shows, and talking with colleagues and other businesspeople, future opportunities can be discovered early.

Environmental

Due to government regulations and potential litigation, opportunities in environmental assessment and problem-solving exist. All commercial buildings require a Phase One environmental assessment prior to obtaining a loan. Testing of soil and removal of underground storage tanks are regulated. Radon, lead, electromagnetic radiation, and asbestos are also governed. These tasks lend themselves well to consulting as few companies have the need for a full-time environmental engineer.

Franchising

Franchising is a highly regulated business that must be properly set up to be legally valid. Since this requires specialized knowledge most business owners do not have, a franchising consultant, often a lawyer, can assist businesses starting to franchise.

Intellectual Property Rights

For those with a law degree, businesses need help protecting their intellectual property. The Internet has made information readily available and companies are concerned about their ownership of ideas. In the legal field, where there are problems, there is business.

International Trade

International trade opens up a number of opportunities for those with appropriate experience. U.S. companies need assistance when entering international markets. They require support in overseas shipping, banking, and marketing. Translators and international protocol consultants may be needed. Currently, China, Vietnam, and Malaysia are countries where many firms are expanding their business.

Companies working through distributors find locating a qualified, ethical representative abroad is challenging. Since the individuals you select will be representing your company, this choice may determine your success in that geographical area. Writing sales agreements and determining compensation may require the assistance of specialists. Product support, including repair, can be tricky in distant locations.

Companies will be doing more business abroad. Expanding your education in international trade, gaining foreign connections by working abroad, learning to speak another language, or interning with an international consulting firm will enable you to gain the experience and credentials needed to specialize in one or more facets of international trade.

Internet

How services will be compensated on the Internet is still being defined. Although it is still unclear how to best use this media for product sales, most businesses feel that it is important to get in early to gain the expertise to move quickly as solutions appear. Consultants, who can guide companies as to how they should approach this new media, are in demand. With such a new area, few have extensive experience, so the field is wide open. Expect much competition, though, due to the lack of entry barriers and the appeal of a new media.

Leadership Skills

In challenging times, the ability to provide leadership and direction for a company may be the determining factor for success. Business owners and CEOs are aware of the need and seek out leadership experts.

Multimedia

Companies are searching for expertise with new media—CD technologies, laser discs, animation, graphics, digital video discs, digital video, interactive television, and online services—to develop products and marketing methods. Multimedia is one of the most rapidly changing areas and keeping abreast of new technology requires continual learning. If you have a graphics or technical background and enjoy a fast-paced, competitive workplace, you'll find opportunities here.

Reorganization

Reorganizations—mergers, buy-outs, takeovers, divisions—require consultants to work through the process. A law degree and accounting background are helpful.

Software: Specialty

Software designers write custom software or work on special projects for companies. Programming languages and design experience are necessary.

Gen X Consultant

Each generation is shaped by its experiences. Those of work age during the Great Depression value thrift and security, having experienced the hardships and job loss following the stock market crash. The Baby Boomers grew up in a growing and more secure economy. They tend to value individualism, but having had more material possessions than their parents, also expect the same comforts. Today's young people are growing up in a work environment without security. They are learning early that they need to be in charge of their own destinies.

Companies are finding today's young people have a different view of their careers. Many companies need advice on how to motivate this generation. Here is a consulting opportunity for a Gen Xer.

Beware of False Consulting "Opportunities"

Some individuals, unable to find equivalent employment, have used consulting to fill their employment gaps giving consulting an unearned bad rap. Not being committed to independent consulting, when a job opportunity becomes available, their consulting career ends. If you are seeking a job and considering consulting in the interim, you will be more successful putting your efforts into upgrading your skills and professionally conducting your job search.

Some of these unemployed individuals have been lured into consulting scams. One of these scams was listed in a sourcebook for home businesses. The listing was for a consulting network. The company claimed that by sending $2,000, you would become a consultant in its network and immediately be given at least 30 projects, paying a minimum of $1,000 a day. Further projects come as referrals from other consultants in the network. Each new consultant is assigned a mentor, to facilitate getting started. Written manuals would be provided to assist in start-up.

The fee for projects goes directly to the consultant. Consultants have multiple profit centers: venture capital, mergers and takeovers, consulting, and human resources. Consultants could work in teams on projects requiring multiple expertise. This consulting network claimed to have consultants worldwide, including all major U.S. cities.

The projects turned out to be general ideas for marketing readily available products, not paying jobs with real companies. The written manuals were photocopied book pages and a book list. Every person was assigned the same mentor. Phone calls to the company number always led to an automated response, requiring callers to leave a message. The company requested that its fee be wired to a bank account. After investigation, the company's main business turned out to be head-hunting, finding job candidates for a fee. The Better Business Bureau in the company's listed home town gave the business an unacceptable rating, with unresolved complaints.

How can a person determine if a business if legitimate?

1. Read the contract carefully. What isn't written is not included even if it is implied. Be careful not to make assumptions, but read the actual wording. The contract from the above company stated the *availability* of consultation with other network consultants, *preparation* of national listings for consulting and human resource directories, *availability* of reference materials and the *opportunity* to work with clients of the networking group. If the contract wording is too vague, rewrite it, then send it back for revision before signing.

2. A direct phone number should be available.

3. Ask for references. Check the credibility of these references.

4. Credentials of new consultants should be carefully verified and candidates met in person.

5. Wiring funds prevents canceling payment on a check. A disreputable firm will not be able to maintain merchant status to accept credit cards, as chargebacks can be made for up to six months. Young companies may not have enough volume to justify credit card acceptance, but if neither checks nor credit cards are accepted, be suspicious.

6. Watch for conflicting information.

7. Verify the company with national trade organizations.

8. Call the Better Business Bureau in the listed city to make sure the company is registered and that complaints have been resolved.

Starting Your Consulting Practice

"Once you make the decision to become a consultant, commit yourself to this no matter what challenges arise," advises Peg Lovell. "Establishing yourself as a consultant is difficult and takes time." As in any business, commitment is the key to being successful.

If you would like to establish a consulting practice, talk to consultants in this specialty. Talk to potential clients. Meet with vendors, who often can offer a different perspective. Watch for special niches where you can offer a contribution. Take work assignments and seminars that give you the in-depth knowledge necessary. Consider working within a group of consultants, at least initially, to learn the mechanics of consulting.

Build your credentials by working towards certification in consulting and in your specialty. Dr. Jerry Eisen, Human Resources Center, explains that certification and education are very important. You are positioning yourself as an expert in your field and need to be able to document your credentials.

To become certified as a management consultant (C.M.C.), you must work full-time as an independent management consultant for five years. Next, detailed case histories of five of your clients are assembled, explaining why you were hired, your action plan, and your results. Having successfully completed these steps, you will take a written two-hour test, then go before a inquiry board of your peers for another two hours. This certification establishes your expertise in, and commitment to, consulting. Through your local chapter and the national organization, educational opportunities are available to increase your competence in topics such as marketing, billing, legal matters, and ethics that are common to all consulting specialties.

Become active in your professional organization. To establish your name, look for highly visible committees and positions. Give seminars at your professional meetings and in the business community. Write articles for your professional publications. You will have to go out and sell yourself. If you cannot sell your services, procure new business, and build referrals, consulting is not a good business for you.

Since consulting is primarily a referral business, time is required to build a reputation. This may mean doing work at low fees or even for free to build references. If you start while you are still employed, you may be able to build your network while keeping your current income. Start taking small consulting jobs in addition to your full-time position. By advance planning, you can build a solid base that will facilitate your transition.

CHAPTER 9

Consumer Retail

*T*he consumer retail market is a huge but tough market. Competing head on with large retailers would probably be foolish, but there are some opportunities left. Look for areas that large retailers are not yet targeting and then ask if these are likely future markets for large corporations. If not, you may have found a business opportunity.

Consider a consumer retail products business if:

❖ You have a unique idea for a retail business that has a narrow market unlikely to interest large retailers.

❖ You enjoy retail sales.

❖ You have enough capital to be able to run this business for a minimum of six months without profit.

❖ You have thoroughly researched your competition and are convinced you have enough market potential to make a reasonable profit.

Despite the competitiveness of retail markets, by finding specialty retail areas, taking advantage of the resale markets, and other strategies, you can find business opportunities. Everything Earthly's market is environmentally-friendly products. Richard Scott has found that continually experimenting with his retail mix enables him to identify which products sell. Different products do well in different stores. What sells well for him, may not sell as quickly elsewhere.

Ann Siner of My Sister's Closet has found that there is a strong market for women's quality resale clothing attractively displayed in a pleasant shopping environment. When the price of new clothing seems unaffordable, women will shop resale.

Everything Earthly

Richard Scott, owner of Everything Earthly, thrives on being able to make a living by promoting what he believes. Everything Earthly sells products that are good for the environment. Extremely knowledgeable on environmental issues, he selects products that are not only environmentally compatible, but from companies with a strong environmental focus. When he finds a good product from a company that is not known to be environmentally-friendly, he uses the product as a springboard to educate the company. Research has shown that profits increase when companies become more environmentally-focused.

Although Scott's educational credentials include an M.A. in philosophy, he has supported himself as an entrepreneur, owning other businesses. Scott's previous businesses did not fulfill his passion for community activism nor did they mesh with his values. With Everything Earthly, his passion is compatible with his business. This has brought him great satisfaction and enabled him to survive in a field that is still struggling for recognition.

Finding suppliers of environmental products has been difficult. A few organizations exist that have been helpful: Co-op America, which publishes *Green Pages*; and Eco Expo, with two trade shows a year and a publication called *In Business*. Scott has recently become president of a group, Green Retailers Association, that helps set up connections between suppliers and retailers in the Western Hemisphere. When bringing new products into his store, he always applies the seventh generation litmus test. This test is derived from Native American culture. The Eastern Federation of Nations, comprising the Iroquois and other Eastern tribes, examined how each decision they made would effect their descendants seven generations removed. If the effect would be negative, the change would be rejected. Scott, too, rejects products that will negatively impact the seventh generation.

Finding what products sell is often a matter of trial and error. In Scott's store, clothing made with naturally colored cotton and hemp is the best seller. The cotton is grown organically, making it environmentally-friendly. The hemp products are very durable and long-lasting. Hemp requires three-quarters less water than growing cotton, conserving valuable resources. Hemp garments, with their soft and silky texture, are the fastest growing area of sales.

Everything Earthly also carries body care products and paper made from kenaf, a plant in the hibiscus family. This paper has an excellent appearance. Maybe in the future, kenaf can help prevent the loss of our forests. Fine paper can also be produced from hemp.

Scott and a partner originally started the business in 1992. They spent a couple of months doing market research by selling products from their homes and at festival booths. This research indicated people were interested in environmentally-friendly products; however, the financial numbers didn't favor a profitable business. Realizing they would need to educate people, they opened a store anyway, believing in the importance of making these products available.

The store has expanded twice in its present location. Scott would like to move to a more visible location, gain space, and expand his product lines. Solar power is an area of interest for him. "My goal is to have the first totally solar-powered store in town," he explains.

With Earth Day, April is a very busy month. Scott participates in many community events related to the environment. He feels that "the efforts are well worth the satisfaction received." The store maintains a special grassroots section that posts free environmental information concerning local groups and how to get involved.

Opening a business in a new market niche requires more patience than something tried and true. Scott is very committed. Being committed keeps him searching for new ways to demonstrate the value of using green products. "I believe I am in a business that actually has the potential to change the way the world does business. Indeed, if we don't change I fear for the future of humankind."

My Sister's Closet

Have you ever been in a store and thought, I could do this, too? Ann Siner, a former director of marketing with a large retail company, was on a business trip to San Antonio when she happened across an upscale resale boutique. Tiring of corporate life and impressed by the boutique she had chanced upon, she decided she could create a similar store. With her retail marketing and sales experience plus an MBA, she had the experience needed to get a fast start.

In January 1991, Siner quit her job and spent about eight months researching the competition, selecting a location and negotiating the lease. She made trips to San

Diego and La Jolla where she queried other upscale resale shops. Since she would not be competing directly with their stores, the owners offered a wealth of information. Siner learned how to price clothing and select a location by researching demographic data with the help of a local librarian and a demographic research company, Advo.

Selecting a location was challenging. Siner wanted to locate in an area with working women from their mid-20s to mid-50s. Research and location selection took about seven months. Many of the good locations did not want a resale store. The negotiation for her present location took three to four months, in part because of controversy on leasing to resale. Siner wrote up a business plan, a necessity for obtaining her lease, but which also proved immensely helpful in getting started. The store's name, My Sister's Closet, is partially a credit to Siner's sisters, Jennifer and Tess, who have assisted in the business and helped extensively with the start-up. Her sisters add artistic talents to Siner's business background and retail experience.

Once the lease was signed, Siner remodeled and opened her store in only a month. By word of mouth via friends, there was already an inventory of clothing. An interior designer was hired for the floorplan and to supervise the build-out. All the work was completed by family, friends, and a retired handyman. Siner had enough money saved so that she did not need to secure a loan. The store opened in August, 1991, turning a profit in one month!

Initially Siner and her sisters ran the store. Now there are 10 employees including a store manager. Opening in 1992, My Sister's Closet II, focused on bridalwear and formalwear, but then expanded to sell all types of dresses and accessories. Recently, the two stores were combined to form a single 3,600 square foot location when space became available adjacent to one of the stores.

My Sister's Closet accepts designer label and natural fiber clothing and accessories that are currently in style. Clothing must be clean and in immaculate condition. Siner has developed a contract for consignees, stipulating all the terms of consignment. The store prices all the clothing. Clothing is priced at roughly a third of retail price and kept for a period of three months, bridal for six months. Pleasing both customers and consignees is often challenging, as both are her clients.

One of Siner's biggest challenges is finding good employees. Newspaper want ads have generally not proved successful. Most employees are found by either word-of-mouth or in response to a sign in the store window. Siner emphasizes the importance of thorough interviewing and reference checks.

The stores reside in a centrally located, upscale shopping center that has benefited from careful selection of merchants. A large bookstore and gourmet shop are two of the major tenants. The location gives the stores high visibility. Siner also advertises in a local monthly women's magazine, a trendy weekly regional newspaper, the style magazine in the city newspaper, and a neighborhood newspaper. Periodic mailings with notification of sales and special events are sent to one of the store's mailing list of customers. Recently, Siner computerized the store, increasing efficiency.

Resale clothing stores have the appeal of finding a real bargain at an excellent price, lower than discount stores. Recycling clothing lets someone else benefit from affordably priced garments that otherwise might be discarded. Even items that don't sell find a second life via donation to a non-profit thrift shop. Consignees get a donation receipt and the non-profit group raises money. My Sister's Closet provides resale shopping in a pleasant, upscale environment.

From the previous examples, you have seen that opportunity in retail exists. Next, you'll learn ways to find these situations.

New Consumer Product Opportunities

Tourist Businesses

If you live in an area that draws a large number of tourists, you have an unique business opportunity. Tourists often plan to bring back gifts or souvenirs. They seek out interesting stores with items that they can't buy at home. Make your store intriguing to draw in curious tourists. In many areas, this may be a seasonal business.

T-Shirts: Specialty

Silk screening is a fairly low cost business opportunity. Because T-shirt design is a major selling point, a creative person can dream up original designs that appeal to local markets or visitors. T-shirts can also be designed and produced for local groups. You can create designs for local schools, businesses, clubs, and churches. Consider screening designs for local sports, for example. Be careful about professional sports, though, because this is big business with mandatory licensing fees. Besides screening T-shirts, consider sweatshirts, jackets, hats, shirts, sweatpants, ties, boxers, shorts, uniforms, towels, bags, mousepads, coffee cups, puzzles, tiles, and plaques.

Clothing for Real People

Although the clothing market has been very difficult for even large stores, a few small companies are thriving. Statistics indicate that people are weighing more, but many large clothing designers still design for the "perfect" body. A market exists for clothing that will fit real people. If this clothing is comfortable and makes an individual look slimmer, people will buy. Clingy knits, cropped tops, tight clothing, hemlines that are halfway up the thigh are the reasons many clothing manufacturers are in dire financial condition. This is a challenging area, but a few small designers are making it by meeting the needs of real people.

Niche Markets

Batteries have become a necessity in our lives, powering many of our electronic gadgets. Several stores sell only batteries. Since most batteries have a limited shelf life, especially nicads, this is a business that many larger companies wouldn't want to hassle with.

The current market for environmentally-friendly products is not big enough for large retailers. However, the potential market is huge as Everything Earthly's owner, Richard Scott, foresees. Stores such as Everything Earthly need more environmental products to stock their stores and gain public awareness.

Several cosmetic companies have specialized in providing products for special markets. Creating cosmetics for a specific ethnic group, hair color, age group, or skin type are examples of niche markets. Larger cosmetic companies sell to broader markets, although some of these niche groups are quite large. Most specialty cosmetic companies sell via their own catalogs, although selling through other catalogs or media may be lucrative.

Liquidation/Surplus

While this used to be a great area with limited competition, these stores now seem to be everywhere. There may be opportunity yet for stores that specialize in one type of merchandise, for instance, sports equipment and apparel. If you know the retail market, investigate specific merchandise areas to look for opportunities. Nearly everyone wants a bargain. Stores that can provide great deals on merchandise have the advantage.

Swap Meets

Swap meets are immensely popular. This can be a low cost way to build a business. Most large cities have multiple swaps. By having a booth at several different swaps, profits can be increased more rapidly. These markets can also be a way to test market products or services. Some products are first introduced at a swap and later turn up in retail stores. Often prices at swap meets are comparable to retail shops because swap market sellers know that people tend to buy on impulse.

Businesses That May Be Dominated by Large Companies

Proceed carefully.

- ❖ Children's clothing
- ❖ Baby stores
- ❖ Maternity clothing
- ❖ Uniforms
- ❖ Wigs
- ❖ Large, small, short, and tall sizes
- ❖ One price stores/Dollar stores
- ❖ Computer-sized clothing
- ❖ Any type of sports equipment or apparel
- ❖ Security products except unique items

Used Consumer Product Opportunities

Used products are great retail businesses for small companies. Larger companies usually don't want the hassle. Look for new markets in used retail.

Used Electronic Media

When individuals tire of a particular audio compact disc, they would rather trade it in on something new. Some companies recycling CDs are used bookstores, music stores, free-standing exchanges, and flea market businesses.

Video and audiotapes, although less sturdy, are another market. Videodiscs are a very small market, but are less prone to damage. Used computer software and video games lose value quickly. However, one large local bookstore seems to do quite well retailing used but current or recent version software and video games. Combining all of these might be the best business opportunity.

Used Clothing

Quality clothing in good condition has good resale value, especially women's clothing. Although you should check out your local competition first, it is amazing how many of these stores a community can support. Create high standards for the condition of consignment clothing to keep your customers coming back.

Children's clothing is one resale niche. Children are constantly outgrowing clothing and new clothing, even children's, is expensive. Some resale stores have specialized in this market, though children's clothing does not have the resale value of women's clothing. To compensate for lower value, consider increasing the quantity.

Savers is a large chain of used clothing superstores that has taken the quantity approach and is doing fine. They buy clothing from local charities, clean it, and resell at a profit. Although the store has a discount, spartan appearance, the volume of goods seems to make the difference. The more clothing that a store stocks, the more likely people will find something that appeals and fits.

Used Furniture on Consignment

Many times a family tires of furniture before it is worn out or they move to a new home where the old furniture doesn't fit. Terri's Consignment is a chain of used furniture stores that has been quite successful. Home furnishings include items from homes, model homes, estates, and liquidations. Furniture is grouped attractively and teamed with accessories such as lamps and pictures. While more expensive than shopping through the want ads or garage sales, the store provides convenience for busy consumers. A store such as this would do best in an area where people move frequently. The chain started with one store and now has five locations. In 1993, it started franchising.

Other Used Equipment

Look for other used products that might create a viable business such as used sporting equipment, children's sports and play products, and home office equipment.

Antiques

The antique business has a devoted customer base. This market requires strong knowledge of antiques and the ability to locate sources of antiques to build an inventory.

Product Rental Opportunities

Special Event Clothing Rental

Most of us do not need dressy clothing often, consequently the cost of this clothing per wearing is high. Wearing the same outfit every time isn't very appealing either. Rental becomes a more attractive option especially for occasions like proms and weddings that are usually one-time events. Rental costs are high, but not as high as buying. Clothing must be cleaned after each wearing which increases costs, but team up with a dry cleaner.

Party Rental

No one wants to keep large quantities of tables, chairs, china, and tableware that are used infrequently. One-time items such as dance floors, margarita machines, helium tanks, grills, champagne fountains, and candelabras aren't practical to buy. Children's party equipment, like inflatables, are popular for birthday parties. Party rental stores provide these items, plus may plan and cater the event as well.

Equipment Rental

Homeowners often find themselves occasionally needing a particular piece of equipment. If the equipment is large or expensive, renting may be a good option. Spend time talking with rental shop owners, preferably in other communities where you will not be viewed as a competitor, before deciding to open this type of business. The cost of opening an equipment business is high and good insurance is required.

Future Opportunities

The consumer retail market is large, but competition, especially from large companies is intense. Usually these businesses have higher start-up costs although consignment stores may be an exception.

CHAPTER 10

Educational Services and Products

hile education does not guarantee a job, individuals who seek a position with decent pay need to be continually re-educating themselves. The rate of change in specialized fields continues to accelerate. More individuals are making multiple career changes, in part due to major shifts within, or total elimination of, job fields. These factors have created a continual demand for training that has opened up opportunities in the educational market. This market extends from very early childhood through retirees.

Consider a business in educational products and services if:

❖ You enjoy helping others and enjoy learning yourself.

❖ You have the ability to take complex information and make it easily understandable to others.

❖ You have a theatrical flair to make learning exciting and fun.

❖ You have teaching experience and have developed effective ways of helping others learn.

❖ You are tolerant of differing abilities, nationalities, and personalities.

❖ You have specialized knowledge that you can clearly communicate.

This is a rapidly expanding sector with many different niches, meeting specific needs. Like most industry sectors, the market is very competitive, but resourceful individuals will continue to find opportunities by finding unserved markets, better teaching techniques, and ways to make learning more convenient. With so many working individuals needing accessible ways of upgrading their skills and knowledge, businesses that make it easy and enjoyable to update skills will be successful.

Arizona School of Real Estate and Business

Occasionally a business develops from a present work position. Bill Gray, president of Arizona School of Real Estate and Business, came to the school in 1978 as a student. He was impressed with the quality of the instructors and, once licensed, offered to teach at the instructor-owned school for free. As a practicing real estate agent, he could rely on the income from his home sales.

The school offers classes to help prepare real estate professionals for their licensing exam and to meet mandatory continuing education requirements. Today the school has expanded, offering classes in other business-related fields. Founded in 1969 by a newly graduated university student, a construction company later took over the school to train its real estate agents. Later, the construction firm sold the school to its instructors.

Interest rates at the time—early 1980s—hovered around 16 percent so home sales were stagnant. This was not a great time to be a real estate agent. One of the instructor-owners asked Gray if he would like to buy out the instructor's portion of the business. Gray arranged a buy-out over a two year period of time. Later, he used a bank loan to buy out the other instructor-owners. Knowing that interest rates fluctuate and that they would eventually fall, he focused on providing quality instructional programs.

At the time Gray bought the school, it was not the largest school in town. Another school had a prime location and dominated local real estate education. Eventually, after relocating and selling out to a new owner, that school closed. Now the Arizona School of Real Estate and Business is the major real estate education provider in the state with 85 instructors, including 14 who are full-time. Each month, 350 classes are offered.

Expanding beyond real estate education, the school now offers classes for contractors, appraisers, loan originators, loan processors, insurance and securities, new home sales, and computer classes. Concentrating on just real estate limits profit potential. Slowly the property around the school has been acquired so that classes are now spread over several buildings. Besides its central location in Scottsdale, classes are given in four other Arizona cities. Gray regularly travels nationwide teaching real estate classes.

A separate corporation was created for the school's monthly newspaper called *Arizona Journal of Real Estate & Business.* This publication lists the courses offered each month plus related articles of interest to real estate and business professionals. The newspaper, over 50 pages in length, earns a small profit through outside advertisers. It is the largest business newspaper in Arizona with a circulation of over 51,000. Receiving the newspaper monthly, the school is ever-present in the minds of professionals requiring continuing education courses.

Courses are offered days, weekends, and evenings with packaged programs that meet all relicensure requirements. These requirements are completed in minimum time, conserving valuable work time. The school is now approved to offer college credit for sales licensing courses. A custom textbook, flash cards, and tapes are published by the school. A number of other related books are available for sale.

Gray attributes his success to a commitment in providing quality instruction. Most students come to the school through word-of-mouth. Paying attention to quality rather than profit is key. He does not mean that costs and profits should be ignored, only that they are not the primary concern.

"Get in there and just do it. Plan your course, but be flexible and ready to change," Gray encourages. He did confess that if he knew at the onset about risks, lawsuits, IRS paperwork, and employee problems, he never would have bought the school.

"Be committed," Gray advises. "Most people start out fine, but when they aren't immediately profitable or successful, they give up before they can achieve success. Be patient. Success will come with commitment to quality." When starting a new program at the school, Gray is willing to take a loss at first because of his commitment to the long-term success of the program.

Rather than competing, he recommends creating your own unique business. When you compete, you are on the defense. Other schools in town have imitated his, but they are already behind by doing so. Create your own vision and carry it through.

When Gray receives calls asking if he is hiring new instructors, he says no. But he tells them if they have something unique to bring to the school, then let's talk. By speaking with prospective instructors, he can tell if they will fit with the school's philosophy. His school continues to grow by expanding into new areas with its focus on quality instruction.

Educational Management Group

Educational Management Group, or EMG, produces customized video and interactive television curriculums for schools throughout the world. Dr. Gail Richardson, a former educator and founder of two previous educationally-related businesses, wants to empower teachers. He believes it is important to identify the truly great teachers and find ways for them to impact larger numbers of students. By using interactive television, now feasible due to refined data compression via phone, satellite links, and a private broadband, wide area network (WAN), students can ask questions directly to the experts.

EMG develops customized curriculums and distributes these video programs to schools via a global network throughout the U.S., Canada, and Mexico. EMG crews travel throughout the world, programming events such as paleontologists on dinosaur digs, plants and animals of the Amazon Rainforest, and archeologists exploring Egyptian tombs. Programming is broadcast on a weekly schedule so schools can tune in to the show of their choice. In addition, the company produces videos, computer programs, and print materials on request from individual teachers to help assist in curriculum planning.

Richardson founded the company in 1988 with four employees. To generate cash flow initially, they produced a series of parenting tapes for schools to distribute to parents via local cable TV. Title 1 grants for reading, math, and parent instruction can be used by schools to purchase these tapes.

Richardson observes that technology has not impacted the way teachers teach. Although he does not think that technology itself is most important, he recognizes that children today are already adapted to learning via television and video. Previously, schools needed to teach students basic skills to prepare them for a single career. Now students must learn a broader range of skills to prepare them for a lifetime of change and managing multiple careers. They need excellent interpersonal skills, independent thinking skills, adaptability to change, and computer skills.

In 1988, the technology was not adequately developed nor was it cost effective to produce the interactive programming available today. EMG grew as this technology improved. Its first video programming was done at a shared studio at the local YMCA. Later EMG developed its own off-site studio. Now, relocated to new and larger facilities, the company plans to expand to 50 studios at its Scottsdale facility with additional studios throughout the U.S.

Richardson assists teachers by providing prepared curriculums to reduce preparation time. He views electronic curriculums as a means to "level the playing field," meaning all children can have access to experiences that would otherwise be unavailable to them. Many difficult concepts can be learned more easily from video. By using interactive television, experts are available to children throughout the U.S. and they can answer questions that may be beyond the teacher's expertise.

Getting schools equipped for technology has been challenging. Schools need to be rewired. EMG equips each classroom or media room with a television, fax machine, color printer and scanner, VCR, video camera, speaker phone, and satellite link via a small dish antenna at the school. EMG technicians set up and maintain this equipment. This same technology is also used to train, communicate, and transfer curriculum materials to teachers.

Schools receive unlimited programming by paying a set rate per student that works out to be 30 to 35 thousand dollars per year for the average elementary school and 150 to 200 thousand for high schools. Equipment and transmission costs are additional. Programming is simulcast in multiple languages. Mexico has been a receptive market, in part due to the need for distance learning in smaller communities. Educational funding has been readily available there.

The company has grown in employees and revenues by 25 percent per year, now with 200 employees, 110 locally and the rest throughout the U.S. In February 1995, Simon and Schuster bought the company to expand its educational technology market. With the added capital available by this purchase, EMG plans to expand to 400 employees by the end of 1996.

Additionally, Richardson is interested in an electronic high school where students take classes at home via EMG's Home Empowerment Network. Students would come on campus for testing, special interest activities, and athletics. He believes this to be a cost-effective means of providing secondary education. Richardson would like to have smaller class sizes in the primary grades where basic reading, math, and language skills are learned. Often, high schools have smaller classes than in the early grades where students need more individual help to master basic learning skills.

The company also is interested in creating recertification programs for professionals who are required to have continuing education, such as in the healthcare field. Programming can be delivered when convenient via cable television. Even the testing process can be automated through the use of voice prints.

Richardson advises potential business owners to choose a business they enjoy so much they would do the work for free. Starting a business requires long hours, which are much easier to bear if you love and believe in what you are doing. Richardson's main motivation is he believes he can make a difference in education.

EMG was started originally with his own funding, but Richardson advises to borrow as much as you need. Cash flow is challenging at first, but he believes the lack of capital can be at least partially offset by quickness in responding to new markets.

✧ ✧ ✧

Arizona School of Real Estate and Business has expanded rapidly due to quality instruction, but also because of its convenient scheduling of courses. Dr. Gail Richardson also understands the importance of quality instruction and convenience. His goal is to provide access to quality instructors for everyone. Distance learning is one solution to make learning more accessible.

Educational Opportunities

Teacher Trainer

Most teachers are highly dedicated and hard working individuals. If you are a master teacher, consider a business working with other teachers to help them become more effective in their instruction. Different teachers have different strengths, but helping them develop these abilities for maximum effectiveness would be to everyone's benefit.

The authors of *How to Talk So Kids Listen and Listen So Kids Will Talk* (Adele Faber and Elaine Mazlish; see Resources) are former teachers who developed methods of communicating to help children learn better. They have written a couple books and developed a business teaching others their techniques.

Getting Technology into Schools

Public schools have had difficulty coping with the rapidly changing needs of businesses. Students need training using computers, but many teachers received their education before computers were widespread. Teachers and students need instruction. Funding the costs of adding computers and other technology is another dilemma. Ideally, all students would have their own computers.

Computer manufacturers are developing lower cost computers. If costs decrease substantially, computers may become affordable for more families. The challenge of keeping pace with technology is difficult. Programs that allow businesses to upgrade systems while donating their previous equipment to schools would be helpful, but schools need to be able to maintain these systems. Networking computers would require fewer peripherals, but wiring needs to be updated.

With more computers, access to the Internet would provide opportunity to communicate with others worldwide and explore individual interests. Video production, an excellent teaching tool, is moving toward editing via computer, nonlinear editing. Previously, a substantial investment in equipment placed editing beyond the budgets of public schools.

Distance Learning

Dr. Gail Richardson founded his company, Educational Management Group, to bring great teachers and experiences into classrooms via technology. His company is involved in distance learning, meaning that students and instructors are in different locations. A single instructor can be brought into multiple classroom locations rather than having to travel to each site, making learning efficient, convenient, and more cost-effective.

Distance learning can bring information to greater numbers of students inexpensively. Once the equipment is in, costs are low. Companies that can assist in programming may find unfilled niche markets.

Rewiring Schools

Most schools are not wired for incorporating distance learning. Businesses that design and install networking systems and ISDN lines have a big market. Other modes of high speed data transmission may be future markets.

Home Schooling

Home schooling is becoming prevalent. Children are schooled at home generally by a parent who is not required to have special training. Most parents who home school their kids are very concerned about the quality of their education. Why not offer training for these parents?

Some companies are producing materials especially for this market. Talk with home schooling groups to see what materials parents need and children want. Perhaps you could also sell used materials or set up a learning materials exchange to help parents reduce costs.

Another idea, perhaps for a charter or private school, is to provide classes, testing, and other services for home-schooled children. Parents often find that trying to teach all subjects is beyond their abilities. Help fill deficits by allowing children to take only certain classes at the school. Children benefit from having multiple teachers with different talents. Special programs can be made available on an elective basis. Classes that require special equipment such as biology, chemistry, art, and others can be provided through the school. Orchestra, band, choral, sports, clubs, and drama groups can be offered. Opportunities for interacting with other children to learn social skills, team work, and similar skills can be provided.

Foreign Language Instruction

Research indicates the best time to learn a foreign language is the primary grades. In today's global business world, those who can speak a second language have an advantage. Computers are an excellent mode for learning a second language, but most software is geared toward adults. To keep proficient in a language, instruction should be reinforced periodically throughout the school years and after.

Second Language Instruction for Businesses

As our population becomes increasingly diverse, businesses become motivated to be able to reach non-English speaking individuals. In the southwestern states—Texas, New Mexico, Arizona, and California—Spanish-speaking educators could provide Spanish instruction to employees. Other languages may be important for businesses doing business internationally.

Career Exploration

Children are often exposed to only a limited number of careers, often those of family and friends. We need to find ways to allow children to experience more of the available choices without locking them into a specific career choice too early. Giving children the opportunity to explore as many different special interests as possible will allow them to discover their true interests.

Many of the career materials available are based on outdated general profiles of jobs. Although there is an abundance of career materials, information that gives a glimpse at the variety of possibilities within a career field is lacking.

Career Counseling

With the shift from one job for a lifetime to many jobs, there is a greater need for career assistance. New career counseling stresses flexibility and the multiplicity of career options available within a field. More effective ways of assisting individuals with the current job market are needed.

Conflict Resolution

Training in conflict resolution is valuable in the workplace and in interpersonal relationships. Tom Snyder Productions has developed a video program to assist elementary and high school teachers in teaching these skills. There is a great need for training in resolving conflicts for all ages.

Communication Skills

Our ability to communicate well with others is one of the most important factors in our success at work and in our personal relationships. Yet lack of effective communication skills seems widespread. Listening well and clearly communicating ideas are skills most people could improve yet public schools do not stress these skills.

Open Universities

Open universities offer courses to all who are interested regardless of educational background. The classes are often similar to special interest adult education classes offered through community colleges, but with a broader range of offerings. Examples of courses may range from white-water rafting through computer courses. If your community does not have a broad adult education program, consider founding an open university.

School Security Consultant

Most schools were built when security was less of a problem. Guns and weapons in schools were not a major problem 20 years ago. Ways to help schools work with these problems while maintaining a safe learning environment are needed.

Continuing Education

Continuing education for fields that require credits for licensure is already a big market, but there is a need for re-education in all fields. Industry has a great need for training, but some of this training is provided in-house. Outside trainers are usually specialists in a given area. Since technology and business are changing so rapidly, training and seminar companies are in a very tough business.

Continuing education, usually mandated on a state-by-state basis, is mandatory for some professions, especially the medical profession. Some states have limited the amount of continuing education that is permissible via home study. Professional organizations provide much of the continuing education. Especially in certain professions, there is opportunity for private companies. Distance learning may open up more opportunity. Perhaps by providing distance learning to facilities rather than directly into homes, the home study classification can be avoided.

Instructional Materials

The instructional materials market has some deep-pocket companies, but there are specific niches for development of materials. Check your areas of expertise to see who is developing materials so you can avoid going up against large companies. CD-ROM and video are popular instructional formats now, but keep your eyes open because technology will continue to evolve.

Companies catering to public schools will find cost is a major factor in purchases. This market is very seasonal with purchase orders mainly in the spring. Orders must be filled by late summer for the next school year.

Private Post-Secondary Schools

The private school market has been very tight since the government placed responsibility for loan repayment on these schools. Many students attend on federal loans so if a school drops below the predetermined loan default rate, the school will not be approved. If you are contemplating a private, for-profit school check with other schools in your region.

Many of these schools provide training for paraprofessionals in medical, technical, and business fields. Schools specializing in technology areas, such as virtual reality and computer-related skills, seem to be thriving now.

Education for the 21st Century

As the pace of change accelerates, educational needs will concurrently increase. To provide continual re-education, more effective teaching methods, many already available, need to be more widely implemented. New technology makes it easier and more convenient to get training.

Public education has often resisted input from the business community, but both sectors must work together so students develop the skills they need to make a living. Many teachers have no experience in business. Teachers should have real world experience in addition to their expertise in educating. Alternating business experience with teaching would increase the effectiveness of teachers, but this is not the trend. Resistance to working together is reflected in the trend toward privatization of education. Business may be able to more effectively educate, but cannot bear all the costs. In some areas privately-owned charter schools have been founded to help meet the needs of children and business, but sometimes students find courses non-transferable. When business and education unite, education will become more applicable and effective. Maybe you will found a business that helps solve this dilemma.

CHAPTER 11

Engineering Services, Products, and Manufacturing

*E*ngineers possess skills that are essential to numerous businesses, especially manufacturing. They conceive and develop many of the products we use every day plus find solutions to many technological problems. Many of the advances in technology originate with engineering professionals.

Consider a business in engineering or manufacturing if:

- ❖ You are an engineer with up-to-date knowledge and a passion for engineering.

- ❖ You have design and management experience in manufacturing.

- ❖ You can assemble a team of individuals with the necessary skills to make your business successful.

- ❖ You are comfortable working with computers and effectively use them in your work.

- ❖ If your sales and marketing skills are lacking, you recognize the need to hire or partner with someone who has this ability.

The companies profiled are in manufacturing design. Two were founded by engineers. All have recognized the need to hire quality individuals possessing skills that were out of the founders' expertise. This balanced team approach has contributed to the success of their companies. The first two companies are only a few years old, but have experienced rapid success because they produce a needed product and have good, innovative management. The third, Western Design Center, has an unique niche discovered by experimentation and driven by a passionate leader.

Air Taser

When Patrick Smith was studying in Belgium as part of his Harvard MBA program, fellow students from around the world spoke of their perception of the United States as a dangerous country to live. Around this time, two of Patrick's friends were murdered during a driving altercation in a parking lot. Because of concern for his mother who was often home alone during her husband's business travel, Patrick and his brother, Tom, a financial consultant, decided to buy her a .357 Magnum for protection. Their mother was not anxious to own a gun and asked them, "Isn't there a better way?" Smith began to research nonviolent, nonlethal crime deterrents.

During his research he encountered a nonlethal technology called a Taser®, being used by police to subdue assailants. The Taser was unavailable for civilian use because gunpowder was used as the detonator and the Bureau of Alcohol, Tobacco and Firearms considers it a concealed weapon. A cartridge is fired which shoots out two probes that attach to the clothing or skin of the assailant. The electrically-charged probes interfere with the neuromuscular system, incapacitating the assailant for about 15 minutes. When Smith tracked down the original inventor and patent holder, Jack Cover, he found that Cover lived nearby. Retired but still inventing, Cover suggested using air instead of gunpowder to fire the unit.

The company designed and now produces the air-powered cartridge for its handheld unit, which resembles a cellular phone in appearance. The Air Taser® shoots out two probes up to a distance of 15 feet. When the probes penetrate clothing or skin, the Taser-waves™ generated act like white noise to the nervous system, causing the assailant to fall to the ground. Although the probes may puncture the skin, the injury is only superficial and there are no residual effects even in individuals with pacemakers. Units generate only 0.4 joules of electricity, barely the amount to light a small bulb. The waves can travel through up to two inches of clothing and are effective even if only one probe should hit its target. An optional laser sight allows precise aim, and the high-tech visual appearance of the laser red dot may help to scare away the assailant. If there are multiple attackers, the unit can also be used as a stun gun.

To keep Air Tasers away from criminals, Patrick Smith devised a clever scheme to identify the user. During use, the air cartridge releases sprinkles of film coded with the unit's identification number. These sprinkles called Anti-Felon Identification (AFIDs) allow police help in tracking the owner of the unit. All units are registered at purchase and records are maintained by Air Taser. Police departments have endorsed the units and identification scheme.

If the Air Taser is used in self-defense, the company recommends the unit be placed on the ground after firing it at the assailant. The Air Taser automatically continues to disperse Taser-waves for 30 seconds, allowing enough time for the victim to escape. This 30 second burst will incapacitate the attacker for a short time, causing disorientation. Air Taser will replace used units left at the crime scene. "The company values the life of the unit's owner more than the cost of the unit," emphasizes Malcolm Sherman, director of sales and marketing.

Units are powered by ordinary nine-volt batteries and a battery indicator lights up when only 70 percent of power remains. This eliminates the unpredictability of batteries and wondering if the unit has sufficient power.

The company has three other security products developed and plans more. The next product released will be a door peephole lens that allows identification of visitors from as far as 15 feet away.

From the start, the Smiths decided not to keep the business as strictly a family enterprise, but to bring in experts to meet company needs. Individuals with expertise in engineering, quality control, marketing, and government affairs were hired. Most companies do not need a government lobbyist, but seven states have laws against electronic weapons which includes the Air Taser. "Although we are restricted in seven states, we aim to change this situation in the penal codes. With our built-in tracing system, we can approach these legislatures with credible reasoning that the Air Taser offers a safe and effective alternative to a firearm. Already we have prevented two bans on the device simply by educating legislatures and law enforcement on the safety issues and its tracing system that promotes responsible use," pledges Steve Tuttle, director of government affairs.

Videos are available to address concerns about safety and effectiveness. The company has created a 30 minute infomercial to air on cable and local television stations. The goal is to make the Air Taser available to all responsible individuals.

Air Taser, founded in late 1993 with the first units sold in 1995, has expanded rapidly into export sales. This international market demands that company personnel work in shifts to cover time differences. Half of the company's sales are outside the U.S. Many sales are to the Orient, where guns are illegal.

Deciding to concentrate its efforts in its expertise, the company produces only the air cartridge units. Production is under strict quality controls. A percentage of each batch is test fired and, if any should fail, the entire batch must be examined to locate the problem. Other components are completed by a circuit assembly plant. A computer distributor handles their distribution. Air Taser has teamed up with some strong distributors such as Sharper Image and uses independent distributors for international sales. Distribution and marketing are the greatest hurdles.

Initial financing was $20 thousand of Patrick Smith's own money. Even now, they have only one outside investor. Key personnel have invested their funds and equity in the company. The Smiths feel that having employees share equity increases results. They have plans to take the company public in two to four years.

Finding dependable employees was difficult, but, through recommendation from a local church, Serbian refugees are employed as assemblers. This solution provides committed employees and assists the refugees, many of whom are still adjusting to the U.S. language and culture.

Air Taser combines a needed product with a solid business plan. Its advance planning and business expertise has enabled the enterprise avoid many problems faced by new companies. Knowing the political and educational hurdles would be substantial, they have made the effort to ensure that quality control, financial concerns, and marketing are under the control of experienced individuals.

As crime rates increase, more people will want to carry a protective device. An Air Taser provides an alternative for individuals who do not want to carry a gun or who want an additional protective device.

Baby Think It Over

The unwed teenage pregnancy problem is one of greatest dilemmas facing this country. Many other problems are rooted here: single parent families, welfare, child abuse, lack of a high school education, and crime. A business that can help reduce a social problem such as unwed teenage pregnancy is not only creating jobs, but is also contributing socially. Baby Think It Over manufactures an infant simulator that is used in the education of teenagers about the responsibilities of parenthood.

A down-sized aerospace engineer, Rick Jurmain, heard about a program designed to help teenagers understand the commitment needed when bearing a child. Teenagers are given a five pound sack of flour to simulate a baby. He was impressed with what they were trying to do, but, having two children himself, thought that sacks of flour were poor imitations of a real baby. His wife, Mary, challenged him to come up with a better substitute. He did—Baby Think It Over.

Baby Think It Over incorporates electronics that simulate a real baby. Actual baby cries were digitized and recorded on a microchip. The results are very authentic.

Students are given a bracelet with a key. When the bracelet is locked on their wrist, only they can respond to the baby's cries. The doll is programmed to cry at random intervals and will stop crying only when the key is inserted in a spring-loaded latch on the baby simulator. The student must hold the key in position for a period of five to 35 minutes or the baby will resume crying. If the cries are ignored or the doll "abused," this abuse is recorded inside the doll so the teenager's parenting skills can be evaluated.

Originally the molds for the dolls were produced in Spain, but delivery was not dependable. Now the dolls are custom molded for the electronics by a U.S. company. Both male and female dolls are available with Caucasian, African-American, Hispanic, and Asian features and skin color. A drug doll, whose cries simulate that of a baby born to a mother using addictive drugs, is also available.

A start-up manufacturing entrepreneurial company has many challenges. The electronic boxes are produced in China. When any manufacturing is located abroad, there are all the aspects unique to importing to consider. In retrospect, the Jurmains might have manufactured these electronic boxes in the United States. Fast response has precedence over lower costs for the limited quantities they need.

Cash flow has been difficult, which has slowed growth. The Jurmains found that venture capitalists wanted a majority of their business in return for funds. Instead, they went to family. Due to the success of their company, this has been a win-win situation.

Working with employees has created difficulties. Mary Jurmain attributes some of the difficulties to their own inexperience as employers. Taking responsibility, her husband says, "It's always management's fault." Their most vital employees are their controller, since finances need especially close attention in a young business, and their operations manager, who makes sure their products get shipped.

Unlike most start-up companies, they have been overwhelmed with publicity and have done very little marketing. Distribution has presented challenges. At first, they responded only to requests. Distributors came to them, asking to sell their dolls. However, this created problems as most distributors could not pay them until they sold the dolls. The wait for payment was lengthy, which is difficult for such a rapidly growing company. Now they use both direct and indirect sales and have just hired a marketing manager.

Independent research studies are in progress to determine if these dolls help deter teenage pregnancy. Research results are sometimes requested to get funding for purchase. However, regardless of study results, an important use of the dolls is to realistically teach parenting skills. Parents, especially young parents, need to learn these skills to effectively raise their children.

The Jurmains believe strongly in their product. Making a difference is what drives their commitment to their products.

Western Design Center

Small business has an abundance of passionate individuals, people who thrive on doing business on their own terms. Bill Mensch, is certainly one of those individuals. In the competitive technology business, his Western Design Center (WDC) succeeds by taking a leadership role.

Used with permission of *Arizona Business Gazette.* Jeff Topping, photographer, July 4, 1996.

Mensch, an electrical engineer, was instrumental in the design of the 6800 computer chip, found in a few early personal computers and Motorola's single board computers, and the 6502, in the Apple, Kim, Pet, and Commodore 64 computers. Building on expertise gained from working at Philco-Ford, Motorola, MOS Technology and Integrated Circuit Engineering (ICE), Mensch has designed custom computer chips derived from the 6502 which he licenses to other companies for special applications. Licensees select their own chip manufacturers.

Mensch's interest in electronics began in childhood when he was growing up on a dairy farm in Pennsylvania. With the long hours and the often unpleasant job of milking cows, he sought a different venture through his local 4-H Club. While others chose raising pigs, sheep, or other traditional farm projects, he selected electronics as his interest. Encouraged by his high school counselor, he was the only person in his family of 10 to attend college. In 1965, during his sophomore year at Temple University, he was introduced to a man from IBM who advised him to "get into computers."

After obtaining his associate degree from Temple in electronic engineering technology, he was elated when hired by Philco-Ford. While at Philco-Ford, he attended engineering classes at Villanova University. During an important project involving a seven-layered board, he successfully solved a temperature-related problem that the engineers had been unable to figure out. This intensified his passion for circuit engineering and he decided to pursue his engineering degree.

After graduation, Mensch joined Motorola, doing Central Processing Unit (CPU) design. He worked on chip design at all levels from basic physics to system design. It was at Motorola that he met Chuck Peddle, another designer. Later, at MOS Technology, they conceived the design for the 6502, used in Commodore and other computers. Jack Tramiel, CEO of Commodore, pushed MOS

Technology to gear up to produce large quantities of the 6502, then abruptly quit ordering the chips, pushing MOS Technology into financial insolvency. Then Commodore bought MOS at a very low price and started using its chips to develop the Commodore computer line. Mensch left.

By 1978, Commodore wanted to re-engineer its calculators from NMOS to CMOS technology. Tramiel wanted Mensch back, but instead Mensch worked out a deal where he would start his own company to work exclusively for Commodore. Mensch signed the contract, but Tramiel neglected to sign. Mensch, valuing honesty, went to work on the project. Even though he was approached by Xerox for part-time consulting, he stuck to his exclusive agreement with Commodore. Xerox went to Commodore offering to share its advanced fabrication technology with Commodore in exchange for some of Mensch's time, but was turned down.

During the alliance with Commodore, Mensch decided to move to new facilities, purchasing a building. When Tramiel heard of his move, he was enraged that he had not been informed. Being an independent company, Mensch did not anticipate Tramiel's reaction. Tramiel canceled their unsigned agreement and took back all equipment from the project. Mensch was left with a new building, a $50,000 note due in a few months with another due six months after the first, but no projects. He was forced to cut staff, uncertain what he would do next.

Remembering Xerox's interest, he contacted them and said he was available. They wanted to meet with him immediately. Being late in the year, Xerox offered to advance him what remained in its R&D budget in return for doing a yet undefined project for them in January. This advance kept his company solvent until the new year. In January, he began training Xerox engineers in microprocessor design.

From 1978 through 1988, the company struggled to gain focus. Mensch tried many ventures; most were not financially successful. Mitel needed a CMOS 6800 which he designed. He developed training programs in IC (integrated circuit) design. Mensch trained individuals in mask design (integrated circuit layout) in the evenings, hoping to eventually employ the students. He just needed to find a way to turn his passion for IC design into a successful venture.

His dream was to develop a CMOS 6502, but he was unable to interest Commodore or other computer manufacturers in developing this chip. Mensch decided to develop the chip anyway. Upon completion, he resolved to try to license this design. Surprisingly, the companies that had been previously uninterested, now were interested in licensing the new chip, the 65C02. Commodore sued WDC over the design, claiming trade secrets from MOS Technology were used. However, the differences between the 6502 and 65C02 were significant enough that the suit was settled out of court.

In 1983, Mensch developed two other chips derived from the 6502. Shortly after design completion, Steve Wozniak from Apple called, wanting to use one chip, the 65C816 for a new computer, the Apple IIGX, that he was designing. Royalties from these custom, patented chips secured WDC's success. Designs continued to be refined. The new game systems such as Super Nintendo, Franklin Digital Books, Commodore accelerator cartridges, and other dedicated applications use WDC's licensed technology.

WDC is a world leader in chip licensing. This was Mensch's elusive key to success. At first, WDC used large, upfront licensing fees. Later, this was changed to a small, per chip charge that made its chips accessible to small companies and individuals.

Since then, Mensch has developed a low-cost, easily customizable computer that is battery powered. The Mensch Computer uses four telephone-style serial ports for a printer, modem, keyboard, and PC link. Additional memory is added through PCMCIA slots.

Mensch attributes his success to his education, passion for his work, focus on CPU design, and adaptability to change. His commitment has enabled him to survive lean and difficult times. He uses examples of discipline and strategy he learned as a cross-country runner. "The best time to pass your competitor is during the most difficult part of the run," he explains.

Mensch's reverence for education is rare. "Education is what got me where I am today," he explains. He spends a significant amount of time and money funding graduate fellowships, high school scholarships, and internship programs. Mensch teaches at Arizona State University without pay and would like to see the university develop a combined MBA/BSEE program. WDC has a World Wide Web page, a portion of which will be devoted to offering internship programs developed around WDC's 8-bit data bus microprocessing and the Mensch computer. Students will post project results online to share information and knowledge.

Another way Mensch gives back to society is his hiring policy, which he smilingly refers to as "Ellis Island." He purposely sought out more than 30 individuals: teachers, nurses, bankers, and bookkeepers in unrelated fields who weren't personally satisfied with their careers and taught them a valuable skill, mask design. Mensch gave them an opportunity to participate in the realization of his dream. Many of these people later found excellent positions in large microprocessor companies such as Intel, Motorola, and NCR.

WDC has developed an organizational structure to enable employees to define their positions. This creates consistency within the company. Mensch feels that a two person start-up business is ideal. One person functions in a creative capacity, developing products or services while being freed from the routine tasks of running a company which are handled by the second person. As the company grows, the positions of Chief Financial Officer (CFO), contracts person, account executive, and distribution are added. To simplify company structure, he prefers a company with fewer than 15 employees.

Mensch prefers to concentrate on creative planning, delegating other functions to his employees. His mission is to design products that fill a need and make a difference. Satisfaction comes from seeing his CPUs used in development of successful products.

"If you can create, create." advises Mensch. "If not, work for someone who does."

Manufacturing businesses may have the advantage of a patentable product. Although getting a patent does not guarantee that your market will not be taken by another product, a patent can help protect a unique product. Deciding whether or not to patent a product depends on a number of factors such as profit potential, product uniqueness, ease of imitation through a work-around, and product market life. Talk to others who have experience in patents before you decide to patent.

Engineering Opportunities

Some fields of engineering are covered in other chapters: agricultural, automotive, biomedical, computer, environmental, and software. Other fields, including chemical, civil, electrical, industrial, and structural with their many subspecialties, we'll discuss here. These fields overlap greatly, but each field has unique training and skills. When engineers complete their training and become employed with a company, they learn another unique set of skills, depending on their employment and interests.

Engineers should consider producing a product or performing a service related to their individual skills. Although engineering is a very broad occupation, individual engineers are often highly specialized. Bill Mensch focuses on the narrow field of microprocessor design. He knows microprocessor design in detail from the physics through the fabrication. By building a business on this unique knowledge and skills, he has been very successful. Not many individuals have this depth of knowledge, so he is able to capitalize on his expertise.

Consider your present employment as paid training. Learn as much as you can while employed by taking advantage of others' experience, special projects, seminars, and professional meetings. When you are in your own business, these costs will all come out of your gross profit. Be on the lookout for opportunities: niches you can fill, products that you can design, or problems you can help solve. If you have the opportunity for a position in an area of demand, consider taking the assignment, to take advantage of the chance to learn while being paid.

Next examine up and coming technology in your field. Could you get training or experience in the necessary skills? Getting into a technology early allows for greater profit margins and less competition. Build up your credentials with participation in special projects, taking or giving seminars, and writing articles.

Consulting

Consulting is an alternative, either in a group of different or similar specialties or on your own. A group has the advantage of being able to share expenses to hire support personnel. Grouping with individuals of different expertise or strengths broadens the scope of jobs you can undertake. Consulting can be a lonely endeavor and working together in a group eliminates some of the isolation.

Automation of Facilities

Now that the cost of computerization has decreased, businesses are automating their plants. Fewer workers will be needed in the plants, but many engineers and technicians are needed to analyze, design, install, and maintain this equipment. This massive automation of facilities has provided business for many small engineering firms. Electrical, industrial, computer hardware, and software engineers analyze the needs of a business then design and implement an automated system to meet those demands. This trend towards automation has opened up a number of specialty fields such as PLACE, programmable logic control engineering.

Product Repair

Engineering technicians may find opportunities in product repair. With products that update rapidly, less demand exists for repairs since often individuals and businesses just buy the newer model in lieu of fixing. Specialize in products that have longevity or high cost. Are these products generally purchased with a service contract? If so, can you get certified to provide this contract work?

Equipment will always have need for repair. By owning your own business, you have the ability to control your career and increase your earnings.

Related Fields

Rick Dixon, Precision Home Inspection, transferred his engineering education and experience to the real estate field by founding his building inspection business. Interested in building inspection, he took a university course and sought out work experiences to prepare him for this business. Is there a related field where you can apply your skills?

Product Design/Manufacturing

Ideas for new products are plentiful, but many never make it to market. Many "new" products are variants of existing products. Others just aren't economically feasible. If your product is targeted to a litigious area such as medical products, your development, approval, and insurance costs may make the product economically unfeasible.

Is your product so easy to copy that you'll have a multitude of competitors before you can get your company solvent? Nurse Pro Pack, the original developer of the apron that nurses wear to carry frequently-used items, was copied almost immediately. Competitors used Third World companies to cut its costs, undermining Nurse Pro Pack's price yet lowering quality. Advertising costs consumed much of the start-up funding. With a product that can be imitated, make sure you have a strategy to capture a large portion of the market quickly.

Producing a new or improved product requires research to determine your competition, economics such as payback of investment costs, product distribution, and investigation of any legal ramifications. Air Taser®, a unique non-lethal personal protection device, was developed after thorough research. Patrick Smith, president, noticed a need for a protective device. He came across the design of the Taser® during his search. Modification was necessary but Smith made sure the device would be safe and approved for consumer use. He then hired a marketing specialist to work out marketing and distribution strategies. Although the device is not yet approved for all states, the company, knowing that education concerning the safety of the Air Taser is needed, hired a political lobbyist to work full-time on educating legislators. All these efforts need to be factored into start-up costs and product pricing.

Know your market and your competition. Trade shows and advertisements in trade journals are excellent sources for researching competing products. Taking the time to thoroughly investigate these sources can save you a lot of money later.

Product development costs are often substantial. Air Taser's key employees have invested in the company. This, and one private investor, covered development costs and allowed these individuals to share in the prosperity of the company. With their own investment at risk, employees have strong motivation to work toward making the company successful.

Many companies in the service business said that they never wrote a business plan. In a manufacturing business, planning is more important. With substantial upfront costs, you need to be sure that cash flow is adequate. If you want a loan, the bank will require a business plan.

Increasingly, manufacturing is taking place in other countries. Baby Think It Over dolls were originally manufactured in Spain and currently gets its electronics from China. Adding international complexities to the difficulties of getting a manufacturing company up and running can be very demanding. Individuals rarely possesses all necessary skills, mandating a team approach.

Engineering and Manufacturing: Support Opportunities

Training for New Technology

Few fields need as much training as engineering. Technology keeps changing and continual updating of knowledge is necessary. While there are training firms already for technology, room is still available for new businesses.

Specialized Job Placement: Short-Term and Consulting Assignments

Since engineers' qualifications are so specialized, finding a person with exactly the qualifications needed is much more difficult. Placement firms with client representatives that have engineering experience may help provide a closer match.

Sometimes an engineer is needed on a interim basis. A firm specializing in short-term assignments could help fill this need. On Assignment, a temporary lab professionals company, found its specialty filling temporary lab positions.

Consultants need assistance in finding work, but often they have to do their own prospecting. An individual with experience in their field could help generate job possibilities. This would ease the frustration of trying to devote full attention to current work while seeking new assignments.

New Product Research

Without product research, companies have no new products and a limited future. Some small companies assign a group solely devoted to investigating new markets.

Competitor intelligence is a growing business as companies scramble to be first to introduce a new product. Knowing in advance what your competition is doing is an obvious advantage. The Internet provides many ways to get this information, such as individualized news services and competitor home pages.

Marketing for Engineers

Engineers, often logical and factual by nature, tend to be reluctant salespeople. An engineer who enjoys marketing may be able to find a niche handling marketing for small engineering companies.

Surplus Equipment

As the pace of change accelerates, equipment becomes outdated quickly. Not all businesses need cutting edge technology so surplus equipment may be a good buy. Businesses that repair equipment need parts to fix equipment. If you are adept with industrial, instrumentation, and computer equipment and live in an area where there is availability of surplus equipment, this may be a business opportunity. Check your competition.

Future Engineering Opportunities

Engineers are the designers of technology. With technology in fast forward, opportunities are available, but intense competition is part of the business. Developing new products involves more risk and often more capital investment, but if you have the necessary skills, opportunities abound here.

CHAPTER 12

Entertainment and Leisure Services

S mall business opportunities abound in entertainment and leisure. Because these businesses are often unique, they lend themselves to the personalized management found in small companies. However, large businesses are aware of the opportunities. Some entertainment and leisure businesses are heavily capitalized.

Consider a leisure and entertainment business if:

❖ You enjoy sports-related activities and don't mind working evenings and weekends.

❖ You enjoy working with people.

❖ You have worked in and enjoy the entertainment business.

❖ You have unique ideas for a leisure business and can get the capital to fund these plans.

The following two businesses are proof that your interests can become your business. Be creative in your thinking of how to provide enjoyment for others. Creativity and uniqueness are especially valuable in the entertainment field.

Mesa Aquatics

Non-profit organizations are often overlooked as a business opportunity. Certain tax advantages are available if you qualify and adhere to the Internal Revenue System (IRS) regulations. The company director, considered an employee of the non-profit, has management control and earns a salary. Any profits stay within the organization. Social, religious, and community groups are often established as non-profit organizations.

Competitive swimming, although not generating the interest of some for-profit sports, prepares children and young adults for work by teaching competition, commitment, and discipline. Mark Taylor, with the title of Head Coach and President, runs Mesa Aquatics, a competitive swimming organization. Taylor controls the organization, which has a board of directors for the swim teams and a second board for the booster organization that organizes fund-raisers. In addition to the swimmers belonging to Mesa Aquatics, he also trains Olympic-quality swimmers from other countries, generating extra funds. Sometimes, he will provide room and food for up to three foreign swimmers at his own expense.

Taylor, a competitive swimmer since age six, has worked his way up in coaching. He was employed for a short time in a marketing firm while volunteering for Swim Florida, a U.S. swim team based in Fort Myers, Florida. Then he was hired to coach in Coventry, England. A year later he had the opportunity to coach his own team in the Burrough of Waltham Forest. The Board of Directors of Mesa Aquatics recruited him from England, in part because of his experience coaching Olympic swimmers in England.

Mesa Aquatics has a synergistic relationship with the local school system and city. The City of Mesa and Mesa Public Schools own the pool, which is outdoors and located at one of the district's junior high schools. The pool is open to the public during the summer months of June through August, but Mesa Aquatics has use of the pool during specific hours and limited use of a portion of the pool during public hours. The remainder of the year, Mesa Aquatics has greater pool time. Heated for year-round use, Mesa Aquatics and the city split the heating costs. The city covers maintenance, chemicals, and electricity.

Previous to Taylor's arrival, former head coaches made errors in filing the non-profit paperwork with the IRS. Consequently, Taylor assumed payback for these previous inaccuracies. Now the organization is careful to have all IRS paperwork checked by an accountant experienced with non-profits. As an alternative, the organization could have been dissolved then re-formed as a non-profit, but this would have taken time.

If you are committed to a cause that does not generate high profits and falls under IRS rules (Publication 557), a non-profit organization may allow you to earn an income and stay true to your values.

Wacky Wires & Wonders:
An Artistic Approach

Margie Frierson's business is difficult to describe in one word, but given that challenge, that word would be fantasy. What she enjoys about her work is that she gets to do what she loves—singing, dancing, and art design—and she meets such wonderful, interesting people. Frierson creates exceptional experiences through balloons, gift baskets, flowers, entertainment, and creative event decor.

An expressive, inquisitive individual, Frierson originally used her artistry in scientific research. As a child she loved to sing and dance, but in a family of nine, lessons weren't an option. Her first opportunity to use her talents came her senior year in high school when she auditioned for the chorus and was accepted. At school, she excelled in classes, so was encouraged to pursue challenging subjects such as science. Adept in the laboratory because of her curiosity and ability to work well with her hands, she earned a degree in biological science.

After graduating from college, Frierson worked for a time as a chemist. Then she seized the opportunity to audition for a singing job with a band, was hired, and made double her salary as a chemist. A subsequent break sent her on tour for five years, a fabulous time for her. Frierson learned to play an instrument and dance. Following this with a role in a musical, she then fell back on her college degree and worked for a cosmetic company, doing cosmetic formulating. The company relocated, but she chose not to move.

Frierson, now seeking work, responded to a vaguely worded help wanted ad. The job was with a new franchise, Eastern Onion, a singing telegram company. Singing telegrams were a huge fad at the time and there was a lot of work available. She helped with writing the parodies, besides delivering singing telegrams. Although she enjoyed the business, she disagreed with some items stipulated by the franchise. "Why not start our own company?" she asked her boss. Her boss was receptive, but Eastern Onion soon got wind of their plans. Either abandon the plan to compete, the owner was told, or Eastern Onion would end the franchise. The owner chose to abandon the plan.

Frierson decided to proceed on her own. With only two phone listings under singing telegrams, Wacky Wires & Wonders, singing telegrams and gifts, became the new business name. She missed the yellow page deadline her first year, 1975. Extensive advertising with flyers and radio got her business going quickly anyway. Using her previous experience doing voiceovers, she knew how to get radio advertising time. She started with one full-time person and by the end of the first year had 10.

The business name became an issue when bidding for a special event design for a Pierre Cardin show. He refused to work with a company named Wacky Wires! Very quickly, a second name was contrived, An Artistic Approach, which made the business acceptable. She uses the name An Artistic Approach with design and floral clients. The new name also gains placement at the beginning of yellow page listings.

Frierson's business has been a natural progression. Her original singing telegram clientele wanted other services. She started with balloons in 1976 and still does a lot of balloon work. Baskets, especially containing food, are always popular. Flowers, event decors, and entertainment became requested additions. Frierson believes in trying new things. If something works, she learns more and adds that to her business.

Once when being interviewed for a popular women's magazine, the interviewer repeatedly asked her what was different about her business. Frierson mentioned several ways, but the interviewer continued to ask. Finally, she made up something on the spot: "I make one pound brownies with a message on them." This appealed to her interviewer and was mentioned in the subsequent article. Calls started pouring in. She didn't even know the size of a one pound brownie! Off the top of her head she quickly put something together. Her flexibility enabled her to capitalize on this surprising opportunity. Calls came in for about a year from that one mention.

Why has she been successful? Timing was great for the singing telegram business, but she does few singing telegrams now. Frierson trusts her own ideas and tries to do things that people can't get elsewhere. With floral arrangements, she works with exotic and highly stylish flowers and, without the overhead of a storefront, can do great things for less money. A building at home is filled with floral coolers and flowers are hand selected rather than phone ordered. Her knowledge of the floral business came by working with a florist who encouraged her to go on her own. By learning as she grew, she avoided preconceived ideas. Her arrangements look different and are creative. Frierson also does welding and plaster work to build the structural elements for her decors. "Ideas are everywhere," says Frierson. Classes in areas such as sculpture and drawing have been invaluable.

Many entertainment businesses are capital-intensive. Frierson thinks this is because owners hire others to do the work. She can do most things herself, but will hire people when needed. She does flower and balloon arrangements, deliveries, puts baskets together plus sings and dances on top of all this!

Christmas is her busiest time and baskets are the big item. The single busiest days of the year are Valentine's Day and Mother's Day. In the earlier years, summers were slow since there are no gift-giving holidays. Her market, primarily corporate now, keeps summers busy.

Several of her faithful clients use small gifts—a cookie basket, special coffee, etc.—to reward their customers and referral sources. These businesses find that the small cost of sending a gift pays back huge rewards. This is great steady business for Frierson. Food, she says, is a gift everyone loves.

Businesses in leisure and entertainment often have very unusual hours. Frierson often finds herself working in the wee hours of the morning when she is cleaning up from a late night event. She has learned ways to expedite decoration removal to help minimize clean-up time. Most events are on weekends. She has adjusted her lifestyle to these hours.

Frierson says that this business works for her because she can do the things she loves to do. She still occasionally sings at a local restaurant. Her entertaining experience has enabled her to build a network of entertainers that she can call upon in her business.

❖   ❖   ❖

Although the media says that leisure time is increasing, the opposite seems to be the reality. With more working hours needed to meet rising costs combined with stagnant wages, average work weeks are increasing in length. More people are holding two jobs. More work is being brought home. Nonwork hours are spent updating skills to keep up with the newest technology, sharpening computer skills. With all this extra work, when leisure time is available, people want to pursue enjoyable activities that provide relaxation and relieve stress.

Entertainment Opportunities

Party Organizing

The party planning business seems to keep growing. Organizing a party requires a lot of work: cooking, running around to get items, then cleaning up afterwards. Margie Frierson of Wacky Wires & Wonders says she can put together an event for just a little more than individuals are able to on their own since she gets flowers and other supplies at wholesale cost. Not only is the price competitive, but with her experience in planning, the results are sure to be superior.

Consider specializing in several specific events such as birthdays, bar mitzvahs, or others. Wedding and anniversary planning are still large markets.

Party Rental

Much of the equipment needed for parties are not items you use frequently. Often large quantities of articles are needed. Party rental stores can furnish this equipment. Party rental combined with party planning makes a good business combination.

Party Entertainment

For those of you with entertainment skills, parties are the perfect place for your services. Musical entertainment such as bands, singers, and disc jockeys can work in combination with party planners, wedding planners, and event planners to put together a memorable event. Mimes, jugglers, clowns, and fortune tellers would also be wise to team with others.

Some small companies rent play equipment for children's parties: inflatables to bounce off energy, tents of plastic balls, trampolines, and other easily set up equipment. If you have unique, workable ideas for party entertainment, consider using these ideas to start your own business.

Laser Light Shows

Although a small market, this business can work if you are willing to travel extensively and have a imaginative, novel presentations. Be creative in defining your market. Conventions and business meetings, outdoor events, admission-based indoor shows are possible markets.

Food

People seem to love to eat no matter what the occasion. Besides catering, there are other options for satisfying this love of food for special occasions and events. You might market your mobile food or ice cream truck to events or even large home-based parties. Renting out grills, margarita machines, shaved ice machines, soda fountains, popcorn and candy cane machines, or a flavored iced tea and coffee cart are a few ideas.

Unique Celebrations

Sometimes the whole idea of celebrating is doing something new and different. Margie Frierson strives to come up with ideas that people haven't seen and that they can't buy in stores.

One business, Flock 'em and Shock 'em, specializes in filling yards with flamingos during the night. You could easily make your own shockers! For a full-time business opportunity, combine this with party planning or rentals.

Games

Billiard halls, video game arcades, and virtual reality game centers are other entertainment businesses, all requiring significant capital investment. The entertainment business can easily have multiple profit centers such as food and beverages, arcade games, pinball, and Japanese slot or pachinko machines from Pachinko Paradise (profiled under import businesses).

Travel-Related Businesses

Although airline travel ticketing is undergoing changes, the tour business is still thriving. This is a crowded field, but if you have experience, great ideas, and a love of the business, give it consideration. Uniqueness and image are important.

Entertainment Parks

Ideal ingredients for a successful entertainment park are a warm climate, so the park may be open year-round, and a tourist locale, providing visitors. While high risk and capital-intensive, a theme park can be a successful and rewarding endeavor. You will need to seek investors to raise the large amount of capital needed. How about a park filled with mazes?

Magic

A shop demonstrating and selling magic tricks is another entertainment idea. A magic store or kiosk would thrive in an upscale area with high walk-by volume such as a mall. Success depends on the magician's ability to relate well with people and pricing sufficient to cover overhead yet allowing for profit.

Sports Opportunities

If you are a sports enthusiast, investigate the opportunities available in your favorite sport. Most sports require some equipment or special apparel. Competing in retail with large sports retailers is difficult, but you may be able to identify a niche that is of little interest to the big retailers. Also, you might consider a retail store in a vicinity that caters to a particular sport, but would not support a large retailer. Enthusiasts may find they need products they neglected to bring with them.

Equipment Rental

Renting equipment might be more lucrative than selling. Renting prior to purchase makes sense. Letting customers try out equipment by renting will assist in sales. Offer a discount for those that buy after renting, or consider applying rental costs to the purchase. Especially in vacation or remote areas where equipment is needed by visitors just during their stay, consider the rental business on its own or as an adjunct to retail.

Training

Training helps individuals improve their skills. Combining training with retail sales can increase business. You might contract your teaching skills to resorts, increasing your chance of continuing sales to the facility.

Focus and competition are skills that sports and business have in common. Participation in sports increases physical fitness. Using the preceding as selling points, try marketing your training to businesses.

Mark Taylor of Mesa Aquatics has developed a career in coaching swimmers. Swimming, unlike sports that draw large numbers of fans, does not have much financial backing. To be able to train swimmers, Mesa Aquatics is set up as a non-profit corporation. Money to pay costs and a salary for Taylor comes from monthly dues and fund raising. Fortunately, he has a cooperative arrangement with the school, where the pool is located, and the city to help pay for facilities. Sports help build focus, determination, and character so schools, churches, and civic organizations may help with funding.

Sports Facilities

Does the sport require special facilities? Often sports facilities require a substantial cash investment which may mean gathering private investors. Golf courses, skating rinks, race tracks, bowling alleys, and bungee jumping usually require a large investment. However, go-carting, indoor wall climbing, archery, model airplaning, and martial arts require less capital. If you love horseback riding, consider owning a riding stable, for example.

Videography

With videography skills, you can team with a sports facility and tape individuals in their moments of glory. Skydiving is often taped. By showing the tape to friends, individuals can prove they actually did jump. Most sports lend themselves well to videotaping so look for your own opportunities.

Promoting

Organizing and promoting events generally requires a substantial financial investment and may involve a large financial risk. The rewards, however, can sometimes be great.

Are any of these sports your hobby? They all have business potential, though some more than others.

aerobics	*four wheel driving*	*scuba diving*
archery	*gymnastics*	*snow skiing, snowboarding*
backpacking	*handball*	
baseball	*hang gliding*	*soccer*
basketball	*hiking*	*spelunking and cave diving*
biking	*horseback riding*	
boating	*hunting*	*surfing*
bowling	*ice skating*	*swimming*
bungee jumping	*indoor wall climbing*	*tennis*
camping	*inline skating*	*racquetball*
car racing	*jet skiing*	*triathlon*
dirt biking/racing	*jousting*	
fencing	*marathons*	*water skiing/jet skiing*
fishing	*martial arts*	*weight training*
flying	*mountain climbing*	*wrestling*
football	*parachuting/skydiving*	*yoga*

For example, consider boating as a recreational activity. If you enjoy boating, you could establish a service cleaning, maintaining, and repairing boats. You might own a marina, rent out boats, or run a charter service. Racing boats is still another possibility. Since boating is seasonal in most locations, you'll need to find ways to produce income off-season. Boat storage, repair, customizing, or sales are off-season sources of income.

Vacation Opportunities

If you live or plan to relocate to a vacation vicinity, other business opportunities become feasible. Tourists have leisure time to take advantage of a variety of activities. Many ideas are seasonal, but there are ways to cope with seasonal businesses. In the off-season, you can pursue a second business, work for someone else, prepare for the next season, or move your business temporarily to a more favorable climate.

Custom Tours

Come up with a unique tour in a unusual vehicle. One company gave tours in an amphibious vehicle. Jeep tours attract tourists in areas that require four wheel drive. Moab, Utah is four wheel drive country with Canyonlands and Arches National Park just outside of town. Some backpacking tours use friendly llamas, who happily eat the trailside vegetation. How about an unique boating tour?

Vehicle Rental

Besides directed tours, some people prefer self-directed excursions. This creates a need for rental of vehicles such as four wheel drive, bicycles, mopeds, vans, motorcycles, and boats.

Accommodations

People who are away from home need lodging. These accommodations include campgrounds, RV parks, vacation rentals, motels, and bed and breakfasts. A bed and breakfast or campground require less upfront costs, but you will need to find cost-effective ways to inform tourists of your accommodations. Other types of lodging require high capitalization, but can be profitable. You could start with one location and gradually add others.

Campgrounds are especially seasonal. Combining a campground with a specialty store or secondary business which would generate year-around commerce.

Future Leisure Markets

Consider catering to mature adult needs. Since the average lifespan has increased, leisure years will allow plenty of time to pursue entertainment, sports, and traveling. Those businesses that successfully cater to retirees can expect greater future demand.

There seems to be an insatiable appetite for sports. Opportunities exist in nonprofessional sports activities for families and individuals. Small businesses can provide products for these sports and opportunities to participate. Sports such as four wheel driving, jet skiing, and inline skating are opening up new opportunities.

CHAPTER 13

Environmental Services and Products

*D*espite decreasing federal regulation of the environment, regulation is being shifted to state and local levels. Although the source of regulation is shifting, laws will probably increase in complexity. The more complex regulations become, the more opportunities will be created to assist in compliance. Even without government regulation, a majority of people feel that the quality of the environment is important. If a more environmentally-friendly product is available at a competitive price, individuals are likely to prefer that product.

Consider an environmentally–related business if:

✦ You have a degree in civil, bio-, or environmental engineering, geology, environmental science, or related fields.

✦ You have one or more environmental certifications.

✦ You have extensive knowledge and experience in a specialized environmental area.

✦ You are intensely interested in environmental issues and have worked on these issues politically.

✦ You have the patience to work with government regulations and paperwork.

Lack of attention to environmental matters, such as the situation in the former Soviet Union, eventually depresses the economy. Being proactive in protecting our environment is more cost effective than expensive and difficult clean-up. The U.S. has learned from the plight of other countries and is assuming the proactive stance. Trojan Technologies, a Canadian company, finds the U.S. very receptive to environmentally-protective technologies.

Trojan Technologies

Hank Vander Laan, VP of a cable television business, decided he wanted to do something different. He began talking with individuals in his community of London, Ontario, Canada. While serving on a committee for his local school in 1976, another committee person told him about a local business owner, Harry Lewis, who wanted to sell his company. The company was a metal fabrication plant, but what interested Vander Laan was a patent the owner held for his invention of ultraviolet (UV) disinfection of water. UV light alters the genetic material in bacteria, viruses, and other pathogens so they cannot reproduce, creating a chemical-free method of purifying water.

Vander Laan, an engineer with an interest in environmental issues, was intrigued with this technology and investigated further. Researching the technology through government agencies and private business, the consensus was that UV water disinfection would be important in the future.

In 1977, with a partner, Vander Laan bought the business, Trojan Metal Products, including patent rights. Initially the metal fabrication business generated a cash flow so that Vander Laan could research the technology. A capable scientist and an engineer, who would work with insight and integrity, was hired to develop the technology.

Although the process had been patented, no units had yet been sold. Vander Laan set up a research program to improve the technology, originally focusing on homeowners and small businesses with private water supplies. Since Vander Laan was raised on a farm where quality water was valued and where there was a awareness of the problems with run-off from farmlands, he knew a need existed for a cost-effective and easy-to-use purification system for private wells. This market turned out to be smaller than original projections, but is growing.

The company has sold its systems internationally from the onset. "Since this technology was applicable globally, we immediately marketed globally," explained Vander Laan. "When you are marketing a product with low initial concentration, you need a large global market." Sales in other countries are made through manufacturers' representatives, some exclusive, others representing multiple products.

Although the original focus was on private well water disinfection, Vander Laan was aware of the possible use of UV disinfection for water discharged from sewage treatment plants. London, Ontario is located close to the Great Lakes. The shores of the lakes are heavily industrialized and many communities dispel water, chlorinated to destroy microbes, from sewage treatment plants into the lake. The same communities bring lake water back into their water treatment plants where it is again chlorinated. Queens University in Ontario recently completed a major study on the effects of drinking chlorinated water. The results of the study indicate a correlation between drinking chlorinated water and increased rates of colon and other cancers.

Wastewater treatment plants process raw sewage by screening and settling out solids followed by biological processes to remove dissolved and colloidal organic substances. Bacteria, virus, and protozoan parasite levels then need to be reduced to acceptable levels prior to release. The traditional way to disinfect water is prolonged treatment with an adequate amount of chlorine. Chlorine is highly toxic and hazardous to transport and store. The Environmental Protection Agency (EPA) has endorsed UV disinfection by recognizing that this technology is at least as good and maybe better for disinfection than chlorine. UV disinfection produces no toxic chemical byproducts and requires a short period of time to disinfect. The timing for this product seems excellent.

Trojan initially delayed dealing with the more complex water discharge from sewage treatment plants because of the higher levels of solids, bacteria, viruses, and other pathogens. More extensive research was needed. During one year, its research costs exceeded earnings. The waste treatment UV system was developed from 1977 through 1982. In 1982, a prototype system, the UV 2000, was installed at a facility of the Ontario Ministry of Environment. The Ministry tested and evaluated the system, which consistently outperformed chlorination.

However, the government was not ready to switch from chlorination. They asked to test the system another year, straining the financial resources of Trojan. Vander Laan says that resistance to new technology has been the greatest obstacle. Although UV disinfection systems have proven their effectiveness, he is constantly asked to verify the system. The tendency is to criticize rather than be open to new technology. "Regulators are very conservative and need 5,000 reasons to change regulations."

Trojan deals with this resistance by thorough research; five to ten percent of the yearly budget is dedicated to research. They seek out risk-takers in the regulatory field. Although in the minority, there are individuals in governmental positions open to new opportunities. Trojan has found less resistance to new technology in the U.S., where the majority of its systems have been placed. "There are more risk-takers and greater awareness of environmental issues, especially in California. Academic institutions in the U.S. have greater funding for environmental studies," Vander Laan points out.

Trojan, like other environmentally-oriented companies, has experienced resistance from traditional technology manufacturers and distributors of chlorine. Some chlorine manufacturers, noticing demand, are becoming involved in the development of their own UV disinfection systems. Demand is also rising in Third World countries, which are just installing waste treatment plants.

Vander Laan supports environmental regulation, believing that it pushes the technology forward. Without enforcement of regulations, there would be decreased demand for their products. Government grants have helped research in the area of UV disinfection. Trojan has been able to obtain some grant money. Product improvements plus lower system costs are the focus of research efforts. Vander Laan understands the economics of environmental products. "Even though your technology might be environmentally superior, you have to be cost-competitive— or at least even, though preferably better."

The first generations of Trojan UV2000 and UV3000 systems have been installed in over 1,000 communities. The latest generation UV4000 system, which uses high-intensity, self-cleaning lamps, is now being installed in major cities worldwide.

Trojan has used partnering arrangements to create win-win working relationships with suppliers. For example, Trojan collaborated with other manufacturers in developing the unique power supply system needed in its UV4000 system. The development of the power supply was split between a North American firm and a European company to encourage sharing of innovative ideas.

Trojan UV disinfection is used by one of the largest water vending machine manufacturers. Their systems are also used in treating water for the food and beverage industry, cooling and wash waters, and to treat growth media used in aquaculture.

In Europe, drinking water disinfection is a growing market. A new system, the UV8000, is specifically designed for the pressurized systems used in water treatment plants. The quality of water in Europe has been a concern. In Holland, well water is taxed so disinfection of water from other sources can be very cost effective.

Trojan has several systems installed there. Existing plants often are older and in need of updating. Conservative policies have limited use of UV disinfection of drinking water in North America. An advantage of chlorine is that small amounts of chlorine stay in the water, preventing new growth of bacteria in water distribution systems. However, UV is a more effective killer of viruses than chlorine.

In response to the need for drinking water purification, Trojan is developing a more sophisticated technology called advanced oxidation, a physico-chemical combination of UV and chemical disinfection, for drinking water. This advanced oxidation process is intended to work on toxic wastes as opposed to the UV disinfection process that acts on microbial contaminants.

"It is important to believe in your business, to have a vision," Vander Laan emphasizes. "If you are only interested in financial results, you won't wait and may walk away from a good idea. Commit to your product with integrity rather than opportunistically and be realistic about the importance of cost effectiveness."

To increase financial resources for distribution and product development, the company went public in 1993. In the past three years, the company has had dramatic growth with increased capital for development of new systems in response to client needs and mounting concerns about the safety of chlorine. The company now employs over 100 people.

National N–Viro Technology

Environmental companies often find themselves at the whim of government regulations. N-Viro is such a company. N–Viro converts and pasteurizes sewage sludge to produce enviro-soil, which is like top soil.

The federal government has set standards for the treatment of sewage sludge. However, there is little enforcement of these standards. Since waste treatment is regulation and cost driven, municipalities may not go to the extra expense of meeting these standards if there is no enforcement. If municipalities do not comply with regulations, there may be run-off problems, with environmental consequences.

Sometimes N-Viro's process can save the municipality money, but usually this treatment is more costly. Sewage sludge can be disposed of by four methods: 1) putting it on the ground as an agricultural fertilizer after minimum treatment 2) converting sludge to compost (N-Viro) 3) burying it in a landfill 4) burning the sludge. In cities where odor, appearance, and social considerations are a problem, burying it in a landfill or conversion to compost may be the only alternatives.

N-Viro invested in the technology to convert sludge to a compost-like material to help municipalities meet government regulations. Sludge is mixed with alkaline material such as lime or kiln dust then sterilized. After this process, the byproduct is no longer waste, but a beneficial agricultural compost. Expecting strong environmental enforcement, the company invested substantially in marketing and went public.

If you are considering an environmental business, it may be wise to depend on cost effectiveness not government regulations. There are many excellent environmental companies that are now struggling due to a back-off in governmental enforcement of environmental regulations.

❖   ❖   ❖

The preceding companies demonstrate the unique challenges of environmental companies. Forces, such as government regulations, resistance to change, and resistance from established technologies are added elements that must be dealt with. Businesses in other sectors, especially agriculture and real estate, also have strong environmental considerations.

Environmental Opportunities

Environmental Assessments and Clean-Up

The market for environmental assessments was created by the government with legislation establishing that liability for past contamination be passed to new owners. All commercial real estate involving a bank loan needs to have an environmental assessment prior to sale. Since passage of an amendment, Superfund Amendments and Reauthorization Act of 1986 (SARA) to the Superfund law, Comprehensive Environmental Response, Compensation, and Liability Act (CERCLA), investors are provided a means to avoid liability for environmental damage. If a purchaser performs due diligence by having a pre-purchase environmental assessment, the "innocent purchaser" clause can be used to avoid liability. Because of this, a market for firms doing environment assessments has emerged. Phase 1 assessments, including a site inspection, are public record searches of the past history of a property. Banks require a Phase 1 assessment for all commercial property loans. The assessment shows if there is anything in the past use of the property to warrant further investigation. Phase 2 assessments involve sampling and testing of soil, at minimum, to determine if there is contamination. Phase 3 assessments determine the extent of contamination and Phase 4 provides resolution of the problem.

Although no specific qualifications are necessary to do these assessments, there is considerable liability. Any individual in this field should be qualified and covered by liability insurance. Knowledge to perform site inspections can be acquired through a background in industrial chemicals, environmental issues, and civil engineering. Specific situations may require a knowledge of geology, groundwater, waste disposal, landfills, and environmental health.

Indoor Air Specialist

With a background in environmental health, heating and air conditioning, chemical or civil engineering, or a team of individuals with these backgrounds, an emerging specialty is indoor air quality. Buildings have become more air tight for energy efficiency while use of air conditioning and chemicals has concurrently increased. Lack of ventilation means occupants will have increased exposure to industrial chemicals, formaldehyde from manufactured wood and carpets, pathogens inhabiting air conditioning systems and ducts, and other chemicals. Diagnosis of the source of health complaints due to substandard indoor air quality can often be difficult, calling for the use of specialists.

Sustainable Construction

The University of Florida at Gainesville has a Center for Construction and Environment where the effects of construction and demolition on the environment are considered. Construction not only consumes a lot of materials and potentially damages the environment, but also uses resources and generates wastes. Creating environmentally-compatible housing is only one issue. Creating a healthy indoor and outdoor environment, minimizing resource consumption, and using environmentally-compatible materials while reducing environmental damage are additional considerations. Building durable structures so continual rebuilding is unnecessary would reduce consumption. Designing energy efficient buildings, maximizing the use of natural energy sources such as solar and wind, reduces environmental damage.

Construction and material companies that use and effectively market environmentally-compatible techniques and materials distinguish themselves from other companies. Consumers are becoming more environmentally aware and will choose these companies and materials if they are cost competitive.

Recycling

Although paper, glass, and aluminum recycling are well-organized in many communities, opportunities still exist for recycling other materials. Recycling various materials into decorative mulch can be profitable. Consider composting: recycling lawn materials and biodegradable food leftovers into compost to be sold. ARBICO, distributors of pesticide alternatives, not only sells compost, but uses the heat generated from its compost pile to warm a nearby building. An adjacent world-class resort chooses to use composting and organic gardening techniques to meet its gardening and landscaping needs. Homeowners and even apartment dwellers can use ARBICO's products and advice.

A seasonal business targeted to homeowners and businesses is collecting and composting leaves in urban areas, using available equipment (See ODB Company, Resources) that quickly sucks in leaves. The property owner pays to have the leaves removed and then you sell the resulting compost.

Recycling fabrics, tires, building materials, plastics, and other materials can produce products which sell at a premium. An upscale shoe line uses recycled materials for its casual shoes. Garbage Collection, an Oakland, California company, uses textile discards of fleece, velvet, cotton, and denim and remakes them into children's clothing. Recycled soft drink bottles made of polyethylene terephthalate (PET) are made into fleece and sold in outdoor apparel from Ecotrek in Amherst, Massachusetts. Ecotrek also recycles foam, nylon, felt, car tires, and other materials into backpacks. Industrial equipment can be refurbished and resold as a profitable business. Electronic Materials and Computers has built a successful business recycling industrial, primarily computer, equipment. Non-profit organizations can recycle older computers to donate or sell at very low cost to lower income families and schools.

Substituting toxic materials with recyclable materials may be cost-effective when considering total costs. Railroad ties soaked in creosote, which is toxic, are difficult to dispose of. An Iowa company, Ames Technology, has developed an alternative material that improves the longevity of the ties and is recyclable. Eco-tie, the alternative, is an aggregate of ash, sulfur, and used tires.

Biodegradable

We're all familiar with that indestructible "popcorn" packaging. Once those styrofoam pellets get loose in the environment, they remain forever. A company, Biofoam, has developed biodegradable packing "popcorn," made from grain. Unlike styrofoam pellets, the biodegradable popcorn does not hold static electricity. Humidity doesn't affect the product either and the costs are nearly even with styrofoam. Making a product biodegradable eliminates the need for recycling.

Sale or Manufacture of Green Products

Everything Earthly specializes in the sale of environmentally-friendly or green products. Richard Scott, Everything Earthly, has formed a Western Hemisphere coalition of merchants, Green Retailers, to seek out environmentally-friendly products to market. Businesses producing this type of product are needed.

Consumers are showing a preference for personal care products that are environmentally friendly. The Body Shop has been very successful selling "green" cosmetics and personal care products. Everything Earthly is expanding its personal care product line.

Customers also support businesses that contribute to the community. Richard Scott is involved in many community organizations and posts information about neighborhood and environmental groups in his store. Body Shop pays employees for time spent volunteering.

Consumers seem willing to pay a reasonable premium for certain products, especially clothing. Richard Scott has found that natural clothing, especially hemp and naturally colored cotton, are his top sellers. Demand for these products will increase, though, as they become more cost-competitive. As prices drop, more consumers will choose "green" products.

Safe Drinking Water

Many water purification systems are on the market though few are both efficient and effective. Concern about drinking water safety continues to grow as the health effects of chlorine are being scrutinized. The next breakthrough in water purification will be to reduce costs. This is a competitive market, but a more cost-competitive product could find a niche.

Trojan Technologies uses ultraviolet light for water disinfection. In Europe, its systems are used for drinking water purification. They are currently designing a new system targeted toward this market. The possible health hazards of drinking chlorinated water are making alternative methods of purification more accepted.

Pollution-Reducing Products

Worldwide, many larger cities have pollution levels that exceed those recommended by health experts. Increased incidence of allergies and aggravation of asthma and other respiratory disorders are signs that we need to take pollution seriously. Auto, truck, gas lawn mower, and other equipment emissions are a serious problem that needs resolution. Development of electric cars and lawn mowers are indications of the demand by consumers to help resolve the problems.

Emissions are just one type of pollution. Use and disposal of hazardous materials is another huge issue. Landfills are reaching their limits for disposal of personal and business wastes. Cost effective ways to dispose of these materials are needed.

Environmentally-Friendly Agriculture

ARBICO and Fox Fibre are two companies that are working in the area of sustainable agriculture by reducing chemical use and substituting more organic growing methods and soil enrichment. Both companies help growers maximize the potential of their land. ARBICO assists with disease control among livestock, pets, and plants. Fox Fibre grows naturally colored cottons to thrive when grown organically, reducing both chemical and water use.

Future Environmental Markets

Cost competitive environmental products, services, and energy sources have great potential. People will choose a product that is good for the environment over one that is not when the cost is similar. With the number of environmental problems, opportunities exist for those who can provide solutions. Some of these problems, like limiting automobile emissions, have huge profit potentials.

CHAPTER 14

Family and Personal Services

With ever increasing numbers of women working plus longer working hours for many people, people have less leisure time and need to rely on small businesses for more assistance. Look for ways to make your services cost effective and convenient for busy families. Businesses that make people more successful, healthy, or attractive are great opportunities.

Consider a business in family or personal services if:

❖ You enjoy working with and helping people.

❖ You have a talent for dealing with people that many would consider difficult.

❖ Your services help save people time or solve problems.

❖ Your services help people to be more successful.

With working people being squeezed for time, opportunity for businesses that provide family and personal services is growing. Workers, feeling less secure about their jobs, are hesitant to take time off from work. Service businesses can help meet their needs. The following two companies have grown by providing necessary services.

Children's Campus

Mary Sue Watson loves children! The child-care business enables her to use her special gift for communicating with children. Although the business is challenging, because of a myriad of regulations and small profit margins, it can also be very rewarding. Watson's motivation is not just profit; she wants to make a difference in the lives of children.

Watson's debut in child-care began when her sister started a new business and needed someone to care for her two little girls. Enjoying children and being home already with her own two young sons, Watson offered to care for the girls. Since she already had these four children, she also kept a friend's baby. With five children less than four years old under her care, she was in the child-care business. For two years, she provided day-care in her home.

Watson's first job was in 1967 at a child-care center. There she learned the basics of the business and was able to have her two sons with her at work.

Watson then decided to open her own center which was a franchise, financed with help from friends and family. The child-care business was in its infancy and the center became profitable immediately. All tuitions were paid directly by the families, with no state funding. Watson enjoyed every aspect of the business. After eight years and with the addition of another child to her family, life was hectic. She decided to sell the business, thinking that finding a buyer would take time. The center sold almost immediately, with all Watson's sales conditions met. Watson retained ownership of the building. That was in 1979, and the center is still operating at capacity.

Hoping that the hours would be more flexible, Watson pursued a career in commercial real estate. One of her first clients was a former "mom" at her child-care center. While searching for a child-care center for this client to buy, she came across a closed center in poor repair and impending bankruptcy. Her client wanted a turn key operation, but Watson and her husband decided to buy the center. She was in the child-care business again!

The Watsons, their family, and friends did most of the renovation work to get the Children's Campus in operating condition. In August 1982, they opened the center, licensed for 116 children. The center is located in a lower economic neighborhood and by October, money reserves were running low. Watson's husband encouraged her by saying, "Mary Sue, you are the marketable difference. Get out and sell it." Using informal home management, parent workshops, and her experience as a working mom, she found her niche.

With the strong incentive of having to meet payroll, Watson was bold. She approached key people at churches, public and private schools, parent-teacher organizations, service clubs, and radio and television stations. "If I could help your employees be more productive and it wouldn't cost you anything, would you let me talk to them during their lunch break?" Watson spoke to these groups, explaining that when their families were happy and their homes well run, research has proven that their productivity increases. During the next month, Watson had over 30 speaking engagements, including several radio and talk shows. Although she was not paid, during these talks she was able to mention Children's Campus and leave literature describing the school. Soon the school reached full enrollment.

In June 1987 Watson became ill and she discovered she was not indispensable. Prior to her illness, she had been reluctant to delegate work. Watson is a stickler for details, which contributes to her success, but also makes it more difficult to delegate to others who may not be as attentive. This realization helped her expand her business to the growth she has now achieved. If a business is to grow, an owner must let go of some of the responsibilities.

In 1991, Watson, her husband, and Joy Bauer formed Kreative Solutions for Childcare, a consulting, management, and training company. Watson and Bauer conduct training courses that enable child-care professionals to get their Child Development Associate (CDA) and Child Care Professional (CCP) credentials. In 1983, Watson did a 30-week national television series on child discipline.

Through an opportunity with People to People, Watson served as a delegate participating in a friendship mission to child-care centers in Soviet-bloc countries. Watson shared information about our child-care and learned that children are the same everywhere. Despite the language barriers, Watson felt a bond with her newly found friends and peers.

The Watsons now manage three schools in addition to Children's Campus. For the school year 1995, one of these schools took advantage of a new opportunity from the state department of education to become a charter school. This school is unique, operating like two separate businesses within one. The charter is funded as a public school, with no cost to the family. This portion includes grades kindergarten (half-day) through sixth grade. The toddler program, preschool, an additional half-day of kindergarten, and pre- and after-school programs are operated for profit.

Pride in Children's Campus and the other centers the Watsons manage is evident. Watson seems constantly planning improvement on some aspect of a center. They know from experience what works and what doesn't. Although they delegate to their center directors, a close eye is kept on each center, especially for cleanliness.

Finding and keeping good employees is especially difficult, due to the inability of child-care centers to offer competitive wages and benefits. Giving employees a great deal on child-care for their own kids can help minimize wage differences. Directors need to be creative in motivating their employees. Watson makes a special effort to know her employees and that they are appreciated. Small gifts or incentives acknowledge this appreciation. When visiting her centers, she makes an effort to speak with each employee. Staggering employee hours so that some employees come in early and others stay late helps decrease costs for covering the approximately 12-hours a day that centers need to stay open.

Child-care centers need to carefully evaluate profitability of their hours. Some centers offer extended hours; a few are open 24 hours a day. An around the clock schedule might be profitable in a hospital or factory-based center. Saturday hours can be profitable in some areas.

Prior to opening a center, working in a good center to learn about this business is helpful. Next, check with your state regulatory agency for child-care to check applicable regulations. Visit other centers, both locally and in other locations, to learn the pitfalls. Watson says that having a support group with other owners is a great way to find solutions and employees. Since centers have a very localized client base, you are not competing with centers located in other neighborhoods. Local and national organizations and associations can provide good information.

There are multiple options available for a child-care business. Some people start with a small, home-based child-care service. Your state will limit how many children, in addition to your own, you can care for in your home. In many states, a license is not required for home-care. Another option is a non-profit center. In an economically disadvantaged area, this might open up additional funding sources. You, as director, earn a set salary paid by the business. Management of a facility within a factory, business, or hospital can provide convenient child-care for on-site workers.

Watson feels that it necessary to own multiple centers with a minimum licensed capacity of 100 children to make a good profit in child-care. With her husband as her business partner, their present goal is to open two to three more centers. Watson credits her success to the support of family and friends, being mentored by several gifted people, hard work, continued education, and God's blessings.

Traco, International

Peter Hill, owner of Traco, International has developed a program to help people, especially women, take more control of their lives through self-knowledge and self-defense techniques. With increased crime and so many women, who are often crime victims, living independently, his program answers a need.

Traco, International started as a martial arts business. When both owners became disabled, the name was sold to the other local branches. Hill, with a partner, started the his independent branch of Traco, International in 1981. His concentration initially was on martial arts. In 1989, he bought out his partner and developed the G.E.T. I.T. program for conflict resolution.

G.E.T. I.T. Together stands for Goal, Emotion, Techniques, Inner Skills, and Test. The program was developed with women in mind. Hill wanted to show women how they could better control their lives so as not to become victims. The program works for personal defense, personal relationships, and other life challenges.

In the classes, which are full- or half-day or a 12-week program, Hill first explains basic conflict resolution then follows up by teaching self-defense techniques. He advises women to quickly assess the goal of the person challenging them and then be able to defend themselves, if necessary. Not all people have good goals! He stresses that a person can lose everything they have, but not who they are. Defend yourself, he teaches, not your property. Women learn to protect themselves without having to depend on others. By learning self-defense and actually breaking a wooden board with their own hands, Hill demonstrates how concentration can maximize their success.

The program is licensed to others all across the U.S. G.E.T. I.T. has been endorsed and used by mediation specialists, ministers, probation officers, psychologists, and facilitators. The Nicole Brown Simpson Foundation and the Southwest Gestalt Institute have reviewed and praised the techniques used in his G.E.T. I.T. manual. Hill cites several recent incidents where the victims would have benefited from this training, and also relates stories of people successfully using these concepts and techniques.

While the G.E.T. I.T. program empowers people mentally, emotionally, and physically for conflict resolution in life, his company also offers additional courses in Tai Chi and other martial arts for a greater variety of body control and self-defense techniques. Hill has been concentrating more on self-defense and less on martial arts. His mission is to help people change themselves and take responsibility for their lives.

His strength is developing programs and teaching. He wrote the course materials. Developing the G.E.T. I.T. program has been his biggest challenge. He admits being weak in marketing and has considered bringing in another person to focus on introducing his program to more people. Traco has one paid part-time employee and his wife does his bookkeeping.

"Attitude," he explains, "is important in meeting our goals. First, we need to set our goals. Then work toward these goals, step-by-step, and enjoy the process." His students are taught that by giving service to others, they will better meet their own goals. Hill's instructors are mostly unpaid. They teach in exchange for lessons or volunteer. This is a way that they can serve others, develop personal and teaching skills, and pass on their knowledge.

Hill is a continual learner. He took Emergency Medical Technician (EMT) training because he felt it would expand his knowledge and, therefore, his teaching. He also has training in Applied Kinesiology. He is well versed in a variety of martial arts and continues to develop integrative training for practical applications.

With so many constraints on their time, people will use small businesses for services in order to gain some leisure time. Find effective, cost-effective ways to publicize your services. Maintain a superb reputation to keep existing clients while obtaining word-of-mouth business.

Family Services Opportunities

Child-Care

Child-care, like many businesses, is becoming increasingly challenging due to more regulations and decreasing profit margins. In Watson's state, welfare spending for child-care has not been increased since 1988. Seasonal changes in enrollment affect revenues, with summers having lower enrollments. Adding summer camp programs on a partial week basis helps maintain cash flow. Chickenpox, until the vaccine is widely available, can dramatically decrease enrollments for short periods. Maintenance costs often eat up profits.

Finding quality, convenient day-care is a major concern for working moms. Child-care can be provided in your own home. Profits will be limited due to the small number, defined by state regulations, of children you will be able to care for at home. However, if you are seeking a very small business or want to provide child-care only when your children are still young, this may be a good option.

To increase your profit potential, think about opening a child-care center. With more space, you may qualify to take a greater number of children. Greater numbers of children may help you to be more profitable. However, your expenses will be significantly higher. Many owners operate more than one center so are able to buy in larger quantities, getting better prices.

Consider adding additional services. Some centers, in areas where parents can afford to pay the additional charges, offer optional programs such as computer training, dance, and acrobatics. Often these services are outsourced. Many centers provide after-school programs for school age children when both parents work. The children are picked up at school and brought to the center.

Some businesses are offering learning programs for child-care centers. These pre-packaged programs eliminate having the teachers doing planning and gathering materials. They can spend their time working with the children. With children at centers up to 12 hours a day, there is little time for curriculum planning.

Adding sick child care to a day-care will mean having a nurse on staff and a physician on call. Missing work because a child is sick is problematic for many working parents. There is a need for this service, but cost and liability are probably preventing availability.

Home Schooling

Home schooling is becoming more popular, in part due to parental concern about their children's education and peer groups. This trend has opened up a new market for teaching materials and programs. Some specialized retail stores provide the same type of learning materials that public and private schoolteachers use in their classrooms. A small company could develop learning materials for this market.

Another need is providing activities allowing home-schooled children to interact with their peers. Children need to develop social skills in addition to learning skills. Some parents form informal groups for this purpose, but children's computer schools give this interaction while teaching computer skills. Some enterprising individuals teach science programs for home-schooled children.

Children's Entertainment

Children's entertainment centers provide a field trip destination for child-care centers. Birthday parties can be hosted. On a smaller scale, many parents might relish a small business that provides activities for children while busy parents complete errands.

Adult Day-Care

Adult day-care is a much different business than a child-care center. Medicare and long-term care insurance policies may cover day-care. Most of your clients will require special care, being either elderly, handicapped, or mentally deficient. As with sick day-care, you'll need an RN on staff and a doctor on call.

Sign Language Interpreter

To be successful in assisting those that are hearing-impaired through sign language interpretation, you'll need to look for creative ways to find paying assignments. The need is there and the work is satisfying, but pay is generally low. Consider providing consulting or training programs for businesses on hearing protection. Grant money may be available for non-profit businesses.

House Cleaning

With both heads of household working and having limited free time, home cleaning services are thriving. Many of these are franchises providing name recognition, but you can start a business on your own. Working for a short time with an existing company will give you ideas on how best to structure your business. Offer a menu of services and a distinct image that make your company unique.

Self-Storage

Many people hate to part with items they might need later. Consequently, we tend to accumulate more than we have room to store. Moving, home-based businesses, and other situations create the need for temporary storage. Self-storage centers have become very popular, but do require a substantial cash investment and an on-site live-in manager. Storage is especially needed in very transient areas, warm climates attracting seasonal residents, and areas where many houses are built on slabs, without basements.

Family Counselor

Family counseling can help families grow stronger and happier. If you have expertise in helping families, there is need for your services. Marketing your services through schools, churches, large companies, pediatricians, and maybe even public agencies will help get your name to those in need of your services. Consider giving free presentations to large companies, teachers' groups, and organizations to become known in your community.

Funeral Director

If helping people under stress appeals to you, consider a career as a funeral director. Talk with people in this field. Most states require licensure. Training to gain licensure qualifications is available at some community colleges. These programs include an apprenticeship with a certified director. Since this work does not appeal to all, be sure to spend some time working with a funeral director before committing to an educational program.

Personal Services Opportunities

Career Consultant

Career counseling is increasingly important with the insecurity of the job market and the number of career and job changes. When a career meant one company for life, the need for career counseling was less. Now people need to assume responsibility for their employment future. What future skills will be needed? What about lateral moves or career changes? How can individuals assure themselves of future employment? The number of issues involved in career counseling has soared.

Although this is not a business you should start without experience, these skills can come from a variety of backgrounds such as human resources, counseling, or education. Work toward acquiring additional specific experience and accreditation in career counseling.

Image Consultant

Most people are not aware of the image they project to other people. Personal image is important for employment and personal relationships. With job markets tight, an image counselor paired with a career counselor would be a powerful combination. Individuals could be videotaped in different situations. Play the tapes back and let individuals make their own observations prior to your own input.

Some individuals will need assistance with speech, dress, and appearance. You may want to team up with people who can assist in these areas as well. The key to this business is to get referrals. Produce a short videotape that you can distribute.

Total Image Salon

Instead of just providing hair and manicurist services, why not have a total image salon? Working in conjunction with an image consultant or on your own, you can function as your own referral source. In the reception area, have videotapes and books that describe all of your services. Besides hair and nails, these services could include: permanent makeup, electrolysis, makeup, wardrobe guidance including figure flattery, weight control, exercise classes, a relaxation studio, massage, speech improvement, image consulting, and personal security.

Permanent Makeup

Application of permanent make-up—eyeliner, eyebrows, lipliner, and lip color—helps individuals look their best with minimal time. Regular make-up rubs and washes off, but permanent makeup stays in place until the sun lightens the tint and the outer layers of skin slough off. Permanent makeup helps reduce wrinkling around the eyes, resulting from repeated pulling of this delicate skin during daily make-up application. An excellent background for this business would be cosmetology, make-up artist, or color specialist.

Personal Security

As crime increases, people become more concerned about their personal security. Traco, International, which began as a martial arts business, is focusing on this need. Peter Hill, president, developed a program called G.E.T. I.T., that helps women have more control of their lives and personal security.

Air Taser has taken another approach to the security problem. Patrick Smith researched personal security devices for individuals who did not want a gun, but wanted protection. In many Eastern countries, gun ownership is illegal. He is marketing the Air Taser® to individuals as a powerful yet safe personal protection device.

Many experts predict that crime will continue to increase. Most of the solutions we have available today to protect personal possessions focus more on reporting an in-progress crime rather than on prevention. Crime deterrents are needed. How can we protect ourselves, then secondly, our homes, cars, and other possessions?

Personal Trainer

Substantial willpower is needed to get yourself down to the gym on a regular basis or to maintain a regular exercise routine. When a personal trainer shows up at your door, you have little choice. A personal trainer can make sure you get regular exercise while providing an individualized program to meet your needs and goals. If you have experience in weight training, aerobics, exercise physiology, or related areas, consider marketing yourself as a personal trainer.

Roommate Matching

For singles who want to share apartment or home expenses, but don't know anyone who needs a roommate, a screening and matching service can be helpful. In addition to full service matching, consider offering screening for those individuals who have a prospective roommate, but would like background check. Market your services through large apartment complexes, health clubs, college campuses, and other places that attract singles.

How about matching single-parent families? Two single-parent families provides the opportunity for two adults in a household, helping to share the child-raising. You'll need to be innovative in your marketing. Perhaps you could work through child-care centers, apartment complexes, children's clothing stores, and schools.

Singles Introductions

From the sheer number of introduction services, there must be a need although, in some areas, this market may be near saturation. Screening applicants thoroughly is very important. Video is an effective tool for prospective introductions.

Upscale Pawn Shop

Pawn shops have had an image problem. By changing the name, locating in a decent neighborhood, presenting an upscale appearance, and target marketing, this could be a good business opportunity.

Other Services that You Might Consider

- ❖ Gift shopping/shipping
- ❖ Credit counselor
- ❖ Child-care payment collector

Service businesses often can be started with a limited amount of funding, however, may find themselves in competitive markets. Constantly look for ways to improve your service and distinguish your company from competitors.

CHAPTER 15

Financial and Accounting Services

*T*he financial business fluctuates with the economy and markets. When the financial markets and economy prosper, financial businesses thrive. When a slump occurs, these same businesses may have a poor year. Budgeting for these cyclic variances can help even out these fluctuations. Accounting businesses are vulnerable to changes in the tax laws, which could substantially decrease their business. In both sectors, the goal is helping people increase their personal net worth.

Personal financial planning used to be a "hot" business, but changes over recent years have made this a tougher field. Online services provide a wealth of financial information, often for free. Mutual funds have made investing in stocks and bonds easy. Financial planning, with its relative ease of entry, has had less than a pristine reputation due to a get rich quick attitude by a few of its planners. Financial markets are unpredictable, but when clients lose money, they look to their planners for responsibility.

Certainly there are opportunities in this field. Some businesses have done very well. Small businesses, with their ability to shift directions quickly, are more able to adapt to changing markets.

Consider a financial or accounting business if:

❖ You enjoy sales and working with numbers.

❖ You have a fascination with the financial markets and marketing skills.

❖ You work in the financial field and enjoy your work.

❖ You have been successful managing your own and others' finances.

❖ You are computer literate.

People will always seek to improve their financial situation. Companies that can assist in them in doing so can be successful. Both of the companies discussed in this chapter help increase profits. The first, The Access Group, works with small businesses while the second, Fidelity Monitor, advises individuals.

Access Group

Small, home-based companies find it difficult to obtain merchant status to accept credit cards. Banks don't want to accept a small business until they have a successful track record. But if a business can't accept credit cards in a marketplace where everyone else does, its chance at success is lower. Often when a small business seeks merchant status from the bank, it is referred to one of the companies listed under credit cards in the yellow pages. Some of these companies have had a reputation for taking your money, but not delivering upon their promises.

The Access Group, a partnership of Dave Dauer and Bob Gerver, was founded in response to the needs of small businesses. Both are ex-Teleflora employees who ventured out on their own when Teleflora stopped setting up merchant accounts. Teleflora, now back in the credit card business, catered to small businesses and has been one of the more reputable ways of getting merchant status.

Dauer and Gerver decided to cater their business to setting up home-based businesses at a fair price. "We represent banks that know home-based businesses," explains Gerver. "By dealing in volume, we can provide the service at lower costs." Both know the difficulties of running a business at home because they, too, work from their homes, living in different states. With their experience, they are able to select the best bank for each business. The Access Group can also provide the software necessary to accept phone credit card orders.

They decided to form a partnership, drawing upon their different strengths, after discovering that they both were in the same business. Dauer was formerly the sales manager with Teleflora and enjoys speaking with people on the phone. Gerver, a former Teleflora independent representative, prefers to do the processing and other back office tasks. Both use other contractors to assist with their end of the business. The company is growing rapidly, mainly on referral. Although they had much negative input about partnerships, they have found their partnership has strengthened their business.

Operating from different locations makes them highly dependent on an efficient phone system that can handle fax and conference calls. Gerver has integrated computers into his end of the business, now motivating Dauer to get set up as well. They are planning to use CompuServe for communications.

Starting business in spring of 1995, Gerver said the first few months were tough. He recommends being very conservative about spending at first. Growing slowly makes it easier to stay financially solvent, he says.

Their mission is to do the right thing for their customers. They strive to develop a personal relationship with each client. Having satisfied clients has made referral their primary means of marketing, saving advertising dollars. The profit per customer is low so they must make their profits by increased volume. Its niche, home- and Internet-based businesses, sets the Access Group apart from its competition.

Fidelity Monitor

Financial newsletters flourished through the late 1980s and early 1990s. One of those newsletters is *Fidelity Monitor*, one of three newsletters focusing strictly on the Fidelity family of funds. Jack Bowers started his newsletter in 1986 and enjoyed a number of years of growth until 1994, when he noticed subscriptions tapering off. Online services provide immediate and often free information. However, the cornerstone of *Fidelity Monitor* is its portfolio recommendations. *Fidelity Monitor's* portfolio has continued to post excellent returns.

Bowers started *Fidelity Monitor* while still working full-time with Hewlett Packard. When he decided he wanted to start a desktop publishing business, he reviewed his interests to determine profit potentials. He had been a fan of Fidelity mutual funds so decided to start a newsletter focusing exclusively on their funds.

For five years he built up the newsletter part-time, still keeping his job and relying on his credit card debt to grow the newsletter. In 1990, the newsletter made a profit. In 1991, he quit his job and has since been devoted full-time to the newsletter. Customer input has shaped the newsletter which, with his undivided attention, has become more diversified. Bowers started small and promoted himself with free publicity through financial magazines and excellent ratings from the *Hulbert Financial Digest*, which rates newsletters. He attributes his success to having an excellent portfolio track record, defining a niche, and choosing a successful fund family. By focusing strictly on Fidelity funds, he distinguishes his newsletter from competitors.

Fidelity has some stellar funds from which Bowers designs his model portfolios. He tracks all the Fidelity funds, but has multiple portfolios to allow for different investment goals. Investors are told specifically which funds to invest in and when to make portfolio changes. Bowers explains that online services provide broad-based information, but do not tell exactly what investments to make and when. Many of his subscribers are over 60 years old, an age group that has only recently begun using online services. His goal is to make his subscribers successful. Because they have thrived, his newsletter has also flourished.

While Fidelity does not endorse the newsletter, public relations has been supportive by arranging manager interviews and giving non-privileged information. Because he is not a market timing (moving money in and out of funds according to the strength of the stock market) newsletter, he has not encountered problems with Fidelity's management. In the past, Fidelity has discouraged newsletters that endorsed market timing. Large numbers of people moving money in and out of funds frequently makes fund management difficult. The relationship of a fund family-specific newsletter can be a win-win situation for both. A newsletter endorsing a family of funds can increase investments in that family and create loyal investors.

Bowers continues to focus on an excellent track record for his model portfolios. He views the success of these portfolios as the key to keeping existing subscribers and gaining new ones.

The heyday of financial newsletters has passed with the increasing use of online services. Although payment for online services is still being resolved, he views now as the time to get established online. If restarting, he would definitely go with an online-only approach since he thinks this is where future profits will be made.

Both of these companies have found a niche where they can be successful. This chapter discusses areas that you can investigate if you are interested and experienced in financial matters.

Financial Opportunities

Retirement Plan Consultant

With a financial planning background plus experience and special training in setting up retirement plans for businesses and families, consider retirement planning. Demand will increase as the large Baby Boomer generation grows closer to retirement age. More people are self-employed and need assistance in setting up annuities, Keoghs, 401K, and profit-sharing plans. Attention to detail is important since plans must comply with IRS regulations.

Benefits Consultant

The number of businesses is increasing, primarily because of the rise in numbers of small businesses. Initially a small business may not have many employees and may not even pay benefits. As these small businesses grow, more will provide benefits to retain quality employees. More small businesses might provide benefits if they could do so more cost-competitively. Resourceful individuals are assisting these companies by forming small business pools. With a larger number of qualified individuals, small businesses can get rates that are more competitive.

Insurance Agent

Insurance is a necessity for most businesses and individuals. Although the market is highly competitive, individuals who enjoy working with people and have marketing skills can build a successful business. New businesses need insurance so the increase in small companies is a boon to insurance agents.

In the insurance business, you will benefit from seeking ways to distinguish yourself from all the other agents out there. Often, just a little more effort can bring great rewards. Once you have a client, make sure you give that person incentives for loyalty. Some agents send small gifts such as personalized address return labels after each insurance payment is received. A small gesture, easily made on a personal computer, but an effective way to keep your clients.

Insurance is very cost competitive, with low cost often being the main decision factor. Term life insurance has become more popular than whole life policies. Many families are surviving on less income. They may feel that insurance is a luxury rather than necessity. Some agents are concerned insurance companies will bypass individual agents by selling directly to customers via the Internet. Talk to agents to get their future predictions for independent agents.

Statistics indicate that many people are not well-suited for this business. Figures indicate that as high as nine out ten individuals trained as insurance agents drop out of the business within a few years. In part, this is due to the intense competition. Differentiating yourself from other agents requires work. Obtaining new clients requires constant effort. Individuals must find ways to generate new clients by referrals. Still, the need for insurance has never been greater.

Incorporating Businesses

The more small businesses, the more need for experienced individuals who can incorporate these businesses. Combining this assistance with other business services would increase your chances of success.

Crime Prevention

Businesses need assistance in planning for security and crime prevention. Employee embezzlement continues to be prevalent. Bad checks, stolen credit cards, forged currency, and product theft are serious problems. With increased use of temporary workers. downsizing, and greater employee mobility, important trade information can be seized. If you have experience in auditing, security, or intellectual law, you will find a need for your services.

Divorce Planning

Financial planners can assist couples in the process of divorce to equitably divide assets. Perhaps you could team with a mediator, providing a complete service.

Short-Term Investor

With stock trading experience, some individuals are making a living doing short-term trading, trades that capitalize on market volatility. Needless to say, you will need money to invest and your earnings will depend on your investing savvy and the markets.

Investment Club Organizer

Investment clubs have become popular, but clubs often are formed by inexperienced investors seeking confirmation of their stock picks by other inexperienced investors. This seems to be a great opportunity for a financial planner to set-up and assist the group while keeping records, advising investors, and executing trades.

The Motley Fool and other Original Ideas

David and Tom Gardner developed an investing forum on America Online that attracts many investors because of its wealth of non-biased information and fun approach. David, the originator of the idea, formerly wrote for Louis Rukseyer's

"Wall Street Week" while his brother, Tom, was an instructor in business and finance at the University of Montana. The two have an online investment portfolio where they post their trades, to allow others to share in profits. As a credit to human ingenuity, their Motley Fool forum and subsequent book, *The Motley Fool Investment Guide*, demonstrates there is always room for a new business idea.

Other financial companies have also used original ideas to build successful businesses. Morningstar started out as a small company that evaluated and rated mutual funds. Now its ratings and software are an industry standard. Mark Hulbert wondered who was tracking the actual performance of investment newsletters. At the time, nobody was. He started a company that monitored, ranked, and published their performance.

Accounting Opportunities

With changes in tax laws a distinct possibility, accountants might be wise to develop areas of specialization now. Areas that you might focus on include:

❖ Audits

❖ Management consulting

❖ Estate planning

❖ Valuations of businesses/business brokerage

❖ Mergers and acquisitions

❖ Litigation support

❖ Reorganizations

❖ Financial planning

❖ International accounting

❖ Representing companies and individuals in IRS audits

❖ Providing general accounting for a specific type of business or sector (such as non-profits)

International Accounting

More companies are doing business internationally. Although international accounting standards are being developed, accountants assisting clients doing business internationally become involved with business and cultural differences. Becoming acquainted with accounting and business practices in different countries involves the same kind of approach as for other businesses expanding internationally. Unless you are using accountants based in these countries, it is probably wise to start with only one or two countries before broadening your scope.

International accounting is a growing need. This market will continue to expand. Most universities now offer courses in international business, which would be a good introduction.

Investigative (Fraud) Accounting

Although it seems that fraud within businesses is becoming more rampant, fraud is probably just being detected more frequently. Computerization may be helping to track down sources of deception. Detecting fraud demands accounting skills, but additional skills and perceptive ability are helpful. You might concentrate on specific business sectors.

Environmental Accounting

Accountants who specialize in environmental accounting do valuations on the probable or actual dollar amounts of environmental destruction. Those individuals with an interest in the environment may find this an interesting specialty.

Estate Planning

As individuals approach retirement age, they are ready to set up trusts to pass their inheritance to chosen recipients. Setting up a trust requires experienced assistance. A lawyer and accountant may team up for estate planning services.

Business Brokerage

Accountants who like working with people may enjoy business brokerage. Income, as in the real estate profession, is sporadic, but a mature business can be profitable. Your ability to shift through the financial numbers and find discrepancies or inconsistencies will prove valuable. A real estate license may be required.

Opportunities in Supporting Businesses

Marketing for Financial Planners and Accountants

Similar to other professionals, financial professionals need to develop a marketing program that will help them be successful. Referral is a primary source of new clients. Help these businesses develop effective referral programs and assist these them with defining their specific markets. Often, due to their focus on facts and numbers, financial professionals may not relish the marketing aspect of the business.

Collection Service

There always seems to be an abundance of people who don't pay their bills, forcing companies into the unpleasant task of collections. Many companies will gladly farm out their past due accounts for a percentage of collections to distance themselves from this job. If you don't have collections experience, why not work for a collections company for a while to see if you have the grit for this business?

Computer Training

When working with numbers, computers are nearly essential. Computers increase accuracy and have become the industry standard. Individuals who think logically have a natural advantage when using computers so professionals in the financial field should be quick learners. You can focus on helping your peers more effectively computerize their business.

Setting up Computer Systems for Financial Professionals

If you have the hardware and software skills, you might specialize in setting up systems for financial and accounting professionals. Each company has unique needs which are best served if you know the business. Financial professionals, with their combination of computer expertise and knowledge of the business, may find they can provide a superior service to their colleagues. Group practices may need assistance in setting up computer networks.

Software for a Financial Niche

Although there is an abundance of general accounting and financial software, consider developing programs for areas such as international, investigative, and environmental accounting. Develop software for business brokerage, business valuation for specific business fields, and trusts. Niche areas still have need for software.

Future for Accounting Businesses

Small businesses tend to outsource accounting until they can afford a chief financial officer. The need for accountants to handle financial affairs, bookkeeping, audits, and financial planning will increase as the number of small businesses grows. Changes in the tax system could dramatically reduce the need for tax work, but this is still very speculative.

CHAPTER 16

Food Services
and Products

*F*ood businesses, especially restaurants, have one of the highest business failure rates. The fast food business may be the most difficult sector of all. When in a rush for lunch, often people will go with name recognition and head to a familiar restaurant. Long hours, lower profit margins, and greater staff turnover than upscale restaurants surely are also contributing factors. Location is extremely important.

Still, people enjoy food and we all need to eat. In addition to restaurants, other opportunities are worth investigation. Look for unfilled needs.

Consider a food product or service business if:

❖ You have worked in the food business in a variety of positions.

❖ You enjoy people, can tolerate long work hours, and have restaurant management experience.

❖ You know and love the food business plus have an unique product or service to offer.

When you think of the food business, restaurants may come to mind. But there are many more opportunities in the food industry with less risk. The following two companies are examples of other possibilities.

Arizona Bread Company

The Benkel family, Carole, Jerry, Andrea, Jeff, Adam, Amy and her husband, Matt Wakser, wanted to build a company they could keep in the family. They looked at many possibilities, searching for a fledgling business niche. While on a trip to visit family in Atlanta, Amy and Matt came across a wonderful little bakery. They discovered they had a family contact who knew the business owner so they were able to speak with him about his business. When they expressed interest in starting a similar business, the owner told them to try baking bread at home and gave them the names of books they should read. If they were still interested later, he suggested they talk with him again. After following his advice and investigating further, they contacted him again and he referred them to professional consultants. They studied the art of premium bread making with professionals and then started researching locations.

Jeff Benkel, a CPA, assisted with market research. While many towns have established, well-known bakeries, Phoenix did not. Market research indicated a demand for superior, distinctive bread in both wholesale and retail markets. The family was familiar with the area, having one family member already living there.

The food and restaurant business is especially challenging for obtaining loans. Banks will not consider a business without a two-year track record. The family approached the Small Business Association (SBA) for a loan. They were amazed at the SBA's reluctance to loan amounts of $200 thousand or less. Considering their audience, most small businesses would not require more money than this to get started, but their smaller loan request complicated the process.

Eventually, after much paperwork and many visits, their loan request was accepted. Mistakenly thinking the difficult part of financing was over, the family started working on the build-out of their leased site. SBA demanded more paperwork and more visits. Every time a worker was on site, they required an SBA representative to be present. If a worker was late, as often happened, the SBA representative often had left and work could not progress. The process became so cumbersome the family realized that opening was going to be delayed for months. And the longer the delay, the more money would be needed. They decided to abandon the SBA low-interest, long payback loan and went to a loan agent. The new loan rate was much higher with a three-year payback, but the savings in time was worth it. They opened The Arizona Bread Company on October 5, 1994. The store was profitable the first year.

The retail business results in about 60 percent of their profits with the remaining 40 percent coming from wholesale sales to resorts, restaurants, and a few independent retail outlets. Matt, with his experience in wholesaling and expertise in working with people, runs the wholesale division and is vice president. Amy, as president, manages the retail store, which sells soups, salads and sandwiches in addition to bread. They are located on a busy corner next to a bank. Especially at first, walk-in traffic from the bank generated a lot of business. Now referrals and excellent write-ups in local newspapers bring in new customers. In 1995, they were selected as making the Best Bread in Phoenix by *New Times*, a popular weekly newspaper.

The store is so successful that a second location was opened in Spring 1996. This store produces cookies, brownies, pastries, and croissants. The two stores will complement each other by selling the other's products in addition to its own. For this store, banks came to them offering loan money.

The family attributes their success to a quality product and being first in their market, giving them much free publicity. They look for employees that take pride in their workmanship since all their products are handmade. Finding good employees has been challenging. Sometimes they have hired friends of friends. Other times they have had prospective employees approach them. New employees are started on probationary terms to be sure they carry through with the quality mission. Jeff does the accounting, and Adam runs production while Amy's mother, Carole, runs the counter.

A third store is planned and then, perhaps, franchising. Arizona Bread Company, in less than a year, has become the local leader in its market.

China Mist Tea Company

Timing can be critical to the success of your business. John Martinson and Dan Schweiker might have had successful coffee businesses if it had been the 1990s. But it wasn't. Dan Schweiker, the first coffee roaster in Phoenix, owned a retail gourmet coffee and tea business in the early 1980s. At the same time, John Martinson had a business selling coffee to resorts and businesses. "We were too far ahead of the curve," explained Martinson. Located in the Phoenix area, hot summers broke their businesses. Iced coffee drinks weren't yet popular. "Dan only had two customers in the summer," quipped Martinson, "the mailman and me."

Schweiker didn't want to go back to practicing law. Martinson needed to find another business. They pooled their resources and decided to go into the business of selling iced tea to resorts and restaurants. The trend was moving away from alcoholic drinks and some beverage needed to take its place. They figured people would be unlikely to switch from alcohol to sweet soda, so guessed iced tea would become popular. Other people they spoke with agreed. In restaurants and resorts, 85 percent of the tea consumed is iced tea. Both had experience with tea from their previous businesses and, mused Dan, "I fell in love with the business."

The pair have complementary skills. Martinson, the right brain of the business, is the master of sales and marketing and Schweiker understands and enjoys the mechanics of running a business. Both men knew they were on to something this time because they were closing 80 percent of their sales calls. Being first in the gourmet iced tea market, China Mist offered service with its complete iced tea program plus point of sale support.

The idea began when Martinson was approached by a sales agent at Bunn-o-matic. That company had developed an iced tea brewer, but was having difficulty finding a marketing niche. When Martinson and Schweiker saw the brewer, they "knew there was a business lurking in the machine."

Originally, Martinson and Schweiker thought they'd lease the brewer and combine it with an already available tea, marketing to high-end hotels and resorts. Martinson, with Schweiker's experience in mind, suggested they become a packager instead, blending their own tea. They then identified the qualities they wanted in a tea: good clarity, smooth and non-bitter with a ruby gold color. China Mist Tea is the result of three years of refining their blend. At first, they kept the fact that they were working on their own tea blend secret. As a small company, the large tea companies that originally supplied them could have squashed their fledgling company. Going by the generic name of Restaurant Tea Service, they worked with their target market of high-end, white tablecloth restaurants and resorts.

Currently, they offer their trademark China Mist tea plus 11 flavored teas, with Passion Fruit as the most popular. Flavored tea is about a third of their business. Restaurants and resorts often choose one of these flavors as their trademark tea or offer a different flavor every day of the week. They also have caffeine-free herbal iced tea, which is a small, but growing portion of the business.

Soon China Mist began receiving calls from other restaurants, including fast food chains, requesting its tea. The two debated on whether to sell to these markets, but finally agreed that they would if those restaurants would pay the same price as their other clients. They have expanded to provide their tea to high-end retail outlets. Distribution now includes Canada, the Caribbean, and Pacific Rim.

Cash flow and finding a bank to work with were challenging. A bank is a partner to a business and if the bankers do not understand your business, they don't want to work with you. Banks need to understand the balance sheets of your business sector. In different sectors, numbers such as capital investments, collections, etc. vary dramatically although they may be healthy within that particular sector.

Hiring capable employees has often been difficult. About two years into the business, they hired a junior in high school as part of a program for home economics occupations. That student, Rommie Dresher, is now vice president of the company in charge of employees, production, and research and development. Martinson explained that while at the time she was inexperienced, they recognized her valuable qualities. "She's a tough negotiator, keeps close tabs on money, is tough on collections, and an excellent manager." He added that "she wasn't hesitant to speak up when she disagreed."

China Mist has had its challenges. Iced tea recently received an undeserved bad rap. Media distorted stories about bacteria in iced tea. Tea leaves do not harbor harmful bacteria, but like other plants such as lettuce have a normal flora of bacteria. These bacteria will not make you sick. A lab testing tea from Cincinnati restaurants gave false positive tests for harmful bacteria. The media jumped on the story before finding that the results were inaccurate.

China Mist did not wait for questions, but chose to respond proactively. Martinson and Schweiker sent a letter to their customers that cited findings from the Center for Disease Control (CDC) that the test results were misinterpreted. Included was a CDC statement that "Tea is a beverage with little history of disease transmission." By the time the media got the story out, China Mist clients knew how to respond to their customers' concerns. Some clients displayed their excellent inspection reports. China Mist has had an anti-bacterial program for 12 years. Company distributors visit customers and grade them on their adherence to the anti-bacterial program. Brewing tea in hot water destroys bacteria in the water. They tell their clients that brewing equipment needs to be cleaned thoroughly like other cooking equipment and recommend that iced tea not be kept for more than eight hours.

This publicity occurred in the winter off-season. "The timing couldn't have been better," indicated Martinson. The publicity opened up opportunities for China Mist because restaurants previously resisting the company's marketing were now eager to hear about its anti-bacterial and service program.

Schweiker, when asked about the current coffeehouse trend, expressed that he felt it is important to get in at the beginning of the curve, not the top. Coffeehouses are popular with Generation X, but soon Gen Xers will have less discretionary dollars as they start families and save up for homes.

Knowing they need to keep on focus while expanding their markets, they have been working with a consultant. They stressed that finding a competent individual whom they could communicate well with is what has made this a positive experience.

China Mist demonstrates that, with the courage to try again and good timing, persistence breeds success.

❖   ❖   ❖

These two businesses have positioned themselves in niches that aren't in direct competition with large companies in the food market. Specialty bread is best marketed locally to ensure freshness. China Mist distributes primarily through restaurants, establishing its own market. Now that the company is established, it has started retailing their teas.

Food Market Opportunities

Capitalizing on Trends

The key to capitalizing on a trend is to get in early and establish your clientele. The coffeehouse trend is a reflection of a move away from alcohol especially during business hours. With this fast-paced society, workers need to be alert, which popularizes caffeinated beverages. People are becoming more health conscious and don't want to consume a lot of calories in their beverages. When thirsty, we need some beverage, but plain old water just doesn't have the appeal.

The founders of China Mist Tea found that you can get into a trend too early. They both went broke in the coffee business in the early 1980s. In their same market area, a few years later, another coffeehouse was very successful. That business, with better timing, went on to establish multiple locations, eventually being bought out by a corporation. With amazing courage, the China Mist founders jumped right back in. This time, a little farther into the trend, they hit success.

Iced tea consumption is still on the rise. Right now the trend is fruit flavored teas. Passion fruit is the most popular flavor in China Mist's line. Maybe in the future, flavors such as ginger, vanilla, clove, wintergreen, cinnamon, or other others will be popular. Herbal teas are still gaining popularity.

Back in the late 1980s, many cities, with the notorious exceptions of Seattle and San Francisco, didn't have a single coffeehouse. Many of these cities today have dozens of coffeehouses. People need places to get together to socialize and make business contacts. However, we are now well into the trend and a new coffeehouse has substantial competition. If you have a great location or an unique idea, you may still be successful, but competition limits your market.

Low Calorie Beverages

The number of beverages available has expanded in the last five years. Still, many of the beverages, including the bottled iced teas, are packed with calories. A zippy beverage with few or no calories is still a largely untapped market. There are some low calorie flavored waters, a few unsweetened iced teas, and the diet drinks, but most of these low calorie beverages are artificially sweetened and way too sweet. The answer may lie in developing a new taste.

Pizza

Pizza's popularity is enormous yet we are stuck with so many me-too pizzas. Develop a unique pizza at a fair price and choose an underserved location. Provide good service and you'll have the basis for a successful business.

Snack Trucks

Convenience is a big factor in food sales. If food is readily available to people, they will buy. Bring snacks and lunches to schools and businesses with a snack truck. You can charge a little more for the convenience. Take the truck to special events for additional sales on weekends and evenings.

Personal Cook

With husbands and wives both working, time to cook meals is drastically reduced. In an upscale area, you might prepare a week's worth of meals for a family. Or how about offering your services for one day a week? To be profitable, you'll need to be highly organized.

Fast Food

In resort areas, unique fast food restaurants have a fair chance at success although this may be seasonal. In an urban location, unless you are in a shopping area or large business complex, fast food restaurants have a more difficult time getting established.

Franchises are often the best bet in this market, especially the new trend towards dual, complementing franchises. Some combinations of franchises that have worked together are: Arby's/Sbarros, Blimpie/I Can't Believe It's Yogurt/Java Coast Coffee, Carl's Jr./Green Burrito, Carl's Jr./Long John Silver, Denny's/Baskin-Robbins, Dunkin' Donuts/Baskin Robbins, KFC/Taco Bell, Rally's Hamburgers/Green Burrito and Taco Bell/TJ Cinnamons. The purpose is to extend menu offerings, share kitchens, and perhaps provide for additional meal coverage.

Make sure you get an adequate, exclusive area when purchasing a franchise. Confirm in advance you'll have the opportunity to buy multiple locations for increased profits. A recent article in *SmartMoney* magazine (see Resources, Franchises) on the pitfalls of franchising, including fast food, is required reading before venturing into franchising.

Healthy Food Store

As people age, they often become more concerned with eating healthy food. Perhaps it is the inevitable health challenges that most of us face as we grow older. In the next 30 to 40 years, we will have a huge population of elderly people.

The adjective "healthy" is used here instead of "health" because health food has a tarnished image. With manufacturers of food supplements touting sometimes outrageous claims for their products, many people have been turned off. By calling your store a healthy food store, you can avoid the stigma. As supermarkets specialize by providing organic fruits and vegetables, ethnic foods, and health foods, this is a competitive market. You might try taking orders for your regular customers by fax or phone, then having the orders ready when they come by or deliver them for a small fee. By focusing on healthy rather than all-hype foods, you may find your store appealing to those who want to eat healthy, but who have been dubious of health food.

Distinctive Bread

Everyone seems to love bread, but that stuff called bread in supermarkets is often marginal, tasteless, and lacking in nutrition. Arizona Bread Company found a large market for its quality bread.

Since bread has a shelf life of only a couple days, there is a need for a business that delivers fresh bread two or three times a week. Many people love fresh bread, but don't have the chance to stop just for bread three times a week. Since bread isn't damaged by freezing, you could fabricate custom containers for home delivery. Your customers wouldn't even need to be home. They could place their monthly orders by phone or fax in advance, with orders billed biweekly or charged to credit cards.

Specialty Foods and Local Brands

Some specialty food kiosks do well. How about an all chocolate or flavored popcorn kiosk? In high density business locations, kiosks can generate substantial sales with reasonable overhead costs. With multiple good locations, kiosks offering distinctive products have excellent income potential. Look for unique, unserved high-volume sites.

Local brands are in vogue. If you have a unique food product, you may be able to develop this into a business. For profitability, you'll need to think about a line of products rather than a single item.

Mystery Shopper

The mystery shopper concept has been around for a long time because it is a very effective means of finding out the quality of service at a restaurant or other service business. The way these services work is an anonymous individual or family goes to an establishment then writes up a review on the restaurant's service. If your town does not have these services or if you have tested ideas on how to make these services better, this may be your business.

Marketing and Consulting

Once you have a restaurant or store open, you'll want to find unique ways to bring in customers. One way you might consider is to host a TV cooking show. If you use public access television, your costs can be almost nothing. After gaining experience on public access, you can approach your public television channel with a pilot. This would be great publicity for a healthy food store. Maybe your product manufacturers would help sponsor the show.

If you start a restaurant and it is family-owned, emphasize this in your marketing. Attitudes are shifting away from big business. Use this to build your business. Once you get customers, concentrate on keeping them as the costs for obtaining new customers are much greater. Find ways to reward your loyal customers: complementary drinks, desserts, etc. Work on a referral program that rewards existing customers for referring new customers. Perhaps you could consult for other restaurants once you have developed an effective program of your own.

Future Food Markets

Since people need and love to eat, food businesses have a stable market. Fast food restaurants are highly competitive and name recognition is important. Upscale restaurants are risky because of the larger capital investment and time needed to become established. These restaurants are also more affected by changes in the economy with the rising diversity of nationalities in the U.S., ethnic restaurants may have a greater chance for success, than their American-style counterparts. The best opportunities in this area are probably non-restaurant businesses.

CHAPTER 17

Franchising

Some franchises are solid business opportunities while others provide little chance to become profitable. Upfront and continuing costs are generally higher than comparable nonfranchise businesses. The same amount of effort and hours are needed for success as with other businesses although, with some franchises, name recognition may be a powerful benefit. For a reality check, find a franchise book that is a couple years old at the library or a used bookstore. Look through to see how many names you recognize. Of the unfamiliar names, try calling some of these businesses. You'll find many have vanished. When considering buying a franchise, ask yourself what you will gain. Could you do this on your own or does the franchise offer something—name recognition, patents, products, or support—that will help your business be successful?

A franchise may be a good option if:

❖ Name recognition is important in the type of business; for example, fast food.

❖ Name recognition and trust are important, for example; automobile repair.

❖ If a franchise has a special patented product(s) or knowledge that has been proven successful.

❖ You are interested in active ownership. Generally you will be the main provider of the service or proprietor in the business.

❖ You have business experience, but do not have a unique product or service. A franchise may provide this product or service.

❖ You have specialized skills related to the franchise, but do not have business experience. A franchise may provide business training and someone to call with questions although you can get both on your own.

Some businesses, such as fast food, rely heavily on name recognition. For these franchises, the name recognition may be worth the costs. You may find that you'll need multiple stores to generate sufficient profits. Make sure from the start you will be able to buy additional local franchises, if desired.

Other franchises are based on a unique product or service. A successful business based on an novel service will be copied. Services cannot be patented. Count on competition from the start. Karen Rego, HEADSHOTS® founder, developed an original idea of combining makeovers with a photographic session. Her concept was very successful and was copied by GlamourShots and others. People, especially women, love the way they are transformed, like fashion models. With the makeover documented by photos, they can show family and friends the results. When competition appeared, prices were slashed, making it difficult for stores to be profitable.

If the franchise has a unique product, is it patented? Patents may not be walls of protection, however. Many patents just don't hold up in court. Patent attorneys have many strategies for destroying the protection granted by a patent. By changing the product slightly, another company can weasel around the patent and market a similar product. To enforce a patent generally means going to court and that means very high costs.

NOVUS has developed its own unique products and techniques for automobile glass repair. Although the franchise has many competitors, NOVUS has name recognition and is known for quality service. The company works with insurance companies that preauthorize repairs. NOVUS continues to develop its repair products and techniques. Franchisees seem happy with the franchise and their earnings.

LemonBusters offers a presale auto inspection service for used cars. Comparable to the home inspection business, its service makes used car buyers more comfortable with their purchase and facilitates negotiating a fair sales price. Rather than hurrying into franchising, the company has carefully perfected its system and plan to start franchising in late 1996.

HEADSHOTS®

Shari Leve: Before

HEADSHOTS®, a contemporary photographic studio, provides a makeover and photo session bringing out each client's best features. Clients may request business photos, family pictures, or glamorous photos for a spouse or friend.

In 1991, Shari and Bob Leve bought a HEADSHOTS franchise. Bob, a former stockbroker, investigated a variety of franchises. He narrowed his list to a few for serious investigation. When Shari saw HEADSHOTS, she knew this was the business for her. Bob, after researching the company, agreed with Shari's decision. The couple borrowed the funds needed to open their franchise.

Shari Leve: After

Shari truly loves this business. She stays involved with all aspects of the client visit from makeovers, which include hair styling and make-up, selection of wardrobe through the photo shoot. Her artistic background is valuable in obtaining attractive results. With no experience in photography, working with expensive camera equipment was at first intimidating, but now is her favorite part. Shari has a wonderful philosophy about the business. Making non-models look glamorous raises self-esteem. Through photography, she shows men and women that they can achieve the same looks depicted by magazine models. She also wants people to know that, although they can look this way, they should not feel they need to go to the efforts of extensive make-up on a daily basis.

The experience, which is designed to be fun, starts with the makeover. Model make-up techniques are used to draw out the client's best features and provide the emphasis needed to photograph well under studio lighting. Wardrobe, chosen from the studio's selection or brought with the client, helps create the desired mood and image. Next, professionally-trained photographers capture the best look through a 12-pose photo session. Using the magic of the Kodak Prism System, video images of the different poses can be viewed immediately after photographing. Clients, with the help of staff, can choose which poses they prefer and order photos the same day.

Stores are located in middle-class areas selected by the franchiser, always in malls. The Leve's store now has nine employees, five full-time. Hiring dependable employees with a good work ethic is their greatest challenge. Bob does the preliminary employment interview. Shari then interviews those who appear to be good candidates. She looks for people who share her enthusiasm for the business and enjoy working with people. Still, they find it difficult to find quality, dependable staff.

Another challenge of this business is that it does not generate a lot of repeat business. The Leves are adapting the business, by providing professional business photography in addition to the trademark glamorous look, to generate multiple visits. Although a client may splurge for glamorous photography infrequently, there is a need for updated business photos much more often.

Bob handles many of the business functions, advertising, and most of the paperwork, freeing Shari to be actively involved with clients. They have arranged the business so they each usually put in no more than forty hours a week. Weekends are workdays, but on some weekdays they let dependable employees take charge. Since both are involved in the business full-time and they have two children, it is important to have a schedule allowing time together for the family.

Bob had the financial background to thoroughly investigate the business so they were aware of the costs and projected profits. They have been happy with the support from the franchiser. Because of good planning and support, the store was profitable the first year.

The most effective marketing is by word-of-mouth. Incentives are given for clients to refer their friends. Special promotions are designed for Christmas, Valentine's Day, Mother's Day, and graduations.

Although the franchiser is actively in business, it has suspended franchising in order to maintain the quality focus of the business. When a business is as personally focused as HEADSHOTS, a franchiser has difficulty ensuring consistent quality.

Shari recommends you choose a business you will enjoy. She is very satisfied with their decision. Coincidentally, the author's picture on the back cover was taken at the Leve's HEADSHOTS location.

HEADSHOTS®: The Franchisor's Perspective

Founded in Hawaii in 1987, HEADSHOTS®, the inspiration of two women, combines a makeover and photo session, bringing out the attractive qualities of individuals. The founders believe the experience itself should be pleasant and comfortable. Starting with very little capital, they were able to sell a mall leasing agent on their concept. The agent agreed to give them temporary mall space to see if their idea would be successful. The store quickly became popular. Karen Rego, one of the founders, attributes their rapid success to the uniqueness and quality of their service. They moved to Austin, Texas and began franchising in 1990.

HEADSHOTS faced a similar situation to that of many new, unique businesses. At first, it seems like growth will continue indefinitely, but eventually a plateau is reached. Other competitors come in and the idea becomes less unique. Price competition lowers everyone's profits.

HEADSHOTS' franchisees with business expertise adjusted to the increased competition by giving better service and product. However, with a service it is often more difficult for clients to see the quality difference.

Rego loves her business, but says that being a franchiser has often been difficult. Although the media often tells the story of franchisees, franchisers have their own challenges. While a franchiser can make suggestions to franchisees, it is often difficult to motivate franchisees to implement this advice. Sometimes judging a prospective franchisee's business savvy is difficult. Then when a franchisee struggles because of a lack of business sense, he or she may simply stop paying the franchise fees. These franchisees may need more business guidance than a franchiser can give. The result may be the franchiser must take back the location as a company store or lose it.

"Stay flexible," Rego says. She thinks that businesses with a unique product are best for franchising. "Service businesses, which do not require products purchased from the franchiser, are more difficult."

For start-up companies, she advises having little debt and being adaptable to change. Rego mentioned the challenges of a labor-intensive business and recommends hiring people with related competencies who enjoy the work.

HEADSHOTS is a great business. The owners know they are in the people business. They strive to make the makeover and photo session fun. A challenge in this type of business is getting customers back after their initial visit. Although happy with the experience, many customers will not feel the need to be re-photographed for quite some time so stores must constantly be bringing in new clients. These clients often do refer friends and family.

NOVUS Windshield Repair®

When considering whether to purchase a franchise, be sure you speak with franchisees of your selected franchiser. For example, two different NOVUS franchisees have repaired windshields on my two cars. Both did excellent work and both were very happy with the franchise.

NOVUS, founded in 1972, began as a windshield repair company. In 1993, NOVUS was acquired by TCG International (TCGI), which has more outlets in

North America than any other auto glass repair and replacement business. NOVUS now offers the option of windshield repair or replacement. TCGI also owns Speedy Auto Glass, a sister company providing similar services. NOVUS franchisees have two options: a retail location or mobile service franchise.

Ninety percent of new franchisees start with a mobile unit, a practical and cost-effective way of doing business. Then, later, they may establish a retail fixed location or add additional mobile units. While most franchisees own a single franchise, one franchisee in Seattle has 22 franchises. He started with a single franchise and has grown through extensive media advertising.

There are 450 NOVUS franchises in the U.S. and an additional 1,200 representatives in 45 countries around the world. One franchisee in Spokane, Washington has been with the company continuously since 1975. He started the business as a second career after retiring from the Air Force. Husband and wife teams often make successful franchisees. Some franchisees are starting over in this business after being laid off. Women have done well, with many excelling in sales. John Hunter, from NOVUS corporate headquarters, says that the prime indicator of success is being easy to get along with. No technical expertise is necessary, but some sales background is helpful. Regional conferences are held every year with a biennial Super Session to update information, share sales and business tips, and network with other franchisees.

NOVUS provides the trademark, tools, sales and marketing materials, factory training, and access to a national network of insurance referrals. With the initial franchise fee, you receive five-and-a-half days of training at the Minneapolis office and are entitled to up to five more days of support with a NOVUS representative in your own area. During the Minneapolis training, new franchisees are taught all aspects of running their business, including technical training, sales and marketing, and business management. They role play contacting potential customers such as fleet owners, trucking businesses, used car lots, and insurance personnel. During the five days of training in the new franchisee's area, franchisees are given additional "hands on" experience in running the business.

The initial franchise fee is $15,000 plus $2,695 for the necessary equipment and supplies. Royalties are eight percent of gross windshield repair sales, five percent of gross windshield replacement sales, or $250 a month, whichever is greater. During the first six months of the franchise agreement, the $250 minimum fee is waived. The franchise term is 10 years with no charge for renewal. Recently, a 75 year old franchisee renewed for another 10 years.

The process of becoming a NOVUS franchisee begins with your initial contact with the company. NOVUS will mail company information to you and then will ask you to call back with your questions. Once you and NOVUS feel comfortable with each other, NOVUS mails out a confidential information form to be completed and returned plus a list of all its franchisees. You select the franchisees you wish to contact. The company does a credit check and sends you the NOVUS Uniform Franchise Offering Circular. After speaking with your selected franchisees, NOVUS then checks to see if you have any additional questions. Next, if you want to pursue buying a franchise, the company will invite you to visit for a Discovery Day at its Minneapolis headquarters where you and key personnel can become acquainted prior to making your decision. A finance program is available for up to $12,000 of start-up costs.

NOVUS does not make income projections since so much depends on the franchisee. Auto glass is a competitive business, however, automobile windshields are constantly being damaged from rocks and other debris so the business is out there. If these damaged windshields are not repaired, temperature changes and hitting potholes puts stress on the glass that may result in more extensive fracturing. NOVUS has built a reputation among insurance professionals and business owners for providing economical, reliable service. This reputation facilitates sales by franchisees. The company maintains its own chemist and laboratory, continually refining its procedures. Repair resins and chemicals are produced within the company. NOVUS has kept pace with new computer electronic data exchange and telecommunications technology used by the insurance industry. The NOVUS motto is "Repair First, Replace When Necessary."

NOVUS provides comprehensive operations manuals for all aspects of the business. The marketing department supplies a complete marketing manual including camera-ready artwork for newspaper and yellow pages ads, direct mail, outdoor advertising, and broadcast-ready radio and television ads. Franchisees can participate in a national yellow pages program that offers a $100 rebate per franchise.

NOVUS, as an international company, works with the differences in standards established by countries for testing auto repairs. The company is working on instituting consistent testing standards worldwide. In other countries, the NOVUS opportunity is sometimes sold as a distributorship. Local distributors are familiar with their country's unique needs.

George Sieg, a franchisee, has a masters degree and worked in computer programming. His job required frequent travel and, after suffering a heart attack, he bought a NOVUS mobile franchise. His son-in-law already owned a franchise so he didn't even bother to investigate other franchises. Sieg loves the flexible hours, contact with people, and says he earns more now than he did as a programmer.

When asked about cost of materials, he thought prices are reasonable. Sieg said that many NOVUS retail locations are going into converted gas stations.

A mobile franchise can be set up using your own vehicle, which must have a white exterior with the standard NOVUS blue vinyl graphics. With a mobile franchise, a cellular phone is a must. You'll speak with local businesses and insurance offices, setting up your own appointments. NOVUS does business with over 50 insurance companies, who will preapprove the repairs. Also, you can do commercial and fleet repairs to build your base of customers.

Styles on Video

Would you like to see how you would look with a new haircut? Or how about 20 pounds thinner? Styles On Video put together computer imaging systems that could change your appearance. You may have seen kiosks that let you choose five to ten hairstyles to try on video before committing to a new haircut, permanent, or haircolor. With this software, you could try on these new styles then record the results to video to take home. Or, with a telephoto lens on the camera, you would get a full body image. Tell the computer how much weight you want to lose, then view the results. What a great idea!

For awhile, the company's growth seemed unstoppable. The company went public and the share price soared. Then recently, noticing the absence of a previous Styles on Video kiosk, a call was placed to shopping center management. "They're gone, out of business." Next Styles On Video's corporate headquarters was contacted. The company was still in business, but with new management. However, a couple months later, the entire company was out of business.

Originally the company sold systems to anyone interested then ventured into franchising. Franchising lasted only three to four months. Then it sold systems primarily to spas and beauty salons. The company was very honest. It had a good product which was successful in salons and spas. But the profits generated from stand alone franchises just didn't meet the expectations of franchisees. Novelty generated business at first, then sales dropped. These systems work better in salons where a client can choose a style, try it on, and then the salon can make money from the services given—cut, style, coloring, and permanents.

The weight loss package, which was developed with a substantial investment, might fit well in a weight loss center to motivate potential clients to sign up for the program. Weight loss businesses have had a high litigation rate. Styles On Video decided not to directly tie itself to such a highly litigious business. Styles also found that people did not necessarily want to see their thinner image. The idea, though it seems good, was not very successful. This failure of its second product combined with market saturation of the Styles on Video systems contributed to the company's demise.

When franchising ceased, the company assisted owners of existing systems who wanted to sell their systems. Styles On Video collected a $3.00 residual for each imaging session. Users bought disks that allowed 220 imaging sessions. After using all these, they had to purchase a new disk. Now, with no one to provide new session disks, are the owners able to use their imaging systems?

When you are working with a new concept, it is difficult to predict if people will buy. Under what circumstances and at which price will people buy? Will they purchase the product or service once or multiple times? Is this a fad? Some Styles On Video system buyers started mail order businesses in which clients send in their photo and get a video showing their appearance with new hair styles. When the imager cannot control the image and is dependent on the quality of the picture sent, it is difficult to get adequate results.

Styles On Video was an excellent idea and they tried to adapt to the market. Ultimately, with a reduced market and competition, the company, once very successful, could not survive. Companies with unique products or services often need to follow a trial and error approach until they find what works. Purchasers of these systems found the business works best in a location where the subsequent services help subsidize the imaging.

A similar situation exists in the use of imaging for home improvement: landscaping and other improvements. Systems have been marketed to be the basis of an imaging-only business. Imaging systems would work best as adjuncts to companies that can provide the improvements. Many people are reluctant to pay for the imaging only, but if part of a home improvement business, costs could be recouped in providing the work.

Water ´n Ice

Water stores, supplies of reverse osmosis processed water, have become popular especially in regions where water taste is problematic. In Arizona, when temperatures hover above 100° and tepid water flows out of cold water faucets, bottled water becomes very popular. Water ´n Ice is a such a franchise. The Phoenix area has over 30 stores. Franchisees were shown profit estimates that appeared very lucrative. The initial franchise fee, around $37,000, included use of the name, training, and use of the water treatment equipment. Franchisees were not able to buy the equipment outright. Supplies had to be purchased through the franchiser at highly-inflated prices.

Arizona franchisees soon found that their profits and costs did not come near the estimates that had been given. They banded together and successfully won a lawsuit, claiming fraudulent disclosure, against the owners. The franchisers had been gambling away profits in Las Vegas and were too short of cash to fight the case. One of the owners walked away, leaving the other to defend the case on his own.

The franchisees won their independence from the franchiser, keeping the name and equipment. They are no longer offering franchising, although they have an independent group to share knowledge and supply costs for the existing stores.

Talking with a former franchisee, he expressed that more time should have been spent talking with existing franchisees prior to buying. Although he felt the profit projections were too high, he didn't spend enough effort investigating actual potential. The franchisers received 20 percent royalties—very high in a low profit margin business. When franchisees discovered suppliers with much lower prices, the franchiser refused to switch. Franchisees were required to buy supplies through the franchiser at inflated prices.

Now that the lawsuit has been settled in favor of the franchisees, their profits have dramatically increased. They can buy their supplies from the most competitive source and no longer pay franchise fees.

Looking at the Water ´n Ice story, those considering buying a franchise can see the importance of doing their own market research and profit projections. Not all franchisees have been as fortunate. The Water ´n Ice case was successful because profit and supply costs were given in writing, substantiating the fraudulent calculations. The fleeing of one franchiser substantiated the claims of wrongdoing. Small businesses quickly become bankrupted by legal action, though the involvement of 30-plus businesses defrayed the costs. The franchisees won more than they spent by getting the equipment, name, and freedom from royalties.

Investigating Franchise Opportunities

Many people who don't know what business to start opt for a franchise. If you find a franchise in a field where you have interest, a franchise will help get you started. If you have little business experience, the franchiser should be available to answer questions along the way. You can get the information on your own, but more time and effort will be needed. But don't choose a franchise just because you don't know what else to do. Find something you'll enjoy that has the potential to earn money and check the opportunity thoroughly before investing.

Evaluate whether your business as planned can ultimately generate enough revenue. Many franchises available would supplement an existing business, adding an additional revenue source. As an example, a landscaping business might add imaging to its services. Imaging franchises are available, but the software needed can be purchased on your own if you have or are willing to learn the necessary skills. Clients bring a picture of their yard—or you take a photo—and this image is scanned into a computer. Using a library of images from your inventory of trees, shrubs, and flowers, you redesign the client's yard, showing in advance how the finished yard will look. Then you can either landscape the yard or sell the client the plan, plants, and directions to do the job independently.

Be leery of franchises that:

1. Claim to be the ideal business. All businesses have challenges.

2. Claim to be so easy that anyone can run this business successfully. All businesses require a variety of skills that must be acquired.

3. Claim that no effort is required. If the business could be run with no effort, why would they franchise it?

4. Have inflated earnings claims. To see if profits are accurately forecast, talk to other franchisees.

5. Are carbon copies of similar, nonfranchise businesses. Franchise costs may cut your profitability making it difficult to compete. Ask why there is an advantage to being a franchise rather than starting the business on your own.

6. Do not have at least one company-owned franchise. If this is such a great business, why aren't they participating? How do the franchisers know that this business will be successful if they don't operate the business? Have the details, marketing, and challenges been worked through?

7. Do not have a unique, patented product or do not have good name recognition. Franchises involve extra costs and a non-franchise business may be able to provide the same service more cost effectively, for example, copy shops.

Researching a Franchise

Researching a franchise is similar to checking out any other business. The problem with franchises is that many people just accept what they have been told by the franchiser, without verifying the information.

Most importantly, talk to present and former franchisees. Confirm the amount of net profit, profit after expenses. If this a very new franchise, fees should be significantly lower due to increased risk. Can you terminate the franchise agreement for legitimate cause without losing your present site? What are the franchise renewal terms? How happy are they with franchiser support? Before you invest:

- ❖ Visit the franchise headquarters and get to know the people you will be working with.

- ❖ Check the credit of the founders and key company executives. Have they been involved with previous franchises? What happened to those franchises? If they have had previous bankruptcies, be especially cautious. The owners may be starting franchises for the money, then abandoning them. Bankruptcies should be disclosed in the Offering Circular.

- ❖ Get the Better Business report for the franchisers from the city where they are headquartered. If there are existing local franchises, check with your local Better Business Bureau as well. Read the Dunn & Bradstreet report, if available.

- ❖ Have a franchise lawyer look over all agreements prior to signing.

- ❖ Get the names of oldest and newest franchisees. Call them.

- ❖ Find out the failure rate for franchisees.

- ❖ Try to get profit and loss statements from existing franchises.

- ❖ Will you be given an exclusive area? Will you be given first right of refusal for additional outlets in your area?

- ❖ Find out the length of the franchise period. Is it renewable? Is there a renewal fee? Make sure this is in writing.

- ❖ Is the franchise transferable to your heirs? Will there be a fee?

- ❖ Ask for a complete disclosure of all costs and fees in writing.

- ❖ Check if there is a local market for the franchise products or services. Who are your competitors, franchises and nonfranchises? Check them out.

- ❖ Read some of the references listed under Resources.

Remember that some franchises make money while others do little more than break even, if that. Tip the scales toward making a reasonable profit by doing your research prior to buying.

CHAPTER 18

Hobby Businesses

S ome of the best opportunities for small businesses are those involving hobbies, crafts, and special interests. These are small, yet often lucrative markets that may be too limited to interest big business. Many of these businesses require some manual assembly which discourages larger businesses, that prefer processes that can be automated. Most hobbies are not fads so it is less likely your market will disappear. Less competition and a stable market are strong advantages.

Hobby-related businesses are usually run by people with a passionate interest. Your customers will expect you to be very knowledgeable in your special interest area. For those who are natural teachers, you will be able to use this talent in conjunction with your hobby business. This can be very satisfying. Being able to make a living doing what you love may be your dream.

There are niche areas within each interest that can be developed. Choosing a niche makes it easier to become an expert in your area. By limiting yourself to a specialty, your business can easily gain a distinctive image. You can more precisely target your advertising to publications and groups with an interest in your products.

If you do not have business management experience, community colleges, Small Business Development Centers, and the Small Business Association have courses to help you gain this expertise. Growing your business slowly will allow you to learn as your business expands. If you want a small or part-time business, the hobby and craft market is especially flexible to allow seasonal, limited hours, home, or one-person businesses. Your customers do not expect you to be a large company and will be more amenable to factors such as a home or post office box mailing address, not accepting credit cards, and the lack of an 800-number. Although having a more professional address and easier ordering will facilitate your success, you may find that you can start-up without these services and add them when volume increases. Lower start-up costs increase your chance of success.

Hobby and craft businesses would be best for individuals:

❖ With a strong special interest.

❖ Who have special talents.

❖ Who would like to work at home.

❖ Who want to start-up with a very small amount of capital.

❖ Who want flexible or unusual hours.

❖ Who want to have a part-time or seasonal business.

❖ Who lack business management experience. You can gain this experience slowly, through business courses, seminars, mentors, and peers, combined with the practical experience of running your business.

Some people have avoided the hobbyist market because they think profits are limited. The following two companies illustrate that hobbyist businesses can be profitable, thriving enterprises.

Nancy's Notions

Do you know someone who loves to sew or quilt? I'll bet they are familiar with Nancy Zieman who hosts a PBS television show called "Sewing With Nancy" and is the owner/president of a thriving sewing retail and catalog business.

Nancy's Notions began in 1979. From her kitchen table, Zieman put together a one-page flyer featuring various sewing-related items. Working first from her in-laws' basement, then, after running out of space, from her own remodeled basement, she has since outgrown three additional locations. Her current headquarters and warehouse in Beaver Dam, Wisconsin encompasses 50,000 square feet. The business now employs 130 people, often processing over a 1,500 orders per day. The 1996 catalog is 168 pages.

Although her *Nancy's Notions* catalog is the heart of her business, Zieman now has a 2,500 square foot retail store that also offers sewing classes. Through the catalog and store, over 4,000 different sewing-related items—notions, patterns, fabrics, books, and videos—are sold. Zieman attributes her rapid growth in part to her PBS television show, "Sewing With Nancy." The show was first taped from her home in 1982, but is now produced at Wisconsin Public Television in Madison, Wisconsin. This is the longest running sewing show on television.

What distinguishes Zieman's business from other sewing businesses is her dedication to education and creativity. Zieman, a home economist with a degree in clothing and textiles, is a natural educator. Sewing methods are explained in an easy-to-follow manner. She encourages others to find creative and timesaving techniques with her featured television segment, "Viewer Hints." Each television program features a hands-on demonstration and responds to viewer questions.

In 1987, Zieman started a Video Club, that now has over 225 sewing videos for sale or rent. Edited versions of her television series are available on video. Zieman has a family herself and understands that fitting sewing into a busy schedule is a challenge. In her store and catalog, you will find sewing notions designed to make sewing easier. Besides videos, Zieman has written a number of sewing books. Many of these are focused on timesaving. Sewing can be very time consuming with selecting and fitting a pattern, cutting out pattern pieces, sewing, and finishing. She has devised innovative ways to create clothing in less time. Her approach is to find simplified, faster methods of sewing.

Her other emphasis is creativity. Via TV, videos, and books, she teaches others how to create custom-designed clothing, quilting, and home decorating. She also designs creative sewing patterns for The McCall Pattern Company, a major pattern producer.

Recently, Zieman focused on ways to inspire children to sew. Zieman started sewing at age 10 as a member of her local 4-H Club. She produced a video/booklet combination, *Sewing With Nancy—Kids!*, which features easy, fun projects.

The home sewing business, as a whole, is difficult. Since more women are working, they have less time for sewing. Prices for fabrics and patterns have risen. To be successful in such a challenging field is notable. Zieman has met this challenge by finding innovative ways to serve her customers. Customers are welcomed with a surprisingly high level of service. Nancy's Notions has built a reputation of superior, reliable service delivering exceptional products. With such attention to detail, her company should continue to thrive.

Roy's Train World

Roy's Train World, started by model train hobbyist LeRoy Honetschlager, is a successful model railroading business. His son, Tim, LeRoy, and other family members run this retail and mail order firm.

Roy's Train World was founded because of difficulty getting products and parts locally. Originally, LeRoy also operated a custom upholstery shop behind the store. Model railroading has became more popular, resulting in expanded product lines. With the increase in products for the hobby, the store has also grown. LeRoy closed the upholstery shop. Now the store has multiple employees; most are family members. Roy's Train World is open from 9 A.M. to 5:30 P.M. (5 on Saturdays, 9 P.M. on Thursdays) six days a week. Mail order is about 10 percent of the business.

Centrally located, Roy's is well-organized, exceptionally clean, and inviting. A broad selection of products is offered: products to build a complete railroad set-up, books, and videos. Although packaged products are shrink-wrapped, customers can bring merchandise to the front if they need to have a product opened for further examination.

Model railroading has grown from a limited choice of products to greater complexity in scale and variety. Electronics has increased the intricacy in putting together a model railroading set-up. Tim Honetschlager attributes their success to product knowledge and service to their customers. Increasing complexity demands they be able to assist their clients.

As part of this assistance, a variety of clinics are offered on various aspects of model railroading. During their busy Christmas season, every customer that purchases a train set receives an invitation to a class that runs for four Saturdays. In the class, they demonstrate how to build a train layout from start to finish. Throughout the year, free classes are offered on model railroading subjects such as wiring, model building and scenery. Attendees receive a coupon for 15 percent off purchases made that same day. These classes make model railroading less intimidating.

Railfan trips on tourist railroads both in and out of state are sponsored to promote goodwill. Other in-store events are periodically held. Recently, a contest ran challenging customers to create a railroad-oriented model on a 6 x 6 inch board. Winners receive store gift certificates.

A neighboring community has a railway museum with rail access. The museum is a publicly held corporation run by a non-profit public corporation and staffed by volunteers only. The site is owned by the city which has given support through on-site work. Tim Honetschlager was part of the founding group and volunteers his time when able. At the store, employees promote the museum by telling their customers about the facility and providing some financial support. They also enjoy working with local railroading clubs. Discounts are given for products used in club projects and club swap meet flyers are distributed in the store.

Located in a tourist and convention locale, Roy's has customers stop in from all over the world. Most hear about the store from its advertising in the trade publications. Honetschlager said that placing ads in the hobbyist train publications, yellow pages, and underwriting the local public television series on railroading brings good response.

He mentioned that those contemplating opening retail stores should be aware that customers can be very demanding. Often they expect to return items that they have used or broken, destroying the product packaging. Owners need to keep regular hours and enjoy people. Evening and weekend hours are necessary for customer convenience.

LeRoy has been able to provide a career for himself and family through his hobby business. Being in a small hobby market, he does not compete with large, heavily capitalized public companies. Working in an area you love and having your own niche are advantages of owning a hobby-related business.

❖   ❖   ❖

Both Nancy's Notions and Roy's Train World sell through retail and mail order sales. How about starting a catalog of specialty crafts? This could be as simple as a brochure with pictures or sketches of your products. Nancy Zieman started with a one page flyer. Next we'll discover ways to incorporate your hobby, special interest, or talent into your own business.

Hobby Business Opportunities

Besides retail and catalog sales, selling products from a kiosk or cart, especially in a prime location, can be lucrative. If you are considering this route, be sure to read *Treasure Trove of Crafts Marketing Success Secrets* by Barbara Brabec (see Resources). Her book presents a realistic and practical guide that uses many real businesses, some successful, others unsuccessful, as examples. Kiosks and carts have certain advantages. Overhead is low and you can rent these for use during prime sale periods. Mobility allows easy location changes so you can experiment to find out which locations are best. In malls, they are in the midst of traffic, a prime location. This is an inexpensive way to have multiple select locations at peak buying times.

Another book, *Marketing Your Arts & Crafts* by Janice West (see Resources), presents a number of unusual but effective ways to sell what you make. Some of the ideas she presents are marketing to professionals, selling to corporate markets and through new home builders, the Arts in Embassies program, sales co-ops, marketing through brochures, and working with hotel gift shops.

Especially if you reside in a tourist area, the numbers of people with leisure shopping time may support your own or a co-op gallery. To draw in customers, you could provide opportunities for artisans-in-residence.

Some crafts, those with broad appeal, work well as franchises. One franchise sells only baskets, for example.

Selling supplies and products is just one way to turn your hobby into your vocation. Here are some other ways, some of which are incorporated in the preceding companies:

❖ *Specialize.* Becoming an expert in one narrow area can be your claim to fame. Your expertise can be your ticket to getting publicity for your business.

❖ *Become an agent for other hobbyists.* Performing arts and craftspeople can increase their success with an agent to market their business.

❖ *Broker the sale of collectibles.*

❖ *Design and build custom craft show booths.* Because of the variability of weather, a booth is almost a necessity for a participant. While some participants design their own booths, others prefer a prefabricated booth. Portability and compact storage are important. Aim for creative design at a reasonable cost.

❖ *Start a shop catering to display of crafts: frame shop, display boxes, and other display items.* People collect all sorts of things and enjoy displaying their collections. Directories, guides and other publications are in demand for specialty areas. Write your own and market it. You will need to be an expert in your specialty.

❖ *Provide a service for hobbyists.* You could appraise the value of or broker the sale of collectibles, critique a screen play or novel, or any other relevant service.

❖ *Repair or maintain hobbyist equipment.* If your hobby is equipment-intensive, there will be a need to repair and maintain that equipment.

❖ *Design special tools, patterns, products, or clothing for your hobby.* Consign your niche products to local and nationwide stores and catalogs. Design a tool or supply for your niche that is unique, something no one else produces. You will be the only source for this item. Send samples to the hobby magazines. Search out those people who are well known as artisans, and send the device to them with a self-addressed stamped envelope for their comments. If their comments are favorable, obtain written permission to use their endorsement. Endorsements from well-known people are most valuable, but try to get endorsements from all your customers.

❖ *Establish yourself as an expert by writing articles for related publications, teaching courses for local public schools, community colleges, art centers, or giving seminars. Write and sell manuals, plans, newsletters, or books.* Offer private lessons or teach special interest classes offered by municipalities. You could even start your own school or go on the seminar circuit. In photography, for example, a few individuals have developed seminar programs that amateur photographers are willing to pay $200 and up for one day! The value of the information presented by you, your teaching skills, and your marketing will determine your success. Become an expert in a niche area of your hobby. Combining seminars with a marketable product such as books or craft supplies can be a successful venture. Teaching local classes combined with a craft business adds revenue and increases the need for your craft supplies.

❖ *Develop a craft business around home parties.* This is a great low overhead way to get sales. Forming a co-op of artisans, you can feature a wide variety of crafts.

❖ *Make videos for your hobby.* Videos not only describe how to do something, they show. Producing a video can be inexpensive if you work with a young video production company, helping to build its credentials.

❖ *Plan, manage, and promote shows for crafts or collectibles.* These shows can be fund-raisers or private for-profit. Depending on the size of the show, you might be responsible for all details from advertising to participants or specialize in just one aspect such as marketing.

❖ *Rent out your workshop or equipment.* Some businesses provide facilities for hobby work. This would apply to hobbies requiring expensive equipment or have need for large work areas. For example, a shop could provide woodworking equipment, give classes, and rent time for using the equipment. You can sell wood and other supplies.

❖ *Start a consignment store in an upscale or tourist area.* Owners have no cash outlay for products. They can charge the artisan a display fee to stock their items plus take a percentage of the sale price. The downside of consignment is getting enough quality crafts to stock your store. You must create a win-win situation between your business and your consignees. Otherwise, they can sell their crafts elsewhere. The success of a store relies on the display of high quality, in-demand crafts. Consignment shops are often most successful in tourist areas, stocking merchandise reflecting the local attractions. Or you might join with other local artists and craftspeople to jointly run a gallery or shop.

❖ *Of course, you can always turn your hobby into your business.* Hobby businesses are ideal to start as part-time businesses and slowly build toward a full-time or retirement business. A photographer can have a photography studio, buy a franchise like HEADSHOTS, work with real estate agents selling custom homes, specialize in aerial photography, or capture images for transfer to T-shirts, mugs or posters. A videographer can offer videotaping of sports, special events, meetings, and corporate functions or specialize in graphics and animation. Tailors can specialize in alterations, custom clothing design, or custom window coverings. A woodworker might design and produce furniture for custom homes or build custom cabinetry for home businesses. Be flexible in your definition of your hobby to find opportunities such as those mentioned.

❖ *Starting part–time allows you to build slowly.* LeRoy Honetschlager turned his interest in model railroading into a profitable business that provides employment for himself and his family. He started part-time, combining his model railroading shop with an upholstery business. The business grew to full-time and he closed his upholstery shop.

Although hobby businesses are generally less competitive, competition in all businesses is increasing as more people crave control of the future by being self-employed. Search for new ways to provide greater customer service for your clients. Design or search out unique products. Learn everything you can about your competitors.

Hobby Categories

Arts and Crafts

Alterations: clothing

Basket making

Batik

Beadwork

Calligraphy

Candlemaking

Ceramics

Computer graphics

Cooking: specialty

Costume design

Custom clothing design

Custom furnishings: a particular style

Custom pattern design for crafts

Doll making

Drawing: pastels, charcoal, pen &
ink, pencil

Engraving

Fabric painting

Fiberarts

Flower arranging

Fountain design and production

Gift baskets

Glass blowing

Graphic design

Greeting card design: regional cards
or other niche

Hat design

Home decorating

Home accessories

Jewelry making

Kaleidoscopes

Knitting/crochet

Lace making

Lapidiary

Lawn decorations

Leather work

Macramé

Magic

Metal working/machining

Metalwork/sculpture

Modelmaking

Musical instrument construction and
repair

Needlepoint

Neon light design

Oil painting

Origami

Papier-mache

Photography

Plastics design

Pottery

Quilting

Rug making

Scroll saw pattern making

Sculpture	Toy making
Seasonal decorations	Watercolors
Sewing	Weaving
Shell crafts	Welding
Sign making	Windsocks and banners
Silk screening	Woodcarving
Stained glass	Wreaths
Stuffed animal construction	Yard sculptures
Tie dying	

Collecting Hobbies

Antiques	Matchbooks
Art	Miniatures
Autographs	Music
Bonsai	Rocks
Classic cars, motorcycles, other vehicles	Shells
Coin collecting (numismatics)	Spoons
Dolls	Sports memorabilia/cards
Firearms	Stamp collecting
	Thimbles

Special Interest Hobbies

These are some special interests that have good potential as a business in themselves:

Auto repair	Model railroading
Amateur radio	Radio controlled planes
Computers	Rocketry
Electronics, electronics repair	Small appliance repair
Furniture repair	Upholstery, upholstery and leather repair
Home improvement	
Investment tracking	Videography

In large cities, a few videographers have found a niche in news footage. Often at night, local news stations have skeleton crews. Individuals pair police scanners with their camcorders. When hearing about an event on their scanner, they rush to the scene and shoot video. This video is sold to local, or at times even national, stations. Consider news taping in conjunction with your video production business. Warning: you may find yourself in some dangerous situations.

This has created another business opportunity, pager networks. Subscribers are provided with alphanumeric pagers and paged when incidents such as major fires, major injury auto accidents, hostage and barricade situations, severe weather alerts, police pursuits, officer-involved shootings, plane crashes, or search and rescue missions occur. The networks send out information concerning the type of incident, agencies involved, incident location, and radio frequencies to listen.

Amateur (ham), shortwave, citizens' band, two-way commercial and marine radio hobbies all have commercial potential. Stores adding repair to their retail sales are most successful. Directories, guides, accessories, and other related items may start as a part-time business and be built to full-time.

These special interests make good part-time businesses. A few grow into full-time ventures:

❖ Genealogy

❖ Astrology

❖ Fortune telling/psychic/numerology

❖ Handwriting analysis

❖ Beer brewing

You can have a special interest in just about anything!

Animal-Related Hobbies

Two areas to consider in animal-related hobbies are breeding and training. Breeding can encompass dogs, cats, horses, rabbits, pot-bellied pigs, birds, turtles, etc. Training any of the above could be an added profit center to your breeding business. Other profit centers could include pet-boarding or grooming. Consider providing house calls to reach people who are homebound.

People love their pets and will buy things for them. Craftspeople may want to specialize in crafts for pets. Books, publications, and catalogs are opportunities. You will want to find a niche to avoid competition from discounters such as PETsMART. However, you might consider selling your products through a large chain.

As a photographer, could you specialize in pet photos? You can leave literature on your unique service at veterinarian offices and pet supply stores. Team up with a groomer to photograph pets at his or her place of business. Transfer your photos to T shirts, other clothing, mugs, jewelry, and other items. Attend dog, cat, horse, or craft shows to exhibit your items. Mail order catalogs that feature unique items, unobtainable elsewhere, can expand sales.

For horse lovers, you can operate a stable, train race horses, and give lessons. If you live in a scenic area, you could organize group trips. You may also want to sell clothing or other supplies for riders. Considering raising llamas instead. They cannot carry as much weight as a horse, but are amiable, easy to raise, climate-tolerant, eat available vegetation, and need less water. Imagine the novelty of a llama tour!

As the population ages, more people will have pets for companionship. Seniors often regard their pets as very important family member. Their pets may be their primary companions. Look for opportunities here.

For All Hobbies

A good way to find out about existing businesses in special interest is to read all the magazines for your interest. Try to find all the subspecialty publications. Read the ads to see what businesses are already in this market then obtain catalogs from these businesses. Remember that the existence of a full-time business in an area usually means there are enough customers to support it. Be a little careful, though, as some of these may be part-time businesses, unless that's what you want. Read the articles, too, for ideas of new products and services. Read books on the subject. Often the books will include an appendix of suppliers.

Visit any retail hobby stores in your town. While visiting, talk with the owners and ask if they have any interest in selling their business. Visit businesses in other towns to get ideas you can use.

Find any groups with this interest in your community. Local stores, community art centers, and schools will be able to help you locate clubs in your area.

How can you make your business stand out? If you are a natural teacher, write how-to articles or books for your niche. When your writing is published, be sure to include information on your business. Tell people how to reach you and make an offer that encourages inquiry, such as your catalog. Encourage them to contact you with questions. This will be the start of your mailing list and help establish yourself as an expert. If you write for a magazine, you may be able to trade advertising space or its mailing list for payment. Insist on getting your business publicized even if you don't get paid.

Nancy's Notions used public television to fuel the growth of her company. The first show was taped in her home. She produces videos of these shows then sells or rents them. Find a start-up video production company to produce videos for your hobby. It is important for the content of your videos to be strong.

Sports and Entertainment Hobbies

These interests are covered in their own chapter: Entertainment and Leisure Services.

Work at Home Advertisements

You have probably seen ads in the back of popular magazines under Business Opportunities that say you can earn money at home assembling products for companies. Are these viable opportunities or just another marketing scam?

Researching these companies by calling their 800-numbers revealed that they do not provide work, but instead sell a book listing companies that "are currently hiring people to assemble products at home." These companies claim that they will refund the book price if the businesses in their book do not provide work. The book publishers have a toll-free customer service line and promise lifetime phone updates listing additional companies. By publishing a book and not actually employing people, these companies are protected from complaints concerning the employers. The product is the book and these companies fulfill the book orders as promised. You are left to deal with the employing companies on your own.

Most of the employing companies listed in these books charge a deposit, an average of $40, for materials to assemble the products. These deposits are supposed to be refundable if you stop working with that company. Some individuals that have contacted the listed companies say the work done is returned, citing unacceptable quality. Operators insist this is rare and that all companies are monitored. If work is unacceptable, it is returned to be redone. But would the work would ever be judged acceptable? People have complained that they could not get refunds unless the employing company refused to send them products. To get a refund for the book, a copy of the rejecting letter is required. Refusal to pay a materials deposit is not an acceptable reason.

If you are considering buying a book published by one of these companies, get the company name and city so you can call the Better Business Bureau to check its history. According to the Better Business Bureaus called, large numbers of complaints have been received concerning some of these companies.

Future Markets for Hobbyist Businesses

People will continue to follow their passions, pursuing their special interests. This provides long-term markets for businesses that cater to these individuals. Hobbyist markets evolve and change like other markets. Continue to experiment and bring in new ideas. Be open to input from others. Sometimes you can become so involved in your business you miss opportunities. Consider a customer advisory board that will help you find new opportunities for your company. Reward your advisors with merchandise credit or other incentives.

CHAPTER 19

Home Improvement, Construction, and Interior Design

A home improvement business can be an easy business to start, but perhaps that is why it is so difficult to find quality businesses. While customer service is important, more important are the basic skills to do quality work. If you are constantly dealing with unhappy customers, the business will not be enjoyable nor, in the long term, successful. While sales skills may win you an individual job, referrals come from satisfied clients. If you can base your business on referrals, you will reduce the need for expensive advertising.

Consider a construction, home improvement, or interior design business if:

❖ You have solid and in-depth knowledge and skills in your specialty.

❖ You have strong ethics and the desire to do quality work.

❖ You can communicate what needs to be done and why to your customers.

❖ You have a strong work ethic.

Because of the frequent lack of quality in this business, home improvement is wide open for those who have the skills, are committed, and have the patience to build a referral business. People with homes in stable neighborhoods will continue to improve their homes. A growing population means a need for more housing. If you live in a growing area, new construction needs quality craftspeople. Examine your field to find out how you can maintain quality while charging a reasonable price.

The following two companies have focused on quality to build successful companies. Both are home improvement businesses that recognize the importance of professional management, effective marketing, and building on customer referrals.

Ky–Ko Roofing Systems

Many companies are started because people feel they can provide a better service than what is available. Obby Hopper has worked in the roofing business for 15 years, specializing in flat foam roofs. His goal was to start a small roofing company and grow slowly.

The roofing business requires substantial investment capital because of necessary equipment, trucks, and materials. In order to start up, Hopper needed private investors for financing. He located investors, but their ideas for the company differed from Hopper's. They wanted to start big, grow fast, and be the largest roofing contractor in the area. The investors' concept for the company won.

An early challenge in the roofing business is working with new construction. Delayed cash flow creates stresses in a new business. Suppliers who knew Hopper were willing to give him terms on the basis of his experience and personal guarantees.

Another challenge was immediately diversifying into multiple roofing materials. "In retrospect, it might have been preferable to start with one type of roof and then diversify," reflected Tony Gabriel, director of new housing.

In the first year of business, the company did $1.5 million of business. Still a small company with three people doing everything, they presented a big company appearance by professionally-done brochures, contracts, mission statement, logo and trademark, customer warranty certificates, and business cards. To establish credibility, they aligned themselves with people who had been in business a long time: Boards of Realtors, large realty companies, Better Business Bureaus, suppliers, national and local roofing contractors associations, Registrar of Contractors, Building Owners Management Association, and the multi-housing association. To build referrals, Ky-ko installed roofs on homes of the top-producing real estate agents.

Hopper knew if he did quality work at a competitive price, he would be successful. Because of the intense summer heat and dryness, roofing is a challenging business in the Southwest. Tile roofs fare best in the extreme summer heat, but are expensive. Foam flat roofs are popular in the territorial adobe-style homes and commercial buildings, but need more frequent maintenance. Recoating is necessary every five to ten years. Without proper drainage, flat roofs can be very problemsome. A roofing company needs to have expertise in these very different roofing systems. Another challenge is rapid growth and low wages tend to create a shortage of qualified workers. Inexperienced workers may incorrectly install roofs.

Now in its third year, the company has expanded to 70 employees. Its goal is $4 million this year. Business is 50 percent residential. Managers concentrate on hiring the right personnel, watch their cash flow, and do extensive marketing. Dan Stoller, director of sales and marketing, uses his broad experience in marketing, sales, and sales management to bring in new clients and recruit and train top sales professionals. For referring another customer, a free dinner for two is given. Ky-ko gives seminars to help educate real estate professionals and property managers on the importance of quality roofing. The company aims to improve the image of the roofing business. The goal is to build the company to $7 or $8 million, then take it public.

Wonder where the name Ky-ko came from? Obby Hopper's two children are named Kyler and Kohl; put together, Ky-ko.

Park Your Pool

Starting a business based on an entirely new concept is more challenging than founding a venture similar to existing companies. Your customers, unaware of your new product or service, will need more information. They may not feel comfortable purchasing something new and may need to gain familiarity with your company before buying. This additional marketing adds substantially to start-up costs. By recognizing that more time and money will be necessary initially, you can plan ways to sustain your company through this start-up period.

Lloyd Brunn found an unmet need in his unused, unwanted backyard inground pool. Besides requiring year-round maintenance and utility costs, the pool needed major replastering work. When seeking solutions for his pool, he spoke with pool builders who told him that other people had a similar need. He recognized that the presence of a pool added value to his home so he just wanted to "park his pool," allowing a future homeowner to be able to use the pool later. Based on this input, he decided to investigate building a business based on an attractive, cost effective method of temporarily storing an inground pool.

The idea he conceived is to remove the water from the pool then build a wood deck, using specially treated wood, over the empty pool. The deck is strong enough for regular use and will support people, furniture, and potted plants. The new deck provides an attractive backyard area for relaxing and entertaining. Maintenance is very low.

Brunn already had business ownership experience. For nearly 29 years, he operated a custom kitchen cabinet business. He knew firsthand about the challenges of starting a business and recognized the special difficulties of starting a unique business. Prior to start-up in 1991, he hired a part-time marketing person for nine months to investigate the viability of the business. She spoke with homeowners, contractors, and others to determine if there was sufficient need and interest. She also did a patent search to determine if there were any applicable filings. The company name, Park Your Pool, was subsequently trademarked, both locally and nationally. Every Monday morning, the two would meet for a brainstorming session. Brunn found this market research and brainstorming to be very valuable. Additionally, he used university students to do further market research. They used direct mail and response was less than through personal contact. Still, useful information was obtained.

Next, he hired a structural engineering firm to draw up plans for the pool deck cover. The cover is designed to be strong yet cost effective. He took these plans to local cities for approval. Prior to getting the structural design, he found that cities had difficulty comprehending what he had in mind.

Brunn was seeking a business to replace his previous custom kitchen cabinet company. Prefab cabinets were overtaking the custom cabinet business, decreasing his business. He stayed with his previous business for two years after Park Your Pool was founded. Contacts made in that business proved helpful in his new company. He found a source for the specially treated wood used in the pool deck through his plywood supplier from the cabinet business. His subcontractor, who does all the labor in building the custom decks, is someone he has known for years through the cabinet business.

Park Your Pool attracted the attention of local newspapers, resulting in several stories. Response from these stories was not great initially, but he still receives calls from individuals who remember reading about the company. Still, he has not had ample response from print and radio advertising. He also tried hiring an individual to cold call pool owners, but found that people disliked being called, resulting in no sales. Initially, a local television station did a segment on the business. He also had a booth for two years at the local Home Show, which enabled customers to see what his business had to offer. When adding up the costs and results from the Home Show booth, he does not feel that it is the best use of company resources.

His best response is from television advertising. On the cable Weather Channel, during the local forecast, he runs a scrolling message on the bottom of the screen, describing the business. He rotates this advertising through the different local market areas. He has expanded advertising on this channel, now using a professionally produced advertisement. Advertising was also run on CNN and A&E, but he did not receive enough added calls using these networks to justify the cost. Brunn observed that it takes about three years to get a unique business such as his solvent.

Brunn speaks with potential customers, makes appointments, does all sales, budgets and authorizes all advertising, designs the deck, and makes out material lists. Eight out of ten people who buy his custom pool covers have pools that need major repair. These people either need to make a major investment in renovating the pool, fill in the pools, or have a custom pool deck built. Some people travel frequently and don't want to worry about a pool nor pay to have it professionally maintained when they are not using it.

Brunn stresses the need for adequate capital in starting a unique business such as Park Your Pool. He does not recommend using a home equity loan on your house to finance your new business. Friends have bought businesses using their home as equity, then their business did not grow fast enough to make payments.

Costs need to watched carefully. Brunn stressed perfecting your ideas, continually improving upon the original concept. "It is important to be totally committed, to be willing to devote as many hours as needed to make the business successful."

The company is currently working on a practical design for temporary coverage of pools during the colder winter months.

❖   ❖   ❖

When speaking to other business owners, some told me that their customers did not appreciate quality. It is true that a few people do want the lowest price regardless of quality although these same people will probably be unhappy later if they select their contractor based on price only. Most people don't appreciate quality because they don't know what to look for. The job of the business owner is to point out differences between high and low quality then explain the effect of these differences.

If you are a painter and competing with lower quality painters who put only one coat of paint on a wall, demonstrate the difference by showing examples. By seeing the difference in durability, people will understand that it is cheaper to paint two coats now while everything is covered and masked than having to go back and repaint later. Remember that you are a specialist in your area. What appears obvious to you is not so apparent to others.

Home Improvement Opportunities

Plumbers, Painters, Electricians, Heating and Air Conditioning

For experienced, quality tradespeople in populated areas, work is always available. Some businesses struggle, though, due to their lack of marketing savvy. Consider developing a specialty, in which you become the local expert, within your field. Look for ways to get the media interested in your business, giving valuable free advertising.

Work on building a referral system by encouraging satisfied customers to send friends and family to you. You might give them a slight discount in price or added service for allowing a company sign in their yard. Ask if you can use their name as a referral. Give them a dinner for two at a local restaurant for referrals that result in new customers. Make sure you build good contacts and reputation with local home improvement centers. As long as your work doesn't detract from their business, they may be a big referral source. Buy materials from a supplier that will give you referrals. Make it easy for them to refer by keeping them supplied with business cards and information.

If appropriate, take pictures of your work for potential customers. Occasionally do public service work where your company name will gain visibility. Make sure your company trucks and cars are nicely painted and that drivers are courteous. When you do a unique project, send a press release to your local newspapers, radio, and television stations. Consider providing employees with clothing and hats with the company logo for a professional appearance.

Specialty Contractors: Custom Work

Long-term success demands competence. By concentrating on one specialty, you can more quickly get the required skills and position yourself as an expert to gain visibility. More frequently, people are adding custom touches to their homes.

Some areas in which to specialize include: stone, stucco, brick or concrete masonry. Stone is the perennial durable material. Many people enjoy bringing natural materials into their homes. Your clientele will be primarily in upscale neighborhoods and commercial buildings. Other specialties include corian, hardwood or other custom flooring, solar technology, custom windows, skylights, wrought iron work, and others.

Focus on remodeling kitchens, bathrooms, or adding decks, porches, garages, or separate home offices. Home offices that are entirely separate from the house more easily qualify for IRS home office deduction. Remember that, although you have seen many projects from start to finish, your clients may have difficulty envisioning final results. By integrating computer imaging into your business, clients can see the completed project in advance. Customer satisfaction, and therefore referrals, will increase as will your profits.

Do-it-Yourself Advisors

Despite lack of time, finances often demand that homeowners do work themselves. Many home improvement stores have capitalized on this strong trend by offering plans and seminars to do-it-yourselfers. Resourceful stores will find that they can offer more. Why not, for a small charge, give on-site consultations prior to starting projects? How about gathering competent contractors who will assist homeowners with the difficult aspects of a job? A small company could work in partnership with a home improvement center to offer these services.

Custom Shutters

Shutters are back in style. Draperies collect dust and may fade. Shutters can last a lifetime and may provide more security and privacy than drapes. A special type of shutter called security shutters is available which secures windows against break-ins. If a family is gone frequently or has windows in high traffic areas, these shutters may be worth their cost by acting as a deterrent.

Custom Furniture

The recent popularity of rustic and southwestern style furniture has led to successful businesses that design and manufacture these furnishings. Unlike intricate older style furniture, these styles are more simply constructed yet unique in appearance. Bookcases always seem to be in demand, especially from businesses that are flexible enough to build custom sizes.

Antiques

Some people love the beauty and craftsmanship of antiques. If you are an antique admirer, multiple business possibilities exist. With a significant investment, you could start an antique store. Brokering the sale of antiques is another way to become involved with sales. Appraisal services are run by experts in the valuation of antiques. Repairing, refinishing, or reproducing antiques are for those with hands-on skills. Combinations of these services work well.

Bathtub Repair

A new bathtub is a major expense. Companies have developed repair materials and liners to delay replacement. This market is becoming crowded in some areas so research your opportunities first. Several franchises have developed their own materials and products for this market.

Regrouting

The task of regrouting tile is tedious. Now a couple of franchises are available to assist homeowners in regrouting. By developing your own methods of revitalizing old tile, you might be able to bypass the franchise route.

Basement Waterproofing

In some areas, damp basements are a real problem. Special expertise is needed to successfully resolve leaking basements. By working with a competent established business, you can gain the necessary expertise before proceeding on your own.

Snow Removal/Swimming Pool Service

Snow removal and pool service are seasonal businesses, but they can be combined with another business to provide year-round work. Snow removal could be combined with parking lot cleaning and striping.

Lawn Care and Landscape Design

Lawn care services should consider expanding their services by adding lawn installation, thatch removal, aerating, fertilizing, pruning, and other services. Focusing on large properties or commercial accounts may help build your business more quickly, but also requires more skills.

Combining a nursery business with landscape design and computer imaging will increase business. Visualizing final results is difficult for your customers, so make it easy with computer imaging. The cost of systems has substantially decreased and the price will be quickly recovered in additional business.

Sprinkler System Design and Installation

An in-ground, automatic sprinkler system is a great convenience, keeping a lawn healthy without much hassle. Properly designed systems can handle all landscaping from grass through trees. Again, this is seasonal in most areas so may need to be combined with a complementary seasonal business.

Storage Sheds

Americans seem to be natural accumulators, often outgrowing basements and garages. Storage sheds provide additional on-property storage. There is room for ingenuity in the development of new designs.

Custom Awnings

This is a great business for the southern states and California where there is an abundance of sun. Awnings are an inexpensive way to dress up a house or business while providing shade. Again, adding computer imaging to your business will result in more sales and realistic expectations concerning the completed appearance.

Employment Firm, Trade School, Referral Service: Construction Work

In fast growing areas, demand for skilled workers often exceeds supply. A trade school to provide skills training for the trades would help meet demand. Another business would be a screening agency where tradespeople could register and their backgrounds checked. Contractors needing workers could hire screened subcontractors from the business. The general public would feel more comfortable with hiring contractors for projects if they had a better way to assess their past work.

Home Security: Beyond Security Systems

Security systems are deterrents, but hardly infallible. Increasing home security requires looking at the entire property. No one system can completely protect property, but by combining multiple deterrents, the risk to the assailant becomes greater. Using landscaping, security lighting, alarms, protected windows, pets, and other deterrents in combination may make the crime not worth the effort. A company that provides a more complete service for home and building protection will find that a large market exists for its services.

Mobile Homes

As the population ages, sales of mobile homes will increase. Demand for mobile home accessories will grow concurrently. Owners will need a place to park these mobile homes, so if you live in a warm climate and own properly zoned land, consider a mobile home park.

Customizing Homes for Elderly and Physically Disabled

As people age, they are more likely to have physical impairments. Falls are a major cause of hospitalization in the elderly. Specializing on customizing homes to help these individuals become more independent or doing preventive remodeling to increase safety will meet a growing need.

House Washing/Gutter Cleaning

With a pressure washer, you can clean homes, office buildings, and gutters. With a little ingenuity, you may find other uses as well, such as washing boats, mobile homes, and aircraft. Combine this with a complementing seasonal business in cold climates.

Carpet Cleaning/Water Clean-up/Odor Removal/Crime Clean-up

While carpet cleaning is an overcrowded field in most vicinities, crime clean-up is a growing market. Although this is not a business for everyone, if you have the grit to handle these situations, there is opportunity. Knowledge of disposal of hazardous materials and adherence to regulations is necessary to protect your business from fines and lawsuits. Expect to work unusual hours. Make contacts with local law enforcement and large apartment complexes.

A Unique Idea

Companies based on a new product or service need to provide lots of information to prospective customers so they understand the benefits. Visual information is most effective. Combine visual aids such as pictures of completed jobs, before and after computer imaging for prospective customers, and a short video. A video could be sent to interested homeowners or played at home shows and home improvement centers. Many potential clients might delay buying because they are uncertain how the finished product will look. Computer imaging alleviates these fears.

These businesses may be more competitive, but are worth consideration:

❖ Interior design company.

❖ Window repair and installation, window tinting, storm windows, custom windows, and sunscreens.

❖ Locksmith.

❖ Septic tank service.

❖ Pool design and installation (lap, beach-type, zero boundary, fiberglass, vinyl, plaster, pebbletech, tile, hot tub, lagoon, fountains, ponds, waterfalls).

❖ Patios, gazebos, patio covers, and misting systems.

❖ Aluminum siding, vinyl siding, stucco, brick and other exterior finishing.

❖ Pest control: choose a specialty for name recognition. Termite inspection and treatment.

❖ Fencing.

❖ Driveway, tennis or basketball court, and parking lot resurfacing.

Future Home Improvement Opportunities

With good technical skills, marketing, and professional management, you can build a referral business that will generate new customers for you. Personable individuals with good communication skills and tact have an advantage. Too many companies in this field lack the professionalism, quality, and basic business sense to be successful. But their deficits open up opportunities for you.

CHAPTER 20

Import and Export Businesses

*M*any opportunities exist for U.S. companies that wish to import or export products. Even very small businesses are able to find opportunities in international markets. Doing business internationally brings many new issues to deal with, but there are ways to minimize the complexities.

Consider an import or export business if:

❖ You have lived in another country, speak the language, have business contacts abroad, and, anticipating entering foreign markets, have gained international business experience.

❖ You wish to expand abroad to increase your potential market.

❖ You have saturated the U.S. market and are looking for ways to grow.

❖ You want to spread your costs over a wider market, achieving greater economies of scale.

❖ You want to find out what your competitors are doing. Direct competition will give you this information quickly.

❖ Clients from other countries are already customers and you wish to expand these markets.

People often think of importing and exporting as the sale of products. Laser Re-Nu, an international company, exports a pre-packaged business to counter large exports of capital from other countries, balancing trade.

Laser Re-Nu

Although Bill Gates started Microsoft in his garage, some say that the day of starting a successful business in your home garage is over. Not so! Laser Re-Nu, a million dollar plus laser cartridge recycling business was started in the garage of its vice president, Ed Karian.

In 1988, Karian was a manufacturer's representative, selling business products. Looking for a new business that would generate more profits, a friend already in the laser cartridge recycling business sold him on that business. To learn the necessary skills, Karian, his son, Christopher, and wife, Sara, took a training course. Then he started up—in his garage. In the beginning, Karian's wife and his son ran the business full-time with Ed still working as a rep, although he spent much time in his new business.

In 1992, Karian made the decision to become involved in the business full-time, moving it out of his garage. He heard that a competitor, Lohr Company, was trying to sell his business so Ed approached the company with the suggestion to merge their businesses. By gaining the additional client base from the second business, the profit potential was adequate to move into leased quarters. Karian used a professional consultant with negotiating experience to set up the merger. He says, in retrospect, that getting professional expertise was a good decision. At this time, his son Christopher Goshkarian, was appointed President and is involved with both U.S. and international operations.

Laser cartridge recycling is an environmental service business. Because cartridges are recycled, they don't pile up in our landfills. Karian, while reading the local weekly business journal, noticed a story about McDonnell-Douglas and a spin-off called Ecotech International. Since Ecotech sounded like an environmental company, out of curiosity he gave them a call to find out exactly what business they were in.

Ecotech specializes in countertrade and offsets. When large companies do business internationally, foreign countries often stipulate that, for the opportunity to do business, the incoming company must create jobs and export potential for the country. When McDonnell-Douglas sells airplanes to a country, it must create opportunities for earnings within the buyer's country to even the trade deficit. This is called countertrade. Ecotech finds opportunities for the foreign country to enable U.S. companies to negotiate their exports. And it just so happened that Ecotech was looking for a laser cartridge recycling company to set up similar businesses in foreign countries.

Through its connections with Ecotech, Laser Re-Nu has set up a turn key operation in Abu Dhabi, United Arab Emirates and Kuala Lumpur, Malaysia. A joint venture has been started in Mexico City, where there is less competition. In a metropolitan area of about 23 million, there were only seven similar businesses. Of these seven, only a couple provide competitive products. Other sites are being negotiated. Laser Re-Nu provides equipment, continuing supplies, raw materials, and training for these international operations. Karian expects the international portion of the business will become the predominate profit center.

Karian has found extensive assistance available for small businesses through the U.S. and State Departments of Commerce, local World Trade Center, and Arizona Department of Commerce. This assistance has saved his company thousands of dollars.

Expanding internationally creates unique challenges. For example, when training individuals for the Abu Dhabi turn key operation, the company encountered problems in getting a temporary visa for the individuals to be trained. Finally, after being unable to resolve the situation, Laser Re-Nu sent one of its own people to Abu Dhabi to train the individuals on-site.

Negotiations with foreign countries take much longer than between domestic companies. Many countries spend much time forming relationships. Foreign companies need to feel comfortable doing business with you and they want to learn more about you personally. Patience is important.

There are now 10,000 to 12,000 laser cartridge recyclers in the U.S. The industry is very mature with several very professional publications including *Recharger* magazine and *R & R*. The existence of these publications has given the industry access to the technical expertise and suppliers necessary to develop quality products. The laser printer manufacturers have created a series of challenges for this industry by making their cartridges difficult for others to recycle. But the recyclers have been able to overcome these obstacles. There are so many recyclers in business now that there is wealth of expertise. This expertise is shared within the business through these publications. Because these companies operate primarily within their own geographic areas, there is not a high level of competition among businesses located in other areas.

Laser Re-Nu has expanded into laser printer service and repair by becoming certified to work on several manufacturers' printers. It recently added a site in Tucson, forming a partnership with an investor/manager that needed Laser Re-Nu's expertise to expand its business. The main operation employs 18 people. The Tucson site has five employees.

A new subsidiary company to provide computer solutions for small- to medium-size businesses called One Source Solutions is scheduled to open in October 1996. The company is certified as a Microsoft Solutions Provider. Classes in Microsoft software products will be held at its location, adjacent to Laser Re-Nu's main location. One Source Solutions will also put together computer systems and provide repairs and service contracts, taking over Laser Re-Nu's service business.

The company views all inquiries as potential opportunities and as a result has been able to find situations that others have overlooked. Karian had an idea for some equipment that would help automate part of the recycling process. He needed an industrial designer to design it. Ed approached the local state university engineering department with no response. One day a young man from the university walked in the door, introducing himself as an industrial design student. Might they have any work for him? Ed sat down and talked with the young man, telling him what he needed. The results were very satisfactory. This equipment is now being used in their turn key plants.

By seeking out opportunities, Laser Re-Nu has become a thriving international business in a very short time.

❖   ❖   ❖

The next two companies fit the more traditional vision of importing and exporting. Maribel Guglielmo used her expertise to start her company, adjusting her business to take advantage of opportunities she has discovered.

Mina International

When you start an import/export business, you face the challenges of domestic companies plus all the added complexities of working with another country. How much and how will you get paid? Currency shifts change your actual compensation. Foreign small businesses come and go; can you trust them? In many other countries, it is necessary to develop a relationship before they will do business with you. This is a slow process. Cultural differences can lead to misunderstanding. Even very large companies have made major cultural blunders, costing them time and money.

Maribel Guglielmo, a former international banker, uses her experience to run Mina International. With her international contacts and excellent reputation, she has built a successful import/export business. Even with her background, she found it took a couple of years to build trust with her manufacturers and three years to make a profit.

The company has four divisions: food, liquor, automotive, and consulting. Mina exports meat—beef, pork, turkey and chicken—to manufacturers in Mexico. From Mexico, she imports finished Mexican food products, then, utilizing a 6,000-square foot warehouse, distributes these products throughout the U.S. Guglielmo, although not of Mexican descent, graduated from a college in Mexico, making key contacts while living there.

The liquor division imports tequila from Mexico and wine from Spain which is sold to U.S. distributors. The automotive division exports GM parts to Mexico added to in-state sales. The depressed Mexican economy has limited automotive exports. Maribel consults for companies interested in exporting and occasionally, importing.

Finances are difficult internationally. Besides working with language differences and fluctuating currency valuations and conversion, you must be sure you will get paid. Working with a bank that has international experience is a necessity. Your banker can be an excellent consultant, often at no added cost.

Despite the added complications of doing business internationally, your company must make it easy to do business. Long distance calls, travel, and shipping are part of the cost of doing business. "Make it as easy for the foreign company to work with you as any of their domestic customers," suggests Guglielmo.

If you are a manufacturer with one or a related line of products, you can afford to sell in many countries. With a lot of products, concentrating on one or two countries is most feasible. Through her first lean years, Guglielmo learned to focus her business. Doing many things just wasn't productive.

Alabaster is the product that got Guglielmo started in business in 1987. She started part-time, expanding to full-time in 1989. Relatives in Spain had originally approached her to sell alabaster in the U.S. She no longer sells the product.

Even with her background, start-up required much perseverance and long hours six to seven days a week. If she could repeat this experience, she would have focused her company sooner. At first, she tried to do too many things and this slowed growth. Guglielmo stressed the importance of having enough financial resources to get you through until you are profitable. In international businesses, more time is generally needed. By 1996, Mina International has grown to seven employees and sales of over $2 million.

Guglielmo noted that many import/export companies are started because an individual can speak another language, has foreign contacts, or has a "hot" idea. All of these are valuable resources, but knowledge of international business is crucial. Companies without this expertise often last only a few months. These fly-by-night businesses create a climate lacking in trust, making start-up for others more difficult. If you are interested in importing or exporting, take international business courses or team with an experienced person, Guglielmo recommends. Bankers are an excellent source of free consulting. She has not received much help from governmental sources.

❖   ❖   ❖

Although Mia Rogers' dad had been in business, Rogers didn't really consider the same business until her husband brought up the possibility. Her father was able to advise them although he initially let them start up on their own.

Pachinko Paradise

Mia Rogers had no intention of pursuing her father's business. As a newlywed in August 1993, she and her husband, Mike, discussed how they would make a living. Mike, with a business degree, and Mia, with a bachelor's degree in child psychology and the intention of earning her doctorate, discussed different job possibilities. Her dad advised them to do something on their own, to start their own business.

In 1972, Mia's father, during a leave to Japan while serving in Vietnam, visited Japanese pachinko parlors. Pachinko is the largest industry in Japan. The owner of Heiwa, one of the largest pachinko manufacturers, is on *Forbes*' list of the richest people in the world. Pachinko machines resemble a vertical pinball machine. Small metal balls are repeatedly launched and ricochet between a complex pattern of nails and spinners, hopefully ending up in a scoring slot, which releases more balls. The metal balls make a tremendous racket which, when added to the additional lights and "slot machine-type" sound effects, contribute to the excitement. In 1972, these machines were flip lever mechanical devices. Her dad thought that pachinko machines would be popular in the U.S. He decided to buy five used pachinkos to bring back home. Confusion, due to language differences, resulted in buying 500 not five machines. Roger's dad wired his wife to raise cash to pay for this purchase.

With 500 machines, he needed to open a business to sell them. The first store was opened in San Mateo, California in 1973. From this store, he opened stores across the country. Sears and Roebuck approached him, wanting to make the machines available through its catalogs. Pachinkos were sold through Montgomery Ward, the Air Force Exchange, and Gemco.

In 1980, the pachinko manufacturers upgraded to computerized machines. Used machines would now cost $800 to $1,000, no longer reasonable for home or arcade use. Her dad received one of the new machines and found it unreliable. He decided to close all the stores and abandon the business. The last store closed in 1984.

The Japanese sent him another pachinko in 1989. This one was much improved and exciting to play. Her dad chose to restart the business from Dallas through mail-order and distributors only. The Japanese replace all the machines in a pachinko parlor every six months to install new models. The used machines must be sold outside Japan.

By 1993, her dad was semi-retired from the business. While Mia and Mike were investigating which business to start, Mike was curious about the pachinko business. Why not try that?

Once they decided they would start their own pachinko enterprise, they were unsure where to locate their business. Professional males between the ages of 25 and 45 are the primary buyers. Roger's mother had recurrent dreams about the Rogers' proposed business. In the past, her mother had been very accurate with her repeated dreams. She dreamed that they would locate in a suburb of Phoenix. Despite hearing her mother's predictions, they researched rapidly growing U.S. cities with their target market and came up with two cities, Phoenix and Austin. Never having visited Phoenix, they decided to take a trip there and liked the area.

Using money saved up for a house, they started their business instead. Moving to Phoenix on November 10, 1993, the business opened November 19. After three months in their first location, they moved to a larger store. Since then they have expanded once into an adjacent suite.

The Rogers sell mainly through catalogs and independent distributors. Retail sales are only two to three percent of their business and limited to holiday seasons. Besides pachinko machines, which account for more of their sales and 50 percent of their profits, they also sell Japanese slot machines, Pachi–slos.

A Pachi-slo is nearly identical in appearance to the American slot machine except the spinning wheels are individually stopped by push buttons. Pachi-slos have bonus cycles which, once entered, result in almost continuous wins. In Japan, people play for prizes rather than money. Pachi-slos use either tokens or quarters.

Roger's sister also opened a store, Pachinko Palace, in Indianapolis. When asked about the pros and cons of a family business, she replied that one of the advantages of this business is she has grown very close to her sister and father, both of whom she speaks with through the business nearly every day. Working with her husband is wonderful, too. Her dad let them figure the business out on their own, finally visiting two months later. Only then did he offer suggestions, which have proved valuable.

Communication has been their chief difficulty in importing. Rogers speaks a few words of Japanese, learned during their yearly visits to Japan. The Japanese have also visited them. Miscommunication has sometimes resulted in interesting situations, such as receiving different models and different amounts than expected. They use primarily fax for communication since written English is commonly understood in Japan.

For the first year, they had no employees, but worked long hours sometimes even sleeping in the store. The business requires drastically varying hours. Some weeks they work 70 hours a week to fill large orders while other weeks are slow. They now have a full-time secretary and warehouse manager plus four part-time employees. Their part-time employees need to flexible to adapt to the variable hours. At first they tried hiring university students, but they were not committed. They have found it helps to hire employees who live nearby.

Once the machines arrive, they need to be converted due to voltage differences, then checked, and occasionally repaired. Shipping from Japan to Phoenix has been easy. Machines are freighted to Los Angeles then loaded on a semi to Phoenix. Shipping within the U.S. is another story, having experienced a great number of problems getting their heavy packages delivered without damage.

Besides yearly trips to Japan, the Rogers also attend five to six conventions a year for surplus dealers and billiards. Billiards parlors are popular places for the pachinko and pachi-slo machines.

❖   ❖   ❖

All of the above companies had either experience (Mina International) or assistance in international marketing. Doing business internationally involves complexities that require special knowledge. Before considering an international business, get the necessary experience or seek assistance prior to start-up.

Import and Export Opportunities

Finding an Agent

Finding an international agent to assist your business in importing or exporting products is similar to selecting any other business consultant. Carefully interview potential agents. This demonstrates your professionalism and commitment.

Questions you might ask:

❖ How long have you been in business?

❖ How many clients have you assisted in importing/exporting?

❖ What countries have you worked with?

❖ How do you bill for your services?

❖ How much time will you devote to providing services for my business?

❖ Are you working with any of our firm's competitors?

❖ Do you have any key government contacts?

❖ Are there any problems in your firm that I should know about?

❖ Can you give me five business contacts of similar companies you have worked with?

Talk to several companies then talk to other import or export businesses to determine what fees are reasonable. You will generally be charged a set fee or a percentage. Pay only for what you actually sell. Be sure to retain the actual negotiating ability for all deals so you remain in control.

Importing

With so many companies today manufacturing abroad, importing is becoming more prevalent. Baby Think It Over manufactures its electronic boxes for the company's infant simulators in China to reduce costs. Lower manufacturing labor costs in other countries have caused many companies to move plants abroad.

Other companies import unique products from abroad. Pachinko Paradise has built its business on imports of Japanese pachinko and slot machines, a product unavailable from U.S. sources. By exporting used machines, the Japanese lower their costs, as machines were previously destroyed.

When importing products, obtain a list of potential producers. The World Trade Center, with locations worldwide, will provide you with a list of companies if you are a member. Becoming a member entitles you to a number of services. If you are actively importing or exporting, you might consider membership.

Check with United States Customs to see if you will need to pay tax or other fees on your product. Is a license required for importing this product? Are there quotas or quarantines? Make sure that you know all the charges that will apply before negotiating a final deal.

Make arrangements for warranty of products in advance. You may be able to negotiate a situation where you are the factory representative and get a percentage for each returned or repaired product. Make sure you will have access to necessary parts.

Exporting

If you already have a successful product or have developed a product with international appeal, you should consider extending your market worldwide. Air Taser, which developed a personal protection device, marketed abroad almost immediately. In some foreign countries it is illegal to own a gun, so an Air Taser® is one of the few alternatives.

Trojan Technologies' UV water disinfection products fill a need for drinking water purification in Europe, where more problems exist with drinking water quality. In Holland, well water is taxed, so using other sources of available water is cost-effective. By spreading costs over a larger market, prices can be lowered to be more cost competitive with existing technologies, a major concern with environmental businesses.

ARBICO sells its beneficial insects worldwide. Soil depletion and growing resistance to pesticides is a global concern. ARBICO networks with U.S. and European producers to provide a broad range of solutions to pest problems. Individual producers can concentrate their efforts on producing large quantities of a few beneficial insects while ARBICO functions as their distributor. In addition, ARBICO is a large producer of beneficial insects, specializing in fly control. Sally Fox, Natural Cotton Colours, has found a worldwide market for her organically-bred natural colored cotton.

Mina International combines importing and exporting, targeting areas where it has discovered a need. Maribel Guglielmo's experience in international banking has proved valuable in gaining the confidence of foreign companies.

Documentation

A number of documents such as a Bill-of-Laden, Certificate of Origin, Commercial Invoice, Consular Invoice, Dock Receipt, Export Declaration, Insurance Certificate, Letter of Credit, and Transmittal Letter are necessary to ensure that your products get to destination and means of payment is clear. Have an experienced person draw up these documents to make sure you get paid. Except for some shipments to Canada, an export license is required. There are different types of licenses, depending on your products. If you qualify to use a general license, you simply need to indicate the proper code on your paperwork. Generally your responsibility ends once the product has been loaded on the ship or plane. The agent in the receiving country is usually responsible for any taxes or fees in his or her country.

Expanding internationally does require patience. Often getting things done takes longer than anticipated, especially in certain countries, due to the culture and bureaucracy. When entering foreign markets, a long-term perspective is helpful. Initially, these markets may not meet your investment costs. But, over time, your commitment can be very rewarding.

Decisions about markets to enter depend on your product. Guglielmo advises selling in many countries if your have a single product or line of similar products. With a variety of products, you should focus on one or two countries so you do not spread your resources too thinly.

Markets outside the U.S. are four times the size of our domestic market. Ignoring foreign markets limits your competitiveness by the lack of your ability to spread costs over a larger market.

Government Financial Assistance

Eximbank, the Export-Import Bank of the United States, offers loan and loan guarantees for up to 85 percent of value for repayment of export credit. The bank provides additional assistance to companies in international business.

Through the Gold Key Program, the Department of Commerce will set up confirmed appointments for you with business owners and key personnel in countries you want to work with and even provide translators. The charge for setting these appointments is very reasonable. Once you have established dates you will be visiting a specific country, they can proceed in setting up your itinerary of appointments.

Your foreign contacts will be impressed if you send advance information and prepare for your appointments by learning as much as possible about the country and culture. Be sure you keep all appointments or call ahead if plans change. Lack of courtesy in notifying the respective companies gives the United States a bad name and jeopardizes your chance of doing business ever with this company. Unfortunately, a few U.S. businesses have not appreciated this wealth of help and the program could be discontinued.

Independent Distributor

Many countries do business internationally via independent international distributors. These distributors are either exclusive distributors, or more commonly, representatives of similar products. Because they concentrate on one or a few countries, they know their markets well and are familiar with local protocols. This is one of the least capital-intensive ways to becoming an international company and a business opportunity for qualified individuals. Trojan Technologies, designers and producers of UV water purification systems, use independent reps to sell to international markets.

Freight Forwarders and Shipping Consultant

International shipping may require a combination of different means of transportation. Products may be transported by truck to the nearest port, loaded on a boat, then picked up at the foreign port and travel again by truck or train to their distribution point or final destination. Arranging this transportation to ensure all paperwork is correct, all parties paid, and that goods arrive on time and in satisfactory condition is a large chore. A freight forwarder, another business opportunity, acts as your agent in getting your products to destination.

Interpreter and Protocol Consultant

In some foreign countries, English is widely spoken while in others language can still be a barrier. In addition to the language differences, there are significant cultural variations between countries. A gesture that means one thing in the U.S. may have an entirely different interpretation abroad. For instance, in Japan, individuals may nod their heads when you are speaking. This means they hear what you say, not that they agree with you. If you misinterpret this nodding, you may think you have a confirmed business deal when you do not. For individuals who have lived in other cultures, you may be able to advise U.S. companies and act as an interpreter.

International Services

Marketing services internationally is still a new frontier. Patent and intellectual rights issues in many companies are far from being resolved. As with other problematic areas, if you are knowledgeable, you may find opportunity to assist companies with their challenges.

Future International Opportunities

More companies will seek out international opportunities. Marketing internationally can be a way to expand your client base or a business in itself. Unless your company is strictly local, learning about international markets may open up new opportunities for your business.

CHAPTER 21

Legal Services and Products

The legal market is perhaps the most difficult field to enter without prior legal experience and inside contacts. Lawyers may be unreceptive to non-lawyers. Gatekeepers—receptionists, legal secretaries and paralegals—abound. If your business will be working directly with lawyers, you will need to establish a relationship with a lawyer who is supportive, preferably one with a wide network of contacts and influence. Perhaps tying your business to another that has already broken into this market would enable your business to become established.

Opportunities abound in this market with its rapid expansion, due to increased numbers of lawyers, rising crime, and growth in litigation. Consider a business in legal products and services if:

❖ You have experience in the legal field.

❖ You have close contacts with lawyers.

❖ You have developed products or services for lawyers and law offices.

Of all countries, the U.S. has by far the largest number of lawyers per capita. While other professions have cut back enrollments to adjust for numbers of practicing professionals, law schools continue to graduate more lawyers. The American Bar Association is the largest voluntary professional association with a membership of over 350,000, creating a huge market for products and services for the legal profession.

Nolo Press

In Latin, "Nolo con tendre" means I do not choose to publish. Ralph Warner, co-founder of Nolo Press, a pioneering publishing company of self-help legal books and software, did not set out to become a law publisher. In the early 1970s, Warner was a California lawyer working for Legal Aid, giving free advice to people who could not afford legal counsel. He found many people needed legal advice and, although they were working and didn't qualify for free aid, could not afford to hire a lawyer. He wanted to provide legal help for these people, as well.

Nolo Press was started in 1971 when Warner and Charles Sherman, a fellow lawyer, wrote two books on self-help law: *How To Do Your Own Divorce in California* and *The California Tenant's Handbook*. Unable to find a publishing company interested in publishing self-help law books, they self-published them.

Nolo Press gives people a choice: either hire a lawyer, do the work themselves, or at least, be informed and savvy legal consumers. By making legal information available in inexpensive books, Nolo Press makes the legal system more fair and accessible to all. Warner recognized a need for low-cost legal advice at a time when this need was not yet defined. The need is still very much present today. Legal services should be more accessible, and not just to those who can afford the cost of hiring a lawyer.

From his own start-up experience, Warner advises, "New business owners should be careful not to spend or borrow too much." Nolo Press was started in a tiny attic in Berkeley. At first, Warner continued to practice as a legal aid lawyer and director for the Contra Costa County Legal Services Foundation. Three years later, after additional books had been written, the business became full-time with a staff of three including his lawyer—now partner and wife, Toni. By 1980, the number of employees had grown to ten.

Over 80 percent of the books are written in-house. Warner decides which topics to publish. He is committed to empowering people with the knowledge to do routine legal work on their own. "Business owners should choose an area of passion for their business," he advises. When you love what you are doing, it is easier to get through the lean years, difficult times, and challenges that you will encounter.

Warner says that he could have ceased business many times, but his confidence in meeting a need kept him moving ahead.

Nolo Press publishes a quarterly catalog, *Nolo News*, of over 100 legal self-help books and software. In tune with their mission to educate non-lawyers on legal issues, practical articles about legal topics and lawyer jokes are included in their catalog. The topics include common legal situations that are encountered in our family and business life. Previous titles are revised frequently to keep pace with constant changes in laws. Willmaker, software to prepare your own will, was first published in 1985 and is updated on a yearly basis. A half million copies have been sold. Every year around 10 new titles are added.

Believing in the importance of growing intellectually and adapting to change, Warner has expanded into legal software and established online sites. Nolo Self-Help Law Center can be accessed on America Online and the World Wide Web. Selected chapters from their books are featured as well as demos of software, *Nolo News* articles, user polls and feedback, information on court decisions and legislation plus their catalog and online ordering. Use the keyword NOLO, for America Online.

Now located in a converted clock factory in Berkeley, the number of employees and catalog of titles has doubled since 1990. Currently, there are 95 employees, of whom 15 are lawyers. In 1996, Nolo Press is celebrating its 25th anniversary. The company has expanded from personal legal issues to small business legal needs. The mission is the same: provide knowledge of legal issues for those who cannot afford the cost of a lawyer. Indicative of the quality of information, Nolo Press has never been sued.

Reading Nolo's books or browsing one of its online sites, you can see these people care about their work. They are committed to producing high quality information that can be understood by non-lawyers. All their books have a 100 percent moneyback guarantee. Warner remains hands-on by writing and editing many of Nolo's books. Besides commitment to his passion, Warner also wants his work to be fun. This attitude carries through to his books, which are easy-to-read with a touch of humor.

One of the factors in the success of Nolo Press is its commitment in staying within their niche. Rather than expanding to non-legal topics, they develop the depth of the self-help legal market. This focus has made the company name synonymous with self-help legal information. Being the first to find a need and fill it provides a niche that can be a pathway to success.

Video Law Services

After deciding to open her own business and move to Jacksonville, Florida, Michaela Miller, a former executive producer for NBC affiliates, opened a video production business. Her company began by videotaping weddings. After being in the news business, Miller felt she was not a good spectator and wanted to do something more substantial. The wedding video business also proved to be stressful because there is no chance to redo a shoot if results aren't satisfactory.

During her first year in business, Miller received a few calls from lawyers inquiring about video work and was fascinated by how they were using video in their field. In 1987, she decided to do a documentary on utilizing video in litigation. *Legal Video Documents*, a three-hour production, was the result.

This production became a springboard for specializing in legal video. Video Law Services was founded. Miller attended a meeting for litigators and then exhibited at trial lawyer seminars. The company produces day-in-the-life documentaries, depositions, and settlement brochures. The brochures give a case synopsis, telling the before and after details of a case. The plaintiff, family, friends, and others involved in the case are interviewed. Physical and emotional results are shown. The brochure is given to the defense and insurance adjusters in the hope of reaching a settlement.

Getting into the legal market is often difficult for non-lawyers. Networking with lawyers to gain support is important. There are many gatekeepers—receptionists, secretaries and legal assistants—to get through prior to speaking with the lawyer. Fortunately, Miller found a supportive lawyer.

"Persistence and knowing your market are keys to success," says Miller. In the video business, equipment purchase mistakes can be very expensive. Miller uses Hi-8 and post-produces in ¾ inch. High resolution is not critical for her business. The company also use a NewTek Video Toaster, for special effects and titling, and Flyer, a non-linear video editing system, in post production.

Miller is responsible for writing and producing most presentations. She has three full-time employees. Jonathan Hartzer is another writer/producer who also doubles as a sales and marketing representative. Bryan Mobley is a videographer and computer animator while Ann Valentine works as an editor. Miller coordinates and goes to all shoots.

Video Law Services maintains its focus on legal work in the southeast U.S. Michaela views document management, using CD-ROMs and other storage media, as a future need in the legal profession. Finding a niche and focusing on it has made Video Law Services successful.

✤ ✤ ✤

Both of these companies fill a need. Nolo Press serves people in need of legal advice while the Video Law Services meets lawyers' needs. Experience or contacts in the legal field will help you find opportunities.

Legal Business Opportunities

Record Storage via CD-ROM or Other Electronic Media

Which profession has the most paperwork? Probably the law profession. Every conversation and remotely applicable piece of information is documented. Letters are used extensively and copies need to be kept on file. Storing all this paperwork takes room, but electronic media has evolved to meet these needs. CD-ROM recorders have dramatically dropped in price so that recording single copy CD-ROMs is more affordable. Other types of electronic media for storage are on the horizon.

By focusing a CD-ROM recording business on the legal market, you can develop efficient ways to get this extensive paperwork archived.

Setting Up Client-Server Networks for Legal Offices

Law offices need networks to tie computer databases together so all computers can access information on all other computers. Computer hardware and software specialists may want to focus on the special needs of legal offices. Privacy protection using multiple levels of security is important. Once you are familiar with the needs of legal offices, you can use this expertise to help set up other offices. By specializing on one market segment, you can work primarily through referrals, cutting marketing costs.

Legal Software

The legal profession, with its intensive use of forms, records, letters, and databases, has potential for specialized software. After researching the available products, you may be able to find an unmet need. Consider developing billing, practice management, and estate software for legal specialties.

Interim Agencies for Lawyers and Other Legal Workers

The law profession, which functions on a per case basis, would seem to be ideal for short-term assignments. When you have overcrowding in a profession as in law, there are many available individuals for short-term assignments. Someone with in-depth knowledge of the profession and inside contacts, a lawyer or paralegal, may want to start his or her own agency. Combining temporary and permanent placement is another option to consider. You might also function as a headhunter for companies seeking a lawyer with special expertise.

Establishing an electronic database of legal employment opportunities paid for by the employer or the prospective employee could be a business. Many lawyers end up working in a non-legal position, so related positions could be also listed.

Marketing Consultant

Lawyers are using more marketing to gain business. If you have marketing expertise combined with knowledge of the legal field, consider targeting lawyers as a marketing consultant.

Litigation Prevention

Companies prefer to avoid litigation, if possible, due to high costs. Consultants with experience in prevention can help companies avoid getting entangled in legal action.

Legal Research

Instead of doing research in-house, using outside researchers to track down information worldwide can be more cost-effective. With law firms beginning to outsource their research, consider founding an independent research company. Legal librarians who lose their positions due to outsourcing can start their own research firms. By shifting to electronic research, the entire process can be expedited.

Expert Witness Directory

Expert witnesses are available in every specialty you can imagine, with more joining the ranks. Many advertise their availability in the back of law journals.

Someone needs to screen, list, and update available expert witnesses. Why not charge potential expert witnesses to be listed in your directory?

Tracing Services

Lawyers often need assistance in finding heirs, policy holders, witnesses, beneficiaries, defendants, debtors, and other missing people. There is competition for this work, but if you have private investigating experience research your local competition.

Using Video in Law

Video production, graphics, and animation professionals may find a niche in doing work for the legal profession. Make contacts and find a way to get your name known. Video Law Services, in Jacksonville, Florida, discovered this market after receiving a number of inquiries from lawyers. Michaela Miller investigated how lawyers were using video. To get established in the field, her company did a documentary on how to use video in litigation. This gave name recognition and generated business for her company, which now specializes in video for the legal profession.

Legal Furniture

If you are in the furniture business or have woodworking skills, consider creating unique furniture for legal offices. Get input from lawyers as to their needs before designing your furniture line.

Collection Service

Collection services are needed by nearly all businesses that offer any form of credit. Businesses generally detest this chore, so if you can effectively collect past due accounts, you'll find businesses that need your help. Collection services may be owned by lawyers who can follow up with legal action against non-payers.

Consulting Service for International Law

Business is moving rapidly to an international marketplace. Legal systems in other countries differ greatly from the U.S. system. Because cases will more frequently involve multiple countries, there will be an increasing need for experts on foreign legal systems.

Since the U.S. has by far more lawyers per capita, a litigious system, and so many contractual agreements, foreign governments and lawyers probably are most in need of lawyer-consultants who can help them deal with our complex system.

Mediation Specialists

Much time and expense can be saved by mediating disputes rather than going to court. Although some lawyers specialize in mediation, mediators are not required to be a lawyer. Those with training in the mental health field do well in this field. Mediation involves interacting with opposing sides as a neutral party. This process has similarities to those in mental health. Lawyers, who often take adversarial positions, may actually be least suited to the role of mediator. Check with your state to find out if certification is available. Some states have a voluntary certification process, but many will eventually establish mandatory certification.

Legal Continuing Education

Continuing education to practice law is required in 38 states. Some fairly sophisticated continuing education businesses exist, but there is probably room for more. Since most other professions with advanced education require continuing education for licensure, the remaining 12 states may eventually impose mandatory requirements, creating more demand.

Translation Services

A translation business with employees or contractors that speak a variety of languages could target its services towards the legal profession.

Additional, But More Competitive or Limited, Opportunities

   ❖ Audio and video tape enhancement (combine with other services)
   ❖ Product testing
   ❖ Franchising consultant
   ❖ Patent and trademark services
   ❖ Videoconferencing services
   ❖ Process serving

Future Opportunities in Law

The legal field, with its size, power, and representation in Congress, has resisted the pace of change that has swept other fields. Change, however, is the means of adapting to an evolving world. The future is likely to bring unforeseen opportunities, but power shifts in the profession and in government will have to occur first.

CHAPTER 22

Marketing and Event Planning

*M*arketing and event planning go hand-in-hand. Opportunity for new businesses and ideas always exist. If you can demonstrate you can effectively increase sales, companies are likely to be receptive to your services and products. Since there are such a variety of individuals in this field and no strong barriers to entry, competition is great, but so is the opportunity.

Consider a business in marketing and event planning if:

- ❖ You are creative and resourceful and have experience in sales or marketing.
- ❖ You have an outgoing, friendly personality and love working with people.
- ❖ You have exceptional communication skills or theatrical experience.
- ❖ You have a degree in marketing with "real company" experience.
- ❖ You have been successful in sales and enjoy selling.
- ❖ You are a master of market research.

If you enjoy marketing or event planning and production, research the opportunities available in these areas. This chapter will get you started. The following two businesses found success by pursuing the founders' interests and talents.

Ala Carte Productions

Sometimes a career leads back to an original dream. For Jerry Hansen, whose training is in acting, opera singing, and dancing, Ala Carte Productions brings his career full circle. Ala Carte Productions presents original productions, musicals, reviews, and murder mysteries for business conventions and meetings. Hansen writes the productions, often with a humorous touch, to key into the goals and challenges of each business.

Hansen trained at Pasadena Playhouse and the Perry-Mansfield School of Theater and Dance in Steamboat Springs, Colorado. Disenchanted with Hollywood, he headed to New York to become a stage actor. He quickly found that he would need a regular job if he was going to avoid starvation.

Cast from a murder mystery: Jerry Hansen is second from the bottom. Photo by Peter Jordan Photography, Scottsdale, Arizona

Taking a job with a display and interior design company, he was immediately made shipping clerk for the holiday season. Then the company owner became ill, so he was promoted to salesman. His theatrical training translated well into sales. About two years later, Hansen started his own company, Hansen Studio, which was located on Fifth Avenue in New York. Consequently, he started a second company, a home furnishings store, Decorating On a Velvet Shoestring. The two stores worked synergistically, making possible significant purchasing discounts. During this time, he kept involved in theatrics and started two musical ensembles.

In January 1976, his only son, Derik, died after a short illness. This was very difficult for the family to accept. His neighbor owned a bus and limousine company and, trying to help Hansen work through his grief, invited him to visit his company one day. As Hansen wandered through the building, he came across a classic deck and a half bus and, after driving the bus, he decided to buy it. Hansen says the bus saved his life. He spent the next six months renovating the bus, converting it into a motorhome. With his family, he toured the U.S. While traveling, his daughter, Kimberlie, decided that she liked the western U.S. and did not want to return to their home back East. For the next year, he commuted back and forth, eventually selling both companies. He traded his bus for a down payment on an 18-unit apartment complex.

Hansen had an acquaintance who owned a hotel, the Grand Inn, near Sun City, Arizona. The hotel was booked during the warm winter months, but the owner was seeking a way to increase revenues during the hot summers. "How about a dinner theater?" suggested Hansen. Hansen eventually opened three dinner theaters, one at the Grand and two at other resort hotels, founding his new company, Ala Carte Productions.

Occasionally the hotels would request a special show for a particular convention. These shows added revenue to the usual Friday through Sunday schedule.

Gradually, Hansen began to notice this convention market was very profitable with no advertising, no ticket sales, and no newspaper reviewers! Around 1989, Hansen began to focus his business exclusively on the convention market.

Productions are audience-interactive and often have a humorous approach. Companies may request a particular theme such as western or Broadway. Hansen maintains a book of shows because often a company asks for a previously performed production. Other times, Hansen writes the show to meet the particular needs of the company. To be effective, companies must be open and honest about their challenges and goals.

Since productions are often part of a convention, they may be presented over a series of days with a short presentation each day, allowing the story to unfold. A presentation may mimic a particular challenge the company is facing, with names and details slightly changed. Hansen uses humor and audience participation to get the attendees totally immersed. The audience reactions can be quite dramatic!

Once, Hansen developed a production for Nutrasweet. The patent on Nutrasweet™, aspartame, was running out, bringing uncertainty as to how this would effect the company. A two and a half hour musical was enacted over five days, a half hour each morning, revolving around a hypothetical Club Swirl. The production, which involved eight cast members, original songs and music, was presented to 2,000 conventioneers, emphasizing success from commitment.

Another production was designed for Copeland, a large manufacturer of air compressors. With the switch from refrigerants such as R-12 and R-22 (freon), the company foresaw significant difficulties for its distributorships due to increased costs in maintaining larger parts inventories. Hansen's custom production for Copeland's distributorship conference revolved around a hypothetical meat-packing plant in Phoenix. The packing plant had its air conditioning compressor go out in August, with outdoor temperatures exceeding 110°. The compressor's manufacturing company, Copeland, air-expressed a new compressor so that the meat would not be ruined. "We only have one thing to sell in this world and that is service," was the message.

Hansen often plays one of the parts in the presentation. He has a musical director, a production coordinator to handle details and casting, plus a marketing agent to assist in sales. With conventions, timing is critical in approaching the presenting companies. Because knowledge is needed of casting and presentation costs, Hansen stays involved with sales.

A couple of years ago, workers were having trouble putting together a display for a big show at the local convention center. The display instructions were in a foreign language and with metric dimensions. His daughter, who is an officer with the Stage Hands Union, called him and asked for his help. Volunteering his services, he assisted in getting the display set up. His expertise was noted by an executive for an exhibit company, Showport. Now Hansen contracts for Showport, in addition to running his own company. The two businesses work well together. Most shows are set up in the mornings and during the week, not interfering with Ala Carte, which has primarily weekend and evening hours. Sometimes exhibitors need entertainment. Hansen gets early word of their needs then Ala Carte Productions can furnish their entertainment.

Hansen says that everything has come full circle. He started in theatrics and now is a theatrical producer. His detour into the display business ultimately brought him back to the display business, now through Showport. He attributes his success to being in the right place at the right time. How does that happen? "You must be in a lot of places," Hansen explains.

Corporate Arts

Corporate Arts, an audiovisual and event production company, has shifted from successful but flat growth to rapid expansion. "We reached a point where it just seemed like we weren't making any new strides, any new progress," explains Gordon Murray, founder and president. "Customers were telling us our work was some of the best they'd ever seen. We started looking around and thought, 'We should be bigger, we deserve to be more successful." In the year since, the company has doubled its sales and number of employees. In the process, the company has relocated to a 10,000 square foot facility, three times larger than its previous location.

Murray attributes his success to listening to the customer. "Find out what the client wants then find a way to deliver," he suggests. The company, starting as a one-person home business in 1986, focuses on the mechanics of producing effective technical presentations.

Murray, with meeting presentation experience gained through working at Mountain Bell and an independent production company, used his skills and networking to found L8 Nite (later Late Nite) Productions. For the first year, working from his home and using his own money for start-up, he did event and slide production work for small companies. By his second year, he moved in with an equipment rental and staging company and worked out an alliance with two other independent producers. The following year, the alliance became a partnership that lasted only a year. During the first years, growth was slow.

As the company grew, Murray began working with larger corporate clients such as Allied Signal, PETsMART, and Motorola. When these companies schedule a meeting, Corporate Arts works with them in planning the presentation, often resulting in staging the entire event. This may include video with graphics and animation, slide shows, or a multimedia presentation. Besides the presentation, Corporate Arts may arrange for room decor, other entertainment, travel, and lodging.

By 1995, growth had plateaued. With its lease expiring, Murray had the opportunity to rethink the company's direction. A book he had read, *E–Myth* (See Resources), focused his thinking on the company structure. When a company is small and all the individuals are highly skilled, structure is understood. As growth occurs, many companies neglect to define their structure, mission, focus, and policies. Here problems may occur. Murray realized the company had matured; now reassessment was needed.

In this review process, he went to his clients with the idea of a company name change. What did they think? Surprisingly, he found that the name Late Nite Productions, chosen to convey dedication and the long hours involved, conjured some negative images. The name was changed to Corporate Arts, for alignment with the client audience while conveying a mix of business and creativity. Murray brought more structure into the company, to assure continuing quality with the increase in employees. During this transitional period in 1995, Corporate Arts shifted from operating as a sole proprietorship to a corporation with a tiered management model divided into senior management, mid-management, and non-management. By making these changes, the company's growth soared. Employees increased from nine to 17. New profit centers—3-D animation and audio production—were added in-house and new strategic alliances were forged.

Instead of focusing solely on new business, sales people now stay with a project throughout to be sure that client company's goals are met. Working as a team with the creative and technical people, the sales person gains a greater understanding about what it takes to carry through a project.

Marketing is primarily by referral and networking supported by direct mail. Creativity and technical skills play a key role, but consistently meeting or exceeding client expectations is paramount. Murray says that the first step in doing this is to really listen to what your clients say they want. Despite how obvious this sounds, he says that many competitors do not do this, making it easier to get new clients. His goal is to be on time and on budget. To meet budgets, he gets everything in writing so there is no question as to the agreement.

Another key to the company's success is its diversity. Client needs vary, often depending on budget. Some companies want the newest technology, others prefer the tried and true. Murray maintains his older equipment while keeping pace with new technology so he can satisfy all company needs.

Corporate Arts, redefining its market, is now venturing into doing more business nationally with large corporate clients. Previously, business has been concentrated locally. Murray's goal is to increase national business from 10 to 50 percent of the total client base. By the end of 1995, national business had reached 25 percent.

The company has also grown by acquisition. When a Chicago slide production company ceased business, Corporate Arts bought its library of pre-produced slide shows and makes them available for rent to companies seeking an inexpensive meeting program alternative. Murray plans to convert the older slide technology to more current media, adding his company's presentations to the library to get additional revenue through royalties.

Bill Scott, brought in as Chief Operating Officer, uses his experience in banking to help with the financial aspects of the business. He says businesses should start small and establish themselves. During this time, they can begin to form a relationship with their local branch manager who may refer them to the bank's small business division. Once established with a good financial record, the bank will consider a loan. "The Money Store may be more flexible to smaller businesses," he suggested.

Corporate Arts has been very active in the local chapter of International Television and Video Association, Association for Multimedia International, and the Meeting Professionals International. Through these organizations, knowledge is shared and independent contractors found. Corporate Arts does pro bono work to help worthwhile charities. Besides the satisfaction gained, this work provides name recognition and references. The company has received numerous awards from local, national, and even international competition.

Murray's goal is to team with a smaller number of large clients, rather than working with a larger group of smaller clients which involves constantly bidding on projects. Emphasis has shifted from new business to expanding the volume of work with existing clients. He continues to strive toward complete client satisfaction so these large clients will not bother considering another company for their productions.

Businesses need assistance in marketing, planning, and staging events. Being able to adapt to varying needs has helped Ala Carte Productions and Corporate Arts become successful. Both companies take a proactive stance in trying new ideas.

Marketing Opportunities

Marketing on the Internet

The newest and most popular new location for advertising is on the World Wide Web. No one really knows the role the Internet will play, but it does seem certain it will be significant. Since so much information is given away, often advertising must be sold to cover the cost of maintaining sites. Companies need assistance in determining how they will use this new media to further their company growth. If you are creative and visionary, this may be the business for you. No need to worry about degrees, but establish your credentials. This is a new frontier.

International Marketing Consultant

Marketing internationally involves additional considerations beyond those necessary for domestic sales. International customers can be sought by a company directly or through indirect means: a U.S. or a foreign intermediary. If you have contacts in other countries, you could function as the U.S. intermediary to your foreign contacts.

Sales Trainer

Some people are natural salespeople, but most can benefit from training. If you are an exceptional salesperson, you may want to teach others the skills of your success. Market your skills to businesses, helping to improve the proficiency of their sales force.

Low Power TV Station

Setting up a low power (short distance range) television station allows your business to broadcast advertising to a closely-targeted audience. To induce viewers to watch, carry local sporting and special events or other special programming on a public access basis. Public access stations get their programming from volunteers who produce the programming at their own cost for the station. Publicity is their benefit.

Swap Meet Organizer or Promoter

Establishing and marketing swap meets is a growing market since people just love getting a bargain, or at least thinking that they are. Marketing at a swap meet provides some unique opportunities. Some swaps have a continuously playing tape advertising vendors' products. A weekly flyer with vendor products can be distributed to all who come. You might include a vendor locator directory. Arrange for a stage area where vendors can demo or talk about their products and charge for the opportunity to do so. Solicit ideas from your vendors for new ways to market and reward the best ideas.

New Survey Methods

Accuracy in surveys depends on getting to your target population and receiving honest answers. By designing creative means of surveying, you'll get better results. Why can't a survey be fun, more like a game? What if, after participation, you could give your volunteers instant information on how others answered questions? Computers allow you to do this. How about entering participants in prize drawings? Consider awarding many small prizes instead of one big prize, increasing the chance of winning.

Business Image Consultant

Some businesses fail because of their image. But image can be changed. An image consultant can analyze which image is best to reach target markets, then help implement the ideal image. Assess company markets, advertising, marketing materials, name, logo, and products or services.

Promotional Videos

For video production companies, consider focusing on promotional videos. Most families have VCRs. For some products or services, viewing a video in homes is an excellent marketing tool. Try different types of companies to see which are most receptive to this form of marketing. Have a demo ready to show what you can do.

You'll need a group of talented individuals to put together a first class product: camerapeople, technicians, producer, post production editor, audio sweetening specialist, and others.

New Locations for Advertising

Finding new sites to place advertising is profitable. Remember when ads were first placed on the backs of your supermarket receipts? Instead of putting billboards on the buses, the entire bus, windows and all, can be painted with the advertising.

Now that is eye catching! Look for new locations to place advertising and develop your strategy into a business.

Local Ad Magazine

Weekly magazines circulated for the express purpose of advertising were quite popular a few years ago. This media needs an overhaul with new ideas. Someone will come up with a new format that works. How about a local magazine on the Internet? Some cities have already implemented this idea.

Bulk Mailing Service

Direct mail remains a popular way to get your products or services known. If you are familiar with postal regulations and bulk mailing, consider a bulk mailing business. Check you local area to research your competition. Find ways to add service or aim for a niche market.

Infomercial Consultant

Infomercials continue to rise in popularity. This media has some great success stories. For a fascinating and realistic view of this business, read *this business has legs* (see Resources). One of the business equipment companies mentioned in this book, Air Taser, is using infomercials to get its product known. If you have experience with producing infomercials, consulting would be a great business opportunity. If not, find a way to get this experience.

Catalog Consultant

Mail order is convenient for busy people so should remain popular. Most mail order businesses use a catalog to showcase their products. Some have put their catalogs on the Internet. If you have experience designing catalogs, why not offer your services as a catalog consultant? Learn how to translate a print catalog to the Internet and you can provide both services.

Mystery Shopper

Mystery shoppers, anonymous individuals who patronize a business to assess service, are performing market research. Mystery shoppers can evaluate your clients' business plus that of their competitors, to get a comparative review. Done well this can be a wonderful and revealing tool that helps clients improve their service.

Market Research and Public Relations Agency

Marketing and public relations are very competitive businesses. Small and home businesses may be the neediest of these services. Find ways to make your services cost effective to this market and you can avoid going head-to-head with the large agencies.

Referral Agency

Many people are self-employed contractors who must spend a large portion of their working hours recruiting new business. These contractors would rather be working in their specialty.

By specializing in one area, you could do the prospecting. Working with a group of contractors, you can contact prospective employers, advertise cost-effectively, and do other public relations work. By keeping a file on each contractor with his or her credentials and specialty, you can match a job with the contractor that is available and best fits the demands of the job. After each job, you can solicit comments from the employer and use these comments to create individual recommendation files.

You'll need to keep strict standards so your company has a respected name. This may require booting unethical individuals. Funding could include a monthly or yearly fee to join then a bonus for each job found.

Ad Agency

Advertising is often too expensive for small businesses. Sharing advertising is one way to get costs down. Look for ways to help lower advertising costs yet provide effective advertising for smaller companies.

Competitor Intelligence

The more competitive business becomes, the more demand there is for competitor intelligence, as everyone is nervous about rival's plans. With electronic databases and other new or refined tools, you can provide information that will help your clients plan their future business strategies.

Fulfillment for Home-Based Businesses

Home-based businesses have a greater need for fulfillment, order packaging, and shipping than other businesses. When operating out of a home, space limits inventory. Packaging products works best in a facility set up for packaging and shipping. Consider assisting small businesses by providing fulfillment services specifically for their market.

Event Planning Opportunities

Ticket Sales

Some small operators in large metropolitan areas have been quite successful in buying tickets to popular events then reselling them at a profit when events become sold out.

Party Organizer

Who has time to organize a party anymore? Small businesses, many operating out of their homes, are finding a good market for their services. In this business, plan on working primarily Friday through Sunday. Rather than trying to meet everyone's needs, you may grow faster by focusing on a particular type of event, business sector, or specialty image.

Fund Raising

Fund raising is a challenging business. Getting people to donate to a cause is often difficult. If changes to the tax code eliminate the charitable contribution deduction, fund raising may become even more formidable. The need for new ideas that work is always welcome.

Corporate Events Planner

The event planning companies mentioned in this book, Corporate Arts, Ala Carte Productions, and Wacky Wires & Wonders, have unique markets. These companies have been successful by catering their services to client needs. Be aware that this type of business can lead to long and rather unusual hours. Margie Frierson says the drawback to the business is cleaning up at two or three in the morning to comply with location requirements.

Trade Shows: Booth Designer

Companies participate in a variety of trade shows. Having a good booth design is important for company image and display of products or services. Companies constantly redesign their booths to accommodate their changing needs. Creative individuals who have practical building skills might want to investigate this market.

Limousine Service

Many areas have an abundance of limousine services. Consider using another distinctive vehicle to transport your clients. Revolve your business around this image to distinguish yourself from competitors. Today sports utility vehicles may have just as much class as limousines.

Event Clothing Rental

In areas with many special events, a clothing rental business may be a good business opportunity. You'll need to keep abreast with apparel needs and carry a sufficient inventory.

Future Opportunities

New ideas are the impetus of businesses in these fields. Experiment with new ideas, keeping those that prove successful. If you are creative, can produce ideas easily, and are ambitious, you may enjoy and find opportunity in this field.

CHAPTER 23

Medical Services
and Products

$\mathcal{M}$edical services is a recession-proof industry. Healthcare needs only increase during stressful times. The ongoing challenge is to provide an affordable yet quality system that allows for the American system of individual choice of practitioners.

Medicine, encompassing dentistry, optometry, podiatry, psychology, and chiropractors, has changed dramatically in the last two years. Most medical expense is paid by insurance companies either through company policies or subcontracted by the government through Medicaid. This has given insurance companies control of the healthcare business. Hospitals, many of which previously were non-profit, have been bought out by large corporations. The now for-profit hospitals must make a profit plus pay CEO salaries.

Cost control is now the overriding factor in the purchase of equipment and services. Hospitals, other care facilities, and practitioners are seeking the lowest bid from suppliers as a result of decreased payments from insurers. Any business in the medical field must have strict cost controls yet maintain quality control.

Lawsuits are common, with sometimes immense payouts. Significant legal reforms were not passed by Congress and liability is great. Products must be extremely well tested in all possible use situations. Services such as medical laboratories need careful quality control. Medical service and product businesses need to carry high limits of liability insurance coverage for protection.

Managed care is motivating physicians to group together in very large practice groups called Independent Physicians Organizations (IPOs) to gain bargaining power

257

when contracting with insurance companies. Patients are often limited to choosing physicians who have contracted with their insurance plan. Health Maintenance Organizations (HMOs) provide medical care using employed physicians who often practice from their facility, usually limiting coverage strictly to their geographic area.

Businesses in the healthcare field would be best for individuals with:

❖ Healthcare experience.

❖ Behavioral health experience.

❖ Health insurance experience.

❖ An existing business that provides services valuable to healthcare professionals.

❖ A partner having any of the above experience.

❖ Any of the above plus a sincere desire to help people combined with attention to detail.

Challenging situations create new opportunities. Here are some companies that have found opportunities in the healthcare field.

Nurse Pro Pack

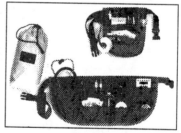

If you've ever been to a hospital or clinic, you've probably noticed the apron packs many nurses wear to carry the variety of supplies and instruments necessary in their work. The original idea for these packs was the brainchild of Kelly Patterson. At the time, Patterson worked as a registered nurse (RN) in a hospital intensive care unit (ICU) and tired of running back and forth for needed items. He modified a carpenter's apron to develop a prototype pack then wore it while working in the ICU. Receiving positive feedback from fellow nurses, he developed the original Nurse Pack in 1987.

In 1989, Patterson and his wife, who is also a nurse, quit their jobs and started Nurse Pro Pack with about $80,000 borrowed from family. Prior to quitting, Patterson had researched and made arrangements with material suppliers and assemblers. Having educated himself on business start-up by speaking with lawyers and accountants, he ran the company.

Patterson placed ads nationally in *Nursing 89*, a widely-read nursing publication, and Mosby's *CardPack*. Advertising in medical publications is expensive. For two months, their bill was $20,000, but they were receiving many orders. In three months, they had used up all their start-up money and both were forced to return to work. However, orders were still increasing.

Patterson continued to operate the company while working as a nurse, but was soon considering bankruptcy. The costs of ordering materials in small amounts, manufacturing, and the 800-number ordering service allowed no profit.

At the same time Patterson's father, Pat, was given early retirement due to downsizing in the defense business in Southern California. Patterson asked his father to take over the company. Deferring bankruptcy, his father put in additional money and began managing Nurse Pro Pack.

His father took over the order-taking, getting rid of the expensive ordering service. Advertising had already ceased. Marketing is now by word-of-mouth through customers and through several U.S. representatives. He switched phone companies, used voice messaging for after-hour calls, worked on new products, and looked for alternative ways to market. They expanded their product line to five designs. There are now three sizes: the large, original Nurse Pack, which comes with or without storage pouch, a Med (medium) Pack, and the Pro Pack, the smallest. The newest design, the EMT Pack, is a Pro Pack with a flap to prevent spillage of the equipment and supplies.

Six months after start-up, competitors started to appear. The Pattersons had developed a quality U.S. manufactured product using 500 or 600 denier Cordova material, double stitching, a strong belting, and a one-year guarantee. A tape loop and triglide are incorporated into the design to hold the loose end belting. The competitors started overseas manufacturing, used single stitched 200 denier nylon, lesser quality belting, and dropped the interior pouch design. They slightly underpriced the Pro Pack. Customers, unable to judge quality from an ad, now had other choices. Meanwhile, labor and materials costs doubled, further undercutting profitability.

His father began working through distributors, expanded retail store sales, and gave packs away free to hospitals. Brochures and re-ordering forms are included with samples and products shipped. For direct orders, the 800-number is stitched into the packs. One of their distributors financed a large ad campaign for their product in 1992 and they hit a high point in sales. Since then, sales have declined, but Pat Patterson is working on new distribution channels to increase sales.

The Pattersons are committed to their products. Yearly design reviews result in continual improvement with new designs. Their packs were used by a number of Desert Storm medical personnel. Quality spurs previous customers to refer clients to them and to reorder. They continue to seek ways to lower their costs and add more distributors. More advertising is needed, but first they need more funding. Ordering materials in larger quantity would decrease costs somewhat, but they want to keep their extensive color line. Although the challenges are great, they feel strongly that their quality products fill a need.

S.C.R.U.B.S.

Although wearing scrubs has become somewhat fashionable, those who work in health care fields often would prefer a more individualized apparel. Sue Callaway, while working as a nurse, sewed her own custom fabric scrubs. Other nurses, admiring her attire, asked her to make scrubs for them. Soon she was sewing for people she didn't even know. At first, she enlisted friends and neighbors to help keep up with the demand. After four years of word-of-mouth referrals, she teamed with her husband and with another couple experienced in the apparel industry to form a company. Sue is the president of the three-year-old S.C.R.U.B.S., whose goal is to make wearing scrubs comfortable, unique, and fun.

S.C.R.U.B.S. stands for "Simply Comfortable, Really Unique, Basic Scrubs." Browsing the S.C.R.U.B.S. catalog, you'll find they live up to their name. The scrubs are colorful, fun, and designed to "brighten your day and bring a smile to someone's face." You'll find scrubs in a variety of patterns including seasonal. Scrubs can be accessorized with matching earrings, surgical hat, S.C.R.U.B.E.E. hair accessory, belt, baseball cap, tie, socks, or boxer shorts. If you're a little less adventurous, just pick a top in the patterns and coordinate with solid color pants. S.C.R.U.B.S. sells high quality, 100 percent cotton scrubs in a rainbow of colors made from chambrays, denim, cotton twill, or cotton sheeting. Who says dressing in scrubs has to be boring?

The by-request catalog is not only vivid and fun to browse, but gives suggestions on how to color-coordinate the tops, bottoms, dresses and accessories to make ordering easy. They promise practical, quality scrubs with bartacked stress points and double needle top stitching. Top this with a 100 percent no hassle, no restriction refund policy.

Occupying a niche and pairing with partners experienced in management and the apparel industry, the company has been able to grow rapidly. Getting capital to cope with this rapid growth has been the only factor slowing expansion. Recently, a retail store has been opened which serves the San Diego market. Besides current styles, discontinued styles are available at the retail store.

As a registered nurse, Callaway recognized that people tire of wearing the same nondescript clothing day after day. Improving your dress improves your mood and the mood of others, too. In healthcare, a little color and fun can help everyone feel better. By filling a void, she has created a successful company. Callaway emphasizes that owning a business takes a lot of work and hours. "The business remains on my mind around the clock, like raising a child," she reflects.

SmartPractice

Semantodontics was founded in 1970 by Jim and Naomi Rhode to provide products for dental practices. They have since expanded into other medical markets, changing their name to SmartPractice. Naomi Rhode is a dental hygienist, an excellent motivational speaker, and a past President of the National Speakers' Association. Her husband, Jim Rhode, has a business background and an expertise in spotting trends.

Naomi began speaking while accompanying her brother, a dentist, on his seminars. Naomi and her husband began presenting their own seminars on dental office management. Often at seminars, dentists would ask where they had found their information. The Rhodes would refer them to books, but were often asked where to purchase these publications. The Rhodes began to sell the publications at their seminars. Shortly thereafter, they founded a book club to meet demand, then started selling infection control products to dental offices. Their product line has gradually expanded to multiple, extensive catalogs.

In dentistry, motivating patients to come in for treatment has been difficult. Many people fear dental treatment and the profession has had poor publicity coupled with a less than caring image. SmartPractice makes products to try to soften this image and motivate patients. Their original products included patient appointment reminders, business cards, dental staff motivational and educational materials: books and cassettes, gifts for referrals, office decor items, and similar products. Stuffed teddy bears are an example of a patient referral gift.

To help medical professionals meet mandates established by the Center for Disease Control (CDC) and OSHA, they market a line of disposable products and protective clothing to meet government requirements.

Another emphasis in their business is personalized, professional communication products such as stationery, cards, and educational patient literature. These products are designed and printed at their facility. A second category of items is those technical products necessary in a dental practice. Many of these products are similar in both dental and other professional medical practices. SmartPractice ensures that all medical products meet the rigorous requirements imposed by the Food and Drug Administration (FDA). Products are sold worldwide, including all of North America, Australia, Germany, Japan, and New Zealand. A division within the company, SmartCare, distributes to hospitals.

Marketing is the key to their success. They have astutely created a need for their products. Both travel extensively, giving seminars, and speaking at dental and medical meetings. Naomi, with her dental background and public speaking expertise, presents a warm, caring image. Her strength is motivational: encouraging and demonstrating how to satisfy patients. Jim Rhode's presentation is all business: you must get your patients to accept treatment for your practice to survive in this competitive world.

Their business has expanded tremendously. Many of the products are now manufactured within the company. They moved to a new custom-designed location in 1987. Graphics design work for their catalog and products is done in-house then printed in their own print shop. The building also includes warehouse space, although a second nearby warehouse building was purchased in 1991. In 1995, a third building was acquired for the human resources department. The company currently employs 265 full-time employees.

Before the abundance of dentists and physicians created by government funding of professional schools, medical professionals did not need to market their services. When an oversupply of dentists was created in the late 1970s, dentists began to have unfilled appointment time and started marketing to increase patient visits. The Rhodes were in the right market at the right time, but they had to teach professionals how to use their products to effectively market their services.

The Rhodes attribute their success to listening to their clients to find out what they want and need. They stay aware of trends so they can provide products and services to meet these needs often even before clients are even aware of the need.

The business now has expanded to include the Rhodes' daughter, Beth Hamann, a dentist, and her physician-husband, Curt. In 1995, the company designed a long-term vision for success and to help focus future efforts. Instead of emphasizing sale of products, SmartPractice focuses on producing products and services that provide solutions for client needs. Their goal is a long-term relationship with clients by getting to know customers so that they can meet their specific needs.

❖ ❖ ❖

These companies have taken advantage of needs they discovered through working within the field. If you already work in the medical field, be attentive to new needs being created by rapid changes in healthcare.

Medical Business Opportunities

Medical Professionals as Entrepreneurs

Physicians, registered nurses, and other health professionals find control over their work and reimbursement decreasing. They may feel they can no longer provide the best patient care. Treatment needs to be approved by the insurance companies whose bottom line is profit. Some will focus on optional treatment such as cosmetic surgery, which is paid directly by the patient. Others will find the situation unacceptable and look for other ways to gain control of their work. These professionals may find medically-related business opportunities such as those discussed in this chapter.

Cost Reduction

Cost reduction consultants are being contracted by care facilities to reduce expenditures. If you have a background in healthcare management and have both medical and business backgrounds, this is an opportunity. Medical knowledge is crucial to maintain quality and gain the cooperation of the professional staff.

Products and services that save time, and therefore money, would fit well in today's tight economic climate. Medical professionals require extensive training and must carry expensive malpractice insurance. Any product that allows a practitioner to provide care more efficiently will help reduce costs. Products that shorten hospital stays cut costs. Laser surgery, although not always faster, reduces the length of a hospital stay for the patient, requiring less nursing and support staff care.

Kelly Patterson of Nurse Pro Pack designed the original nurse apron to help him work more efficiently at his job as an RN in the ICU. By being able to carry frequently used items with him, he is able to work more effectively.

In a hospital, employees and patients are often stressed, leading to lower work efficiency, slower recovery of patients, and a less enjoyable work environment. S.C.R.U.B.S.'s designer, Sue Calloway, with her colorful and unusual scrubs, brightens up this environment, adding a little levity.

Medical treatment is often uncomfortable. By reducing discomfort or helping a patient relax, the treatment can be completed quicker and often with better results.

Virtual reality goggles that promote relaxation have been marketed successfully for dental offices. The patients report a more pleasant visit with less anxiety and discomfort. The dentist is able to work faster, more easily, and the patients are more likely to return for the completion of the treatment.

Inventory and cost-tracking software for hospitals and private offices is needed to keep track of expenditures and compare prices. Inadequate and excess inventories add to costs.

Even if medical procedures are followed accurately and the best treatment given, if these procedures are not documented, the professional is open to a malpractice suit which adds to expenses. Automatic recording of as many procedures as possible prevents omissions. In emergency situations, documentation may be sparse as all efforts are devoted to saving a life. Automatic documentation records treatment so professionals can concentrate on the patient. Computerized, bedside recording systems are being implemented to help avoid omissions and reduce the volumes of paperwork.

Patients must be informed of major risks associated with procedures. Computerized systems that could expedite informed consent while documenting disclosure are needed. Legality must be considered. Patients who cannot read, can't use a written system. How about voice delivery?

Prevention

Prevention reduces costs! Smoking results in more medical costs than any other preventable factor. Billions of dollars would be saved each year if enough people stopped—or young people didn't start—smoking. Companies that can help people break the smoking habit or find ways to deter young people from beginning to smoke have a large market. Companies with viable ideas should investigate obtaining grants for research to substantiate their results.

Many preventive products have less liability potential. Products that reduce the incidence of bed sores, for example, save dollars in treatment time, medications, and products. Special beds and padding plus periodic position changes reduce the frequency of bed sores.

Malpractice cases add to costs and are time-intensive. Devices that prevent errors, which also increase treatment time, reduce costs. For example, color coding prefilled syringes of medications reduces medication errors.

Although disposable products may add to initial costs, the savings in liability and time may make disposables cost-effective. Disposables help prevent contamination and reduce the need for additional sterilization and subsequent treatment. When designing a product, consider whether it is practical to make the item disposable.

Devices that prevent accidents will save healthcare costs. Design products that people are motivated to use. Companies that produce safety products find that convincing people to use preventive products is key to their success. In demand are devices that help prevent carpal tunnel syndrome, back and foot problems, and other conditions.

With our noisy society and so many older individuals, there will be many more hearing impaired people. Even with amplification though hearing aids, an individual may no longer be able to understand normal speech. Prevention is the best answer. Several groups are lobbying for Workmen's Compensation to cover workplace hearing loss. If increased coverage is obtained, workplaces will scramble to provide more hearing protection for their employees.

Health promotion programs that show results are in demand with the rise in HMOs. Since these organizations operate with a fixed budget depending on the number of people enrolled, more treatment costs result in less profit. Developing effective health prevention programs is a challenge as people are resistant to changing habits. Low cost ways to monitor healthy behavior are needed to assess compliance with prevention programs.

Some businesses have developed prevention videos for medical reception rooms. With a captive audience, the practitioners can choose which health-related topics they want to emphasize with their patients while saving the time of explanation. Staff can follow-up by inquiring if the patients have any questions concerning the presentation.

Due to loss of productivity, increased healthcare costs, and accidents related to drug abuse including alcoholism, required drug testing will become more prevalent as a condition of employment. Laboratories that can cost-effectively perform drug testing have an expanding market.

Providing Specialized Equipment and Personnel

Certain types of medical equipment such as lasers and blood-conserving equipment are provided by companies on an as-needed basis. Companies need a large investment to buy the equipment and personnel must be on call 24 hours a day, seven days a week for availability when needed.

Allergy Consultant

People with allergies often suffer unduly. By avoiding the substances that they are allergic to, they can feel better. Many people are allergic to substances found in homes: dust mites, chemicals, and fragrances. By replacing items containing these allergens with non-allergenic materials, a consultant can help these people live healthier lives.

Spread word of your services to allergists, family practice physicians, businesses, and insurance companies. Businesses can benefit by having more productive employees with fewer sick days. Your company can provide the products and construction services or form agreements with outside contractors.

Home Diagnostic Products

Many people do not seek medical treatment when a problem is first noticed. When treatment is delayed, treatment costs increase and the patient's prognosis worsens. Products such as test kits for pregnancy, blood sugar, and fecal blood allow people to confirm the problem and help motivate them to seek care.

Home Health Care Products and Services

Hospital stays are becoming shorter due to mandates from insurance companies. Often it is cheaper to treat patients at home. These patients can still be very sick and require medical products and services while recuperating at home. Products may need to be designed differently for use by non-professionals. Automatic blood pressure cuffs are an example.

These patients may need continuing professional care at home. This has led to a dramatic increase in home healthcare companies. These companies employ nurses to visit patients at home. Nurses also instruct patients and their families to provide self-care. Products are needed that are designed for this market. An opportunity for video production professionals would be to team with a home healthcare company to produce videos demonstrating how to do self-care procedures. Patients easily forget the details of these procedures. Most people have a VCR. Being able to review the procedure on tape would save an additional visit. These tapes could be marketed to other homecare services.

Rehabilitation Services and Assistive Devices

As the population ages and the need to reduce disability costs increases, the demand for rehabilitation services rises. There will be increasing demand for products, equipment, and services to meet this demand. The more we enable individuals to function independently by use of assistive devices, the further costs are reduced while bettering the quality of life for the patient. Assistive devices for the hearing-impaired, back-injured and carpal tunnel syndrome are examples of opportunities.

Short- and Long-Term Care Facilities

Some patients may have no one to care for them at home. They may need short-term care to bridge the transition between the hospital and home. Sometimes only day-care is needed. Other patients will require assistance for an indefinite period of time beyond what can be provided at home.

Older Americans are demanding coverage for nursing homes to accommodate their needs when they are no longer able to live at home. Presently, they must exhaust most of their savings before being qualified for Medicare coverage. This situation may change. It is unclear how this care will be funded, but these facilities will probably need to further reduce costs. The best businesses in the long-term care market will need to work through the cost problem.

Long-term care facilities may qualify for non-profit status. Many larger facilities are non-profits, but smaller homes often may be for-profit. Consider starting a facility if you are compassionate and respectful of seniors and their limitations. Multiple locations will increase profitability. Healthcare experience is needed. Opportunities exist for products, services, and consulting.

Patient Advocates for Insurability

As insurance companies are allowed to take over the healthcare business, patients will need help to resolve treatment disallowment and nonpayment disputes. Doctors and nurses, your former patient advocates, are often not able to be advocates without insurance companies threatening to cut them from their network. Unless the situation reverses itself, you may find yourself spending the dollars that once went for treatment toward trying to get that treatment.

This is an area which already has potential, but political forces could change this by limiting the power of the insurance companies. For a person with health insurance experience, consider consulting as a patient insurance advocate. American Medical Consumers', founded by Dr. Vincent Riccardi, mission is to give subscribers a Personal Medical Advocate so they can be informed HMO clients.

Consultants to Aid States in Forming Medicaid Programs

It appears that the federal government will turn healthcare for the indigent and possibly Medicaid over to the states to form their own programs. If you have experience in managed care and health program administration, this could be a lucrative area. Make political connections now.

Healthcare Facility Services

With the rise in drug abuse and carrying of weapons, security needs are increased. Products that aid in increasing security will help decrease insurance, and possibly additional personnel, costs. A small business can provide background checks on employees, decreasing the chance of hiring mistakes which can result in lawsuits against a facility.

Healthcare facilities rely on an abundance of equipment that requires routine maintenance checks and occasional repair. In a hospital, this equipment is often under a service contract. To provide a repair service, a company would need to subcontract. In medical and dental practices, many repairs are provided by independent small businesses.

Transcription Services

Medical records must be legible to be readable by the variety of medical professionals who rely on patient records. A misread record could result in an error that endangers the patient. Many professionals use transcription services, which translate taped transcription to word processors. In the past, this has been a profitable home business. The trend is presently toward voice recognition where voice is translated to text by computer, eliminating manual transcription. Systems are available yet they have not yet replaced manual transcription. However, this is probably not a good time to begin a transcription business.

If you have an engineering background, you might consider exploring available systems and keep an eye out for enhancements in voice recognition technology that will make these systems more acceptable. Voice recognition is the inevitable future.

Virtual Reality Training Programs

Healthcare requires continual continuing education in addition to the extensive initial training. Cardiac Pulmonary Resuscitation and Advanced Cardiac Life Support annually or biennially are required for most healthcare professionals. Performing mouth-to-mouth resuscitation on models has infection control implications. For this training and other procedures, there is a need for virtual reality systems to streamline required continuing education.

Counseling and Behavioral Health Services

Trends in society such as increased population mobility, underemployment, job stress, single parent families, and crime continue to increase needs for behavioral health professionals, psychologists, and psychiatrists. Facilities will need to be added to meet these needs. This is a very challenging area with strict licensing requirements and regulations. More programs that reduce stress, alleviate depression, and facilitate personal relationships are needed.

Auditing Fraud

Fraud has three sources: practitioners, insurance companies, and patients. Since healthcare costs have become such an important issue, fraud cannot be tolerated. Insurance companies already have systems to monitor practitioner fraud. Practitioners lack systems and mechanisms for remedying insurance company fraud which occurs in the form of delayed or inaccurate reimbursement. Patient fraud, including falsified information, false claims of disability, and malingering will be the most difficult to resolve. Opportunity exists in resolving these dilemmas.

Services for Busy Medical Professionals

Accounting, tax preparation, and financial planning are services needed by most health care professionals. To work with these professionals, it is important to be competent, prompt and honest, qualities respected in health care.

Credentials are valued. Start by working with a small, single practitioner office. Make sure that your work is accurate and thorough. Act as a consultant, giving timely financial advice. Make sure you are recording all business expenses. Most physicians have a large number of professional expenses. Ask for referrals after you have proven your competence.

The increase in two-physician families has created a need for child-care, house cleaning, shopping, and related services. Obstetricians may have around the clock child-care needs, requiring a live-in nanny. Other professionals may need extended hours day-care with centers located near large medical facilities. Your business could cater to their needs.

Medical and Dental Billing

"Electronic medical and dental billing—the opportunity of the 90s!"—the ad screams. Turn key systems for medical and dental billing are readily available. Is this a viable business opportunity? To find out, you could survey medical and dental offices. Before you consider any business, it is important to talk with your potential clients. But let's look at this situation first.

In the past, most medical and dental offices have submitted their own insurance claims by mail. Submission involves checking patient's eligibility for insurance, knowing the coverage of all the local insurance plans, translating medical treatment into insurance codes and following up on slow payment and requests for additional information from insurance companies. Translation of treatment to insurance codes has been simplified in many offices by use of a superbill which has the appropriate code next to the treatment. Often this superbill is simply submitted, eliminating the need for translation to codes.

Medical and dental offices have software to electronically submit their own forms and they are accustomed to doing their own billing. Medical knowledge is needed to respond to insurance company questions. Becoming familiar with all the different plans and learning about the different procedures is the most difficult aspect.

Some physicians traditionally have used billing companies to do their billing because they are not office-based, but work individually or in groups from hospitals: radiologists, nuclear medicine specialists, anesthesiologists, emergency medicine physicians, and pathologists. Their billing companies often provide additional services as well such as group malpractice coverage and contract negotiation. Are you competent to compete with established billing companies by providing these services?

All offices need to have a procedure for working with overdue accounts. Calling patients to work out payment is part of billing. This is where inexperienced individuals can get into big trouble. The most common initiation of a malpractice lawsuit is during collection of an account. If this is not handled in a sensitive and competent manner by a medically knowledgeable person, legal action can be triggered.

Without a medical, billing, and collection experience, it is unlikely an individual can build a successful billing business. Is a medical professional going to trust a new and inexperienced business to handle all of his or her accounts? In-office software packages have levels of security built in so fraud can be detected. This is a strong reason to keep billing within the practice.

Even if you can establish trust and competence, the opportunities are limited. Managed care with HMOs, PPOs, IPOs, and capitation are changing the way physicians are paid. Already, many of the large billing companies are cutting staff. This is an ominous indication the business is on the decline.

Future Opportunities

The demand for healthcare will increase with the rise in the more mature population. As we grow older, we have more healthcare needs. The medical profession is challenged to meet this growing need with less cost while continuing progress in research and technology. Significant changes and advances will be necessary if this goal is to be met.

CHAPTER 24

Network Marketing

Network marketing is often called multi-level marketing or, for short, MLM. Network marketing companies sell products and services through independent distributors. Commissions are paid on a tiered scale, based on product sales plus bringing additional people into the business.

Network marketing appeals to individuals who want to start a business to earn extra money, but aren't sure which business to start. Since this is the same group that this book is targeted toward, some of you may have investigated one or more of these companies.

Consider a network marketing business if:

- ❖ You want to start a part-time business that may, in time, become full-time.
- ❖ You realize this business will require sustained effort and are willing to commit for the long-term.
- ❖ You have made a substantial effort to investigate a network marketing company.
- ❖ You would buy this company's products at their prices even if you were not a distributor.
- ❖ You feel comfortable recruiting people that you know—friends and family—into this business.
- ❖ And—you are enthusiastic about a company's products or services.

The concept of network, or multi-level, marketing, goes back to 1945 with a nutritional supplement company, Nutrilife. Nutrilife compensated salespeople based on recruiting others, but also paid commissions on products sold. Additional compensation levels were added to reward the original recruiters when their new recruits reached the pay levels of their sponsors. Shaklee was founded in 1956. Two Nutrilife distributors founded Amway in 1959. Interestingly, all these companies are still in business, but Nutrilife is now a subsidiary of Amway.

With the current disdain for large corporations, network marketing companies offer the hope of greater control of your career and financial future. Is network marketing for you? When considering becoming a representative for a MLM, use the same criteria as you would for any other business. Is this a business in which you are truly interested? Are you committed, enough to approach friends and family for sales, to the products or services you sell? Are you prepared to run this like a business, devoting as much time as necessary to become successful?

For help in answering these questions, let's look at two young network companies. One, Excel Telecommunications, sells long-distance phone services; the second, Nutrition for Life, is based on an extensive product line.

Excel Telecommunications

Excel differs from many other network marketing companies by selling a service—long-distance communications. This eliminates the need to stock products, continually re-sell to the same people, deliver product, and handle collections. Once a person is signed up for the service, Excel does all the billing and collections plus keeps track of these for your downline as well. Founded in 1988, Excel has grown rapidly in the last couple years and went public in May, 1996.

Long-distance phone service is a necessity for many people. In 1996, Excel is the fourth largest telecommunications company. Excel differs from AT&T, Sprint, and MCI because it is a reseller of phone service. It does not own its own phone lines, but leases them from the three just-mentioned companies. Excel's corporate offices would not verify when or if employees will have their own lines.

You may sign up people as customers only, non-distributors. There are no quotas to be met in order to get paid. However, this is not very lucrative. To do well with Excel, as in other network marketing companies, you must sign up new distributors.

To become a managing representative, the entry level for receiving commissions from recruiting new distributors, there is an initial cost of $195 that covers record-keeping and a monthly newsletter. Additionally, there is a $180 yearly renewal fee. Nearly a fifth of Excel's income comes from its representatives, through these entrance and yearly fees.

To become eligible for commissions, you need to sign up one managing representative. According to company literature, as of April 1995, the average monthly commission check for managing representatives was $235.16. For every recruited representative who brings in three more reps within 60 days, a bonus of $100 is earned. To receive commissions on the long-distance usage of the distributors you have recruited, you must maintain the required number of customers for that commission level. Then depending on your level, commissions are paid for each new distributor recruited plus up to two to five percent, depending on whether they sign up as a residential or commercial customer, of their long-distance billing.

If you want to earn extra money doing training, you may also become an area coordinator, a $395 additional payment initially plus $100 renewal. Yearly training, provided for a fee, is required to continue instructing others. For each person you train, Excel pays $40.

With each tier reached, higher commissions, annual customer retention bonuses, and incentives are offered. To reach the second tier of Senior Managing Representative, you must sign up three area coordinators, plus have 12 managing reps within your downline. The third level, Regional Director, requires a total of six area coordinators and 12 managing representatives. At the fourth level, Senior Director, the business becomes more lucrative, with bonuses increasing to $340 for each recruited representative signing on three more reps. This multiplying downline is where escalating profits are made. Through their own recruiting, downline representatives earn the opportunity to create their own chain. To achieve this success, you'll need to commit yourself long-term to the business. Excel's representative retention rate is slightly better than the industry's average one year retention of 10 percent.

In comparing actual phone rates from 1995 company literature, Excel's rates were nearly identical to current MCI, Sprint, and AT&T personal rates when the monthly service charge, $1 to $3, was included. Rates are continually changed and vary depending on the dollar amount of long-distance calls. A personal 800-number and worldwide service are extra.

Bill Davis, an Excel area coordinator, had favorable experience as a Shaklee representative, but was unable to increase commission checks beyond $1,000 dollars a month. A friend introduced him to Excel Telecommunications in June, 1995.

Davis is fully committed to Excel. He describes himself as a very shy individual who does not like to sell. Davis and his wife run their Excel business professionally, devoting specific times for training and giving overviews of the Excel opportunity. A separate business phone line and business cards enable him to conduct business professionally. Although a part-time business at present, Davis has achieved the second commission level, Senior Managing Representative. His income comes from training, commissions, and signing on new managing reps and area coordinators.

Davis acknowledges certain people are turned off by network marketing. This is okay, he says. He just goes on to someone else who is interested. When individuals make comments that lead him to believe they would be interested in Excel, he asks them if they know anyone who might be interested in the business. He feels that it is insulting to ask directly if they are interested, as this could imply they are needy of income. His sales approach is low key; he simply explains the opportunity to see if there is interest. Davis is in the business for the long-term. He has definite goals and knows that reaching those goals depends on recruiting committed people into his downline.

Excel, although based on an unique concept, has some future challenges. Because the company does not own its own phone lines, it may have less control over its destiny. Excel also lacks total control over its distributors, some who have "slammed", changed an individual's long-distance service carrier without permission, long-distance subscribers. In some states, Excel has been fined for slamming. Although this is directly the fault of its distributors not the company, the company pays.

Nutrition for Life

Many representatives think one of the keys in selecting a network marketing opportunity is choosing a company that has consumable everyday products. Nutrition for Life's product line consists of over 300 items ranging from shark cartilage capsules to nutritional drinks to cleaning products. One unique product is a drinking straw filter, with a two-part replaceable filter, which functions as a portable water filter. Vitamins, personal care, weight management, homeopathy, cleaning, plus air and water filtration products are included in their extensive catalog. Merchandise is ordered directly, so distributors do not need to stock inventory and fill orders. The company uses outside contracted vendors to produce its products.

Nutrition for Life began over a dozen years ago under the name of Consumer Express, a marketer of nutritional products based in Lake Charles, Louisiana. In 1989, Consumer Express acquired Nutrition for Life, a Los Angeles-based company, and changed its name to Nutrition Express. When researching the ability to trademark the name Nutrition Express internationally, the company ran into barriers. Consequently, Nutrition for Life International was formed by a merger of companies in 1993, using the previously trademarked name. The company, publicly traded on NASDAQ, develops, markets, and distributes products through its multi-level network marketing organization. The combination of the company expansion, a public offering, and an approximately 50 percent increase in distributors in 1995 have dramatically pushed ahead company growth. Their distributor network includes the entire U.S., Puerto Rico, Guam, and other Pacific Islands, and Canada.

The original founders, David Bertrand, President, and Jana Mitcham, Vice President, both former teachers, still manage the company. Longevity is one way to assess the company's commitment. Wes Spiegel, Nutrition for Life's marketing director, explained, "Public reputation is another way to evaluate commitment. Ask distributors and acquaintances of management about the reputation of the owners. Look for a wide variety of products, not just one product which may currently be hot, but later fall out of favor. Does the company offer training? Then ask, What do I need to do to keep getting commission checks?"

Tom Schreiter of KAAS Publishing, a publisher of MLM publications, says that a good sign of commitment for a network marketing company is how it deals with a crisis. A top distributor of Nutrition for Life was written up in *The Wall Street Journal* concerning his criminal past. Spiegel acknowledged this had caused problems for some distributors. The company used fax and its weekly teleconferencing sessions to explain the facts behind the story. Lack of control over distributors is a big challenge for MLMs.

In most organizations, distributors provide the majority of support for their downline. Nutrition for Life has a technique called duplication. It encourages distributors to pass along their level of knowledge to their downline so new distributors become comfortable about building their business. In 1995, Nutrition for Life introduced a Business Building System, consisting of a videotape explaining the company, an audio tape, and series of publications that give step-by-step instructions for building your business. For use as a recruiting tool, they publish *Freedom Magazine*, which explains the business, product line, compensation plan, and the concept of a home-based business.

Nutrition for Life has a team of copywriters and graphic artists who put together promotional literature, available in three languages. Satellite broadcasts (requires a $199 satellite dish) and weekly teleconferences bring information about the company into homes and offices worldwide. Management, through these media, can talk directly to distributors and potential recruits. Announcement of new products, training, and marketing information are distributed quickly and consistently.

The compensation plan is built around maintaining your downline. If it is difficult for your distributors to maintain enough minimum monthly volume ($40) to receive commission checks, they will drop out. When distributors in your down-line leave, earnings for those distributors above them decrease. This creates a domino effect, decreasing everyone's income and resulting in more drop-outs. Initially, many people start their Nutrition for Life business by buying products at distributor cost then reselling these items at retail cost.

The compensation plan has seven levels. The goal is to reach Executive status where you start to earn bonuses. Executive status can be earned by any one of these three methods:

❖ Cumulative sales volume of $1,500.

❖ Cumulative sales of $1,200 and enrollment in the Order Assurance Program (OAP), which automatically debits your credit card to meet the monthly $40 minimum requirement.

❖ Cumulative sales of $1,000, enrollment in the OAP at $100 per month, and subscribing to the monthly audiotape education series, Master Developer Series ($20/month), or a single order of $1,000, the same OAP enrollment, and purchase of a Distributor Success Kit ($35).

The first way to earn bonuses as an Executive is by receiving a 20 percent (25 percent if enrolled in OAP) bonus on all purchases by individuals you sponsor that have not yet reached Executive status.

Then once you generate a monthly personal sales volume of $200 and over $300 for yourself and your non-Executive recruits, you collect bonuses based on a formula. Combine 50 percent of the total bonus volume, based on bonus values assigned to products, of your recruits then add your personal bonus volume. Subtract $300. You receive 40 percent of the remainder.

The third way to earn bonuses is through the Seven Level Executive Organization. You receive a bonus on the first $300 in sales of every executive, ranging from one to 10 percent in the first six levels. The seventh level varies from three to 18 percent. These bonuses extend through your downline seven levels once you have achieved Level Four. Beyond these incentives are a Platinum and Platinum Plus status that have special requirements and bonuses.

In its 1995 Annual Report, Nutrition for Life states that it is "committed to a long-term strategy of growth and profitability."

❖   ❖   ❖

These companies, one based on services and the other on products, provide a representation of how network marketing companies work. Each network marketing company is unique and must be investigated as you would any other business. Let's look at considerations in reviewing a network marketing business.

Researching Network Marketing Opportunities

The key to being successful in a network marketing organization is finding a reputable company with fairly priced, consumable products or services, staying committed for the long-term, and the ability to recruit others into your network. Many network marketers never support themselves through their earnings. Of those that do, most find that to reach this level requires years of sustained effort. Since much of your profit comes from signing up other distributors, building this network, or downline, of distributors is paramount to your success. Many in your downline will drop out, becoming discouraged with the time, selling, and patience needed. Your success depends on sponsoring people who will be committed. When developing their downline, many distributors say that they cannot predict who will stay with the business. Industry-wide, after one year, only one in 10 are still in the business.

Small company success is best related to being committed and passionate about your business. Network marketing companies realize this and try to instill this passion through meetings that appeal to the emotions. But sustained passion needs to come from following your interests and values. If you are not passionate about a company and its products, if you are only in this for the money, your chances of success are limited. Does selling the company's products or services fit your interests?

Products

You will want to find a company that has products you can endorse since legally the prime reason for being in business must be the sale of products or services. If signing on distributors is the only or primary activity, this may be a pyramid scheme and is illegal.

Ask yourself, are these products you would buy anyway, but from a different source? Are the products worth the cost? Or are you paying an exorbitant price for products just to participate in the multi-level commissions? A legitimate company could survive by sale of products or services only. Ask if most people would buy the company products or services without the multi-level commissions. Make sure products are cost-competitive, at least equal in cost and, if possible, priced lower.

Some companies sell items that are just prepackaged products available at lower cost elsewhere. Does the company actually make its products? If it uses outside vendors, are the products made exclusively for this company or repackaged versions of products sold at lower cost elsewhere? Will the company accept product returns if the customer isn't satisfied? Does the product lend itself to repeat business? The companies that seem to do the best sell consumable everyday products.

Choose a company with products that will not bring up legality issues. Gold and silver coin network marketing companies have nearly a 100 percent failure rate. Most coin marketing companies have lasted less than two years. Distributors may promote these coins as investments. Selling investment securities requires a securities license. By claiming the coins as investments and making exaggerated earnings claims, distributors push these companies under scrutiny for sale of unregistered securities.

Services

Network marketing has been primarily a product business, but now service companies are in the business. Excel is the fourth largest provider of long distance service. However, commissions from long-distance services are very small in comparison to the product commissions from many other companies. Recruiting and providing training add to earnings.

Travel services have also been offered through network marketing. Research these companies thoroughly, as many have failed. Remember, if the company doesn't survive, you will never reach your income goals.

Discount Buying Clubs

Discount buying clubs, in which distributors recruit other members for profit and include a multi-level commission plan, are a form of network marketing. Before signing up with one of these clubs, research the history of previous clubs. Nearly all have failed.

Hype

Some network marketing companies hype an easy, no-work business. Network marketing is not any easier than any other business. To be successful, you must be committed to the business and run it in an organized, professional way. Neither products nor services sell themselves. When you sign people into your downline, you will be responsible for helping and training them. You'll need to meet with your distributors and show them how to run the business. When distributors find they must work hard to be successful, they often drop out. Companies have found that unless their distributors are making at least $300 a month after a year, they will probably leave. Deceiving people leads to false expectations and harms the industry reputation.

Hype is a big problem with networking marketing companies. Chuck Huckaby (*Profit Now*—See Resources) and Len Clements (*MarketWave*—See Resources) are working to make accurate information available. In his newsletter, *Profit Now*, Huckaby reviews and rates network marketing companies. Both authors are invaluable sources to check before choosing a network marketing company. Ultimately, mistruths harm the credibility of all network marketing companies. Giving out accurate, realistic information will bring more good people into network marketing. Misinformation only causes people to avoid the business and attracts disreputable individuals.

Often it is not the network marketing company responsible for the hype, it is the distributors. Network marketing companies cannot easily control the claims made by their distributors. Both Excel and Nutrition for Life have encountered problems because of disreputable distributors. Since the background of distributors is not checked, recruitment will include anyone that wants in. A few disreputable distributors can damage the company reputation for all.

Selling to Family and Friends

Selling to family and friends is one of the biggest objections to network marketing. All businesses involve selling, but having to approach friends and family not only to sell products or services, but to recruit and train them as distributors is objectionable to some people. With other types of businesses, friends and family generally seek out your products or services when needed and you are not trying to recruit them into your business.

Network marketing businesses, built on relationships, take a long time to establish. Because of the relationship building inherent in the business, network marketing is growing in popularity in certain geographic areas such as the Pacific-basin and Eastern countries where relationship selling is part of their culture.

Selecting a Company

If you like the concept of network marketing, search for a company with good, reasonably priced products that people want or need. Pick a company that has been in business at least five years, preferably longer. Look for a company that has been through a crisis or two. Did they stay committed to their business? Tom Schreiter of KAAS Publishing says that although network marketing consultants will tell you to look for companies with four-color advertising, managers with a financial background, and high capitalization, many companies with these attributes are no longer in business. Some entered the business only for the money and, when they had reached their monetary goal or encountered their first crisis, they pulled the plug. Schreiter points out that both Amway and Shaklee, probably the most successful long-term network marketing companies, were started by individuals who had neither business experience nor great funding. Amway was started by two cropdusters and Shaklee, by a chiropractor. They were, however, committed to their business. He suggests looking for companies with a track record.

Company management is the most important factor in selecting a company. Management can implement changes and adjustments in the company to make the distributors more successful. They can change the product line, compensation plan, or company image. Starting part-time to allow time to build your business without having to rely on the low initial earnings for total support is also recommended.

Criteria for Choosing a Company

❖ *Select an established company that has proven itself with at least a five-year track record.* With an established company, you can check past history, distributor drop-out rate, and company credit rating. You can talk with distributors who have been in the business a while and find out how successful they have been. Look at the company history. All companies experience challenges. How has management dealt with these problems?

❖ *Choose a company with a quality, cost competitive line of products that you feel comfortable endorsing and that are consumable.* Products are second only to management. Consumable products require continual repurchasing. You get new orders without additional recruiting. Avoid companies that require you to carry inventory. Make sure products are 100 percent returnable, at least for a limited time period. Companies that charge a restocking fee are likely to make your customers unhappy.

❖ *Limit your risks.* Companies requiring inventories, order taking, large monthly minimums, and collecting payment leave you responsible for payment for goods not sold.

Compensation plans tend to be complex, with a variety of types. You'll hear terms like matrix, unilevel, binary, stairstep/breakaway, progressive, hybrid, and Australian. Few new distributors truly understand how they will be paid. While the exact compensation plan is not the most important factor in selecting a company, this may make a difference in how you run your business. Refer to Resources for sources to get information on compensation plans. Tom Schreiter explains that although a multitude of plans exist, the bottom line is that most pay fifty cents on every dollar. He does not feel that the type of compensation plan is significant to choosing your company.

Before you commit, know the answers to the following questions. Often the decision to join one of these organizations is made on impulse, without good information to answer these important questions.

✤ What happens if your production level drops?

✤ Are there continuing or yearly fees? Insist for complete disclosure of costs.

✤ What are the minimum purchase requirements for yourself and your downline at each level?

✤ When you lose members of your downline, which inevitably you will, does this change your level of reimbursement?

✤ When you have maintained a level of production for a long period, say 10 years, will you retain that level so that you can eventually retire or at least cut back?

✤ How old is the company? Have the owners started any previous network marketing companies? If yes, what happened to the others?

✤ Do you agree to all the company policies? Is this an ethical company?

✤ Does the company make earnings projections? Your success is dependent on your efforts. Beware of inflated projections.

✤ What is the distributor drop out rate? How is this calculated?

✤ What are the average earnings per distributor?

✤ Call the Better Business Bureau in the company's home office city to check the company record.

✤ If you can visit company headquarters prior to signing on, this will give you more insight concerning the company.

✤ Do credit checks on the company owners. This can be done through a company that maintains credit records, such as TRW, for a small cost.

Talk to other distributors, not just to those who are recruiting you. Ask around and go to company meetings to locate distributors who will speak honestly with you.

✤ How much are they really making?

✤ How much time do they devote to the business?

❖ How has the business affected their lifestyle?

❖ Does the company pay commissions on time?

❖ These distributors represent the company. Do they appear professional and honest?

Network marketing companies are regulated by states. Some states more strictly regulate the business than others. Some activities are illegal and you would be wise to avoid a company engaging in any of these. Profit cannot be made on the sign-up fee. Companies should not emphasize recruitment over sales. Companies cannot require participants to buy product upfront; only a sales kit can be required.

Select a Good Sponsor

If you decide to pursue a networking marketing business, select a sponsor who can train and help you. Check with other members of the sponsor's downline to see if they are pleased with the help they have received. Find someone whom you get along with, is successful in the business, and will give you as much training as you need.

Support Products for Network Marketing

Since many people entering network marketing have little business experience, they look to others for advice and support. This has created a demand for software, videos, and newsletters. By reading some of the publications listed under Resources, you can find out what is available. People need information on how to start and run their business.

Network Marketing Consultant

With network marketing flourishing, those who have had experience in management of MLMs may be interested in serving as consultants for new companies.

Expectations

If you decide to become a distributor, treat it like any other business. At first, expect only a small income from the business. It takes time to build the business. Commit the time necessary. Have realistic financial expectations based on talking with other people in the business. Be patient and keep your full-time employment until you can support yourself with your new business. Network marketing has provided supplemental income for some people and a few people have done exceptionally well.

CHAPTER 25

Personal Transportation: Automobiles and More

$\mathcal{E}$ specially in the United States, but also in other developed countries, personal transportation is a high priority. Most people are so dependent on a vehicle, they have difficulty doing without it even for a short period of time. Because of the importance an automobile in our lives, many vehicle-related businesses are recession-proof. In fact, when funds are short, we keep our old transportation, repairing rather than buying new.

Consider the personal transportation sector if:

❖ You are mechanically-inclined and enjoy car repair, maintenance, customizing, services, or related areas.

❖ You love to design products for vehicles, have engineering ability, and have or will obtain marketing expertise.

❖ You have a passion for cars, motorcycles, boats, or other vehicles and have business experience, have a partner with experience, or are willing to take business courses to gain experience.

Personal transportation, being a necessity in the American culture, is a staple industry. While new car sales flourish in good economic times, car maintenance is a more stable business. The following two companies, one in manufacturing and the other in service, demonstrate ways that enterprising individuals have created specialty automotive businesses.

Husco Engineering Company

While visiting his son at Michigan State in 1980, Dick Husta bought a new Honda Accord in Detroit. He found the long ride back to his home in Connecticut to be quite uncomfortable. The new car lacked a center armrest for his right arm and, due to arm fatigue, he found himself driving with one hand. On his return home, his engineering background provided the impetus for him to design, then install, a center console-mounted armrest.

Following installation, he was often surprised to find other Accord owners waiting at his car to ask where he got the armrest. Sensing an opportunity, he and his wife started producing armrests in their basement. Initial sales were through direct mail using small print ads. Sales also resulted from flyers left on windshields in parking lots.

Husta, with a mechanical engineering degree, had worked for a large corporation in the fuel additive business. His career required several transfers, and in 1980, he was asked to move to Houston. With an elderly family in the East and great love for Connecticut, he decided not to accept another relocation.

As a result of a small announcement he saw in an oil industry publication, he approached a subsidiary of a major corporation, Xerox, which was about to develop a computer-based petroleum trading network. Husta fit their need for someone with a petroleum products background. He began working for them on a consulting basis from an office in Connecticut, and traveled weekly to the operating office in Massachusetts, a three-hour drive. In 1984, the company asked him to move to Massachusetts. Again reluctant to relocate and foreseeing changes in the petroleum industry, he made the decision at age 57 to pursue his growing armrest business full-time.

From his 36 years of corporate experience, Husta had gained a broad background in areas necessary to an entrepreneur such as research, patents, sales, and finance. He has pulled all these skills together to found Husco Engineering Company, Inc., a Subchapter S corporation. Recognizing the importance of image as an adjunct to product quality, Husta utilizes well-written product literature, attractive packaging, and prompt, professional response to inquiries and orders. While creating this big company appearance, Husta operates from an office in his basement and a 2,000 square foot warehouse.

The company has two niche automobile products: the TracTop® armrest and TracPad™. The TracTop®, introduced in 1984, gives support for a driver's right arm and incorporates dual pullout cupholders with a splashproof coffee mug. This armrest has an aluminum mounting topped with a urethane molded, leather–grained covered cushion. TracTop® slides out of the way when the center handbrake is used. In 1985, Husco added dual pullout cupholders, preceding the automobile industry's inclusion of beverage holders by nearly 10 years. The TracPad™ adds a sliding cushion and dual pullout cupholder to a car with an existing, but poorly placed lidded center console. It is a great solution when the existing console is too low and too far back by adding additional height and forward arm support. Although a small company employing Husta, his wife, and part–time employees, Husco is an international business, the largest manufacturer of custom armrests in the world.

Husco is a supplier to Original Equipment Manufacturer (OEM) companies BMW and Volkswagen North America. Products are also sold through automobile dealers. Direct mail activities are being phased down to permit concentration on expanding OEM and dealer sales. The constant increasing cost of print advertising, primarily in automotive publications such as *Car & Driver*, and *Automobile* Magazine, has contributed to Husco's reduction of direct mail efforts. Husco has received much publicity, providing free marketing. Press releases are sent to business publications and newspapers.

As with many small companies, employee management and associated paperwork requirements are probably the greatest challenge. Due to the somewhat cyclical nature of the automotive side of the business, Husta uses part–time employees as required for large orders.

Possessing an engineer's inventive instincts, Husta has created another product named the F1®, after the F1 "Help" key on computer keyboards. The F1®, or "Quick-Flip Reference Organizer" attaches to the computer monitor, permitting the user to keep necessary information within easy viewing. Can't remember that World Wide Web Site? Just record it in the organizer under WWW and you'll find it quickly next time. Recognizing the growing importance of the World Wide Web, Husta has created a home page for his automotive product line.

"It is important for a small business to stay away from generic, 'me-too' businesses. Having an unique, patentable, quality product decreases direct competition. Carefully think through new product ideas. Is the product marketable and can the product be manufactured for a profit? With automotive products, safety considerations are important," advises Husta. He does not recommend franchise-type operations. "A service business must compete with other companies providing the same service, increasing price competition," Husta contends. He pays close attention to cost control and efficiency, highly computerizing his business.

After spending years in the corporate world, Husta has loved every minute of his new entrepreneurial career. Not regretting the decision to start his own business, he emphasizes the fact that it is not for everyone, especially those unwilling to recognize the risk involved. "But," he quickly adds, "as an employee in today's large business environment, there is also plenty of risk and insecurity."

Husta, who is 68, realizes that the time is approaching when he must consider selling all, or part of his business. To fully exploit the opportunities he envisions will take more than one person. It will take a combination of technical, sales, and operating skills that will be found either among compatible individuals, or a company already in the automotive field.

Husco continues to develop unique accessories for the automobile, trucking, and computer markets. All products are manufactured in the U.S. and are distributed worldwide via original equipment manufacturers, branded dealers, and selected distributors.

LemonBusters

LemonBusters, an Austin, Texas-based car inspection service, provides a detailed written inspection report for potential buyers of used cars. "Buying a car without an inspection is like buying a house without an independent review—foolish," says John Adams, Franchise Director.

Barry Sprague, the company founder, has 28 years experience repairing cars. He operated a mobile repair service and a portion of his business involved pre-purchase inspections of used cars. Seeing a need for inspections to protect buyers and facilitate used car sales by reducing risk, he started LemonBusters in 1990.

LemonBusters is an unique company, doing only inspections, no repairs. Currently, there are four LemonBusters, all in Texas. Although many people do a cursory inspection of a car prior to purchase, LemonBusters follows a systematic inspection procedure, diagnosing all systems. This procedure has been constantly refined to produce an accurate estimate of a car's condition. In the inspection process, cars that have been wrecked, clipped, water damaged, or repossessed are usually discovered. When the actual condition of the car is known, fair negotiations on the car's selling price can occur.

The company started franchising, but then backed off. Their present focus is on building a strong reputation and refining systems and procedures. They expect to start franchising in late 1996, with 16 cities targeted for expansion.

LemonBusters has received free national publicity by performing inspections for the television show "20/20." The show investigated the accuracy of disclosures concerning the history of used cars. Used car dealers have a tremendous political lobby. Ralph Nader unsuccessfully worked for accurate disclosure of the presale condition of used cars.

John Adams said other companies have attempted to copy LemonBusters, but the business is filled with potential land mines. He advises new businesses to expect costs to be double what they predict to avoid undercapitalization. "Expect everything to take longer than expected. Expect the unexpected. Business owners need perserverance and should anticipate long hours," he counsels.

Adams recommends franchises for those with no expertise in the field. LemonBusters uses American Service Excellence (ASE) certified technicians. When starting a new business, you must immediately compete with other businesses and get clients. Your business needs to be credible and able to distinguish itself from the competition.

The previous companies demonstrate the need for automotive products and services. The current popularity of utility vehicles, four-wheel drive sports vehicles, trucks and vans has expanded the market for accessories and service. Recreational vehicles are increasing in popularity as the average lifespan increases, resulting in more retirement years for enjoyment of these vehicles. With the rise in the mature population, the sales of these vehicles will increase.

Personal Transportation: Products and Services to Explore

Maintenance: Personal Vehicles

Automobile repair, especially specialty repair shops, is a necessity in our lives. If you have the skills and desire, this can be a good business. Besides a reputation for ethical diagnosis of needed repairs, consistent quality, and reasonably-priced service, providing additional services will help your business grow. Pick-up and delivery back to the place of your client's employment, providing loaner cars, or having a courtesy vehicle is important. A clean shop and waiting area gives a quality image. Calls to clients to determine their service satisfaction is a good marketing tool.

Extended car warranties have added to dealerships' repair business and they have taken away business from independent shops. There are voids independent repair shops can fill. Specialize in repairs that aren't covered by warranties or in cars that are out of warranty. Consider concentrating in repair of other vehicles such as motorcycles or boats. Recreational vehicles (RVs) are generally kept in service for longer time periods than cars so they will need more repair.

Automotive repair businesses seem to have a high failure rate. Repair shops need a steady stream of business to be profitable and many owners lack the marketing skills needed to build business. If you lack marketing expertise, find ways to get these skills. Consider taking classes or working with a small-business consultant. In most cities, you can find this help at little or no charge. Build a base of referral sources such as car washes, other repair businesses, and nearby businesses. Keep a file of recommendations from satisfied customers.

A disadvantage of owning a repair shop is that stricter environmental laws necessitate careful disposal of potentially toxic materials such as used oil, freon, asbestos, and other materials involved in an automobile repair business. Before purchasing such a business, you would be wise to insist on an environmental inspection by an independent qualified consultant. If you buy a business that has contaminated the property, you will inherit the financial responsibility to clean it up. This can be very costly! It is less expensive to properly dispose of these materials initially.

Specializing in a specific make of car may help your business stand out in a competitive market. If you have experience working for a dealership, this would be a natural transition and capitalize maximally on your skills.

Customizing

An automobile is part of your image. Many people are willing to pay for specialty paint designs, pinstriping, and custom moldings plus other details to make a car unique. Referrals can come from repair shops, dealerships, car washes, and detailing businesses. Perhaps you can work as a subcontractor with one or more of these businesses. Consider customizing other vehicles: motorcycles, boats, and RVs.

Salvage

Automobile salvage businesses will always be needed. Because of the need for a substantial inventory, this will require a large capital investment initially. With the requirement for a large parcel of land and zoning laws, salvage businesses are often located in outlying areas where land is less expensive. Some auto lots are building multilevel storage areas to maximize land use. Old or wrecked cars can yield a wealth of recyclable parts. Computerized search systems for locating specific parts has essentially expanded inventory for all such businesses.

How about specializing in recycled parts for RVs, trucks, boats, or motorcycles? Check how competitive these markets are in your area. The RV market would be most lucrative in retirement areas where more residents own these vehicles.

Self-Service Vehicle Wash

Consider a self-service car wash in an area where many people live in apartments, not having access to a source of water to wash their own cars. In areas that use salt to de-ice roads in winter, in dusty locations, or in four-wheel driving sites, vehicles need frequent washing. Cars in high air pollution locales need regular washing to protect the paint finish. Make sure you have a bay to accommodate larger vehicles like RVs and trucks, which need frequent washing. Or you may want to specialize in cleaning certain vehicles.

Auto Detailing

Some people demand that their cars have an immaculate appearance. Other people who use their cars extensively in their business, such as real estate agents, need a well-kept car. Auto detailing businesses meet this demand. This is a low-cost business to start. Space can be leased at existing repair or auto wash locations.

Window Tinting

In the southern states, demand for window tinting is high. In the summer, hot air trapped inside cars, trucks, and RVs can raise temperatures uncomfortably. Tinting reduces the amount of sunlight entering through windows, thereby lowering the inside temperature. Tinting needs to be applied indoors, in a dust-free environment. The tint, which is actually a film applied to the inside of the windows, is adhered to a wet surface. Any air trapped under the film must be removed before the surface dries. This tint is not as easy to remove as to apply, so correct application is important.

Towing Service

If you live near a major highway or own an auto repair business, a towing service might be a good opportunity. Check to see how busy existing businesses are and what they charge. Long hours are involved so you would be wise to bring in a partner.

Used Vehicle Inspection Service

Car prices have risen faster than many people's earnings, creating a demand for used cars. Many people would prefer to buy a used car, but are hesitant because they fear inheriting a lemon. One company, LemonBusters, provides mobile, used car inspections. All car systems, mechanical, electrical, and body, are inspected. The prospective buyer is given a thorough report of the car's condition. This reduces the risk in used car buying. Buyers can negotiate a fair sales price because they know the true condition of the car. LemonBusters is presently opening company stores and negotiating contracts to increase the value of future franchises.

When planning a vehicle inspection business, include inspection of RVs. Since these are higher cost vehicles, the need for inspection is even greater. How about inspecting motorcycles, sports-utility vehicles, or boats?

Specialty Products

Many people spend a considerable portion of their time driving. Especially for these people, accessories that make the car more comfortable or usable are in demand. Husco Engineering found a business opportunity resulting from the founder's own uncomfortable driving experience. Eventually, this led to his full-time business, Husco Engineering, which has since expanded its product line.

Other innovative products transform your car to a mobile office. Work for many people involves substantial travel. The need to use technology on the road continues to produce new products.

The RV vehicle market promises to grow in the future as Baby Boomers retire. Although there are already many products designed for RVs, clever individuals will develop new creations. Custom products for other vehicles such as small aircraft, motorcycles, boats, mopeds, and bicycles will find markets.

Van or Four-Wheel Drive Conversions/Customization

Vans are very versatile vehicles, adaptable for hauling passengers or loads. Some owners convert vans into campers or mobile business vehicles. Vans are also customized to meet special needs of individuals, especially the wheelchair-dependent. If you have unique ideas that can implemented at reasonable cost, you may find a business opportunity customizing vans.

Sports-utility vehicles continue to soar in popularity. People are willing to spend money customizing their vehicles, so consider ways to develop this market.

Trunk Organizers and Pickup Truck Storage

A common scenario for sedan owners is retrieving groceries spilled all over their car trunks. Attempts at products to organize car trunks are available, but none are optimal. Here is an unmet need that requires solutions.

Pick-up truck locked storage is also available, but most have very limited space. Short of adding a cab or an unlocked cover, most of the space is open. Resourceful individuals will find ways of providing secured space.

Windshield Repair/Replacement

Windshield repair is becoming more commonplace. Insurance companies can save money by encouraging owners with severe nicks to repair their windshields before the damage spreads, requiring costly replacement. NOVUS has built a successful franchising business by developing products and techniques that enable its franchisees to successfully repair windshields. Since being purchased by TGI International, it now can provide windshield replacement.

Paint Touch-Up

If windshields are being damaged, you can imagine the damage to vehicle paint. Most vehicles have numerous nicks that, if left unpainted, will rust in most climates. Rust damage is insidious, unsightly, and expensive to repair. There is opportunity for a business specializing in yearly, routine, and cosmetic nick repair and repainting. There are more obstacles in paint nick repair than with windshields. While insurance comprehensive coverage covers windshields, it doesn't cover nicks and rust. So a nick repair business would need to be compensated by individuals. Is this a viable business? If not in itself, an auto painting company might try this as an added service. Properly marketed, this could be an added profit center.

Accident Reduction

Vehicles have become more sophisticated, but accident prevention is still a wide open field. Fewer drivers seem to use turn signals and preventive driving techniques. More drivers run red lights, enter traffic without stopping, make frequent and unnecessary lane changes, and ignore speed limits. Technology has focused on making cars safer in accidents rather than accident prevention. Accident prevention might be more cost effective.

Several companies have devised photo radar systems that take a picture of the license plates of speeding cars and cars that run red lights. These companies make their profits off a percentage of the tickets issued rather than the sale of equipment.

By using this approach, the equipment is more likely to be purchased by cash-strapped city governments who pay nothing. American Traffic Systems, in Scottsdale, Arizona, is one of the major manufacturers of photo radar equipment. The business is extremely competitive, with rival companies vying for business. This is one possible solution to rising accident rates. Perhaps you can design other strategies.

Other Opportunities that May Be Worth Consideration

❖ Driveaways: transportation of vehicles between distant locations.

❖ Special event leasing of vehicles.

❖ Vehicle painting: customizing for personal and business use.

❖ Bodywork.

❖ Locksmith: mobile including cars, homes, businesses. Competitive.

❖ Video accident reconstruction.

❖ Electric car consultant.

❖ Natural gas car consultant.

❖ Vehicle design consultant.

❖ Vehicle repossessing.

❖ Specialized repairs: brakes, transmissions, heating and air conditioning.

❖ Bumper reclamation.

❖ Sunroof installation.

❖ Alarm system sales and installation.

❖ Restoring classic cars, motorcycles, fire engines or other vehicles.

❖ Swap meets for RV and classic car parts.

Automobiles and other transportation vehicles are necessities in most of our lives. Since many existing businesses have not put client needs first, there is ample opportunity for well-run companies. Provide quality, cost-competitive service. Ask your customers about their needs. Realize that your clients are dependent on their cars and provide an alternate means for them to get to work while their car is being repaired. Dealerships have greatly improved their service, but often prices are high for non-warranty work. This is the void that independent shops can fill. Consider maintenance such as bodywork that is not covered by warranties. Think about specializing in vehicles other than cars.

CHAPTER 26

Publishing Businesses

*O*nline services have dramatically affected the publishing business, yet books and periodicals are alive and well. Electronic and print publications each have their market, often supplementing each other. Book-on-demand publishing, still in its infancy, will help the publishing industry control expenses by printing only the number of books ordered. As a nation of information junkies, the explosion of information seems likely to increase. Organizing and sorting out quality information presents new business opportunities.

Consider a publishing business if:

+ You have written a book that you can develop into a line of similar books.

+ You have written a book for a niche market that you can expand upon.

+ You have a regional line of books.

+ You have publishing industry experience. Electronic publishing skills are especially valuable.

+ Through working in the business, you have contacts in the publishing field.

Competing with large publishers for limited bookstore space is difficult. The two businesses profiled next found niches within the publishing field, building their own successful businesses without direct competition.

Mike Byrnes and his partner, Devorah Fox, took their previous job functions and created their own business. Desktop publishing gave them the tools to make their business profitable.

Mike Byrnes and Associates

Mike Byrnes and Associates is a professional group of writers, editors, educators, artists and field specialists providing instructional material in English and Spanish for the trucking, passenger, transport, and heavy equipment business. The company is a partnership between Mike Byrnes and Devorah Fox. The two had worked together at a vocational school. In 1985, the government cut Title Four funding to private schools, which dramatically decreased operating budgets. About the same time, repayment of student loan enforcement was increased by holding schools responsible for getting repayment. Because of the cutback, Byrnes lost his position at the school.

Byrnes decided to start his own business and Fox joined him. Both had been involved in writing instructional home study manuals for the school. Fox had publishing expertise, Byrnes had a wealth of contacts and knowledge through previous experience. They were able to obtain contracts for instructional manuals with two competing schools. This provided enough income for their first year in business. Because of the initial contracts, adequate start-up money was available and the company has had sufficient revenues to avoid borrowing.

The first publications that had been written while both were at the school were put together using traditional methods: transcribing written material to type. The process took a year and involved 75 people. From the beginning, Byrnes and Fox decided to use desktop publishing, which was in its infancy, to enable them to produce the publications at one-fourth the cost.

By 1987, changes in regulations shifted training from home study to in-resident (at schools). Byrnes foresaw a new opportunity. The company shifted its publications to in-school use. Their flagship publications are called: *Bumper-to-Bumper, The Complete Guide to Tractor-Trailer Operations* and *Bumper-to-Bumper, The Diesel Mechanics Student's Guide to Tractor-Trailer Operations*. The company also writes Barron's guides for the commercial driver's license, bus driver's test, and truck driver's test.

Changes in trucking regulations due to NAFTA created another opportunity. By 1999, Mexican trucks will be allowed in all U.S. states. Currently, trucks are allowed only in border states. Mexican drivers will need to conform to U.S. regulations. Publications were translated into Spanish to meet this need. The company decided to copyright its publications in Mexico for extra protection. They found the Mexican copyright process much more time-consuming than the simplified procedure for U.S. copyright. Several trips to Mexico were required. Doing business in other countries requires time and patience.

Marketing is primarily through Byrnes' contacts and telemarketing. Advertising in publications and through cards left at truck stops did not generate sales. A quarterly newsletter including a catalog of publications is sent to schools, training programs, and trucking companies. Byrnes belongs to the American Trucking Association, Diesel Association, and Association of Public and Private Schools. Due to a shortage of qualified drivers, there is a demand for training.

Publications are priced affordably for easy availability with the goal of improved driver safety. Their goal is to get the publications to as many drivers as possible, including the independent drivers who are least likely to have formal training. Currently, trucking schools, whose students are most likely to be hired by trucking companies rather than work independently, and libraries are their main clients. Publications are continually revised. Besides Byrnes and Fox, the firm employs a graphic artist.

Fox advises new businesses to know their industry and the market for their products. "Be prepared for changes. Allow a cushion for unexpected needs."

John Reinhardt finds it easy to discover opportunities. Sunflower Sales is his second business. His first, a group venture, was an immediate success, but went bust when big bucks competitors saw how well his company was doing. Failing in one business increases your chances for success in the second if you have the courage to try again and learn from your first venture.

Sunflower Sales

John Reinhardt looks for opportunities and pursues them. A former Intel executive, he wanted to get out of the corporate rat race. He and a few other Intel employees started a fresh poultry and seafood store in Sacramento. Sales were great at first. Then supermarkets noticed how well they were doing and opened seafood centers within their stores, undercutting prices. The store was forced out of business and Reinhardt was back at Intel.

Reinhardt loves to fish. When Intel tried to convince him to relocate to Arizona, he at first refused. Picturing a dry desert, he didn't realize that Arizona has many lakes and a diverse climate. While still living and fishing in California, he relied on a book, *Recreational Lakes of California*, for local fishing information. That book has sold nine million copies. Finally he did relocate, but he was unable to find a similar book to help him find the best fishing lakes in Arizona.

After relocation, he became weary of 65 hour work weeks and being on the road. He remembered the lack of an Arizona recreational lakes book. Determined to break out of the corporate routine, he started writing a similar book for Arizona. He would work on it a few months, get frustrated, and throw it in the closet. This cycle repeated itself for about a year. Finally he just hunkered down and finished it. During this time, he educated himself about book publishing. Reinhardt joined a local self-publishing organization, Arizona Book Publishing Association. He talked with bookstores and printers. By the time the book was completed in December 1993, he had the necessary information to self-publish the book.

Regional publishing is a market that is more accessible to self-publishers. Marketing books is the most difficult part of publishing. Traveling all over the U.S. to market is expensive, but local markets are within driving range. Building up your own marketing network is possible without using distributors. Reinhardt's network exceeds 150 outlets. "Determination," explains Reinhardt, "is the key to building this network."

From his first book, Reinhardt has developed other regional products. His Arizona Quick Guides are moderately priced, laminated "brochures" focusing on southwestern recreational subjects such as golf, camping, hiking, the Grand Canyon, southwestern cooking, and the Apache Trail. "When Arizona titles are exhausted, I'll move on to other states," adds Reinhardt.

Sunflower Sales uses press releases and complementary copies for publicity. Since his titles are all regional, once retailers carry one title, they will likely carry new titles. Building a catalog of similar titles saves developing new outlets for publications. Reinhardt builds on his profits for each retailer by introducing titles from other authors to his network. He now is a distributor as well as a publisher. He has learned how to get to key people in an organization to place his titles. When he speaks to a retailer, he asks who else might be interested in his publications.

Sunflower Sales is a one-person business, but he is expanding by contracting other people to write titles for him. He has trademarked the name Arizona Quick Guides. By using the same name for a series of guides, he has name recognition and easier retail placement. "Local interest publishing works," emphasizes Reinhardt.

❖   ❖   ❖

By using your unique experience and ideas, you can find ways to build a publishing business that does not compete head on with the large publishers. Electronic publishing and the Internet are opening up new opportunities. The publishing industry has new frontiers where the future is yet to be defined. A few small companies may become future leaders.

Publishing Opportunities

Regional Publisher

John Reinhardt of Sunflower Sales has built his business around regional publications. He knows that marketing is a key to success. Because his products are targeted to the local market, he has been able to build up a network by personally visiting many of the stores. Marketing nationwide is a much more formidable task.

Have you ever had trouble tracking down a resource? That's how John Reinhardt's business started. Perhaps that source you couldn't find is a business opportunity. Some individuals have built local publishing businesses based on regional directory publishing. Directories exist for topics as diverse as listings of area businesses to resources for children. Sometimes these are tied into associated businesses.

Niche Market Publisher

Dan Poynter, author of *The Self Publishing Manual*, which is now in its eighth edition, started his business, Para Publishing, by writing about hang gliding. He self-published the books because of the limited audience. Self-publishing turned out to be another niche market. His business now revolves around teaching others about self-publishing. New niche markets are being created by change. Find one on which to base your publishing business.

Catalog Designer and Publisher

Direct mail is convenient and can be targeted to specific groups. Companies that want to sell their products by direct mail often need assistance in designing their product catalogs. Some very successful catalogs offer information or tantalizing stories about the merchandise. These are proven techniques to boost your catalog sales and increase customer loyalty. Do you have a market that would be amenable to a distinctive catalog? If you have desktop publishing or graphics experience perhaps you can tap into this market.

The catalog market is highly competitive. Postage and paper costs have dramatically increased. By closely defining those individuals who would be interested in your products, costs can be reduced.

ARBICO, with its biological insect control products, developed a catalog of its own and other distributors' products in 1990. The catalog has been very effective in familiarizing interested people about ARBICO's products and mission.

Book-on-Demand Consultant

Book-on-demand publishing is replacing traditional self-publishing. Those who are first in the business can serve as consultants for the later entries. *Flash Magazine*, a journal for desktop printing, is focusing on this new technology and has just published, using book-on-demand, a book on this subject (see Resources). With self-publishing, writers paid a premium to print small quantities. Many books that are self-published, although certainly not all, are targeted toward a limited audience. By being able to print books a copy at a time, small quantities of books become cost-feasible to print.

Small Press

For authors who need larger runs of books, small presses are a great option. Small publishing houses often focus on a special type of book. This enables them to use similar marketing channels for all their publications. Many small presses are now eliminating the traditional set-up process by accepting and printing books electronically. Anyone wishing to start a small press should incorporate electronic publishing.

Online Book Marketer

A retail bookstore has high overhead, but how about an online location? BOOK-ZONE, a virtual bookstore, is located on the World Wide Web. You can browse online, search for a book topic, or even read chapters from a book. While BOOKZONE carries all categories of books, there may be room for specialty bookstores.

Specialty Bookstore

One bookstore, Poisoned Pen, specializes in mysteries only and has been quite successful, with a nationwide clientele. Other bookstores specialize in computer, science, or medical books. A catalog, *Courage to Change*, sells books for "life's challenges." Bookstores have lots of competition from the big chains so finding ways to offer unique service is important. Sometimes this can be done with atmosphere, by having a store that is fun to visit. One bookstore in Columbus, Ohio is located in a multi-story home in the German Village area. New rooms are tucked away off other rooms, hidden staircases lead to more rooms full of book treasures.

Used Megabookstore

A single, small used bookstore is unlikely to be able to carry enough books to be successful. There is a statewide chain of privately-owned used megabookstores called Bookman's. The original store was founded in Flagstaff, with three additional stores in other cities. The stores are huge, the size of a large chain drugstore. Books can be traded for cash or credit. If you choose credit, you get twice the dollar amount of cash. The stores also carry used magazines, CDs, computer software, games, videos, and audio tapes.

Literary Agent

If you have publishing connections and a good eye for what makes a book successful, consider offering your services as a literary agent. Many agents live in New York, but with electronic communications, this shouldn't matter.

Graphic Designer

Graphic designers can find work in the publishing business illustrating books and designing book covers, graphics for online publishing sites, logos, marketing materials, and catalogs.

Postcards and Greeting Cards

Publishing scenic postcards and regional greeting cards is a way to break into the greeting card business, which is dominated by a few huge companies. With unique ideas and a regional market that allows you to market your own products, you may build a successful niche. A couple companies specialize in Western cards, starting with Christmas cards. Now they are developing these regional cards for other occasions. Some of the larger greeting card companies are realizing that they are missing a big market and have started designing their own regional and theme cards, but these smaller companies have already established their outlets.

Fax or E-Mail Newsletter

A number of businesses have sprung up that offer daily customized news via e-mail or fax for specific markets: computer, government legislation, and telecommunications, where timeliness of information is critical. Some are successful, others have had difficulty. If you are interested, research what is currently available and see how you can offer better service.

NewsEdge uses an electronic server to sort and distribute news, sending it directly to clients' offices. Key words and codes are used to select which news is directed to each client. The company, Desktop Data, Inc., founded in 1989, earned its first profit in 1995. Offering a new service, the company has grown slowly, having to demonstrate the value of its service. In the summer of 1995, Desktop Data went public, raising $26 million. Other tough competitors, Dow Jones, Reuters, and more, are either already in or considering this market.

Print Newsletters

The newsletter business may be cheap to get started, but the costs of soliciting subscribers, printing, and mailing will take much of your profits. Those that are successful in this business pursue one of two strategies: 1) Have many different newsletters, especially aiming at subspecialties or 2) Use the newsletter as a vehicle for selling a line of products that are the primary profit makers. Business newsletters command much higher subscription rates, but have a smaller audience. Consumer newsletters need to keep subscription rates low, but may have a broad market. When the problems of piracy and electronic payment are solved, publishing via the 'Net may create new opportunities.

Unique Ideas

Anyone can write poetry, at least they can try. A Minneapolis cab driver, Dave Kapell, has built a business around his product, Magnetic Poetry. To fine tune lyrics, Kapell wrote words on paper scraps then rearranged them until he was satisfied with the result. Only problem were his allergies. Sneezing often dispersed his carefully rearranged lyrics. The solution? Kapell attached the words to magnets, where they stayed effectively adhered to a pizza tin. But when friends wanted pizza, he had to move the word collection to his refrigerator. While he was baking pizza, his friends had a great time rearranging his words!

Kapell noted the opportunity for a product, hence, Magnetic Poetry. His product, sold worldwide, has generated nearly a half million dollars in sales with a substantial profit margin. Now he is developing similar products.

A bookstore that sells just one book title? In Bisbee, a mining town turned retirement, artist, and tourist haven, One Book Bookstore was located in the business district, which is nestled between mountainous slopes. The store's owner, until his recent death, sold almost exclusively a book he had written about growing up in Bisbee, *Me 'n Henry*. In a tourist town, novelty businesses can survive that might not be viable elsewhere. This may not be for you, but you can appreciate the power of a gimmick. While copying someone else's idea is playing catch-up, there are always original thinkers with new ideas.

CHAPTER 27

Real Estate-Related Businesses

*T*he real estate sector aids businesses and individuals in finding suitable property, a necessary service. Although the real estate industry tends to fluctuate with the economy, shelter is a necessity and the industry, in the long-term, does well. Competition is generally intense in this business because it has few entry barriers. However, committed individuals can thrive because the less persistent will become discouraged and drop out.

Consider a business in real estate if:

❖ You enjoy working with and genuinely like most people.

❖ You like flexible hours and don't mind working weekends.

❖ You have natural sales ability.

❖ You budget your earnings so you can survive between sales.

The real estate sector includes many opportunities beyond being a real estate agent. Besides selling real estate, you can be an investor, buying real estate for resale, leasing, or renting. In the past, more people have made fortunes in real estate investing than by any other means, although this may not be true in the future.

Services for real estate provide other business opportunities. Two businesses, both providing services to real estate agents and homeowners, are profiled.

303

Precision Home Inspection

Buying an existing company can give your business a fast start. With an established name and an existing referral base, you have immediate clients. Rick Dixon, a civil and structural inspector with training and experience in commercial and home inspection, relocated out-of-state, purchasing an existing business to get a quick start.

This was not his original plan. Dixon had relocated from the East Coast to Phoenix, partly because of low home prices. He was anxious to own a home, at first planning to build, but home prices were exorbitant in Massachusetts. On a short vacation to Arizona, he found a house and put a small down payment on it. He also checked out the local home inspectors, having already determined he would start his own inspection business. The home inspectors were so busy doing just code violations they were doing few home inspections. He concluded the market was wide open.

Dixon's original plan was to work full-time and start his business on the side. Although he found work with municipalities inspecting road construction, the stock market crash of 1987 resulted in a hiring freeze, ending that plan. At the same time he found an ad in the paper for the sale of a home inspection company. One of the company's major contracts, a real estate company, was on the verge of bankruptcy. Dixon bought the home inspection business.

He was busy from the start, although he had no previous experience as a business owner. He had worked in apartment maintenance while in engineering school. Then, after graduation, he was a concrete inspector and a structural inspector for a major company. Dixon had taken courses in home construction, including home and commercial inspection.

Here he came upon an article about a person with a home inspection business. He took courses to prepare himself for this business which, at the time, was unique.

He uses trial and error to find effective ways to get his company's name visible, using radio, print, and even television, scripting his own ads. Although he has found he has a knack for effective advertising, his primary source of clients is referrals.

Dixon attributes his success to his desire to help his clients save money. Although it may be a deal breaker, home inspections are recommended by real estate agents for disclosure of existing problems to prevent subsequent lawsuits. When the buyers know the true condition of the house, they feel more comfortable with their purchase. Many real estate contracts state that the seller must correct any defects found during the inspection.

Today the home inspection business is crowded with people of varying qualifications. Although there are several membership organizations for the industry, only one, American Society of Home Inspectors (ASHI), professionally certifies its members. To become certified, an individual must perform 250 paid inspections, take three three-hour examinations and pass peer review, which examines that candidate's home reports. ASHI also sets ethics and standards for the inspection business. Dixon is very active in this organization, serving on committees and in leadership positions. One of the challenges in this business is to distinguish yourself from less qualified individuals.

Another challenge has been his subcontractors. Dixon has found that each person he brought in and trained has left within six months to start his or her own business. Now he has a subcontractor who has been with him four years, but he, too, has his own inspection business.

Real estate agents often create difficult situations, especially when they are representing both the buyer and seller, whose interests often conflict. Dixon strives to concentrate on a fair and thorough inspection despite agent pressure.

Although he originally had an office, he has found that this business is operated just as successfully from home. He retains mail and phone service through a business suite address for a low monthly charge to maintain a professional image. Dixon also feels that being incorporated and registering with the Better Business Bureau contribute to his business image.

Working from home also presents challenges, says Dixon. His children sometimes need to be reminded to be quiet when he takes business calls. Being at home provides distractions. He considers himself a workaholic, acknowledging that he spends long hours at his business. Doing what he enjoys keeps him going. Dixon recommends "working in a field you truly enjoy. Then you don't have a job. You have a career and successful business."

Realty Executives

Although now a large company, Realty Executives started as one person's vision and without a lot of capital. The vision of Dale Rector, the founder, is simple. Let real estate salespeople run their careers as their own business. Realty Executives' mission is to provide the services salespeople need to run their business.

Photo by Roxanne England

Dale and June Rector are flanked by their sons, Rich (left), president and CEO, and Gary, director of the company management information system.

306 ♦ *Which Business?*

In today's business world, we are advised to manage our own careers. Real estate agents, like other business professionals, are advised to think of themselves as a mini-business. This idea is similar to that on which Dale Rector based his company in 1965. Imagine how unique and innovative this concept was then!

Dale Rector began as a sales agent. After relocating to Phoenix in 1961 because of the growth boom, he bought a 30-agent real estate brokerage. He found that although the real estate market was booming, running a brokerage had many challenges. Once his agents became successful, they usually started their own brokerages. Rector began to think about how an ideal brokerage would operate. He wanted to work with experienced, successful agents so he designed his ideal agency to attract these individuals.

In traditional real estate offices, a typical arrangement is the designated broker takes a percentage of the commissions of both listing and selling agents. At Realty Executives, the agents receive their full commissions. Office overhead is split among the agents instead of being taken from the broker's portion. This system eliminates the ceiling on agent earnings. Experienced, productive salespeople thrive under this arrangement. Part-time, new, or unproductive agents, who earn little because of few sold properties, are not likely to seek out this type of office.

This concept was not an instant success. Rector knew that he needed to build a credible business before agents would take the chance of signing on. Uncertainty made agents reluctant. The no cost up front, but a percentage of their commissions, was like a safety net even to the most successful agents. For a few months, no one signed on, but slowly a few courageous agents made the switch. When others saw how much more they could make, the company began to thrive although growth was slow at first.

Besides the 100 percent commission concept, Rector made another major change. Traditionally, company names were predominate on agency signs. Rector, in harmony with agents running their own business, made the agent's name largest, with the agency name in smaller print. This may seem like a small change, but the reaction from the Real Estate Commission was a new regulation specifically saying the company name must be larger. So Rector made the X in Realty Executives larger to get around the ruling!

Realty Executives is now a dominate agency in the state. One of the company's former agents started Re/Max Realty, based on similar concepts to Realty Executives.

John Foltz, first an agent and now vice president, embodies Realty Executives' principles. Foltz's father was a physicist who made his living as a real estate agent.

Foltz had no plans to be an agent. He saw all the weekends his dad worked. Instead, he became an accountant, specializing in real estate finance. But he didn't like being away from people where he had little chance to use his natural sales ability.

Foltz believes that to be successful in business you should do something you like to do. "The other alternative is to choose to like what you do. Have fun. Remember that the client's ego, not the salesperson's, is what counts. Find a need and fill it. Be of service," advises Foltz.

Realty Executives is in the real estate support business. The company views both its salespeople and its clients as company customers. Foltz says clients are asked what they want. Questions such as "What do you like best about the company? What do you like least about the company? If you were president, what would you change? How can we help you be successful?"

Foltz relates that people don't like uncertainty. He does not make promises he cannot keep, but instead makes promises he can exceed. He says that running a successful business involves doing more of what's working and eliminate what does not.

Most salespeople come from other companies. Each salesperson essentially has his or her own business. Many hire their own assistants. New agents can work with mentors using the Intern or Transition program. Mentors are compensated for the time spent with new agents by getting a percentage of that agent's earnings.

Realty Executives began franchising in 1987. Before then, the concept had been sold under the name ExecuSystems. Using *Real Trend*'s, an industry newsletter, Top 250 Brokerages Annual List, Realty Executive agents had the highest productivity as a group, with more sales per year than any other realty.

When Rich Rector sits down with new Realty Executive agents, he explains they are his customer. The company will provide the services they need. If they are happy with those services, tell their friends about Realty Executives because the company loves new customers. If they are unhappy, come to him and he will work to improve services offered.

By changing the way real estate agents are paid, Dale Rector created his own unique business—real estate support services. Look around in your business to see if you can find better ways of doing business.

When considering opportunities in real estate, keep both the home, commercial, and multi-family housing markets in mind. Each market has unique challenges and opportunities.

Real Estate Opportunities

Real Estate Agent

Being a real estate agent is still a good business. Agents today have a wealth of tools to assist them and the benefit of 100 percent commission companies to help committed agents be more successful. To get a home listed in the Multiple Listing Service (MLS) through which many home sales are made, it is necessary to go through a broker. Homes that are listed by owners tend to languish on the market since most serious buyers go through an agent to buy a home. Often the owner, through inexperience in negotiation and sales, is the worst salesperson. Agents work through the MLS to search for homes for buyers. Computers, and now the Internet, have streamlined the search process and automated record keeping.

Getting established takes time, as in any other business. Since the business relies heavily on referrals, you must build your referral network. Agents who specialize in certain types of homes or neighborhoods may be able to build their business more quickly. Some agents only sell luxury homes. Others specialize in vacation homes, lakefront or horse property, or relocations.

Successful agents often work in pairs or with a licensed assistant to make sure coverage is always available. If an agent is unavailable, the client will often just go to someone else. Some agents use an unlicensed assistant to handle clerical tasks and phone calls then they can devote their time to aspects of their work that require a licensed agent. Real estate agents can earn a broker's license and build their own companies, hiring other agents. In a small company, the broker may both run the business and sell.

Being able to create loyalty from your clients, through establishing confidence you are representing their best interests, is important for success. Recently, the concept of an agent representing both the buyer and seller has come under fire. Although agents have balanced the interests of both parties in the past, commissions are generally paid as percentage of the sales price by the seller. A new group of agents called buyer-brokers has dedicated themselves to providing the best service to buyers. Often, these buyer-brokers still split the commission with the selling agent, but sometimes they are paid by the buyer.

Disclosure by sellers is also gaining new attention. Many lawsuits in real estate result from owners hiding property defects. Agents recommend that all buyers get a home inspection. Also, sellers should fill out a disclosure statement on the condition of their property. Agents are responsible for informing their clients of known defects or environmental hazards such as lead paint, asbestos, radon, or environmental contamination.

Property Inspection

Because of legal concerns and for the best interest of buyers, property inspections are now nearly routine in real estate transactions. Although presently there is not mandatory licensure for inspectors, ASHI has developed its own certification process so consumers have a means of determining competency. Home inspectors would benefit from an engineering, especially civil or structural, background with experience in building construction. Many people enjoy the process of building their own home, but lack the time to oversee this process. If you already have a home inspection business, this would be an added service you could offer.

Rick Dixon, Precision Home Inspection, has this experience. When he became interested in property inspection, he took courses and sought work experience that would prepare him for this business. Realizing the changes occurring in real estate, he continues to educate himself on issues related to the business. This kind of commitment is important for success. Dixon says he enjoys helping people get a fair deal by knowing the true condition of the property they are buying.

The inspection business has become competitive, but qualified, committed individuals can still thrive.

Home Warranty

Along with home inspections, home warranties are common. A warranty covers repairs on major systems of a home for one year, renewable at buyer's expense, after a sale. Often the seller will offer to pay for the warranty to reassure the buyer. If repairs are needed, the home warranty company calls a repairperson to fix the system for a small deductible. Owning a warranty business does entail risk. If major repairs are needed, your company would be responsible, as written in the contract. Before a warranty is given on a property, the warranty company generally does its own inspection.

Services for Home Sellers

Small companies can help sellers get their property in good condition for a quicker sale. Landscapers might offer a spruce-up deal targeted to sellers. Painting often dramatically improves a home's appearance. How about a service that assesses the appearance of homes than suggests cost-effective ways to make a home more salable? Market your services to real estate agents who may be delighted to have an independent business assess their clients' homes to facilitate sales. You could work out arrangements with landscapers, painters, repairpersons, maid service, and decorators. Just adding flowers and foliage can make a difference. Now that the importance of aromatherapy is known, try adding scent dispensers to a home.

Other business opportunities can be targeted toward vacant homes. Since most agents agree that an occupied home sells faster, a few businesses, sometimes run as a side business by agents, let families occupy vacant homes in return for utilities and maintenance. Since this is unlikely to be a full-time business in itself, the service could be added to a home rental business. Another business possibility is routine checks and cleaning for vacant homes. Perhaps this could be a service offered by maid service companies.

Continuing Education for Real Estate Professionals

To renew real estate licenses, continuing education may be required. Check with your state for requirements for agents, brokers, appraisers, loan originators, and contractors.

Arizona School of Real Estate and Business, which has expanded into other business areas, became successful by offering quality, convenient licensure and relicensure classes. Offering classes of consistent quality and mailing a monthly newspaper, itself profitable, which lists the schedule of all classes helps make this school dominate real estate education in the state.

Consider providing sales and motivational seminars or newsletters for the profession. Some companies have tied these to their real estate product line, with the majority of profit coming from product sales. Ask agents and brokers about their needs. Most real estate professionals are computerized and, while many software programs have been developed, there is always room for an exceptional product that serves an unmet need.

Agent Safety

Safety of agents, who are often alone showing homes, has been a reoccurring concern. Can you design a product or service that would help protect agents? Air Taser® (See Air Taser, Engineering/Manufacturing) has a product that incapacitates assailants without harming them.

Homeowners' Association Management

In some areas of the country, especially fast-growing areas, communities have established homeowners' associations to ensure continued quality and maintenance within the neighborhood. In large communities especially, there may be need for outside management. By going to an outside firm, residents avoid personal conflicts between neighbors.

Apartment Locating

In communities with many apartment units, an apartment locating service may be a business option. Many states require a real estate license, considering this business as a form of property management. Negotiate with apartment property owners that you will bring pre-qualified renters to them for a fee. The prospective renters pay nothing for this service instead a percentage is collected from apartment complex owners.

Property Management

Because of the hassles, and there are many, involved in apartment rentals, many people avoid this business. But property management is a large market with many opportunities. The key in property management is to build up a portfolio of properties, be highly organized, and retain competent advisors and subcontractors.

Make sure that you have a lawyer on retainer and a good accountant. Incorporate your business to maximize write-offs. Some owners build a network of repairpersons. Then they post the contractors' numbers in each unit so when there is a problem on a holiday weekend, it goes straight to the person who can handle it. One owner I know videotapes each unit while walking through with the new renter. That way the renter knows that there is documentation of the initial condition of the property. Make sure the time and date stamp are activated on your camcorder. Another person screens all initial inquiries on vacant units with an answering machine, giving the unit address and instructing the party to call back after driving by the property. This eliminates uninterested and unmotivated parties.

Before getting into this business, talk with others already in property management. Working as a property manager in an apartment complex will give you experience as to what problems you might face. Drugs and guns are added concerns. Owning single family homes may bring better renters, but has its own problems. Talk to an attorney who works with property managers and find out how others deal with the difficulties. As always, when many people avoid a business, opportunities are opened up for the committed.

Leasing Broker

Rental of business property is another related business. When working with business property, your clientele will be more sophisticated, so you will need more experience and knowledge. A good way to start in this business is to work as a leasing agent for a leasing company. Once you have the experience, you can consider starting your own business. A business background, previous business ownership, sales, or accounting experience is good preparation for leasing.

Business Broker

The same background that is helpful for leasing is excellent for building a business brokerage. A business broker negotiates the sale of businesses, working with the selling owners and perspective buyers. Check with your state to see if a real estate broker's license is required. Although there are franchises in this field, working as an agent for an existing company is the best experience.

Estate Sales

Estate sales can include everything from property through possessions. A business specializing in estate sales needs to work closely with an appraiser for property valuation.

Success in Real Estate

Plan on working weekends, especially in the home sales and multi-family housing markets. Building up your business may take a long time, which is one reason so many people leave the business. Talk with others in your region who are already in real estate. Successful individuals enjoy working with people, are ambitious, stay motivated even when a big deal falls through, and find ways to adapt to the variable hours.

Resources

$\mathcal{T}$his section includes a variety of resources—organizations, periodicals, books, and directories—to assist you in your search for your own venture. Contact the organizations representing your business field for information on conferences, mentors, research, and publications. Subscribe to one or more of the related periodicals. Check your library for the books and directories. Subscription and book prices have been omitted since they are frequently changed. Call the organization or company for current information. Also, if you have Internet access, try using a search engine such as Lycos or Yahoo with the organization name as your keyword. Many of these organizations are establishing online sites where you can find immediate, current information.

If your new company would like to do business with any of the companies mentioned in this book, contact information is given. If you are seeking a mentor, contact your representative organization for companies located near you so you may personally meet with your mentor. Please remember that most of the companies in this book are very small and would be overwhelmed if many people contacted them.

If you own or know of an interesting, successful company that started small, write or e-mail: Nancy Drescher, P.O. Box 779, Mesa, AZ 85211. E-mail: N.Drescher@alice-compusytems.com

Later editions of this book will incorporate other innovative small companies located worldwide. If your organization is interested in having the author as a speaker, please contact Oasis Press at 800-228-2275 ext. 135.

Contact information is current at final editing, but companies and organizations frequently move and a few may even cease existance. If information has changed, call directory assistance. Use the home city telephone yellow pages or a current CD-ROM phone database, both available at most libraries.

Chapter 1
How to Choose Your New Venture

Non-Profits

Make sure that you file the appropriate forms to obtain approval for tax exempt status, if appropriate for your organization. Check with an accountant who specializes in non-profits. Underestimating the importance of correct completion of the necessary forms may result in your organization paying penalties. Your accountant can help you complete the forms. Call the IRS for more information. Ask for Publication 557 from their order hotline, (800) TAX-FORM (800-829-3676).

Finding a Niche

Choose one or two characteristics from the following list to help define the niche that your business will serve:

Convenience
  Location
  Hours
  No standing in line
  Multiple ways to buy and pay
  Faster
  Time-saving
  Less bureaucracy
  "Can do" service
  Pick-up or delivery service
  Page when ready service: Give out pagers.
Personal, Individualized Service
  Custom service
  Custom product
  More choices in color, style, design, size, fabric.
  Specialize in specific population group:
    by nationality
    by age
    by sex

    by interests
    by background
  Use customer profile to recommend purchases
Unusual
  location
  packaging
  product
  service
Unique or new approach
Distinctive appearance
More fun to use or buy
Increases customer status
Higher quality
Added amenities
Superior service
Solutions to problems/unserved needs
Reduces client's fears
Increases client's earnings
Partial or full solution to a problem
  Increases client's safety and security
  Less litigious
Unserved or underserved customers
Lower price at adequate (in mind of client) quality
Improved system for providing service
New service, product, or design
New color, format, materials, style
Inside contacts
Easier to use
More efficient
Better results
Expanded product line, most complete inventory
Improves client's life and/or career
Improves client's appearance
Improves client's health

Recycling
Automated
"Natural"
"lowfat"
Environmentally-friendly
Recycled

BOOKS

Start Your Business: A Beginner's Guide
Compiled and edited by Vickie Reierson, 1995
Oasis Press/PSI Research
300 N. Valley Drive
Grants Pass, OR 97526
541-479-9464
(800) 228-2275
Fax: 541-476-1479

Develop and Market
Creative Business Ideas
Dale A. Davis, 1995
Oasis Press/PSI Research
300 N. Valley Drive
Grants Pass, OR 97526
541-479-9464
(800) 228-2275
Fax: 541-476-1479

Chapter 2
Market Research: Increase Your Chances of Success

BOOKS

Customer Engineering
David B. Frigstad, 1995
Oasis Press/PSI Research
300 N. Valley Drive
Grants Pass, OR 97526
541-479-9464
(800) 228-2275
Fax: 541-476-1479

Diary of A Small Business Owner:
A Personal Account of How I Built
a Profitable Business
Anita F. Brattina, 1996
AMACOM, a division of American
Management Association
135 West 50th Street

New York, NY 10020
(212) 586-8100

The E Myth: Why Most Businesses
Don't Work and What To Do About It
The E Myth, Revisited
Michael E. Gerber, 1986 and 1995
Ballinger Publishing Company/Harper
Business
10 E. 53rd Street
New York, NY 10022
(212) 207-7581
(800) 242-7737

I Could Do Anything
If Only I Knew What It Was
Barbara Sher, 1995
Dell Publishing
1540 Broadway
New York, NY 10036
(212) 354-6500
(800) 223-6834

Know Your Market
David B. Frigstad, 1995
Oasis Press/PSI Research
300 N. Valley Drive
Grants Pass, OR 97526
541-479-9464
(800) 228-2275
Fax: 541-476-1479

Making a Living While
Making a Difference
Melissa Everett, 1995
Bantam Press, Division of Bantam,
Doubleday, Dell
1540 Broadway
New York, NY 10036
(212) 354-6500
(800) 223-6834

The Max Strategy, How a Businessman
Got Stuck at an Airport and Learned to
Make His Career Take Off
Dale Dauten, 1996
William Morrow and Company
1350 Avenue of the Americas

New York, NY 10019
(212) 261-6500
(800) 843-9389
Highly recommended for both entrepreneurs and employees. Presents a strategy for keeping your company or career competitive.

Chapter 4
Agricultural Businesses

COMPANIES
ARBICO,
Arizona Biological Controls, Inc.
Rick Frey and Sheri Herrera de Frey
PO Box 4247
Tucson, AZ 85738-1247
(520) 825-9785
(800) SOS-BUGS (800-827-2847)
Fax: (520) 825-2038
www.usit.net/hp/bionet/ARBICO.html

Natural Cotton Colours, Inc.
Sally Fox
PO Box 66
Wickenberg, AZ 85358
(520) 684-7199
Fax: (520) 684-7299

ORGANIZATIONS
Contact the following organizations to obtain information about their services and publications. Most have regular conferences where you can meet others with similar interests while learning about new techniques. Alliances may be formed and mentors found.

Agricultural Electronics Association
10 South Riverside Plaza, # 1220
Chicago, IL 60606-3710
(312) 321-1470
Fax: (312) 321-1480
E-mail: aea-emi@ix.netcom.com
AEA Connector (newsletter)

Ag/INNOVATOR (Precision farming)
1716 Locust Street
Des Moines, IA 50309-3023
(800) 564-4005
Internet: http://www.agriculture.com

American Association of Nurserymen
1250 Eye Street NW, # 500
Washington, DC 20005
(202) 789-2900
Fax: (202) 789-1893 Fax
Newsletters, Annual conference: July-August

American Botanical Council
PO Box 201660
Austin, TX 78720
(512) 331-8868
(800) 373-7105
Fax: (512) 331-1924
Herbalgram (newsletter)

American Breed International Association, Inc.
306 S Avenue A
Portales, NM 88130
(505) 359-0944
American Breed Cow News and *Bull News*

American Dairy Goat Association
PO Box 865
Spindale, NC 28160
(704) 286-3801
Fax: (704) 287-0476
Newsletter

American Farm Bureau Federation
225 Touhy Avenue
Park Ridge, IL 60068
(312) 399-5700
Fax: (312) 399-5896
Farm Bureau News, Meeting: mid-January

American Feed Industry Association
1501 Wilson Blvd. #1100
Arlington, VA 22209
(703) 524-0810
Fax: (703) 524-1921
Feedgram (newsletter)

American Horticulture Society
7931 E. Boulevard Drive
Alexandria, VA 22308
(703) 708-5700
(800) 779-7931
Fax: (703) 765-6032
American Horticulturist (magazine)

American Society of Agronomy
677 S. Segue Road
Madison, WI 53711
(608) 273-8080
Fax: (608) 273-2021
Agronomy News

American Sod Producers Association
1855 A Hicks Road
Rolling Meadows, IL 60008-1215
(708) 705-9898
(800) 405-8878
Fax: (708) 705-8347
Business Management Newsletter; Turf News

American Wine Society
3006 Latta Road
Rochester, NY 14612
(716) 225-7613 (voice and fax)
American Wine Society News

**Association for Farming Systems
Research Extension (AFSRE)**
University of Arizona,
Office of Arid Land Studies
845 N. Park Avenue
Tucson, AZ 85719
(520) 621-8582
Fax: (520) 621-3816
Newsletter and on farm systems research

Bonsai & Orchid Growers Association
26 Pine Street
Dover, DE 19901
(302) 736-6781
Fax: (302) 736-6763
Green World News (newsletter)

Florida Citrus Mutual
PO Box 89
Lakeland, FL 33802
(813) 682-1111
Fax: (813) 682-1074
Triangle (newsletter)

Green Retailers Association
Contact: Richard Scott, Founding President
Everything Earthly, Inc.
414 South Mill Avenue, #118
Tempe, AZ 85281

(602) 968-0690
Fax: (602) 968-0087
Network of environmental products retailers
formed to locate like producers.

Hydroponic Society of America
PO Box 3075
San Ramon, CA 94583
(510) 743-9605
Fax: (510) 743-9302

International Apple Institute (IAI)
6707 Old Dominion Drive, # 320
McLean, VA 22101
(703) 442-8850
Fax: (703) 790-0845
IAI Apple News (newsletter)

**International Association of Fairs and
Expositions (agricultural)**
3043 E. Carro, PO Box 985
Springfield, MO 65801
(417) 862-5771
Fax: (417) 862-0156
Fairs & Expositions (newsletter)

Lawn Institute
1309 Johnson Ferry Road NE, #190
Marietta, GA 30062-8122
(616) 977-5492
Harvests (newsletter)
Results of current research on lawns and
sports turf.

Milk Industry Foundation
888 16th Street NW
Washington, DC 20006
(202) 296-4250
Milk Industry Foundation News Update

National Cattleman's Association
5420 S. Quebec Street
Englewood, CO 80111
(303) 694-0305
Fax: (303) 694-2851
Beef Business Bulletin

National Cotton Council
PO Box 12285
Memphis, TN 38182

(901) 274-9030
Fax: (901) 725-0510

National Farmers Union
PO Box 372790
Denver, CO 80237-7914
(303) 337-5500
(800) 347-1961
Fax: (303) 368-1390
Washington Newsletter

National Hay Association, Inc.
102 Treasure Island Causeway
St. Petersburg, FL 33706
(813) 367-9702
(800) 707-0014
Fax: (813) 367-9608
Hay There (newsletter)

National Live Stock and Meat Board
444 N. Michigan Avenue
Chicago, IL 60611
(312) 467-5520
Fax: (312) 467-9729
Pork Industry Group Letter (free)

National Meat Association
1970 Broadway, #825
Oakland, CA 94612
(510) 763-1533
Fax: (510) 763-6186
E-mail: nms @ hooked.me
Lean Trimmings (newsletter)

Professional Plant Growers Association
PO Box 27517
Lansing, MI 48854
(517) 694-7700
(800) 647-7742
Fax: (517) 694-8560
Growers, wholesalers, retailing, conference and publications.

Society of Municipal Arborists
PO Box 364
Wellesley Hills, MA 02181
(617) 235-7600
Fax: (617) 237-1936
City Trees (Journal), for landscape architects,

horticulturists and nursery personnel, municipal foresters, park planners.

Soil and Water Conservation Society
7515 N.E. Ankeny Road
Ankeny, IA 50021
(515) 289-2331

Soil Science Society of America
677 South Segoe Road
Madison, WI 52711
(608) 273-8080

Wholesale Nursery Growers of America
1250 I Street, NW, # 500
Washington, DC 20005
(202) 789-2900
Fax: (202) 789-1893
The Grower (newsletter), Horticultural Research Institute, *New Horizons* (newsletter)

BOOKS

E Factor
Joel Makower, 1993
Times Books: Division of Random House
201 E. 50th Street, 22nd Floor
New York, NY 10022
(800) 733-3000
(212) 751-2600

State of the World (published yearly)
Vital Signs
Lester R Brown
Worldwatch Institute
W.W. Norton & Company
500 Fifth Avenue
New York, NY 10110
(212) 354-5500
(800) 233-4830 Orders

PUBLICATIONS

Subscribing to a publication in your market is one of the best ways to keep abreast with news and new technology.

AGExporter
U.S. Department of Agriculture
Foreign Agricultural Service
Information Division, Room 4638-S

Washington, DC 20520-1000
(202) 720-3329
Magazine on international trade and trade opportunities

The Cranberry Vine (free)
Washington State University
Route 1, Box 570
Long Beach, WA 98631
(206) 642-2031

Economic Research Service
United States Department of Agriculture (USDA)
1301 New York Avenue, NW
Washington, DC 20005-4788
USDA is a source for many periodical publications for agricultural businesses including:
Agricultural Income and Finance Situation & Outlook Report
Aquaculture Outlook
Cotton and Wool Situation and Outlook Report
Dairy Outlook
Fruit and Tree Nuts Situation and Outlook Report
Livestock, Meat and Wool Market News
Livestock and Poultry Update
Livestock and Poultry Situation Outlook Report
Sugar and Sweeteners Situation and Outlook Report

ERS-NASS
341 Victory Drive
Herndon, VA 22070
(800) 999-6779
Fax: (703)-834-0110
Lots of information, although not easy to wade through.

Farming & Ranch Living
Subscription Fulfillment
PO Box 5288
Harlan, IA 51593-0788
(800) 344-6913

Farming For Profit (newsletter)
Doane Information Service
111701 Borman Drive, #100
St. Louis, MO 63146
(314) 569-2700
Fax: (314) 569-1083

Farm Journal
Centre Square West
1500 Market Street, 28th Floor
Philadelphia, PA 19102-2181
(215) 829-4700
(800) 331-9310

Industrialization of Heartland Agriculture: Challenges, Opportunities, Consequences, Alternatives (conference proceedings)
December 1995
Department of Agricultural Economics
Agriculture Experiment Station
North Dakota State University
Fargo, ND 58105-5636
(701) 231-7441

National Honey Market News
USDA
2015 S. 1st Street, Room 4
Yakima, WA 98903
(509) 575-2494
Fax: (509) 457-7132

Pro Farmer
Professional Farmers of America, Inc.
Oster Communications, Inc.
219 Parkade, PO Box 6
Cedar Falls, IA 50613–9985
(319) 277-1278
(800) 635-3931
Fax: (319) 277-7982
E-mail: profarmer@aol.com
Excellent, easy-to-read newsletter with very useful information for professional farmers on market trends and prices plus agricultural news. Strongly recommended.

Progressive Farmer
Box 830069
Birmingham, AL 35283-0069

(205) 877-6494
(800) 292-2340

Successful Farming
1716 Locust Street
Des Moines, IA 50309-3023
(515) 284-3000
(800) 374-3276
Fax: (515) 284-3563

Chapter 5
Business Equipment, Supplies, and Transportation

COMPANIES
Electronic Materials and Computers
Bud Levey, President
Bill Woosley, Vice President
3102 W. Thomas Road
Phoenix, AZ 85017-5301
(602) 272-3200
Fax: (602) 269-3265

ORGANIZATIONS
Aircraft Owners and Pilots Association
421 Aviation Way
Frederick, MD 21701
(301) 695-2000
(800) 872-2677
Fax: (301) 695-2375

American Rental Association
1900 19th Street
Moline, IL 61265
(309) 764-2475
(800) 334-2177
Fax: (309) 764-1533

American Trucking Association (ATA)
2200 Mill Road
Alexandria, VA 22314
(703) 838-1700
(800) ATA-LINE
Fax: (703) 684-5720

Equipment Leasing Association (ELA)
1300 N. 17th Street #1010
Arlington, VA 22209
(703) 527-8655

Fax: (703)-527-2649

Independent Truck Owner/Operator Association (I(TOO)
PO Box 621
Stoughton, MA 02072
(617) 828-7200
(800) 628-4866
Fax: (617) 828-6606

BOOKS
Bumper To Bumper: Complete Guide to Tractor-Trailer Operations

Barron's How To Prepare for the Commercial Driver's License Truck Test

Barron's How to Prepare for the Commercial Bus Driver's Test

Bumper to Bumper: The Instructor's Guide

Bumper to Bumper, The Diesel Mechanics Student's Guide to TractorTrailer Operations
Mike Byrnes and Associates
PO Box 8866
Corpus Christi, TX 78468
(512) 980-8337
Fax: (512) 980-0781
Also publishes a newsletter for truck drivers and diesel mechanics training professionals: *Down the Road*

Making $70,000 a Year As a Self–Employed Manufacturer's Representative
Leigh Silliphant, 1988
Ten Speed Press
PO Box 7123
Berkeley, CA 94707
(510) 559-1600
(800) 841-2665

Chapter 6
Business Services

COMPANIES
BEST Institute, Inc.
Jerry Beougher
5236 S. 40th Street

Phoenix, AZ 85040
(602) 437-4779
(800) 874-8137
Fax: (602) 437-4283

Staff One Search
Ronni Anderson
2800 N. 44th Street, # 340
Phoenix, AZ 85008
(602) 952-9060
Fax: (602) 952-8792

On Assignment, Inc. (Individual offices
called Lab Support®)
Tom Buelter
26651 West Agoura Road
Calabasas, CA 91302
(818) 878-7900
Fax: (818) 878-7930

ORGANIZATIONS
American Chemical Society
1155 16th Street NW
Washington, DC 20036
(202) 872-4600

**American Institute
of Chemical Engineers**
345 East 47th Street
New York, NY 10017
(212) 705-7338
Chemical and Engineering News

American Management Association
135 West 50th Street
New York, NY 10020
(212) 586-8100
(800) 538-4761
Fax: (212) 903-8168

American Society of Civil Engineers
1015 15th Street NW
Washington, DC 20005
(202) 789-2200
Journal: *Civil Engineering*

American Society for Industrial Security
1655 N. Fort Myer, #1200
Arlington, VA 22209
(703) 522-5800

American Society of Safety Engineers
1800 E. Oakton Street
Des Plaines, IL 60018
(708) 692-4121

**American Society for Training and
Development**
1640 King Street, Box 1443
Alexandria, VA 22313-2043
(410) 516-6949

**Association of Ground
Water Scientists and Engineers**
6375 Riverside Drive
Dublin, OH 43017
(614) 761-1711

Board of Certified Safety Professionals
208 Burwash Avenue
Savoy, IL 61874
(217) 359-9263

Center for Hazardous Materials Research
320 William Pitt Way
Pittsburgh, PA 15238
(412) 826-5320

Institute for Industrial Engineers
25 Technology Park
Norcross, GA 30092
(404) 449-0460

National Business Incubators Association
114 N. Hanover Street
Carlisle, PA 17013
(717) 249-4508

PUBLICATIONS
Human Resource Development Press
22 Amherst Road
Amherst, MA 01002
(800) 822-2801

*Profitable Personnel Services: Start
and Run a Money Making Business*
Kristi Mishel, John Thomas, 1995
TAB Books, Division of McGraw-Hill
PO Box 40
Blue Ridge Summit, PA 17294-0850
(717) 794-2191
(800) 233-1128

NONPROFITS

Society of Nonprofit Organizations
6314 Odana Road, Suite 1
Madison, WI 53719-1141
(608) 274-9777
(800) 424-7367
Nonprofit World magazine (bimonthly)

FRANCHISES

Dynamark Security Centers
Residential and commercial security systems
linked to central monitoring station.
19833 Leitersburg Pike, PO Box 2068
Hagerstown, MD 21742-2068
(301) 797-2124
(800) 342-4243
Fax: (301) 797-2180

Chapter 7
Computer Services and Products

COMPANIES

Granite Computer Solutions
Chris Piraino
55 N. Hibbert Street
Mesa, AZ 85201
(602) 649-7749
Fax: (602) 649-9566

Training á la Carte
Microcomputer Training
Janet Corbosiero and Fran Novak (Founders,
not current owners)
2111 E. Highland, Suite 250
Phoenix, AZ 85016
(602) 224-9911
Fax (602) 224-9912

ORGANIZATIONS

**Association for Computing Machinery
(ACM)**
1515 Broadway
New York, NY 10036-5701
(212) 869-7440
Fax: (212) 944-1318

Association of Shareware Professionals
545 Grover Street

Muskegon, MI 49442-9427
(616) 788-5131
Fax: (616) 788-2765

**The Computer Leasing and Remarketing
Association**
1212 Potomac Street NW
Washington, DC 20007
(202) 333-0102
Fax: (202) 333-0180

**Independent Computer Consultants
Association**
1933 Gardenview Office Parkway
St. Louis, MO 63141
(314) 997-4633
(800) 774-4222
Fax: (314) 567-5133

**International Television Association
(ITVA)** includes video production
6311 N. O'Connor Road #230
Irving, TX 75039
(214) 869-1112
Fax: (214) 869-2980
Video Systems (magazine)

National Association of Broadcasters
1771 N Street, NW
Washington, DC 20036-2891
(202) 429-5350
(800) 368-5644
Fax: (202) 775-3515
Sponsor of large annual exhibition (NAB)
yearly in April in Las Vegas.

Optical Publishing Association
PO Box 21268
Columbus, OH 43221
(614) 442-8805
Fax: (614) 442-8815

PUBLICATIONS

Building a Successful Software Business
(book)
Dave Radin, 1994
O'Reilly & Associates
90 Sherman Street
Cambridge, MA 02140

(617) 354-5800
(800) 338-6887

Byte Magazine
McGraw-Hill Companies, Inc.
PO Box 552
Hightstown, NJ 08520
(609) 426-7676
(800) 232-2983
Internet: http://www.byte.com

Lan Times
1900 O'Farrell Street, Suite 200
San Mateo, CA 94403
(609) 426-7070
(800) 525-5003

New Media
PO Box 10639
Riverton, NJ 08076-0639
(415) 573-5170
Fax: (415) 573-5131
Internet: http://www.hyperstand.com

Videography
2 Park Avenue, Suite 1820
New York, NY 10016
(212) 213-3444 ext. 145
Fax: (212) 213-3484

Videomaker
PO Box 4591
Chico, CA 95927
(619) 745-2809
Internet: http://www.videomaker.com

Chapter 8
Consulting

CONSULTANTS
Jack Akin
Environmental Management Consultants
(EMC)
715 NE 6th Street
Grants Pass, OR 97526
(503) 474-9434
Fax: (541) 474-5884

Dr. Jerry Eisen
Human Resources, Inc.

President, Arizona Chapter of Institute of
Management Consultants
4620 N. 16th Street, Suite 109
Phoenix, AZ 850
(602) 265-0096
Fax: (602) 265-0099

Peg Lovell
Dental consultant
Vice President, Arizona Chapter
of Management Consultants
610 E. Bell Road, Suite 2-111
Phoenix, AZ 85022
(602) 493-1787
(800) 280-1284
Fax: (602) 861-0199

ORGANIZATIONS
American Management Association
135 West 50th Street
New York, NY 10020
(212) 586-8100
(800) 538-4761
Fax: (212) 903-8168

**American Consulting Engineers Council
(ACEC)**
1015 15th Street NW
Washington, DC 20005
(202) 347-7474
Fax: (202) 898-0068

**American Society for Training and
Development**
1640 King Street, Box 1443
Alexandria, VA 22313-2043
(410) 516-6949

Institute of Management Consultants
521 Fifth Avenue, 35th Floor
New York, NY 10175-3598
(212) 697-8262
Fax: (212) 949-6571

**Independent Computer Consultants
Association**
1933 Gardenview Office Parkway
St. Louis, MO 63141
(314) 997-4633

(800) 774-4222
Fax: (314) 567-5133

PUBLICATIONS

CD–ROM Professional
Subscription Department
462 Danbury Road
Wilton, CT 06897-9819
(800) 222-3766
Fax: (609) 488-6188
Internet:
http://www.onlineinc.com/cdrompro

The Complete Marketing Handbook for Consultants
Schrello Enterprises
555 E. Ocean Boulevard
Long Beach, CA 90802
(310) 435-1789

Consultants & Consulting Organizations Directory
Gale Research, Inc.
835 Penobscot Building, 645 Griswold Street
Detroit, MI 48226
(313) 961-2242
(800) 877-GALE
Fax: (313) 961-6083

Consultants News Directory of Management Consultants
Kennedy Publications
Templeton Road
Fitzwilliam, NH 03447
(603) 585-6544

The Contract & Fee-Setting Guide for Consultants and Professionals
Howard Shenson, 1990
The 10 Hottest Consulting Practices: What They Are, How to Get Into Them
Ron Tepper, 1995
John Wiley and Sons, Inc.
605 Third Avenue
New York, NY 10158-0012
(212) 850-6000
(800) 225-5945 (Orders)

Chapter 9
Consumer Retail

COMPANIES

Everything Earthly, Inc.
Green Retailers Association, Founding President
Council For Sustainable Living, Executive Director
Richard Scott, President and CEO
414 S. Mill Street #118
Tempe, AZ 85281
(800) 968-0690
(602) 968-0690
Fax: (602) 968-0087

My Sister's Closet
Ann Siner
2033 E. Camelback Road
Phoenix, AZ 85016-4710
(602) 553-0566
Fax: (602) 957-9221

Terri's Consignment World
1826 W. Broadway Road, #3
Mesa, AZ 85202
(602) 461-0400
(800) 455-0400
Fax: (602) 969-5052
Franchisor: Quality, used furnishings

ORGANIZATIONS

National Association of Resale and Thrift Stores (NARTS)
20331 Mack Avenue
Grosse Pointe Woods, MI 48236
(810) 294-6700
(800) 544-0751
Fax: (810) 294-6776

Gift Retailers, Manufacturers and Representatives Association
1100-H Brandywine Blvd.
PO Box 2188
Zanesville, OH 43702-2188
(614) 452-4541
Fax: (614) 452-2552

BOOKS

Retail in Detail
Ronald L. Bond, 1996
Oasis Press/PSI Research
300 N. Valley Drive
Grants Pass, OR 97526
541-479-9464
(800) 228-2275
Fax: 541-476-1479

Chapter 10
Educational Services
and Products

COMPANIES

Arizona School of Real Estate and Business
William Gray, President
7142 E. First Street
Scottsdale, AZ 85251
(602) 946-5388
Fax: (602) 949-5918

Educational Management Group
Dr. Gail Richardson
6710 E. Camelback Road
Scottsdale, AZ 85251
(602) 970-3250
Fax: (602) 970-3460

Tom Snyder Productions
80 Coolidge Hill Road
Watertown, MA 02172-2817
(617) 926-6000
(800) 342-0236
Fax: (617) 926-6222
Interactive learning and conflict resolution programs.

ORGANIZATIONS

Association for the Development of Computer-based Instructional Systems (ADCIS)
1601 W. 5th Avenue #111
Columbus, OH 43212
(614) 487-1528

Association for Educational Communications and Technology (AECT)
1025 Vermont Avenue, NW, #820
Washington, DC 20005
(202) 347-7834
Fax: (202) 347-7839

Educational Dealers and Suppliers Association
711 W. 17th Street, #J-5
Costa Mesa, CA 92627
(714) 642-3986
(800) 654-7099
Fax: (714) 642-7960

Educational Media Producers Council
ICIA Educational Technologies Division
3150 Spring Street
Fairfax, VA 22031-2399
(703) 273-7200
Fax: (703) 278-8082

Home Study Exchange
PO Box 2241
Santa Fe, NM 87504
(505) 471-6928
For home-schooled students.

National Alliance for Safe Schools (NASS)
9344 Lanham Servern Road #104
Lanham, MD 20706
(301) 306-0200
Fax: (301) 306-0711

National Head Start Association (NHA)
201 N. Union Street #320
Alexandria, VA 22314
(703) 739-0875
Fax: (703) 739-0878

National Home Study Council (NHSC)
1601 18th Street, NW
Washington, DC 20009
(202) 234-5100
Correspondence schools.

International Tele-Education (Intel-ED)
4619 Larchwood Avenue

Philadelphia, PA 19143-2107
(215) 898-8918

PUBLICATIONS

ERIC Review
ACCESS ERIC
1600 Research Boulevard
Rockville, MD 20850
(800)-LET-ERIC (For free subscription)
Internet: http://www.ed.gov
Educational database of information sources.
For a list of public Internet access points to
ERIC database with step-by-step log in
instructions, send an e–mail message to:
ericdb@aspensys.com.

*How to Talk So Kids Will Listen and Listen
So Kids Will Talk (Book)*
Adele Faber and Elaine Mazlish, 1982
Avon Books
1350 Avenue of Americas
New York, NY 10019
(212) 261-6800
Fax: (212) 532-2172

*The Teaching Marketplace: Make Money
With Freelance Teaching, Corporate
Training, and On the Lecture Circuit* (book)
Bart Brodsky and Janet Gers
Community Resource Institute
PO Box 7880
Berkeley, CA 94709
(510) 526-7190

Technology and Learning
330 Progress Road
Dayton, OH 45449
(513) 847-5900
(800) 543-4383

Chapter 11
Engineering Services, Products, and Manufacturing

COMPANIES

Air Taser, Inc.
Patrick Smith, President, Director of
Corporate Strategy
Tom Smith, Director of Finance
Malcolm Sherman, Director of Sales and
Marketing
Steve Tuttle, Director of Government Affairs
7339 E. Evans Road, #1
Scottsdale, AZ 85260
(602) 991-0797
(800) 978-2737
Fax: (602) 991-0791

Baby Think It Over, Inc.
Rick and Mary Jurmain
4330 Golf Terrace
Eau Claire, WI 54701
(715) 830-2040
(800) 830-1416
Fax: (715) 830-2050

Western Design Center, Inc.
William D. Mensch, Jr.
2166 E. Brown Road
Mesa, AZ 85213
(602) 962-4545
Fax: (602) 835-6442
E–mail: wdesignc@indirect.com

ORGANIZATIONS

American Electronics Association
1225 Eye Street, NW, Suite 950
Washington, DC 20005
(202) 682-9110

American Institute of Chemical Engineers
345 East 47th Street
New York, NY 10017
(212) 705-7338
Chemical & Engineering News

American Society of Civil Engineers
1015 15th Street NW
Washington, DC 20005
(202) 789-2200
Journal: *Civil Engineering*

**American Society of Heating,
Refrigerating and Air Conditioning
Engineering (ASHRAE)**
1791 Tullie Circle NE

Atlanta, GA 30329
(404) 636-8400
(800) 5-ASHRAE
Fax: (404) 321-5478

American Society of Home Inspectors (ASHI)
85 W. Alqonquin Road
Arlington Heights, IL 60005
(708) 290-1919
Fax: (708) 290-1920

American Society of Safety Engineers
1800 E. Oakton Street
Des Plaines, IL 60018
(708) 692-4121

Electronic Industries Association
2001 Pennsylvania Avenue
Washington, DC 20006
(202) 457-4900

Institute of Industrial Engineers (IIE)
25 Technology Park
Norcross, GA 30092
(404) 449-0460
Fax: (404) 263-8532

Inventors Workshop International Education Foundation (IWIWEF)
7332 Mason Avenue
Canoga Park, CA 91506
(818) 340-4268
Fax: (818) 884-8312
Interesting publications for inventors.

National Association of Broadcasters
1771 N Street, NW
Washington, DC 20036
(202) 429-5373
(800) 368-5644
Fax: (202) 775-3515

National Society of Professional Engineers
1420 King Street
Alexandria, VA 22314
(703) 684-2800
(703) 684-2802
Fax: (703) 836-4875

PUBLICATIONS

Circuit Cellar INK
The Computer Applications Journal
PO Box 698
Holmes, PA 19043-9613
(800) 269-6301

Computer Aided Design
Dean L. Taylor
Addison Wesley
One Jacob Way
Reading, MA 01867
(617) 944-3700
(800) 238-9682

Computer Design
Circulation Department
Box 3466
Tulsa, OK 74101
(918) 831-9554

EE (Evaluation Engineering): The Magazine of Electronic Evaluation and Test
Nelson Publishing
2504 Tamiami Trail
Nokomis, FL 34275-3482
(941) 966-9521
Fax: (941) 966-2590

Electronic Engineering Times
CMP Publications
600 Community Drive
Manhasset, NY 11030
(847) 647-6834
Fax: (847) 647-6838

Midnight Engineering, Resources and Insight for the Entrepreneurial Engineer
William E. Gates
1700 Washington Avenue
Rocky Ford, CO 81067
(719) 254-4558
Fax: (719) 254-4517
The magazine itself is an entrepreneurial endeavor.

Nuts and Volts, Exploring Electronics and Technology for the Hobbyist and Professional
430 Princeland Court
Corona, CA 91719
(909) 371-8497
(800) 783-4624 Subscriptions only
Fax: (909) 371-3052
E-mail: 74262.3664@compuserve.com

Portable Design, Strategies, Technologies and Products for Mobile Computing and Communications
PennWell Publishing Company
1421 South Sheridan Road
Tulsa, OK 74112
(918) 835-3161
Fax: (918) 831-9497
Internet: http://www.penwell.com

Chapter 12
Entertainment and Leisure Services

COMPANIES

Mesa Aquatics
Mark Tayler
P.O. Box 2071
Mesa, AZ 85214
(602) 827-1964 Fax and phone

Wacky Wires & Wonders:
An Artistic Approach
Margie Frierson
12430 N. 65th Place
Scottsdale, AZ 85254
(602) 483-1999

ORGANIZATIONS

Aircraft Owners and Pilots Association
421 Aviation Way
Frederick, MD 21701
(301) 695-2000
(800) 872-2677
Fax: (301) 695-2375

American Recreational Equipment Association
PO Box 395
Mason, OH 45040
(513) 398-3663
Fax: (513) 398-2815

American Recreational Gold Association (ARGA)
PO Box 417-120
Chicago, IL 60641-7120
(808) 453-0080
(312) 283-3880
Fax: (708) 453-0083

American Society of Travel Agents (ASTA)
1101 King Street
Alexandria, VA 22314
(703) 739-2782
Fax: (703) 684-8319

Balloon Federation of America (BFA)
PO Box 400
Indianola, IA 50125
(515) 961-8809
Fax: (515) 961-3537
Thermal and gas ballooning.

Casino and Theme Party Operators Association
2120 G.S. Highland Drive
Las Vegas, NV 89102
(702) 385-2963

International Association of Tour Managers—North American Region
65 Charnes Drive
East Haven, CT 06513-1225
(203) 466-0425
Fax: (203) 787-6384

International Magic Dealers Association (IMDA)
Hank Lee Magic
PO Box 789
Medford, MA 02155
(617) 391-8749

National Association of RV Parks and Campgrounds
8605 Westwood Center Drive
Vienna, VA 22182
(703) 734-3000
Fax: (703) 734-3004

National Health Club Association
12596 W. Bayaud Avenue, 1st Floor
Denver, CO 80228
(303) 753-6422
(800) 765-6422
Fax: (303) 986-6813

National Sporting Goods Association (NSGA)
Lake Center Plaza Building
1699 Wall Street
Mount Prospect, IL 60056-5780
(708) 439-4000
Fax: (708) 439-0111

Recreational Vehicle Dealers Association of North America
3251 Old Lee Highway #500
Fairfax, VA 22030-2515
(703) 591-7130
(800) 336-0355
Fax: (703) 591-0734

RV Business
TL Enterprises, Inc.
29901 Agoura Road
Agoura, CA 91301
(818) 991-4980

Sporting Goods Manufacturers Association
200 Castlewood Drive
North Palm Beach, FL 33408
(407) 842-4100
Fax: (407) 863-8984

Travel Industry Association of America
1133 21st Street, NW
Washington, DC 20026
(202) 293-1433

NONPROFITS

Society of Nonprofit Organizations
6314 Odana Road, # 1
Madison, WI 53719-1141
(608) 274-9777
(800) 424-7367
Nonprofit World magazine (bimonthly)

Chapter 13
Environmental Services and Products

COMPANIES

Trojan Technologies, Inc.
Hank Vander Laan, President and CEO
3020 Gore Road
London, Ontario, Canada N5V 4T7
(519) 457-3400
Fax: (519) 457-3030

National N ViroTechnology, Inc.
122 S. Wilson Avenue, Drawer D
Fremont, OH 43420
(419) 535-6374
(419) 334-3801
Fax: (419) 332-1534

Ames Technologies, Inc.
Ames, IA 50010
(515) 233-2632

ARBICO (Arizona Biological Controls), Inc.
PO Box 4247 CRB
Tucson, AZ 85738-1247
(520) 825-9785
(800) 827-BUGS (2847)
Fax: (520) 825-2038

Biofoam Corporation
2345 E. Thomas Road, #220
Phoenix, AZ 85016
(602) 954-3626
Fax: (602) 954-8221

EcoMall
350 Fifth Avenue, Suite 7712

New York, NY 10118
(212) 289-1234
Email: ecomall@internetmci.com

Ecotrek
PO Box 9638
Amherst, MA 01059
(800) 858-1383

**Everything Earthly/Center for
Sustainable Living/Green Retailers**
Richard Scott
414 S. Mill Avenue, #118
Tempe, AZ 85281
(800) 968-0690
(602) 968-0690
Fax: (602) 968-0087

Natural Cotton Colours
Sally Fox
PO Box 66
Wickenberg, AZ 85358
(520) 684-7199
Fax: (520) 684-7299

Garbage Collection
Kelly Gode
954 60th Street
Oakland, CA 94608
(206) 453-8322

The ODB Company
Leaf Collection Systems
5118 Glen Alden Drive
Richmond, VA 23231
(804) 226-4433
(800) 446-9823
Fax: (804) 226-6914

ORGANIZATIONS

Air and Waste Management Association
PO Box 2861
Pittsburgh, PA 15230
(412) 232-3444

**American Academy of Environmental
Engineering**
130 Holiday Court #100
Annapolis, MD 21401

(410) 266-3311
Fax: (410) 266-7653

American Water Works Association
6666 W. Quincy Avenue
Denver, CO 80235
(303) 794-7711
Journal: *American Water Works Association*

American Chemical Society
1155 16th Street NW
Washington, DC 20036
(202) 872-4600
Journal: *Environmental Science and
Technology*

American Institute of Chemical Engineers
345 East 47th Street
New York, NY 10017
(212) 705-7338
Chemical & Engineering News (newsletter)

American Society of Civil Engineers
1015 15th Street NW
Washington, DC 20005
(202) 789-2200
Civil Engineering (journal)

American Society of Safety Engineers
1800 E. Oakton Street
Des Plaines, IL 60018
(708) 692-4121

**Association of Ground Water Scientists
and Engineers**
6375 Riverside Drive
Dublin, OH 43017
(614) 761-1711

Board of Certified Safety Professionals
208 Burwash Avenue
Savoy, IL 61874
(217) 359-9263

Center for Hazardous Materials Research
320 William Pitt Way
Pittsburgh, PA 15238
(412) 826-5320

Environmental Careers Organization
286 Congress Street, Third Floor

Boston, MA 02210-1009
(202) 347-7834
Fax: (202) 347-7839

Environmental Information Association (EIA)
3805 Presidential Parkway, #106
Atlanta, GA 30340
(404) 986-2760
Fax: (404) 986-2768
Environmental risks in buildings.

Green Retailers Association
Contact: Richard Scott, Founding President
Everything Earthly, Inc.
414 South Mill Avenue, #118
Tempe, AZ 85281
(602) 968-0690
Fax: (602) 968-0087

Institute for Industrial Engineers
25 Technology Park
Norcross, GA 30092
(404) 449-0460

Institute of Packing Professionals
11800 Sunrise Valley Drive, # 212
Reston, VA 22091
(703) 318-8970
Fax: (703) 318-0310

Institute of Scrap Recycling Industries
1627 G Street, NW #1000
Washington, DC 20005
(202) 466-4050
Fax: (202) 775-9109

National Association of Environmental Professionals
PO Box 15210
Alexandria, VA 22309
(703) 660-2364

National Environmental Health Association
720 S. Colorado Blvd.
970 South Tower
Denver, CO 80222
(303) 756-9090
Journal of Environmental Health

National Materials Exchange Network
(Online)
Attn: Bob Smee
E-mail: nmen@eznet.com
Internet: http://www.earthcycle.com
(509) 466-1532
Fax: (509) 466-1041
Extensive free local and international online marketplace for recycling surplus equipment and goods funded through a grant from the EPA. Recycling of virtually all materials, both hazardous and non-hazardous.

National Recycling Coalition
1727 King Street, #105
Alexandria, VA 22314-2720
(703) 683-9025
Fax: (703) 683-9026

National Solid Wastes Management Association
1730 Rhode Island Avenue, NW
Washington, DC 20036
(202) 659-4613

Society of Environmental Toxicology and Chemistry
1101 14th Street, NW, # 1100
Washington, DC 20005
(202) 371-1275
Internet listing of recycling associations:
http://www.recycle.net/recycle/Associations/AssnIndex.html
There are specific recycling organizations for paper, metals, packaging, tires, batteries, plastics, petroleum, textiles, glass, etc.
Another recycling Internet site is http://granite.sentex.net/recycle

PERIODICALS

BioCycle, Journal of Composting & Recycling

In Business, the Magazine for Environmental Entrepreneuring
Compost Science and Utilization
Book: ***Composting Source Separated Organics*** (composting opportunities)

Book: *BioCycle Guide to Maximum Recycling*
Book: *BioCycle Guide to the Art & Science of Composting*
JG Press
419 State Avenue
Emmaus, PA 18049
(610) 967-4135

Environmental Business Journal
Environmental Business Publishing, Inc.
827 Washington
San Diego, CA 92103
(619) 295-7685

Hazmat World
Tower–Borner Publishing, Inc.
800 Roosevelt Road
Glen Ellyn, IL 60137
(708) 858-1888

Pollution Engineering
8773 S. Ridgeline Blvd.
Highland Ranch, CO 80126-2329
(303) 470-4445 Subscriptions
Fax: (708) 390-2636 Office

BOOKS

Business Environmental Handbook
Martin D. Westerman, 1993
Oasis Press/PSI Research
300 N. Valley Drive
Grants Pass, OR 97526
541-479-9464
(800) 228-2275
Fax: 541-476-1479

E Factor
Joel Makower, 1993
Times Books: Division of Random House
201 E. 50th Street, 22nd Floor
New York, NY 10022
(800) 733-3000
Fax: (212) 751-2600

Harrison's Illustrated Guide: How to Screen Residential Properties for Apparent Environmental Hazards, Guidelines for

Environmental Appraisal Addendum
Henry Harrison, Julie Harrison, 1995
The H Squared Company
New Haven, CT 06511
(203) 562-3159
Fax: (203) 624-5841

State of the World, A Worldwatch Institute Report on Progress Toward a Sustainable Society (updated yearly)
Lester Brown
W.W. Norton & Company, Inc.
500 Fifth Avenue
New York, NY 10110
(212) 354-5500
(800) 233-4830 Orders

Chapter 14
Family and Personal Services

COMPANIES

Children's Campus
Kreative Solutions for Child Care, Inc.
Consulting, Staff Training, On-Site Management
Mary Sue Watson
2830 North 43rd Avenue
Phoenix, AZ 85009
(602) 233-2218 (Children's Campus)

Traco, International
Peter Hill
1140 S. Country Club Drive #110
Mesa, AZ 85210
(602) 969-4701
Fax: (602) 969-7753

Air Taser, Inc.
7339 E. Evans Road, #1
Scottsdale, AZ 85260
(602) 978-2737
(800) 978-2737
Fax: (602) 347-7839

ORGANIZATIONS

American Counseling Association (ACA)
5999 Stevenson Avenue

Alexandria, VA 22304-3300
(800) 347-6647
Fax: (800) 473-2329
Divisions: Career counseling: National Career Development Association (NCDA) and National Employment Counseling Association (NECA).

Institute of Personal Image Consultants
10 Bay Street Landing #7F
Staten Island, NY 10301
(718) 273-3229

For-profit child-care centers:
The NECPA Commission, Inc.
1029 Railroad Street
Conyers, GA 30207
(800) 543-7161
Fax: (770) 388-7772
CCP (Certified Childcare Professional) credentialing

For-profit and non-profit centers:
National Academy of Early Childhood Programs
1509 16th Street, NW
Washington, DC 20036-1426
(202) 232-8777
(800) 424-2460
Fax: (202) 328-1846
Catalog of publications available; NAEYC accreditation program.

Home-based child-care:
National Association for Family Day Care
1331-A Pennsylvania Avenue, NW, #348
Washington, DC 20004
(515) 282 8192
(800) 359-3817

Council for Early Childhood Professional Recognition
1341 G Street, NW, #400
Washington, DC 20005
(800) 424-4310
Fax: (202) 265-9161
CDA (Childcare Development Associate) credentialing

PUBLICATIONS
Childcare Information Exchange
PO Box 2890
Redmond, WA 98073
(206) 883-9394
(800) 221-2864
Fax: (206) 867-5217
A beautiful, informative bimonthly magazine for childcare professionals. Looks at childcare from a more holistic perspective.

How to Open and Operate a Homebased Day-Care Business (book)
Dan Ramsey, 1995
TAB Books
PO Box 40
Blue Ridge Summit, PA 17294-0850
(717) 794-2191
(800) 762-4729

Start and Run a Profitable Home Cleaning Business (book)
Susan Bewsey, 1995
Self Council Press
1704 N. State Street
Bellingham, WA 98225
(360) 676-4530
(800) 663-3007

Chapter 15
Financial and Accounting Services

COMPANIES
The Access Group
Dave Dauer, Sales Manager
Bob Gerver, Operations Manager
P.O. Box 293
E. Longmeadow, MA 01028-0293
(800) 480-6694
Fax: (908) 449-6291

Fidelity Monitor, The Independent Newsletter for Fidelity Investors
Independent Fidelity Investors, Inc.
Jack Bowers
P.O. Box 1270

Rocklin, CA 95677-7294
(800) 397-3094
(916) 624-0191

ORGANIZATIONS

American Accounting Association
5717 Bessie Drive
Sarasota, FL 34223-2399
(813) 921-7747
Fax: (813) 423-4093

American Association of Certified Public Accountants
1211 Avenue of Americas
New York, NY 10036-8775
(212) 596-6200
(800) 862-4272
Fax: (212) 596-6213

American Institute of Certified Public Accountants
1455 Pennsylvania Avenue, NW #400
Washington, DC 20004
(202) 737-6600

American Insurance Association
1130 Connecticut Avenue, NW #1000
Washington, DC 20036
(202) 828-7100

Certified Financial Planner Board of Standards
1660 Lincoln Street #3050
Denver, CO 80264
(303) 830-7543
Fax: (303) 860-7388
CFP Certification

Independent Insurance Agents of America
412 First Street, SE #300
Washington, DC 20003
(202) 863-7000

Institute of Tax Consultants
7500 212th SW, #205
Edmonds, WA 98026
(206) 774-3521
Fax: (206) 672-0461

International Federation of Accountants
114 W. 47th Street, #2410
New York, NY 10036
(212) 302-5952

International Association for Financial Planning (IAFP)
Two Concourse Parkway #800
Atlanta, GA 30328
(404) 395-1605
(800) 945-IAFP
Fax: (404) 668-7758

International Association of Professional Financial Financial Consultants (IAPFC)
4127 W. Cypress Street
Tampa, FL 33607
(813) 832-5532
Fax: (813) 875-7352

National Association of Personal Financial Advisors (NAPFA)
1130 Lake Cook Road, #150
Buffalo Grove, IL 60089
(708) 537-7722
(800) 366-2732
Fax: (708) 537-7740

National Association for Financial Planning
Two Concourse Parkway, #800
Atlanta, GA 30328
(404) 395-1605

PUBLICATIONS

The Future of the Accounting Profession: A Global Perspective
Kenneth S. Most, 1993
Quorum Books, Greenfield Publishing Co.
88 Post Road West
Westport, CT 06881
(203) 226-3571
(800) 225-5800

Investigative Accounting: Techniques and Procedures for Determining the Reality Behind the Financial Statements
Kalman A Barson, CPA
Van Nostrand Reinhold Company

Order Distribution Center
7625 Empire Drive
Florence, KY 41042-2978
(606) 525-6600
(800) 842-3636

Marketing for CPAs, Accountants and Tax Professionals
William J. Winston, Editor, 1995
The Haworth Press
10 Alice Street
Binghamton, NY 13904-1580
(607) 722-5857
(800) 342-9678

Chapter 16
Food Services and Products

COMPANIES
Arizona Bread Company
Amy and Matt Wakser
7000 E. Shea Boulevard, Suite 101
Scottsdale, AZ 85254
(602) 948-8338
Fax: (602) 922-4486

China Mist Tea Company
John Martinson, President
Dan Schweiker, Chairman, CEO
7435 E. Tierra Buena Lane
Scottsdale, AZ 85260
(602) 998-8807
Fax: (602) 443-8384

ORGANIZATIONS
American Institute of Food Distributors
2812 Broadway
Fairlawn, NJ 07410-3913
(201) 791-5570
Fax: (201) 791-5222

American Society of Brewing Chemists
3340 Pilot Knob Road
St. Paul, MN 55121-2097
(612) 454-7250
Fax: (612) 454-0766

Beer Institute
1225 Eye Street NW, #825
Washington, DC 20005
(202) 737-2037
Fax: (202) 737-7004

Brewers Association of America
P.O. Box 876
Belmar, NJ 07719
(908) 280-9153
Fax: (908) 280-9000

Food Marketing Institute
800 Connecticut Avenue, NW
Washington, DC 20006
(202) 452-8444

Food Processing Machinery and Supplies Association
200 Daingerfield Road
Alexandria, VA 22314
(703) 686-1080
(800) 331-8816
Fax: (703) 548-6563
Focus on Food & Beverage (newsletter)

International Bottled Water Association (IBWA)
113 N. Henry Street
Alexandria, VA 22314-2973
(703) 683-5213
Fax: (703) 683-4074

International Food Service Executives Association
1100 S. State Road 7, #103
Margate, FL 33068
(305) 977-0767
Fax: (305) 977-0874

National Association of Concessionaires (NAC)
35 E. Wacker Drive #1545
Chicago, IL 60601
(312) 236-3858
Fax: (312) 236-7809

National Food Processors Association
1401 New York Avenue NW
Washington, DC 20005
(202) 639-5994
Fax: (202) 637-8068
Information Letter

National Restaurant Association
1200 17th Street, NW
Washington, DC 20036
(202) 331-5900

Specialty Coffee Association of America
1 World Trade Center, # 800
Long Beach, CA 90831-0800
(310) 893-8090
Fax: (310) 893-8091
In Good Taste (newsletter)

Tea Association of the USA (TA)
230 Park Avenue
New York, NY 10169
(212) 986-9415
Fax: (212) 697-8658

PUBLICATIONS
Beer Marketer's Insights Newsletter
Beer Marketer's Insights, Inc.
51 Virginia Avenue
West Nyack, NY 10994
(914) 358-7751
Fax: (914) 358-7860

Beverage Alcohol Market Report
Peregrine Communications
160 E. 48th Street
New York, NY 10017
(212) 371-5237

Beverage World Magazine
Keller International Publishing Corporation
150 Great Neck Road
Great Neck, NY 11021
(516) 529-9210
Fax: (516) 829-5414

Gourmet Retailer
Specialty Media, Inc.
3301 Ponce de Leon Blvd. #300

Coral Gables, FL 33134
(305) 446-3388
Fax: (305) 446-2868

The Republic of Tea: Letters to a Young Zentrepreneur
Mel Ziegler, 1992
Doubleday Publishing
PO Box 5071
Des Plaines, IL 60017-5071
(212) 354-6500
(800) 223-6834

Chapter 17
Franchising

COMPANIES
HEADSHOTS®
Shari and Bob Leve
2064 Fiesta Mall
1425 W. Southern Avenue
Mesa, AZ 85202-4814
(602) 833-4597

Karen Rego
HEADSHOTS® Corporate Office
P.O. Box 5
Cedar Park, TX 78630
Currently not granting additional franchises.

NOVUS Auto Glass Repair and Replacement® (windshield repair and replacement)
NOVUS Windshield Repair® (windshield repair only)
NOVUS Franchising, Inc.
10425 Hampshire Avenue South
Minneapolis, MN 55438
(612) 944-8000
(800) 328-1117
Fax: (612) 944-2542

Styles On Video, Inc.
No longer in business.

Water 'n Ice
No longer franchising. Former franchises, based in Arizona, are individually owned.

ORGANIZATIONS

Forum on Franchising, American Bar Association
750 N. Lakeshore Drive
Chicago, IL 60611
(312) 988-5000
(800) 621-6159

International Franchise Association
1350 New York Avenue #900
Washington, DC 20005
(202) 628-8000
Fax: (202) 628-0812
Franchise Opportunities Guide: The Official Guide Published by the International Franchise Association.

BOOKS

Directory of Better Business Bureaus
Council of Better Business Bureaus
4200 Wilson Blvd. #800
Arlington, VA 22209
(703) 276-0100
Fax: (703) 525-8277

Franchise Bible: A Comprehensive Guide
Erwin J Keup, 1995
Oasis Press/PSI Research
300 N. Valley Drive
Grants Pass, OR 97526
541-479-9464
(800) 228-2275
Fax: 541-476-1479

Franchise Buyer
Crain Communications, Inc.
740 N. Rush Street
Chicago, IL 60611
(708) 679-5500
(800) 323-4900
E-mail: info@franchise/.com

The Franchise Handbook
Andrew Sherman, 1993
American Management Association
135 W. 50th Street
New York, NY 10020
(800)-538-4761

Franchise Opportunities
Sterling Publishing Company, Inc.
387 Park Avenue
New York, NY 10016
(212) 532-7160
(800) 367-9692

Franchising: The Bottom Line
Richard Bond, 1995
Source Book Publications
PO Box 12488
Oakland, CA 94604
(510) 839-5471
Fax: (510) 547-3245

The Rating Guide to Franchises
The Encyclopedia of Franchises
Dennis L. Foster, 1991
Facts on File, Inc.
460 Park Avenue South
New York, NY 10016
(212) 683-2244
(800) 322-8755

The Sourcebook of
Franchise Opportunities
Bond, Robert E. and Jeffrey M.
Irwin Professional Publishing
1333 Burr Ridge Pkwy
Burr Ridge, IL 60521
(708) 789-4000
(800) 634-3961

Worldwide Franchise Directory
Gale Research, Inc.
835 Penobscot Building, 645 Griswold Street
Detroit, MI 48226
(313) 961-2242
(800) 877-GALE
Fax: (313) 961-6083

PUBLICATIONS

Franchise Update Publications
PO Box 20547
San Jose, CA 95160
(408) 997-7795
Fax: (408) 997-9377
Magazine and other publications

SmartMoney Magazine
April 1996: Franchising
Customer Service Department
PO Box 7538
Red Oak, IA 51591
(800) 444-4204
This article is a must read before buying a franchise, a very realistic look at franchising.

Chapter 18
Hobby Businesses

COMPANIES

Nancy's Notions
333 Beichl Avenue, PO Box 683
Beaver Dam, WI 53916-0683
(800) 833-0690 Catalog Orders
Fax: (800) 255-8119
Internet: http://www.nancysnotions.com

Roy's Train World
Tim Honetschlager
1033 S. Country Club Drive
Mesa, AZ 85210
(602) 833-4353
Fax: (602) 833-9286

ORGANIZATIONS

Encyclopedia of Associations (updated yearly)
Standard Periodical Directory (updated yearly)
Small Business Sourcebook, 1994
Gale Research, Inc
Edited by Denise Allard
PO Box 33477
Detroit, MI 48232-5477
(800) 877-GALE
Fax: (800) 414-5043
Internet: 72203.1552@compuserve.com

Hobby Industry Association of America
319 E. 54th Street
Elmwood Park, NJ 07407
(201) 794-1133
Trade association for hobby and craft suppliers.

BOOKS

Card Sharks: How Upper Deck Turned a Child's Hobby Into a High Stakes Billion Dollar Business
Pete Williams, 1995
Promoting & Marketing Your Crafts
Edwin Field, Selma Field, 1993
Macmillan Publishers
100 Front Street, Box 500
Riverside, New Jersey 0875-7500
(800) 223-2336

Cart Your Way To Success
How To Make Money With Crafts
Birdhouse Enterprises
110 Jennings Avenue
Patchogue, NY 11772
Write for information.

Automobile Quarterly's Complete Handbook of Automobile Hobbies
Automobile Quarterly, Division of Kutztown Publishing Company, 1981
PO Box 348, 15040 Kutztown Road, Kutztown, PA 19530
(800) 523-0236
If you are interested in vintage transportation from fire engines to motorcycles to autos, this book has a wealth of information. Also publishes the periodical, *Automobile Quarterly*, concerning vintage cars.

Crafts Business Encyclopedia
Leonard D. DuBoft, revised edition: Michael Scott, 1993
Harvest Books
6277 Sea Harbor Drive
Orlando, FL 32887
(800) 543-1918

Hobby Business Guide
Holmes F. Crouch, 1994
Allyear Tax Guides
20484 Glen Brae Drive
Saratoga, CA 95070
(408) 867-2628
(800) 992-6656

Tax and financial considerations for a hobby business. Special chapters on Animal Breeding and Showing, Farms, Orchards, Vineyards, Vacation Property, Research and Exploration, Sports, Travel and Theatrics, Creators and Collectors. Very useful.

How to Be a Weekend Entrepreneur—Making money at craft fairs and trade shows
Susan Ratliff, 1991
Marketing Methods Press
1413 E. Marshall
Phoenix, AZ 85014
(602) 793-5000
(800) 775-1700

The How-To's of Gift Baskets: Growing a Successful Gift Basket Business
Carol Starr, 1993
Green Falls Investment Company
8045 Antoine, Suite 147
Houston, TX 77088
(713) 956-5190

How to Make Cash Money at Swap Meets, Flea Markets, etc.
Jordan Cooper
Loopanics
PO Box 1197
Port Townsend, WA 98368
(360) 385-5087
(800) 380-2230 Credit card orders

How to Recognize and Refinish Antiques for Pleasure and Profit
Jacquelyn Peake, 1984
Globe Pequot
PO Box 833
Old Saybrook, CT 06475
(203) 395-0440
(800) 243-0495

Marketing Your Arts & Crafts, Creative Ways to Profit from Your Work
Janice West, 1994
The Summit Group
1227 West Magnolia, Suite 500

Fort Worth, TX 76104
(800) 875-3346
Fax: (817) 274-1196
Chapters include Alternative Spaces, Museum and Hotel Gift Shops, Corporate Art Markets, Co-op America Business Network, Selling to Professionals, Special Outlets for Senior Citizens, Resources for Artists with Disabilities. Fifty chapters featuring many unusual ways of marketing your arts and crafts.

Promoting & Marketing Your Crafts
Edwin Field, Selma Field, 1993
Audel Books, MacMillan Publishing
100 Front Street, Book 500
Riverside, NJ 08075-7500
(609) 461-6500

A Treasure Trove of Crafts Marketing Success Secrets
Barbara Brabec, 1986
Barbara Brabec Productions
P.O. Box 2137
Naperville, IL 60566
Chapters on Craft Fairs (contacts given), Selling to Shops and Galleries, Wholesaling, Party Plans, Holiday Boutiques, Craft Coops and Networks, Craft Organizations, Suppliers and Resources.

Writer's Market (Updated yearly)
Writer's Digest Books
F&W Publications
1507 Dana Avenue
Cincinnati, OH 45207
(513) 531-2690
(800) 289-0963

PERIODICALS
The Craft Report
300 Water Street
Wilmington, DE 19801
(800) 777-7098
(302) 656-2209
Emphasis is on helping artisans find markets.

Index to How to Do It Information: A Periodical Index
Norman Lathrop Enterprises
2342 Star Drive
Box 198
Wooster, OH 44691
(216) 262-5587
Periodical index for hobby magazines. Excellent source of how-to articles.

Niche—Magazine for Progressive Retailers
3000 Chestnut Avneue, Ste. 304
Baltimore, MD 21211
(410) 235-5116
(800) 642-4314
Specialized periodicals can be located by advertisements in related magazines and newsletters, talking with others in your hobby, getting on suppliers' mailing lists and reading bibliographies in hobby books. The library is a good place to start your search.

Online
All the large online services have forums for hobbyists. Most offer a package including free online time for about ten dollars a month, including Internet access. Usenet groups can be an excellent resource.

Chapter 19
Home Improvement, Construction, and Interior Design

COMPANIES

Ky-ko Roofing Systems
Obby Hopper, Field Operations
Dan Stoller, Director of Sales and Marketing
Tony Gabriele, Director of New Construction
2149 West Mountain View
Phoenix, AZ 85021-1814
(602) 944-4600
Fax (602) 944-5931

Park Your Pool
Lloyd Brunn
3634 North 52nd Place
Phoenix, AZ 85018

(602) 840-2642
Fax: (602) 840-3475

ORGANIZATIONS

Air Conditioning Contractors of America
1712 New Hampshire Avenue NW
Washington, DC 20009
(202) 483-9370
Fax: (202) 234-4721

American Painting Contractors
American Paint Journal Company
2911 Washington Avenue
St. Louis, MO 63103
(314) 534-0301

American Society of Interior Designers
608 Massachusetts Avenue NE
Washington, DC 20002
(202) 546-3480

American Subcontractors Association (ASA)
1004 Duke Street
Alexandria, VA
(703) 684-3450
Fax: (703) 836-3482

Association of Builders and Contractors (ABC)
1300 N. 17th Street
Rosslyn, VA 22209
(703) 812-2000

Association of General Contractors of America (AGC)
1957 E. Street NW
Washington, DC 20006
(202) 393-2040
Fax: (202) 347-4004

Association Landscape Contractors of America (ALCA)
12200 Sunrise Valley #150
Reston, VA 22091
(703) 620-6363
Fax: (702) 620-6365

Garden Council (GC)
10210 Bald Hill Road
Mitchellville, MD 20721-2836
(301) 577-4073
Fax: (301) 459-6533
Retailers, growers, manufacturers, distributors, and suppliers.

**International Interior
Design Association (IIDA)**
341 Merchandise Mart
Chicago, IL 60654
(312) 467-1950
Fax: (312) 467-0779

**International Intelligent
Buildings Association (IIBA)**
PO Box 683
East Brunswick, NJ 08816
(908) 249-4159

**Log Home Builders Association
of North America (LHBANA)**
22203 SR 203
Monroe, WA 98272
(206) 794-4469

**National Association
of Home Builders**
1201 15th Street NW
Washington, DC 20005
(202) 822-0200
Fax: (202) 822-0559

**National Association of Plumbing,
Heating, and Cooling Contractors
(NAPHCC)**
180 S. Washington Street
PO Box 6808
Falls Church, IA 22040
(703) 237-8100
(800) 533-7694
Fax: (703) 237-7442

**National Association of Women
in Construction (NAWC)**
327 S. Adams Street
Fort Worth, TX 76104
(817) 877-5551

(800) 552-3506
Fax: (817) 877-0324

**National Lumber & Business
Materials Dealers Association**
40 Ivy Street, SE
Washington, DC 20003
(202) 547-2230

**Painting and Decorating
Contractors of America**
3913 Old Lee Highway #33B
Fairfax, VA 22030
(703) 359-0826
(800) 332-7322
Fax: (703) 359-2576
Specific organizations exist for building contracting specialties. See the Directory of Associations from Gale Research.

BOOKS

*How to Succeed With Your
Own Construction Business*
Stephen and Janelle Diller, 1990
Plumbers' Handbook
Howard Massey, 1985
Craftsman Book Company
Box 6500
Carlsbad, CA 92008
(619) 438-7826
(800) 829-8123
Fax: (619) 438-0398

National Plumbing Code Handbook
R. Dodge Woodson, Editor, 1993
McGraw-Hill Publishing
1221 Avenue of Americas
New York, NY 10020
(212) 512-2000
(800) 722-4726
Fax: (212) 512-2821

Professional Builder (semi-monthly)
8773 South Ridgeline Blvd.
Highlands Ranch, CO 80126-2329
(303) 470-4445

Chapter 20
Import and Export Businesses

COMPANIES
Mina International, Inc.
Maribel Guglielmo
11202 N. 24th Avenue #103
Phoenix, AZ 85029
(602) 943-9311
Fax (602) 943-9375

Pachinko Paradise, Inc.
Mia and Mike Rogers
1425 E. University, Tempe, Suite 107
Tempe, AZ 85281
(602) 966-9800
Fax (602) 966-2292

ORGANIZATIONS
American Associations of Exporters and Importers (AAEI)
11 W. 42nd Street
New York, NY 10036
(212) 944-2230
Fax: (212) 382-2606

International Traders Association (IT)
c/o The Mellinger Company
6100 Variel Avenue
Woodland Hills, CA 91367
(818) 884-4400
Fax: (818) 594-5804

BOOKS
The Arthur Andersen North American Business Sourcebook—The Most Comprehensive Authoritative Reference to Expanding Trade in the North American Market
Triumph Books
644 South Clark Street
Chicago, IL 60605
(312) 939-3330
Fax: (312) 663-3557

A Basic Guide to Exporting
United States Department of Commerce, International Trade Administration

United States Government Printing Office
Superintendent of Documents
Mail Stop SSOP
Washington, DC 20402-9328

Business Germany: A Practical Guide to Understanding the German Culture
Peggy Kenna, Sondra Levy, 1994
NTC Publishing Group
4255 West Touhy Avenue
Lincolnwood, IL 60646
(708) 679-5500
Also editions for China, France, Japan, Korea, Mexico, Spanish, Taiwan.

Business Handbook How to Succeed in Japan: Access Nippon 1994
Access Nippon, Inc., 1994
Tsauku Bldg.
1-24-11 Sugamo, Toshima-ku,
Tokyo 170, Japan
+81-3-5395-4800
Fax: +81-3-5395-4803
Profiles Japanese companies.

Demographic Yearbook
United Nations Publications
Two United Nations Plaza, Room DC2-0853
New York, NY 10017
(212) 963-8302
(800) 252-9646

Doing Business in Russia: Basic Facts for the Pioneering Entrepreneur
Vladimir Kashin, Robert Johnstone, Tankred Golenpolsky, 1995
Oasis Press/PSI Research
300 North Valley Drive
Grants Pass, OR 97826
(541) 479-9464
(800)-228-2275
Fax: (541) 476-1479

Doing Business With Japanese Men: A Woman's Handbook
Christalyn Brannent and Tracey Wilen, 1993
Stone Bridge Press
PO Box 8208
Berkeley, CA 94707

(510) 524-8732
(800) 947-7271

The Do's and Taboos of International Trade
Roger Axtell, 1990
John Wiley and Sons, Inc.
605 Third Avenue
New York, NY 10158-0012
(212) 850-6000
(800) 225-5945 (Orders)

Export Import
Joseph Zodl
Betterway Books
1507 Dana Avenue
Cincinnati, OH 45207
(513) 269-0458
(800) 289-0963
Fax: (513) 531-4082

Exportisie
Small Business Foundation of America
20 Park Plaza Avenue
Boston, MA 02116
(617) 350-5096

Export Now, A Guide For Small Businesses
Richard L. Leza, 1993
Oasis Press/PSI Research
300 North Valley Drive
Grants Pass, OR 97526
(541) 479-9464
(800) 228-2275
Fax: (541) 476-1479

The Export Yellow Pages
US West Communications
(800) 422-8793
Lists 17,000 exporters in the United States.

A Guide to Successful Business Relations With the Chinese—Opening the Great Wall's Gate
Huang Quanyu, PhD, Richard S. Andrulis, PhD, and Chen Tong, 1994
International Business Press, A Division of Haworth Press
10 Alice Street
Binghamton, NY 13904-1580

(607) 722-5857
(800) 342-9678
Also: **International Business Handbook**, V.H. Kirpalani
The Global Business: Four Key Marketing Strategies, Edited by Erdenor Kaynak
Euromarketing: Strategies for International Trade and Export, Edited by Erdenor Kaynak, Pervez Ghauri.

Import/Export—A Guide to Growth, Profits, and Market Share
Howard Goldsmith
Prentice Hall, 1989
113 Sylvan Avenue, Rt 9W
Englewood Cliffs, NJ 07632
(201) 592-2000
(800) 922-0579

Importing From India, A buyer's manual for selecting suppliers, negotiating orders and arranging methods of payment for more profitable purchasing
Trade Media Ltd. Asiamag Limited, 1990
GPO Box 12367
Hong Kong,
(852) 555-4777
Fax: (852) 873-0488
US Phone number (708) 475-1900
Also available: Guides for Hong Kong, China, Korea, Taiwan, Thailand and the Philippines from the same publisher. Company also publishes Asian Sources Group of trade magazines.

Intercultural Business Communication
Lillian H. Chaney and Jeanette S. Martin, 1995
Prentice-Hall
113 Sylvan Avenue, Rt 9W
Englewood Cliffs, NJ 07632
(201) 592-2000
(800) 922-0579

International Marketing Handbook
Gale Research, Inc.
835 Penobscot Bldg.
Detroit, MI 48226

(313) 961-2242
(800) 877-GALE
Fax: (313) 961-6241
Three volumes of marketing profiles for foreign countries.

The Portable Encyclopedia for Doing Business with China
World Trade Press
1505 Fifth Avenue
San Rafael, CA 94901
(415) 454-9934
(800) 833-8586
Fax: (415) 453-7980
Series includes books about Argentina, Australia, Hong Kong, Japan, Korea, Mexico, Singapore, Taiwan and the USA. Also: ***A Basic Guide to Exporting, Importers' Manual USA*** 1995-96. Call for info on CD-ROM products.

Profitable Exporting: A Complete Guide to Marketing Your Products Abroad
John Gordon and J.R. Arnold
John Wiley and Sons, Inc.
605 Third Avenue
New York, NY 10158
(800) 225-5945
Step-by-step guide to taking your business internationally.

Put Your Best Foot Forward—Asia: A Fearless Guide to International Commerce and Behavior
International Education Systems
26 East Exchange Street
St. Paul, MN 55101
(612) 227-2052
Also Europe, Canada, and Mexico.

Winning in Foreign Markets, Your Global Guide
Michele Forzley, 1994
Crisp Publications, Inc.
1200 Hamilton Avenue
Menlo Park, CA 94025

(415) 323-6100
(800) 442-7477

PERIODICALS

Export Today (magazine)
733 15th Street, NW, #1100
Washington, DC 20005
(202) 737-1060
Fax: (202) 783-5966
"How to" magazine for doing business internationally.

Countertrade & Barter
Metal Bulletin, Inc.
220 Fifth Avenue
New York, NY 10001
(212) 213-6202

Foreign Trade Magazine
6849 Old Dominion Drive, #200
McLean, VA 22101
(703) 448-1338
Fax: (703) 448-1841
Trade information including financing and shipping.

International Business Magazine
American International Publishing Corporation
500 Mamaroneck Avenue, Suite 314
Harrison, NY 10528
(914) 381-7700
Fax: (914) 381-7713

Journal of Commerce
Two World Trade Center, 27th Floor
New York, NY 10048
(212) 837-7000
Export opportunities, agricultural trade leads, shipyards, and other foreign trade information.

Trade and Culture
PO Box 10988
Baltimore, MD 21234-9871
(301) 426-2906
Fax: (301) 444-7837

GOVERNMENT ASSISTANCE

U.S. Department of Commerce

Bureau of Export Administration: export licenses.
(202) 377-1455

International Trade Administration (ITA)

14th Street & Constitution Avenue, NW
Washington, DC 20230
(202) 377-3808
Provides information—sales leads, counseling, statistics, videos—concerning foreign markets. Assists in locating and getting access to foreign markets.

Export–Import Bank of the U.S. (Eximbank)

811 Vermont Avenue, NW
Washington, DC 20571
(202) 289-2703
(800) 424-5201
Loan, loan guarantee and insurance programs for foreign trade. Regional offices: Chicago, Houston, Los Angeles, Miami, and New York.

U.S. Customs Service

1301 Constitution Avenue, NW
Washington, DC 20229
(202) 566-8195
Fifty-one additional offices across U.S.

PRIVATE SECTOR INTERNATIONAL ASSISTANCE

World Trade Centers

One World Trade Center, 55th Floor
New York, NY 10048
(212) 775-1370
This is a network of over 160 world trade centers worldwide, with over 40 U.S. centers. By joining, you gain access to information and educational seminars on world trade and facilities and exhibit halls for use with international clients.

Chapter 21
Legal Services and Products

COMPANIES

Nolo Press

Ralph Warner
950 Parker Street
Berkeley, CA 94710
(800) 992-6656
(510) 549-1976
Fax: (510) 548-5902
Internet: http://www.nolo.com

Video Law Services, Inc.

Michaela Miller
1533 Lakewood Road
Jacksonville, FL 32207
(904) 399-8625
Fax: (904) 396-0256
VideoLaw@aol.com

ALI–ABA Committee on Continuing Professional Education

4025 Chestnut Street
Philadelphia, PA 19104
(800) CLE-NEWS
Fax: (215) 243-1664
Continuing education for the legal profession.

Legal Self Help Center

Ryanwood Square
2024 58th Avenue
Vero Beach, FL 32966
(407) 567-1120
Fax: (407) 567-7744
E–mail: lawgix@iu.net
Internet: http://www.legal.net/Idn2.htm
Legal consulting over the Internet.

Practicing Law Institute

810 Seventh Avenue
New York, NY 10019-5818
(800) 260-4PLI
(212) 824-5710
E–mail: info@pli.educ

ORGANIZATIONS

American Academy of Family Mediators
1500 South Highway 100, Suite 355
Golden Valley, MN 55416
(612) 525-8670
Fax: (612) 525-8725
Internet: afmoffice@igc.apc.org

American Bar Association
750 LakeShore Drive
Chicago, IL 60611
(312) 988-5000
(800) 621-6159
Fax: (312) 988-6281
Also: National Association of Women Lawyers (same address)
(312) 988-6186
Fax: (312) 988-6281
ABA Journal, extensive publications list.

American Intellectual Property Law Association
2001 Jefferson Davis Highway #203
Arlington, VA 22202
(703) 415-0780
Fax: (703) 415-0786

National Federation of Paralegal Associations (NFPA)
PO Box 33108
Kansas City, MO 64114-0108
(816) 941-4000
Fax: (816) 941-2725

PUBLICATIONS

The Bordwin Letter
Ounce of Prevention, Inc.
PO Box 610282
Newton, MA 02161-0282
(617) 330-7033
(800) KNOW-HOW
Fax: (617) 527-1905
Prevention of litigation.

Catalyst Newsletter
National Crime Prevention Council
1700 K Street NW, 2nd Floor
Washington, DC 20006-3817

(202) 466-6272
Fax (202) 296-1356
Free. Forum for crime prevention.

Marketing for Lawyers
Leader Publications, New York Law Publishing Company
345 Park Avenue South
New York, NY 10010
(212) 545-6170
(800) 888-8300
Fax: (212) 696-1848

Privacy Journal
Robert Ellis Smith
PO Box 28577
Providence, RI 02908
(401) 274-7861

Research Advisor
Alert Publications
401 W. Fullerton Pkwy, # 1403E
Chicago, IL 60614
(312) 525-7594
Fax: (312) 525-7015
For law researchers, legal secretaries and librarians.

BOOKS

The Independent Paralegal's Handbook
Ralph Warner, 1995
Nolo Press Self-Help Law Books & Software
950 Parker Street
Berkeley, CA 94710
(510) 549-1976
(800) 992-6656
Fax: (510) 548-5902

Chapter 22
Marketing and Event Planning

COMPANIES

Ala Carte Productions
Jerry Hansen
1525 E. Clarendon Avenue
Phoenix, AZ 85016
(602) 285-5564 Phone and fax

Corporate Arts
Gordon Murray
5110 N. 44th Street, Ste. L160
Phoenix, AZ 85018
(602) 840-4027
Fax: (602) 840-3380

ORGANIZATIONS

American Compensation Association (ACA)
14040 N. Northsight Road
Scottsdale, AZ 85260
(602) 951-9191
Fax: (602) 483-8352

American Marketing Association (AMA)
250 S. Wacker Dr. #200
Chicago, IL 60606
(312) 648-0536
(800) 262-1150
Fax: (312) 993-7542
Multiple journals including: *Journal of Marketing* and *Services Marketing Today.*

Direct Marketing Association (DMA)
1120 Avenue of Americas
New York, NY 10036-8096
(212) 768-7277
Fax: (212) 768-4547

Hospitality Sales and Marketing Association International (HSMAI)
1300 L Street, NW, # 800
Washington, DC 20005
(202) 789-0089
Fax: (202) 789-1725

International Advertising Association
342 Madison Avenue, 20th Floor, #2000
New York, NY 10173-0073
(212) 557-1133
Fax: (212) 483-0455

International Association of Sales Professionals
13 E. 37th Street, 8th Floor
New York, NY 10016-2821
(212) 683-9755
Fax: (212) 725-3752

National Association of Broadcasters
1771 N Street, NW
Washington, DC 20036
(202) 429-5373
(800) 368-5644
Fax: (202) 775-3515

National Association of Temporary Services
119 S. St. Asaph Street
Alexandria, VA 22314
(703) 549-6287
Fax: (703) 549-4808

Photo Marketing Association
3000 Picture Place
Jackson, MI 49201
(517) 788-8100
Fax: (517) 788-8371

Professional Pricing Society
3277 Roswell Road, # 620
Atlanta, GA 30305
(770) 509-9933
Fax: (770) 520-1963

Public Relations Society of America
33 Irving Place
New York, NY 10003-2376
(212) 995-2230
Fax: (212) 995-0757

Sales and Marketing Executives International (SMEI)
Statler Office Tower, #977
Cleveland, OH 44115
(216) 771-6650
Fax: (216) 771-6652

BOOKS

"this business has legs" How I Used Infomercial Marketing to Create the $100,000,000 Thighmaster® Craze
Peter Bieler with Suzanne Costas, 1996
John Wiley and Sons
605 Third Avenue
New York, NY 10158-0012
Read this book to get an insight of the vulnerability of patents.

Complete Guide to
Special Event Management
Ernst and Young
John Wiley and Sons, Inc.
605 Third Avenue
New York, NY 10158-0012
(212) 850-6000
(800) 225-5945
Fax: (212) 850-6088
Management, marketing, and financing of special events, entertainment, and sports.

PUBLICATIONS

Creative: The Magazine of
Promotion and Marketing
37 West 39th Street
New York, NY 10018
(212) 840-0160
Fax: (212) 819-0945

Marketing Tools, Information-Based
Tactics and Techniques (magazine)
American Demographics, Inc.
P.O. Box 68
Ithaca, NY 14851
(607) 273-6343
(800) 828-1133
Fax: (607) 273-3196
Books from American Demographics:
Market Mapping: How to Use
Revolutionary New Software to Find,
Analyze, and Keep Customers
The One to One Future: Building
Relationships One Customer at a Time
The Insider's Guide to Demographic
Know-How
Segmenting the Mature Market:
Identifying and Reaching America's
Diverse Booming Senior Markets
Segmenting the Women's Market

Chapter 23
Medical Services and Products

COMPANIES

Nurse Pro Pack, Inc.
Kelly Patterson, Pat and Barbara Patterson

808 S. Revere Street
Mesa, AZ 85210
(800) 284-3449

S.C.R.U.B.S.
Sue Calloway
8665 Argent Street
Santee, CA 92071
(800) 231-5965
Fax: (619) 448-0306

SmartPractice
Jim and Naomi Rhode, Beth and Curt Hamaan
3400 East McDowell Road
Phoenix, AZ 85008-7899
(602) 225-9090
(800) 522-0800
Fax: (602) 225-0245

Empower! The Managed Care Patient Advocate (Internet website)
http://www.comed.com/empower/what.spml
Mark Braly created this thorough, honest, and realistic overview of managed care as a labor of love due to his own experiences with treatment under managed care. The site provides intelligent information on ratings for HMOs, patient satisfaction, review processes, state laws; HMO CEO compensation, and just about everything else you need to know about managed care with links to other relevant sites.

ORGANIZATIONS

National and state medically related associations have yearly meetings that feature new products and services. The national associations can give you the address and number of your state association. These organizations publish monthly journals, but they are more oriented to research and practice articles than new products and services.

American Auditory Society
1966 Inwood Road
Dallas, TX 75235
(214) 330-4203

**American Association of
Homes for the Aging (AAHA)**
901 E Street NW, Suite 500
Washington, DC 20004-2037
(202) 783-2242
Fax: (202) 783-2255

American Chiropractic Association
1701 Clarendon Blvd.
Arlington, VA 22209
(703) 276-8800
(800) 986-4636
Fax: (703) 243-2593

**American College of
Healthcare Administrators**
325 S. Patrick Street
Alexandria, VA 22314
(703) 549-5822
Fax: (703) 739-7901

**American College of
Healthcare Executives (ACHE)**
1 N. Franklin, Suite 1700
Chicago, IL 60606-3491
(312) 424-2800
Fax: (312) 424-0023
Directory, biennial. Multiple journals.

American Dental Association (ADA)
211 E. Chicago Avenue, Suite 1100
Chicago, IL 60611-2691
(312) 440-2500
Annual meeting: October.

American Medical Association (AMA)
515 N. State Street
Chicago, IL 60610
(312) 464-5000
Fax: (312) 464-4184

American Naturopathic Association
1377 K Street NW, Suite 852
Washington, DC 20005
(202) 682-7352
Fax: (202) 448-2657

American Nurses Association (ANA)
600 Maryland Avenue, SW; Suite 100N
Washington, DC 20024-2571

(202) 651-7000
Fax: (202) 651-7001

American Optometric Association (AOA)
243 N. Lindbergh Blvd.
St. Louis, MO 63141
(314) 991-4100
Fax: (314) 991-4101
Annual meeting: June.

American Osteopathic Association (AOA)
142 E. Ontario Street
Chicago, IL 60611
(800) 621-1773
(312) 280-5800
Annual meeting: October.

**American Podiatry
Medical Association (APMA)**
9312 Old Georgetown Road
Bethesda, MD 20814
(301) 571-9200
Fax: (301) 530-2752

American Psychological Association (APA)
750 1st Street NE
Washington, DC 20002-4242
(202) 336-5500
Annual meeting: August.

**American Speech-
Language-Hearing Association**
10801 Rockville Pike
Rockville, MD 20852
(301) 897-5700 Voice or TDD
Fax: (301) 571-0457

**American Veterinary
Medical Association (AVMA)**
1931 N. Meacham Road, Suite 100
Schaumberg, IL 60173-4360
(708) 925-8070
(800) 248-2862
Fax: (708) 925 1329
Two journals, annual meeting.

American Physical Therapists Association
1111 N. Fairfax Street
Alexandria, VA 22314
(703) 684-2782

Association for the Advancement of Medical Instrumentation
3300 Washington Blvd., Suite 400
Arlington, VA 22201-4598
(800) 332-2264
(703) 525-4890
Fax: (703) 276-0793
Trade show: Advancement of Medical Instrumentation Manufacturing and Exhibits.

Health Industry Manufacturing Association
1200 G Street, NW. Suite 4000
Washington, DC 20005
(202) 783-8700
Fax: (202) 783-8750

Health Industry Distributors Association
225 Reinekers Lane, Suite 650
Alexandria, VA 22314
(703) 549-4432
Fax: (703) 549-6495

American Dental Trade Association
4222 King Street, W
Alexandria, VA 22302-1597
(703) 379-7755

Dental Manufacturers of America
Fidelity Building
123 S. Broad Street, Suite 2531
Philadelphia, PA 19109-1025
(215) 731-9975

PUBLICATIONS

If you have a nearby medical and/or dental school, try its library for these and other references.

Buyers Guide for the Health Care Market
American Hospital Publishing, Inc.
737 N. Michigan Avenue, Suite 700
Chicago, IL 60611-2615
(800) 621-6902
(312) 440-6800
Fax: (312) 951-8491

Medical Device Register (updated yearly in January)

International Medical Device Register (updated yearly in December)
Subacute Healthcare Register (updated yearly in May)
Product Development Directory (updated yearly in May)
HMO/PPO Directory (updated yearly in October)
U.S. Home Healthcare Register (Spring 1995)
U.S. Home Healthcare Register Pricing Guide (1995)
Directory of Healthcare Group Purchasing Organizations (Updated Oct)
Medical Economic Data
5 Paragon Drive
Montvale, NJ 07645
(800) 222-3045
(201) 358-7500
Fax: (201) 573-4956

Medical and Health Information Directory
Gale Research, Inc.
PO Box 33477
Detroit, MI 48232-5477
(800) 877-GALE
Fax: (800) 414-5043
Internet: 72203.1552@compuserve.com
Volume I: Medical associations, institutions, government agencies, HMOs, PPOs, insurance companies, pharmaceutical companies, research centers and medical schools.

Operational Policy and Procedural Manual for Long Term Care Facilities (Four volumes), December 1995
Heaton Publications
105 Madison Street, Suite B
Albertville, AL 35950
(205) 875-0986
(800) 221-2469

PERIODICALS

Dentistry Today (Free to individuals in the dental field)
26 Park Street

Montclair, NJ 07042-3483
(201) 783-3935

Hearing Health, The Voice
On Hearing Issues
PO Drawer V
Ingleside, TX 78362-0500
(512) 776-7240 Voice/TTY

HomeCare, The Business Magazine
of the Home Health Care Industry
Miramar Publishing Company
6133 Bristol Parkway
PO Box 3640
Culver City, CA 90231-3640
(800) 543-4116
(310) 337-9717
Fax: (310) 337-1041

Medical Product and Manufacturing News
Medical Device & Diagnostic Industry
Both free to qualified individuals
Canon Communications
3340 Ocean Park Boulevard, Suite 1000
Santa Monica, CA 90405-3207
(310) 392-8839
Fax: (310) 392-4920

Physicians' Marketing and Management
Clinical Health Consulting, Inc.
Box 740056
Atlanta, GA 30374-0056
(404) 262-7436
Fax: (404) 352-1971

Physicians Travel and Meeting Guide
Excerpta Medica, Inc.
105 Raider Blvd.
Belle Meade, NJ 08502-1510
(908) 874-8550
Fax: (908) 874-0707

Chapter 24
Network Marketing

COMPANIES
Excel Telecommunications, Inc.
P.O. Box 744114

Dallas, TX 75374
(214) 705-5500
(800) 875-9235 Customer Service
Fax: (214) 705-5501

Nutrition for Life International
David Bertrand, President
Jana Mitcham, Vice President
9101 Jameel
Houston, TX 77040
(713) 460-1976
Fax: (713) 460-9049

ORGANIZATIONS
Direct Selling Association (DSA)
1666 K Street, NW #1010
Washington, DC 20006-2808
(202) 293-5760
Fax: (202) 463-4569

Multi-Level Marketing International
Association (MLMIA)
119 Stanford
Irvine, CA 92715
(714) 854-0484
Fax: (714) 854-7687

PUBLICATIONS
Big Al's Recruiting Newsletter
Tom Schreiter
KAAS Publishing
PO Box 890084
Houston, TX 77289
(713) 280-9800
Fax: (713) 486-0549
E-mail: bigalmlm@aol.com

Chuck Huckaby's *PROFIT NOW*
PO Box 4245
Barboursville, WV 25504
(304) 736-2413
Fax: (304) 736-3230
E-mail: HuckabyCPH@aol.com
Huckaby's PROFIT NOW newsletter strives to provide information without hype. The newsletter independently reviews network marketing companies. Reviews include evaluation of products, market potential, company

strength, support, marketing, and compensation plans. Huckaby's background is in financial planning and he views network marketing as a means of helping people generate extra earnings. He has written a series on compensation plans.

Huckaby also sells a computer program "Fast Five" that allows individuals to set up targeted mailings, bypassing available franchise mailers. Contact him for more information.

MarketWave

Beyond the Veil (book, video)
Case Closed (generic recruiting tape)
Len Clements
2126 East Shea Drive
Fresno, CA 93720
(800) 688-4766
For a wealth of information on network marketing, visit Len Clements' online site: http://www.networkmarketing.com/marketwave.html. He lists his ten top picks in network marketing companies, best books and periodicals, and other information. Clement's goal is to expose the sham companies while giving exposure to the reputable ones. Recently, he has become a full-time distributor for a new network marketing company so his expose mission is now part-time. Clements has written a report entitled *Network Marketing Compensation Plans Explained.*

MLM Woman (newsletter)

Linda Locke
Regent Press
2073 N. Oxnard Blvd. Suite 251
Oxnard, CA 93030
E–mail: MLMWOMAN@aol.com or
CompuServe 73672,2762
WWW: http://www.west.net/~regent/mlm-woman
Locke assists women in building their network marketing businesses. She feels that women often have a different approach to the business. Contact online.

Multi-Level Marketing: A Legal Primer: A Handbook for Executives, Entrepreneurs, Managers, and Distributors

Mario Brossi, Joseph Marino, 1991
Order from *Profit Now* or *Big Al's Recruiting Newsletter.*

The Network Trainer (magazine)

PO Box 57723
Webster, TX 77598
(713) 280-9800
Fax: (713) 486-0549

BOOKS

Multi-level Marketing, The Definitive Guide to America's Top MLM Companies

The Summit Publishing Group, 1994
1 Arlington Center
1112 E. Copeland Road, 5th Floor
Arlington, TX 76011
(817) 469-6054
(800) 875-3346 Ext. 131, 132, or 133

MultiLevel Money

Jeffrey Lant
JLA Publications
PO Box 38-2767
Cambridge, MA 02238
(617) 547-6372
Fax: (617) 547-0061

Successful Network Marketing for the 21st Century

Rod Nichols, 1995
The Oasis Press/PSI Research
300 North Valley Drive
Grants Pass, OR 97526
(541) 479-9464
(800) 228-2275
Fax: (541) 476-1479
A complete guide to starting a network marketing business from compensation plans through building your downline. The explanation of compensation plans is easy to understand.

Upline (newsletter)

Wave 3, The New Era
In Network Marketing
Richard Poe, 1995
Prima Publishing
P.O. Box 1260BK
Rocklin, CA 95677
(916) 632-4400

Chapter 25
Personal Transportation:
Automobiles and More

COMPANIES

Husco Engineering Company, Inc.
Richard P. Husta
17 Calvin Road
Wilton, CT 06897
(203) 762-3181
(800) 752-3181
Fax: (203) 762-3427
Internet: http://www.spav.com/husco/
E-mail: bpkg31a@prodigy.com

LemonBusters, Inc.
Barry Sprague, President and Founder
John Adams, Franchise Director
5818 Balcones Drive #201
Austin, TX 78731
(512) 454-5999
Fax: (512) 454-8322

American Traffic Systems
4141 N. Scottsdale Road
Scottsdale, AZ 85251
(602) 994-3529
Photo radar equipment.

ORGANIZATIONS

Automobile Fleet and
Leasing Association (AFLA)
2512 Artesia Blvd.
Redondo Beach, CA 90278
(310) 376-8788
Fax: (310) 798-4598

Automotive Parts and
Accessories Association
4600 East-West Highway

Bethesda, MD 20814
(301) 654-6664

Automobile Service Association (ASA)
1901 Airport Freeway #100
Bedford, TX 76095-0929
(817) 283-6205
(800) 272-7467
Fax: (817) 685-0225

Automobile Service Industry Association
25 Northwest Point
Elk Grove Village, IL 60007-1035
(708) 228-1310
Fax: (708) 228-1510

Automotive Parts and
Accessories Association
4600 East(West Highway #300
Bethesda, MD 20814
(301) 654-6664
Fax: (301) 654-3299

National Vehicle Conversion Association
(NVCA)
2W Main Street #2
Greenfield, IN 46140
(317) 462-5033
Fax: (317) 462-7525

National Truck
Equipment Association (NTEA)
37400 Hills Teck Drive
Farmington Hills, MI 48331-3414
(810) 489-7090
(800) 441-NTEA
Fax: (810) 489-8590

National Association of Automobile
Trim and Restyling Shops (NAATRS)
6255 Barfield Road #200
Atlanta, GA 30328-4300
(404) 252-8831
Fax: (404) 252-4436
Auto, marine, and aircraft.

National Institute for Automotive
Service Excellence
13505 Dulles Technology Drive
Herndon, VA 22071-3415

(703) 713-3800
Fax: (703) 713-0727

**Towing and Recovery
Association of America (TRAA)**
2200 Mill Road
Alexandria, VA 22314-4677
(703) 838-1895
(800) 327-8542
Fax: (703) 684-6720

BOOKS

Auto Detailing For Show and Profit
*Ultimate Auto Detailing: Your hands-on
guide to the professional concourse winners' secrets*
David H. Jacobs. Jr., 1986
Motorbooks International
PO Box 1
729 Prospect Avenue
Osceola, WI 54020
(715) 294-3345
(800) 866-6600

PERIODICALS

Automobile
K-III Magazine Corporation
Box 55752 (Subscriptions)
Boulder, CO 80322
(800) 289-2886
Fax: (212) 447-4778 (NY office)

Auto Week
Subscriptions: 965 E Jefferson
Detroit, MI 48207
(800) 678-9595
Fax: (313) 446-6777
Internet: http://www.autoweek.com

Car and Driver Magazine
PO Box 52906
Boulder, CO 80322-2906
(212) 767-6000 Orders
Fax: (212) 767-5619

Car and Parts Magazine (Vintage cars)
PO Box 482
Sidney, Ohio 45365-0482

(513) 498-0803
(800) 448-3611

Motor Trend
PO Box 155279
Boulder, CO 80321-5279
(513) 498-0803
Fax: (513) 498-0808

Off-Road
PO Box 453
Mt. Morris, IL 61054-0453
(310) 820-3601
(800) 877-5602

Chapter 26
Publishing Businesses

COMPANIES

Mike Byrnes and Associates
Mike Byrnes, Devorah Fox
2025 North Third Street, Suite 155
Phoenix, AZ 85004
(602) 252-4868
Fax: (602) 252-8120

Sunflower Sales
John Reinhardt
P.O. Box 50328
Phoenix, AZ 85076-0328
(602) 893-6092 Phone and fax

BOOKZONE (Online Bookstore, Small
Publisher Access)
Internet: http://ttx.com:80/bookzone/

**Courage to Change, Catalog for Life's
Challenges**
318 Oak Grove Court
Wexford, PA 15090-9569
(800) 440-4003
Fax: (412) 935-2757

Magnetic Poetry
1304 University Avenue NE
Minneapolis, MN 55413
(612) 378-7697

Poisoned Pen, A Mystery Bookstore
7100 E. Main Street
Scottsdale, AZ 85251
(602) 947-2974

ORGANIZATIONS

Arizona Book Publishing Association
PO Box 40105
Phoenix, AZ 85067
(602) 274-6264 Message line

Association of Directory Publishers (ADP)
105 Summer Street
Wrentham, MA 02093
(508) 883-3688
Fax (508) 883-3717

The International Association of Independent Publishers (COSMEP)
Box 420703
San Francisco, CA 94142-3303
(415) 922-9490
(800) 546-3303
Fax: (415) 922-5566

Newsletter Publishers Association
1401 Wilson Blvd. #207
Arlington, VA 22209
(703) 527-2333
(800) 356-9302
Fax: (703) 841-0629

Optical Publishing Association
PO Box 21268
Columbus, OH 43221
(614) 442-8805
Fax: (614) 442-8815

Publisher's Marketing Association (PMA)
2401 Pacific Coast Hwy., # 102
Hermosa Beach, CA 90254
(310) 372-2732
Fax: (310) 374-3342
Publishes PMA newsletter, monthly. Provides a cooperative marketing organization for small to medium sized publishers.

Suburban Newspapers of America (SNA)
401 N. Michigan Avenue
Chicago, IL 60611
(312) 644-6610
Fax: (312) 321-6869

PUBLICATIONS

Book-on-Demand Publishing (book)
Rupert Evans

Flash Magazine,
The Premier Journal of Desktop Publishing
Riddle Pond Road
West Topsham, VT 05086
Fax: (802) 439-6463
E–mail: walter@flashmag.com
Internet: www.falshmag.com
Fax on demand:800-Flash06
Contact online, by fax, or mail.

The Self-Publishing Manual
Dan Poynter
Para Publishing
PO Box 2206
Santa Barbara, CA 93118-2206
(805) 968-7277
Fax: (805) 968-1379
E-mail: 75031, 3534@compuServe.com

Chapter 27
Real Estate-Related Businesses

COMPANIES

Precision Home Inspection
Rick Dixon
6900 East Camelback Road, Suite 700
Scottsdale, AZ 85251
(602) 941-HOME (4663)

Realty Executives
Founder: Dale Rector
President: Rich Rector
Vice President: John Foltz
4427 North 36th Street
Phoenix, AZ 85018
(602) 957-0444
Fax: (602) 468-1762

ORGANIZATIONS

American Society of Home Inspectors ASHI
85 W. Alqonquin Road
Arlington Heights, IL 60005
(708) 290-1919
Fax: (708) 290-1920

Apartment Owners and Managers Association of America (AOMA)
65 Cherry Plaza
Watertown, CT 06795-0238
(203) 274-2589
Fax: (203) 274-2580

Building Owners and Managers Association (BOMA)
1201 New York Avenue NW #300
Washington, DC 20005
(202) 408-2662
Fax: (202) 371-0181

National Apartment Association (NAA)
1111 14th Street NW #900
Washington, DC 20005
(202) 842-4050
Fax: (202) 842-4056

National Association of Real Estate Brokers (REALTIST)
1629 K Street NW #602
Washington, DC 20006
(202) 785-4477
Fax: (202) 785-1244

National Association of Realtors (NAR)
430 Michigan Avenue
Chicago, IL 60611
(312) 329-8200
Fax: (312) 329-8576

National Association of Master Appraisers (NAMA)
303 W. Cypress Street
PO Box 12617
San Antonio, TX 78212-0617
(210) 271-0781
(800) 229-6262
Fax: (210) 225-8450

PUBLICATIONS

Environmental Site Assessments and Their Impact on Property Value: The Appraiser's Role
Robert Colangelo and Ronald Miller, 1995
Publisher: Appraisal Institute
Brownfield Development Corporation
875 N. Michigan Avenue, Suite 2400
Chicago, IL 60611-1980
(312) 335-4100
E–mail: 103064.1030@compuserve.com

Profits in Buying and Renovating Homes
Lawrence Dworkin
Craftsman Press
6058 Corte del Cedro
Carlsbad, CA 92009
(619) 438-7828
(800) 829-8123

Index

Establish A Framework For Excellence With The Successful Business Library

Fastbreaking changes in technology and the global marketplace continue to create unprecedented opportunities for businesses through the '90s. With these opportunities, however, will also come many new challenges. Today, more than ever, businesses, especially small businesses, need to excel in all areas of operation to complete and succeed in an ever-changing world.

The Successful Business Library takes you through the '90s and beyond, helping you solve the day-to-day problems you face now, and prepares you for the unexpected problems you may be facing next. You receive up-to-date and practical business solutions, which are easy to use and easy to understand. No jargon or theories, just solid, nuts-and-bolts information.

Whether you are an entrepreneur going into business for the first time or an experienced consultant trying to keep up with the latest rules and regulations, The Successful Business Library provides you with the step-by-step guidance, and action-oriented plans you need to succeed in today's world. As an added benefit, PSI Research / The Oasis Press® unconditionally guarantees your satisfaction with the purchase of any book or software program in our catalog.

YOUR SUCCESS IS OUR SUCCESS...

At PSI Research and The Oasis Press®, we take pride in helping you and 2 million other businesses grow. It's the same pride we take in watching our own business grow from two people working out of a garage in 1975 to more than 50 employees now in our award-winning building in scenic southern Oregon.

 AFTER ALL, YOUR BUSINESS IS OUR BUSINESS.

CALL TO **RECEIVE A FREE CATALOG** OR **TO PLACE AN ORDER**

1-800-228-2275

All Major Credit Cards Accepted

PSI RESEARCH

300 North Valley Drive, Grants Pass, OR 97526 (800) 228-2275 (541) 479-9464 FAX (541) 476-1479

Select The Tools Your Business Needs From The Following Resource Pages

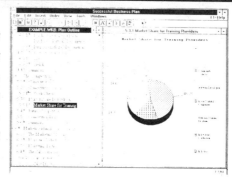

BOOKS TO SAVE YOU TIME AND MONEY

START YOUR BUSINESS: A BEGINNER'S GUIDE

From the editors at The Oasis Press® comes this guide for the beginning business owner. This all-in-one business book lists the major requirements and issues a new business owner needs to know, including;
• Start-up financing
• Creating a business plan
• Marketing strategies
• Environmental laws
Also available with step-by-step software. The perfect combination for any beginnning business looking for current information. Runs on Windows 3.1 or higher.

Start Your Business Book & Disk Package   **Pages: 198**
Paperback $24.95   **ISBN: 1-55571-363-7**

INSTACORP: INCORPORATE IN ANY STATE

The mechanics of forming a corporation or an LLC is a relatively simple and routine task that can be performed by anyone. This book shows you step-by-step how to incorporate in your state, as well as gives you an understanding of basic legal and tax ramifications of various corporate structures, and how you may best utilize their frameworks. Software is included to help you further by providing eight easy steps of incorporation. Runs on Windows 3.1 or Windows 95!

InstaCorp Book & Disk Package   **Pages: 130**
Paperback $24.95

SECRETS TO BUYING AND SELLING A BUSINESS

Prepares a business buyer or seller for negotiations that will achieve win-win results. Shows how to determine the real worth of a business, including intangible assets such as "goodwill." Over 36 checklists and worksheets on topics such as tax impact on buyers and sellers, escrow checklists, cash flow projections, evaluating potential buyers, financing options, and many others.

Secrets to Buying and Selling a Business   **Pages: 266**
Paperback $24.95   **ISBN: 1-55571-398-X**

STARTING & OPERATING A BUSINESS... series

Our bestseller for 15 years – still your best source of practical business information. Find out what new laws affect your business. No other publication can provide a beginning business such complete, hands-on information – designed especially for each state's unique regulations. There's an edition for every state in the United States, plus the District of Columbia.

Starting & Operating a Business in... series   **Pages: varies**
Paperback $24.95   **Binder: $29.95**   **Please specify state**

AVAILABLE FOR ANY OF THE 50 STATES PLUS WASHINGTON DC

TO ORDER CALL **800 228-2275**   **PSI RESEARCH**
FAX **541 476-1479**   300 NORTH VALLEY DRIVE, GRANTS PASS, OR 97526

BOOKS TO SAVE YOU TIME AND MONEY

ESSENTIAL LIMITED LIABILITY COMPANY HANDBOOK

This book tells you everything you need to know about setting up LLCs or converting an existing business. It presents difficult financial and legal concepts in simple language and answers the questions most asked by entrepreneurs and small business owners about LLCs. Includes a certificate of formation and a sample operating agreement.

The Essential Limited Liability Company Handbook
Paperback $19.95   ISBN: 1-55571-361-0   **Pages: 236**

FRANCHISE BIBLE

An up-to-date guide to franchising for prospective franchises or for those who want to franchise their businesses. Includes actual sample documents, such as the latest FTC-approved offering circular, plus worksheets for evaluating franchise companies, locations, and organizing information before seeing an attorney. This book is helpful for lawyers as well as their clients.

Franchise Bible
Paperback $19.95   ISBN: 1-55571-367-X   **Pages: 274**

RETAIL IN DETAIL

Takes readers through all the steps of planning, opening, and managing a retail store of their own, beginning with an honest assessment of whether they are really suited to running a business. Contains practical information on planning a store opening, from selecting a product line and hiring employees to buying an intial inventory and obtaining the required permits, licenses, and tax numbers. Instead of offering theories, this book goes into detail on handling day-to-day store operations.

Retail in Detail: How to Start and Manage a Small Retail Business   **Pages: 150**
Paperback $14.95   ISBN: 1-55571-371-8

HOME BUSINESS MADE EASY

Thinking of starting your own business at home? This book is the easiest road to starting a home business. Shows you how to select and start a home business that fits your interests, lifestyle and pocketbook. Walks you through 153 different businesses you could operate from home full or part-time. The process has been boiled down to simple steps so you can start to realize your dreams.

Home Business Made Easy
Paperback $19.95   ISBN: 1-55571-164-2   **Pages: 252**

TO ORDER CALL **800 228-2275**   **PSI RESEARCH**
FAX **541 476-1479**   300 NORTH VALLEY DRIVE, GRANTS PASS, OR 97526

ORDER DIRECTLY THROUGH THE OASIS PRESS
The Oasis Press® Order Form

Call, Mail or Fax to: PSI Research, 300 North Valley Drive, Grants Pass, OR 97526 USA
Order Phone USA & Canada (800) 228-2275   Inquiries and International Orders (541) 479-9464   FAX (541) 476-1479

TITLE	✔ BINDER	✔ PAPERBACK	QUANTITY	COST
Bottom Line Basics	☐ $ 39.95	☐ $ 19.95		
The Business Environmental Handbook	☐ $ 39.95	☐ $ 19.95		
Business Owner's Guide to Accounting & Bookkeeping NEW EDITION!		☐ $ 19.95		
Buyer's Guide to Business Insurance	☐ $ 39.95	☐ $ 19.95		
California Corporation Formation Package and Minute Book	☐ $ 39.95	☐ $ 29.95		
Collection Techniques for a Small Business	☐ $ 39.95	☐ $ 19.95		
A Company Policy and Personnel Workbook	☐ $ 49.95	☐ $ 29.95		
Company Relocation Handbook	☐ $ 39.95	☐ $ 19.95		
CompControl: The Secrets of Reducing Worker's Compensation Costs	☐ $ 39.95	☐ $ 19.95		
Complete Book of Business Forms	☐ $ 39.95	☐ $ 19.95		
Customer Engineering: Cutting Edge Selling Strategies	☐ $ 39.95	☐ $ 19.95		
Develop & Market Your Creative Ideas NEW EDITION!		☐ $ 15.95		
Doing Business In Russia NEW EDITION!		☐ $ 19.95		
Draw The Line: A Sexual Harassment Free Workplace		☐ $ 17.95		
The Essential Corporation Handbook		☐ $ 19.95		
The Essential Limited Liability Company	☐ $ 39.95	☐ $ 19.95		
Export Now: A Guide for Small Business	☐ $ 39.95	☐ $ 19.95		
Financial Management Techniques For Small Business	☐ $ 39.95	☐ $ 19.95		
Financing Your Small Business		☐ $ 19.95		
Franchise Bible: How to Buy a Franchise or Franchise Your Own Business	☐ $ 39.95	☐ $ 19.95		
Home Business Made Easy		☐ $ 19.95		
Incorporating Without A Lawyer (Available for 32 States) SPECIFY STATES:		☐ $ 24.95		
The Insider's Guide to Small Business Loans	☐ $ 29.95	☐ $ 19.95		
InstaCorp – Incorporate In Any State Book & Software NEW!		☐ $ 29.95		
Keeping Score: An Insider Look at Sports Marketing		☐ $ 18.95		
Know Your Market: How to do Low-Cost Market Research	☐ $ 39.95	☐ $ 19.95		
Legal Expense Defense: How to Control Your Business' Legal Costs and Problems	☐ $ 39.95	☐ $ 19.95		
The Loan Package	☐ $ 39.95			
Location, Location, Location: How To Select The Best Site For Your Business NEW!		☐ $ 19.95		
Mail Order Legal Guide	☐ $ 45.00	☐ $ 29.95		
Managing People: A Practical Guide NEW EDITION!		☐ $ 19.95		
Marketing Mastery: Your Seven Step Guide to Success	☐ $ 39.95	☐ $ 19.95		
The Money Connection: Where and How to Apply for Business Loans and Venture Capital	☐ $ 39.95	☐ $ 24.95		
People Investment	☐ $ 39.95	☐ $ 19.95		
Power Marketing for Small Business	☐ $ 39.95	☐ $ 19.95		
Profit Power: 101 Pointers to Give Your Small Business A Competitive Edge NEW!		☐ $ 19.95		
Proposal Development: How to Respond and Win the Bid	☐ $ 39.95	☐ $ 19.95		
Raising Capital	☐ $ 39.95	☐ $ 19.95		
Retail In Detail: How to Start and Manage a Small Retail Business		☐ $ 14.95		
Safety Law Compliance Manual for California Businesses		☐ $ 24.95		
Company Illness & Injury Prevention Program Binder (or get a kit with book and binder $49.95)	☐ $ 34.95	☐ $ 49.95 kit		
Secrets to Buying & Selling a Business	☐ $ 39.95	☐ $ 19.95		
Secure Your Future: Financial Planning at Any Age	☐ $ 39.95	☐ $ 19.95		
Start Your Business (available in a book and disk package – see back)		☐ $ 9.95 (without disk)		
Starting and Operating A Business in... book INCLUDES FEDERAL section PLUS ONE STATE section —	☐ $ 29.95	☐ $ 24.95		
PLEASE SPECIFY WHICH STATE(S) YOU WANT:				
STATE SECTION ONLY (BINDER NOT INCLUDED) – SPECIFY STATES:	☐ $ 8.95			
FEDERAL SECTION SECTION ONLY (BINDER NOT INCLUDED)	☐ $ 12.95			
U.S. EDITION (FEDERAL SECTION – 50 STATES AND WASHINGTON, D.C. IN 11-BINDER SET)	☐ $295.00			
Successful Business Plan: Secrets and Strategies	☐ $ 49.95	☐ $ 24.95		
Successful Network Marketing for The 21st Century		☐ $ 14.95		
Surviving and Prospering in a Business Partnership	☐ $ 39.95	☐ $ 19.95		
TargetSmart! Database Marketing for the Small Business NEW!		☐ $ 19.95		
Top Tax Saving Ideas for Today's Small Business		☐ $ 15.95		
Which Business? Help in Selecting Your New Venture NEW!		☐ $ 18.95		
Write Your Own Business Contracts	☐ $ 39.95	☐ $ 19.95		

BOOK SUB-TOTAL (FIGURE YOUR TOTAL AMOUNT ON THE OTHER SIDE)

OASIS SOFTWARE   Please check Macintosh or 3-1/2" Disk for IBM-PC & Compatibles

TITLE	3-1/2" IBM Disk	Mac	Price	QUANTITY	COST
California Corporation Formation Package ASCII Software	☐	☐	$ 39.95		
Company Policy & Personnel Software Text Files	☐	☐	$ 49.95		
Financial Management Techniques (Full Standalone)	☐		$ 99.95		
Financial Templates	☐	☐	$ 69.95		
The Insurance Assistant Software (Full Standalone)	☐		$ 29.95		
Start A Business (Full Standalone)	☐		$ 49.95		
Start Your Business (Software for Windows™)	☐		$ 19.95		
Successful Business Plan (Software for Windows™)	☐		$ 99.95		
Successful Business Plan Templates	☐	☐	$ 69.95		
The Survey Genie - Customer Edition (Full Standalone)	☐		$149.95		
The Survey Genie - Employee Edition (Full Standalone)	☐		$149.95		
SOFTWARE SUB-TOTAL					

BOOK & DISK PACKAGES   Please check whether you use Macintosh or 3-1/2" Disk for IBM-PC & Compatibles

TITLE	IBM	MAC	BINDER	PAPERBACK	QUANTITY	COST
The Buyer's Guide to Business Insurance w/ Insurance Assistant	☐		☐ $ 59.95	☐ $ 39.95		
California Corporation Formation Binder Book & ASCII Software	☐	☐	☐ $ 69.95	☐ $ 59.95		
Company Policy & Personnel Book & Software Text Files	☐	☐	☐ $ 89.95	☐ $ 69.95		
Financial Management Techniques Book & Software	☐		☐ $129.95	☐ $119.95		
Start Your Business Paperback & Software (Software for Windows™)	☐		$ 24.95			
Successful Business Plan Book & Software for Windows™	☐		☐ $125.95	☐ $109.95		
Successful Business Plan Book & Software Templates	☐	☐	☐ $109.95	☐ $ 89.95		
BOOK & DISK PACKAGE TOTAL						

AUDIO CASSETTES

TITLE		Price	QUANTITY	COST
Power Marketing Tools For Small Business		☐ $ 49.95		
The Secrets To Buying & Selling A Business		☐ $ 49.95		
AUDIO CASSETTE SUB-TOTAL				

OASIS SUCCESS KITS   Call for more information about these products

TITLE	Price	QUANTITY	COST
Start-Up Success Kit	☐ $ 39.95		
Business At Home Success Kit	☐ $ 39.95		
Financial Management Success Kit	☐ $ 44.95		
Personnel Success Kit	☐ $ 44.95		
Marketing Success Kit	☐ $ 44.95		
OASIS SUCCESS KITS TOTAL			

COMBINED SUB-TOTAL (FROM THIS SIDE)

SOLD TO: Please give street address

NAME:

Title:

Company:

Street Address:

City/State/Zip:

Daytime Phone: E-Mail:

SHIP TO: If different than above give street address

NAME:

Title:

Company:

Street Address:

City/State/Zip:

Daytime Phone:

PAYMENT INFORMATION: Rush service is available. Call for details
International and Canadian Orders: Please call for quote on shipping.
☐ CHECK Enclosed payable to PSI Research

Card Number:

Signature:

YOUR GRAND TOTAL

SUB-TOTALS (from other side)	$
SUB-TOTALS (from this side)	$
SHIPPING (see chart below)	$
TOTAL ORDER	$

If your purchase is:	Shipping costs within the USA:
$0 - $25	$5.00
$25.01 - $50	$6.00
$50.01 - $100	$7.00
$100.01 - $175	$9.00
$175.01 - $250	$13.00
$250.01 - $500	$18.00
$500.01+	4% of total merchandise

Charge: ☐ VISA   ☐ MASTERCARD   ☐ AMEX   ☐ DISCOVER

Expires:

Name On Card:

WHICH BUSINESS?12/96

Use this form to register for an advance notification of updates, new books and software releases, plus special customer discounts!

Please answer these questions to let us know how our products are working for you, and what we could do to serve you better.

Which Business? Help in Selecting Your New Venture

This book format is:
☐ Binder book
☐ Paperback book
☐ Book/Software Combination
☐ Software only

Rate this product's overall quality of information:
☐ Excellent
☐ Good
☐ Fair
☐ Poor

Rate the quality of printed materials:
☐ Excellent
☐ Good
☐ Fair
☐ Poor

Rate the format:
☐ Excellent
☐ Good
☐ Fair
☐ Poor

Did the product provide what you needed?
☐ Yes ☐ No

If not, what should be added?
_____
_____
_____

This product is:
☐ Clear and easy to follow
☐ Too complicated
☐ Too elementary

Were the worksheets (if any) easy to use?
☐ Yes ☐ No ☐ N/A

Should we include?
☐ More worksheets
☐ Fewer worksheets
☐ No worksheets

How do you feel about the price?
☐ Lower than expected
☐ About right
☐ Too expensive

How many employees are in your company?
☐ Under 10 employees
☐ 10 - 50 employees
☐ 51 - 99 employees
☐ 100 - 250 employees
☐ Over 250 employees

How many people in the city your company is in?
☐ 50,000 - 100,000
☐ 100,000 - 500,000
☐ 500,000 - 1,000,000
☐ Over 1,000,000
☐ Rural (Under 50,000)

What is your type of business?
☐ Retail
☐ Service
☐ Government
☐ Manufacturing
☐ Distributor
☐ Education

What types of products or services do you sell?
_____
_____
_____

What is your position in the company?
(please check one)
☐ Owner
☐ Administrative
☐ Sales/Marketing
☐ Finance
☐ Human Resources
☐ Production
☐ Operations
☐ Computer/MIS

How did you learn about this product?
☐ Recommended by a friend
☐ Used in a seminar or class
☐ Have used other PSI products
☐ Received a mailing
☐ Saw in bookstore
☐ Saw in library
☐ Saw review in:
   ☐ Newspaper
   ☐ Magazine
   ☐ Radio/TV

Where did you buy this product?
☐ Catalog
☐ Bookstore
☐ Office supply
☐ Consultant

Would you purchase other business tools from us?
☐ Yes ☐ No

If so, which products interest you?
☐ EXECARDS® Communications Tools
☐ Books for business
☐ Software

Would you recommend this product to a friend?
☐ Yes ☐ No

Do you use a personal computer?
☐ Yes ☐ No

If yes, which?
☐ Macintosh
☐ IBM/compatible

Check all the ways you use computers?
☐ Word processing
☐ Accounting
☐ Spreadsheet
☐ Inventory
☐ Order processing
☐ Design/Graphics
☐ General Data Base
☐ Customer Information
☐ Scheduling

May we call you to follow up on your comments?
☐ Yes ☐ No

May we add your name to our mailing list? ☐ Yes ☐ No

If you'd like us to send associates or friends a catalog, just list names and addresses on back.

Is there anything we should do to improve our products?
_____

Just fill in your name and address here, fold (see back) and mail.

Name _____

Title _____

Company _____

Phone _____

Address _____

City/State/Zip _____

E Mail Address (Home) _____ (Business) _____

If you have friends or associates who might appreciate receiving our catalogs, please list here. Thanks!

Name_____   Name_____

Title_____   Title_____

Company_____   Company_____

Phone_____   Phone_____

Address_____   Address_____

Address_____   Address_____

FOLD HERE FIRST

‖‖‖‖

NO POSTAGE
NECESSARY
IF MAILED
IN THE
UNITED STATES

BUSINESS REPLY MAIL

FIRST CLASS MAIL PERMIT NO. 002 MERLIN, OREGON

POSTAGE WILL BE PAID BY ADDRESSEE

PSI Research
PO BOX 1414
Merlin OR 97532-9900

‖₁.‖₁.‖.‖.‖₁.‖₁.‖₁.‖₁.‖₁.‖₁.‖₁.‖₁.‖₁.‖₁.‖

FOLD HERE SECOND, THEN TAPE TOGETHER

✂
Please cut
along this
vertical line,
fold twice,
tape together
and mail.